PRINCIPLES
OF
ADMINISTRATIVE LAW

By

Keith Werhan

Ashton Phelps Chair in Constitutional Law
Tulane University School of Law

CONCISE HORNBOOK SERIES®

Mat #40170299

Concise Hornbook Series, *WESTLAW* and West Group are
trademarks registered in the U.S. Patent and Trademark Office.

© 2008 Thomson/West
    610 Opperman Drive
    St. Paul, MN 55123
    1–800–328–9352

Printed in the United States of America

ISBN: 978–0–314–14934–3

 *TEXT IS PRINTED ON 10% POST CONSUMER RECYCLED PAPER*

For my students—past, present, and future

*

Preface

There is a frustrating paradox that clouds the study of administrative law. On one hand, administrative agencies are ubiquitous at every level of government. No institution of government touches our lives as frequently or so pervasively. Every lawyer surely deals with administrative agencies, and thus with administrative law, in some way, at some time, during her or his practice. So do law students who venture into such courses as environmental law, labor law, and communications law.

On the other hand, this eminently practical field of law can be one of the most abstract and elusive subjects in the law-school curriculum. This abstractness is the product of the ubiquity of administrative agencies. Administrative law principles must be stated abstractly because they must apply to myriad agencies, which come in a variety of shapes and sizes. Each agency has a distinctive history, organizational structure, policy agenda, arsenal of powers, and set of limitations on the exercise of those powers. Because of this diversity, generalizations about administrative agencies are treacherous, and the task of developing meaningful and functional legal principles applying to the full range of agency action is no mean trick. And in addition to accommodating the wide diversity among agencies, administrative law must cope with the considerable variety and complexity of agency decisionmaking processes as well.

Administrative law is challenging for another reason: It is ambitious. The aspiration of administrative law is nothing less than to control the exercise of governmental power within the rule of law. Administrative law, like constitutional law, superimposes a legal framework on an incorrigibly political process. Administrative law and constitutional law thus experience similar difficulties in mediating the uneasy relationship between law and politics in American government.

A final challenge in studying administrative law is that agencies, for all their familiarity, seem like alien creatures under the law. Although agencies do things that resemble what legislatures and courts do, they are decidedly different in makeup, and therefore in outlook, from those more familiar institutions. Agencies seem to inhabit the shadows of the three constitutional branches of government. And yet, understanding administrative law requires at least a basic sense of what administrative agencies are and what they do.

This book is written with the purpose of assisting law students and lawyers in overcoming these difficulties in the study of administrative law. Its goal is to organize and to develop the core components of administrative law in a way that renders this legal system both comprehensible and usable. With that goal in mind, I have discussed throughout the book (1) the historical development of administrative law and the administrative state; (2) the evolution of the essential principles of administrative law, with an emphasis, of course, on current doctrine; and (3) the contemporary controversies in administrative law. I also have included in each chapter diagrams that provide a visual organization of administrative law and the administrative process.

The "concise hornbook" concept has provided an ideal format to develop the essential principles of administrative law in the manner that I believe is appropriate for the study of this subject. This book covers what I consider to be the core of administrative law. I have attempted throughout the book to examine in an accessible yet sophisticated manner the subject areas and the principal cases that virtually every law school course in administrative law covers. In my 25 years or so of teaching administrative law, I have come to believe that the successful students are those who understand the essentials of the administrative law system. If students understand the logic of that system, as well as the fault lines within the system, they have a usable framework for handling any administrative law problem that may come their way.

In closing, I would like to express my appreciation to the editors at Thomson West for their patience and support when my work on this project was delayed by Hurricane Katrina and its aftermath, and to Emory Law School, which graciously allowed me the use of its facilities to continue work on this book when I washed up in Atlanta after the storm. I also am grateful, as always, to Lo and Ben for their understanding and support. Finally, I would like to thank my assistant, Gail Nelson, for her work in bringing my diagrams to life.

KEITH WERHAN

NEW ORLEANS, LOUISIANA
JULY 2007

Summary of Contents

Table of Contents

PRINCIPLES
OF
ADMINISTRATIVE LAW

*

Chapter 1

AN INTRODUCTION TO THE STUDY OF ADMINISTRATIVE LAW

This introductory chapter sets the table for the principles of administrative law that follow. It begins by offering basic answers to several preliminary questions one might bring to the study of administrative law—such as, what is administrative law? What are administrative agencies? And what motivates agency action? The chapter then briefly introduces the "traditional model" of administrative law, which provides a helpful point of departure for analyzing administrative law problems. The chapter concludes with a history of the administrative state in the United States that, although necessarily brief and somewhat simplified, is more extensive than one often finds in administrative law texts. Some sense of history is necessary to an understanding of administrative law because much of this jurisprudence has developed over a long period of time and on the run, in a continuing effort to keep up with the evolution of the administrative state.

§ 1.1 What Is Administrative Law?

Administrative law, as its name suggests, is the law of government administration. It is the system of general legal principles

1

that lawmakers and judges have devised over the years to legitimate, as well as to control, the actions of administrative agencies. Administrative law prescribes the ground rules for creating administrative agencies; it defines the power of those agencies; it structures the processes of agency decisionmaking; and it shapes the rights of individuals to participate in those processes as well as to challenge agency decisions in court. The Administrative Procedure Act of 1946 ("APA") provides the basic framework for federal administrative law and functions as something of a sub-constitution for federal agencies.[1]

Administrative law is limited by several important boundaries. The first and most fundamental limitation is that administrative law by and large applies only to the actions of administrative agencies that alter the legal rights and obligations of individuals. Because of this limitation, there are many things that agencies do that clearly are "administrative" in nature but that are not directly controlled by administrative law. Indeed, it is fair to say that *most* agency activities do not directly affect individual rights and therefore are not subject to administrative law. For example, agency officials, as part of the administrative routine, determine their priorities, establish enforcement strategies, form working groups and task forces, analyze and process information, recommend budgets, provide congressional testimony, give speeches, meet with members of various interest groups, and engage in myriad other activities that are necessary to fulfill their responsibilities, but that do not have a direct impact on individual rights. Administrative law by and large has little to say about such activities.

Administrative law also has little to say about the substance of agency action. Although "administrative law" might aptly describe the considerable amount of law that administrative agencies produce on a day-to-day basis, the conventional understanding of administrative law as a category of jurisprudence relates to *how* agencies make their decisions and *how* courts review those decisions, and not to the content of agency decisions as such. Administrative law is process-oriented. It focuses on the power of agencies to act with the force of law, and the procedures they must follow when taking such actions. The substantive laws that agencies make, as well as the substantive law they enforce, provide the subject matter of such kindred subjects as labor law, environmental law, communications law, and so forth.

Administrative law is also general rather than specific. Its interest is the general legal principles that apply across-the-board

§ 1.1

1. 5 U.S.C. §§ 551–559, 701–706. The APA is discussed briefly in § 1.5(d) and is introduced in detail in Chapter 4. The provisions of the APA are examined throughout this book.

to the actions of all agencies, and not to the idiosyncratic procedures that particular agencies follow. For example, the Environmental Protection Agency, as an administrative agency, is shaped and controlled by the general requirements of administrative law. The EPA, though, like most every agency, has adopted special procedures that are uniquely suited to its regulatory responsibilities. While those procedures are important components of environmental law, they are meaningful in the study of administrative law only to the extent they relate to the decisionmaking procedures of agencies in general.

This book, like most texts on administrative law, has imposed one final limitation on its subject matter: It is confined to *federal* administrative law. Each state has its own complement of administrative agencies, and with them, its own body of administrative law. A "comparative study" of the administrative law of the various states, together with that of the federal government (not to mention other nations), has much to offer, but so too does a limited focus on the federal administrative system. Because federal administrative law has influenced the development of administrative law in the states, and because the jurisprudence at both levels of government shares much in common, one who understands the federal system knows a great deal about state systems as well.[2]

Despite these limitations, the scope of administrative law remains quite broad. Administrative law is implicated whenever the activities of government agencies or officials affect individual rights. Moreover, it speaks not only to the power of agencies themselves, but also to the respective roles of the principal constitutional actors—Congress, the president, and the courts—regarding the exercise of agency authority. Administrative agencies, however, are the primary subjects of administrative law.

§ 1.2   What Are Administrative Agencies?

From the foregoing discussion, it makes sense to think of an agency, at least for the purposes of administrative law, as any governmental entity with the authority to take actions that alter the legal rights and obligations of individuals. And indeed, that is pretty much the definition of "agency" provided by the Administrative Procedure Act, with one important modification. The APA excludes the principal institutions of the federal government— namely, Congress, the president, and the federal courts—from its definition of agency (APA § 551(1)(A)-(B)).[1] With that exception

---

2. See Arthur Earl Bonfield, *The Federal APA and State Administrative Law*, 72 VA. L. REV. 297, 303–34 (1986). The leading law-school casebook integrating federal and state administrative law is MICHAEL ASIMOW, et al., STATE AND FEDERAL ADMINISTRATIVE LAW (2d ed 1998).

§ 1.2

1. Although the APA does not explicitly exclude the president, the Supreme

noted, the APA's definition of "agency," which determines the coverage of the Act, broadly includes "each authority of the Government of the United States, whether or not it is within or subject to review by another agency" (APA § 551(1))[2]

The APA language makes clear that agencies can be either freestanding units of the government or subunits within agencies. For example, the United States Department of the Interior, a cabinet-level agency, contains a number of subunits, such as the U.S. Fish and Wildlife Service, the Bureau of Indian Affairs, the National Park Service, the Bureau of Reclamation, and the Bureau of Land Management. Each of these subunits would qualify as an "agency" if it were considered an "authority of the Government of the United States." It is irrelevant to their standing as "agencies" that these units are within the Department of the Interior or that their decisions are subject to review by the Secretary of the Interior.

The key term in the APA definition of agency, therefore, is "authority," which the Act left undefined. A Senate report that forms part of the legislative history of the APA provides a glimpse into the congressional thinking, however. The report defined "authority" to include "any officer or board, whether within another agency or not, which *by law has authority to take final and binding action* with or without appeal to some superior administrative authority."[3] This Senate report suggests that we define "agency" functionally rather than formally. Any unit of the federal government, indeed, according to the legislative history, any officer of the federal government, should be regarded as an agency of the United States, and therefore subject to the APA, if it has legal authority to take "final and binding action," that is, action with the force of law.

While all administrative agencies share in common the power to take legally binding actions, they otherwise exhibit a wide variety of form and function. Congress possesses broad authority when creating an administrative agency to devise an institutional design that best enables the agency to fulfill its mission. At the

Court has held, primarily on separation of powers grounds, that the APA's definition of agency does not extend to the president. Franklin v. Massachusetts, 505 U.S. 788, 800–01 (1992).

2. See Pickus v. United States Board of Parole, 507 F.2d 1107, 1111 (D.C.Cir. 1974) (APA definition of agency should be given "broad, inclusive reading"). The APA definition makes several exceptions in addition to those for Congress and the courts. The excluded enti-

ties all are of a special nature, such as territorial governments and certain military authorities (see APA § 551(1)(C)-(H)).

3. Senate Comparative Print (1946), quoted in *Attorney General's Manual on the Administrative Procedure Act* 9 n.1 (1947), reprinted in WILLIAM F. FUNK, et al., FEDERAL ADMINISTRATIVE PROCEDURE SOURCEBOOK 33–171 (3d ed. 2000) (emphasis added).

outset, though, it is useful to highlight two basic distinctions that help to categorize the forms and functions of administrative agencies.

As to form, the basic distinction is between "executive agencies" and "independent agencies," the latter of which are sometimes referred to as "independent regulatory commissions." As the names suggest, executive agencies are designed to be responsive to the political and policy direction of the president, while independent agencies are somewhat insulated from presidential control. A single individual who serves at the pleasure of the president typically heads executive agencies. Independent agencies generally are led by a collegial group of individuals (usually five or seven) whose membership is closely balanced between the two major political parties. The members of the leadership group serve fixed and staggered terms and are subject to removal by the president only "for cause." While personal friction and policy disagreement are acceptable reasons for the president to remove the head of an executive agency (indeed, the president needs no reason at all for such a removal), those reasons would not provide legitimate "cause" to remove a member of the governing board of an independent agency. In order to remove a member of an independent agency, the president typically must demonstrate that the member suffered some disability or engaged in misconduct. Independent agencies thus have more freedom than executive agencies to develop and to implement their own policies. But aside from this difference in political independence, the distinction between independent and executive agencies is seldom relevant in administrative law. Both types of agencies have similar functions and procedures.[4]

As to function, administrative law provides that agencies can act with the force of law in one of two ways. They can either issue a "rule" through "rulemaking," a process that resembles legislative lawmaking, or they can issue an "order" through "adjudication," a process that in its most formal version resembles a judicial trial. The rulemaking-adjudication distinction is central to administrative law, and we shall consider it in detail and notice its echoes throughout the course of this book.[5] For now, it is sufficient to note that a rule, like a statute, creates a legal norm that governs the conduct of a defined category of individuals, while an order, like a court decision, reflects an individualized application of a legal norm to specific individuals.

Through the processes of rulemaking and adjudication, administrative agencies carry out functions that run the full gamut of

---

4. The distinction between executive and independent agencies is discussed in § 2.4(b).

5. The distinction between rulemaking and adjudication is discussed in §§ 3.1, 4.1.

governmental authority. They regulate the behavior of individuals and of the entities individuals create, license individual activity, dispense benefits, set rates, let contracts, collect taxes and fees, maintain and control the use of federal property, and on and on. When agencies take such actions with binding effect, that is, with the force of law, they must comply with administrative law.

§ 1.3 What Motivates Agency Action?

Scholars have developed a number of theories concerning agency behavior, and there is no consensus support for any one view. Three theories have attracted powerful support over the years, though, and each retains a significant contemporary following. One of these is often labeled "public interest" theory, which as the name suggests, posits that agencies act in order to further public values and the general good, as either the legislature or agency officials have defined them. According to this view, Congress creates agencies as a means of addressing public problems that existing institutions, including the economic marketplace, have been unable to resolve. Agency decisionmaking processes thereafter provide a forum for public deliberation on the proper resolution of those problems. The public interest theory of government administration has deep roots in American political thought. James Madison, for example, identified "the supreme object" of government as "the public good, the real welfare of the great body of the people."[1] Such sentiments were commonplace during the founding era, and they have remained a staple of American political discourse ever since. Much of contemporary administrative law reflects an effort by legislators and judges to hold administrative government to the public interest ideal.[2]

The other two leading theories of agency behavior reject the public interest theory as naïve and present themselves as more realistic, alternative accounts of the motivations that drive government administration. The first challenger to the public interest ideal is "interest group" theory. This account describes agencies as political brokers. In this view, agencies make decisions by trading off claims for preferential treatment pressed on them by special interest groups. According to interest group theory, the decisionmaking process of an agency does not provide a forum for public deliberation, but rather a field of competition among interested

---

§ 1.3

1. THE FEDERALIST NO. 45, at 299 (James Madison) (Modern Library ed., 1941).

2. For varying expositions of the public interest theory, see Robert B. Reich, *Public Administration and Public*

Deliberation: An Interpretive Essay, 94 YALE L.J. 1617 (1985); Mark Seidenfeld, *A Civic Republican Justification for the Bureaucratic State*, 105 HARV. L. REV. 1511 (1992); Cass R. Sunstein, *Interest Groups in American Public Law*, 38 STAN. L. REV. 29 (1985).

parties. Every agency decision selects "winners" and "losers" from among those competitors. Interest group theory reached its high-point in the 1960s and 1970s, after the belief took hold that many agencies did not act in the public interest because they had become "captured" by the very interests they had been created to regulate. Agency capture appeared to be the inevitable result of a rigged game in which special interests aggressively competed for agency favor, but in which the public interest, as such, lacked representation. A significant amount of administrative law that Congress and the courts developed during the 1960s and the 1970s was a response to this diagnosis of regulatory failure.[3]

The second primary rival to public interest theory is "public choice" theory. This account is closely related to interest group theory, and in many ways is a successor to it. The distinguishing feature of public choice theory is its use of an economic model to explain public policymaking. According to public choice theory, agency action is a "good" that is distributed in a regulatory "market" according to the laws of supply and demand. In this view, Congress creates agencies not in an effort to solve public problems, but rather in a bargained-for exchange among members of Congress and interest groups that believe the agency will operate to their mutual advantage. Following interest group theory, public choice adherents claim that each of the many "market participants" in the governing process seek individual benefits, or "rents," rather than the public interest or the interests of others. But instead of viewing agency decisionmakers as passive brokers among the competing claims of interest groups, as interest group theory would have it, public choice theory posits that agency officials make decisions in order to maximize their own self-interest, which usually is described as enhancing their power or retaining their office. Public choice theory depicts agency decisionmaking processes not as a forum for public deliberation, but as an economic marketplace in which those whose interests are at stake, including agency officials themselves, rationally negotiate a "deal" that reflects their relative power, the nature and intensity of their interests, their "transaction costs," and always, their individual assessments of how their own interests are best served. Public choice theory thus discounts administrative agencies as public facades for the pursuit of private gain. Not surprisingly, this bleak explanation of agency behavior has led many, but not all, adherents of public choice theory to advocate deregulation. From a public choice per-

---

3. The leading exploration and critique of the interest group theory is Richard B. Stewart, *The Reformation of* *American Administrative Law*, 88 HARV. L. REV. 1667 (1975).

spective, the regulatory markets created by administrative agencies are a poor substitute for the real thing—free economic markets.[4]

Each of the three theories of agency behavior offers different accounts of how the decisionmaking of administrative agencies responds to the critical interaction that shapes public policy, that between the particular interests of individuals and the common good of society. According to public interest theory, agency officials must subordinate the "special interests" of individuals, including themselves, to the public values and interests that unite all members of society. In interest group theory, government policymaking requires agencies fairly to "aggregate" the interests of the individuals and groups with a stake in the decision in order to maximize social benefits. Public choice theory holds that regardless what one believes agencies *should* do when making public policy, what they *actually* do is transfer public resources to private individuals and their groups.

In recent years, public choice theory has eclipsed interest group theory and has put tremendous pressure on those who cling to the public interest ideal. Like public interest theory, public choice theory has roots that extend to the origins of the American republic. The founding generation tempered its embrace of the public interest ideal of government action with the realistic concern that self-interested behavior was more in line with human nature. They thus attempted to design a special system of governance that fostered the selection of "a chosen body of citizens, whose wisdom may best discern the true interest of their country, and whose patriotism and love of justice will be least likely to sacrifice it to temporary or partial considerations."[5] Those who adhere to public interest theory see themselves as carrying on in that tradition. Public choice theorists tend to see that effort as futile.

Although there is obvious merit in each of the three leading accounts of agency behavior, none is fully convincing. Each theory explains some, but not all, agency actions. While public interest theory is too idealistic, public choice theory is too cynical. Although agency officials sometimes reach decisions simply by brokering the

---

4. The public choice literature is vast. For a good introduction to public choice theory with a critical bite, see DANIEL A. FARBER & PHILIP P. FRICKEY, LAW AND PUBLIC CHOICE: A CRITICAL INTRODUCTION (1991). For early, leading expositions of the theory, see JAMES M. BUCHANAN & GORDON TULLOCK, THE CALCULUS OF CONSENT: LOGICAL FOUNDATIONS OF CONSTITUTIONAL DEMOCRACY (1962); Richard A. Posner, *Taxation by Regulation*, 2 BELL J. ECON. & MGT. SCIENCE 22 (1971); George J. Stigler, *The Theory of Economic Regu-*

lation, 2 BELL J. ECON. & MGT. SCIENCE 3 (1971). For recent efforts to use public choice theory to reform regulatory law rather than to abolish regulation, see JERRY L. MASHAW, GREED, CHAOS, & GOVERNMENT: USING PUBLIC CHOICE TO IMPROVE PUBLIC LAW (1997); David B. Spence & Frank Cross, *A Public Choice Case for the Administrative State*, 89 GEO. L.J. 97 (2000).

5. THE FEDERALIST No. 10 *supra* note 1, at 59 (James Madison).

interests of the affected parties, they base other decisions on their sincere understanding of public values or the common good. The best resolution of this theoretical impasse might well be to appreciate that the public interest, interest group, and public choice theories each provide important, but importantly limited, insights into agency behavior.[6]

§ 1.4 The "Traditional Model" of Administrative Law

Just as no one theory of agency behavior can adequately account for the variety and complexity of contemporary government administration, no simple legal model can faithfully depict contemporary administrative law. There nevertheless exists a traditional model of administrative law that provides a helpful starting point for analyzing administrative law problems. Because a considerable amount of contemporary administrative law can be understood as an elaboration of this model, it is worth introducing its essential elements. (See Figure 1–1.)

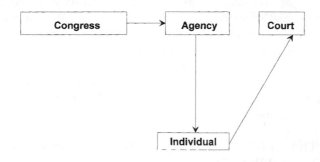

Figure 1-1: The Traditional Model of Administrative Law

The traditional model begins with the requirement that Congress create administrative agencies by statute. Administrative lawyers refer to these statutes as "organic" or "enabling" acts, and this book uses those terms interchangeably. These acts operate as a kind of corporate charter for the agency. They contain provisions

---

6. For an excellent analysis of the leading theories of agency behavior, coupled with an argument that none of the theories adequately describes actual agency decisionmaking, see Steven P. Croley, *Theories of Regulation: Incorporating the Administrative Process*, 91 COLUM. L. REV. 1 (1998).

that empower the agency to act as well as provisions that limit the agency's authority to act. These provisions are binding on the agency. Any agency action that exceeds the authority that Congress has provided it, or that is inconsistent with any provision in the enabling act, is *ultra vires* (that is, beyond the agency's scope of authority) and thus invalid. The traditional model enforces the *ultra vires* principle by providing for judicial review over agency action that alters the legal rights of individuals.

The essential dynamic of the administrative process prescribed by the traditional model of administrative law, then, involves a legislature delegating power to an agency, which exercises that power subject to judicial review.

§ 1.5 A History of the American Administrative State and of American Administrative Law

Although theorists of agency behavior disagree over the reasons why Congress creates administrative agencies, all would agree that legislators do so on pragmatic grounds (whatever those grounds might be), and not as a conscious exercise of any political theory. The historical development of administrative agencies has to a large degree been a history of improvisation. The same can be said of the development of administrative law, which has developed in response to the ever-shifting conception of the role of administrative government in the United States. Because the histories of the administrative state and of administrative law are intertwined, they both are considered in this section, albeit briefly.[1]

(a) The Antebellum Era and the Pre-modern Administrative State, 1789–1860

The framers of the Constitution aimed to create a national government that was energetic, but limited, effective, yet safe. Notwithstanding the tension that is inherent in those dueling aspirations, members of the founding generation understood their commitments to energetic government and to individual liberty as mutually reinforcing. Their goal, in short, was to produce balanced government. America's Revolution had been fueled, at least in part, by the colonials' fear that the English government had lost its balance, and thus that their traditional liberties were threatened by an increasingly tyrannical power. The chief culprit, as the colonials saw it, was the "gluttonous ministry" of England, which was using, or rather abusing, the prerogatives of the Crown to compromise the

---

§ 1.5

1. This history relies heavily on Robert L. Rabin's leading article, *Federal* *Regulation in Historical Perspective*, 38 STAN. L. REV. 1189 (1986).

independence of Parliament, and eventually, of the English people themselves.[2]

The pragmatism of the delegates of the Constitutional Convention of 1787, however, left no room for doubt that there would be a new federal government housed in the Executive Branch. Creating such a government, of course, was the immediate purpose of the federal constitution. The delegates believed that one of the failures of the early state constitutions had been to over-learn the lesson of executive tyranny by providing for dominant legislatures and impotent chief executives. The framers' determination to right the balance between legislative and executive power in the federal government came through in the provisions for a single chief executive rather than a plural executive; the selection of the president by the people of the United States, albeit indirectly through an electoral college, rather than by Congress; and a "considerable"[3] presidential term of office of four years, without term limits.[4] Each of these provisions represented conscious changes from many of the original state constitutions. The intent underlying the delegates' design was to create an energetic Executive Branch. Alexander Hamilton, writing in *Federalist 70*, explained the thinking, "Energy in the Executive is a leading character in the definition of good government," and is "essential to the steady administration of the laws."[5]

The text of the Constitution made clear that its drafters understood that the president and the vice president, the only two executive offices created by the document, would not be the only officials responsible for "the steady administration of the laws." The Constitution charged the president with the duty to "take care that the Laws be faithfully executed," and not that the president personally execute the laws (art. II, § 3). Moreover, Article II of the Constitution referred on a couple of occasions to Executive "Departments" (§ 2, cls. 1, 2) and prescribed the method for selecting "Officers of the United States" (art. II, § 2, cl. 2). The Constitution essentially stopped there, however. It said nothing about the identity or the organization of the "Departments" that will constitute the Executive Branch.[6] The Constitution instead placed a continu-

2. BERNARD BAILYN, THE IDEOLOGICAL ORIGINS OF THE AMERICAN REVOLUTION 95, 130 (1967); see *id.* at 94–143; GORDON S. WOOD, THE CREATION OF THE AMERICAN REPUBLIC, 1776–1787, 18–43 (1969).

3. THE FEDERALIST NO. 72, at 469 (Alexander Hamilton) (Modern Library ed., 1941).

4. The Twenty-second Amendment added the current two-term limit on the presidency in 1951.

5. THE FEDERALIST NO. 70, *supra* note 3, at 454 (Alexander Hamilton).

6. The Constitutional Convention considered, but rejected, a proposal that would have created several named departments, with the secretaries of those departments constituting a "Council of State" in order "to assist the President in conducting the Public affairs." II MAX FARRAND, ED., THE RECORDS OF THE FEDERAL CONVENTION OF 1787, at 335–37 (1911).

ing responsibility for fleshing out the structural details of the federal government on the institutions the document created—Congress, the president, and the federal courts. In shouldering that responsibility, Congress has taken the lead by virtue of its potent necessary-and-proper power (art. I, § 8, cl. 18), which enables the national legislature "[t]o make all Laws which shall be necessary and proper for carrying into Execution" not only the legislative powers delineated in Article I, but also "all [of the] Powers vested by this Constitution in the Government of the United States, or in any Department or Officer thereof."

When the First Congress took up the task of organizing the executive departments in 1789, it resembled a second constitutional convention continuing the work of the delegates who had met two years earlier in Philadelphia.[7] The First Congress rose to the occasion, engaging in a thoughtful debate over the first principles that should guide their installation of the federal government. The Continental Congress had created the Departments of Foreign Affairs, Treasury, and War, and it was a foregone conclusion that the new Congress would re-constitute them. In dispute was the appropriate organization of those departments under the new constitutional system. For example, members of Congress disagreed over whether the executive departments should be led by a single individual or by a governing group. They also debated whether the president should be able to remove department heads on his or her own or only with Senate approval. Congress eventually wrote organic acts that organized the original executive departments in line with what contemporary administrative lawyers describe as the model for "executive agencies," that is, the original executive departments operated under the personal leadership of a single official who was removable in the sole and unlimited discretion of the president. In these first organic acts, the First Congress thus settled a fundamental structural question that the Constitution had left unresolved: The president would control the actions of the executive departments.

The First Congress supplemented the original three cabinet-level departments with additional executive offices to handle matters of federal concern, including the Post Office, the Patent Office, the office of the Attorney General, and the U.S. Attorney offices. President Washington appointed around 350 executive officers to get the government of the United States up and running. The small scale of the Executive Branch created by the First Congress makes plain that the founding generation's conception of the range of government administration was far narrower than is the contempo-

---

7. For a recounting of the structural work of the First Congress, see David P. Currie, *The Constitution in Congress:* *The First Congress and the Structure of Government, 1789–1791,* 2 U. OF CHI. L SCH. ROUNDTABLE 161 (1995).

rary understanding. The political preferences of the antebellum era created a kind of double-default rule against federal regulation. The first default rule preferred the private, self-regulation of free markets over any government regulation. When political leaders became convinced that some market failure made government regulation necessary, the second default rule came into play: Americans tended to opt for state rather than federal control. The federal government thus did not assert a strong regulatory presence before the Civil War. The primary object of the national government of the antebellum era was to spur economic development, but the states took the lead even in that endeavor. National law enforcement was centered on revenue collection and the enforcement of judgments entered by the federal courts.

Administrative law remained in its infancy throughout the antebellum era. Because Americans preferred the private, self-regulation of free markets, the primary "government regulator" was the judiciary, which "regulated" individual behavior through its enforcement of the common law in lawsuits between private parties. On those occasions when Congress believed it necessary to enact laws that altered common law understandings, the legislators typically looked to the courts, rather than to administrative agencies, to enforce those laws.

(b) The Progressive Era and the Birth of the Modern Administrative State, 1860–1932

The double-default rule against federal regulation (the preference for market controls over government regulation coupled with the preference for state over federal regulation) began to recede after the Civil War. The War itself, together with the Reconstruction of the South that followed, consolidated power in the national government to a degree that had been nearly unthinkable in antebellum America. In addition, the transition of an agrarian United States to an urbanized society with an industrialized economy accelerated after the War. Urbanization exposed and exacerbated social problems across the nation. And industrialization encouraged the development of outsized economic firms that many Americans found alarming.

As the antebellum understanding would have it, the first regulatory responses to the societal anxiety triggered by the changes of the late nineteenth century came from the states. But individual states proved unable to control enterprises that had organized on a national scale, had created a transcontinental system of railroads, and had developed an increasingly interdependent economy. Nor could states sensibly address social problems that were national in scope. Congress responded to this combination of market and state regulatory failure in measured terms. True to the double-default rule, the national legislators carefully picked their spots, authorizing federal regulation only as a last resort. But it more frequently seemed necessary for Congress to select the final option of federal regulation for economic and social problem solving.

The "railroad problem" of the late nineteenth century created a perfect storm for federal regulation on these grounds. The national economy depended on the railroads, and yet it seemed that every interest affected by them cried out for federal regulation. The central problem was that market forces drove the railroads to engage in discriminatory rate setting. As a result, shippers often paid drastically different prices for the same service. These rate differentials, in turn, had a rippling effect on individuals, industries, and towns that relied in some way on the shipping and receiving of goods by rail. Common law principles of unfair competition did not address discriminatory rates, and state rate-regulation laws, which began to appear in the 1870s, offered piecemeal solutions at best. The Supreme Court exacerbated the railroad problem in 1886 when the justices on commerce clause grounds prohibited states from regulating the intrastate segments of interstate lines.[8] By this process of elimination, federal regulation was the only means left standing for addressing discriminatory railroad rates.

After a decade of debate and deliberation, Congress took on the railroad problem by adopting the Interstate Commerce Act of 1887.[9] The Act created the Interstate Commerce Commission ("ICC"), which is widely recognized as the first modern administrative agency. Robert Rabin explains, "For the first time, a national legislative scheme was enacted that provided wide-ranging regulatory controls over an industry that was vital to the nation's economy—the railroads. Moreover, regulation of the industry was committed to an institutional mechanism that was virtually untested on the national stage, the independent regulatory commission. The modern age of administrative government had begun."[10]

This conventional view, however, understates how tentative Congress was in its creation of the ICC. The House version of the Interstate Commerce Act did not provide for the creation of an administrative agency at all. It proceeded in the antebellum fashion by delineating a series of legal restrictions on the pricing practices of railroads and by providing for the enforcement of those restrictions by lawsuits in federal court. This was the path Congress would choose several years later in its next major regulatory

---

8. Wabash, St. Louis & Pacific Railway v. Illinois, 118 U.S. 557 (1886).

9. Act of Feb. 4, 1887, 49th Cong., 2nd Sess., ch. 104, 24 Stat. 379.

10. Rabin, *Federal Regulation in Historical Perspective, supra* note 1, at 1189.

statute, the Sherman Antitrust Act of 1890.[11] But the Senate insisted on the creation of an administrative agency to get a handle on the railroad problem, and the House acceded.

Still, the tentativeness of Congress's first step into modern regulatory government permeated the final Act. On one hand, Congress gave the ICC authority to investigate and to enforce a host of pricing prohibitions that the Act imposed on the railroads, including a general requirement that rates be "reasonable and just." On the other hand, the Act did not provide this new agency with the power to set railroad rates.[12] The Commission originally functioned similarly to a court in the sense that it evaluated whether the pricing practices of the railroads violated the Act's restrictions in administrative proceedings modeled on a judicial trial. But unlike a court, the Commission had authority to launch its own investigations of the pricing practices of the railroads.

The innovation of the Interstate Commerce Act lay not only in the regulatory role that it conferred on the ICC, but also in the institutional design of the Commission. The organization of the ICC differed sharply from the First Congress's design of the original executive departments. The new agency was led by a collegial body of five commissioners (rather than by a single official), no more than three of whom could share membership in the same political party. The commissioners served fixed, six-year terms, and were removable by the president only for "inefficiency, neglect of duty, or malfeasance in office."[13] In modern parlance, Congress had chosen to make its first modern regulatory agency "independent" rather than "executive" in nature. But in another indication of congressional hesitance over its new direction, the Act made the commissioners' decisions on staff hiring, as well as their expenditures to cover expenses, subject to the approval of the Department of the Interior, a cabinet-level executive department.[14] Congress removed the ICC from the control of the Interior Department in 1889, perhaps in an effort to protect the Commission from the incoming president, Benjamin Harrison, a former railroad lawyer.

The independent agency model of the ICC reflected, as it reinforced, what legal historian William Nelson has described as a general institutional shift in the last third of the nineteenth century from an overtly political, party-dominated governance to a more bureaucratic design that emphasized specialization and expertise.[15]

---

11. Act of July 2, 1890, 51st Cong., 1st Sess., ch. 647, 26 Stat. 209.

12. Congress gave the ICC rate-setting authority in the Hepburn Act of 1906. Act of June 29, 1906, 59th Cong, 1st Sess., ch. 3591, 34 Stat. 584.

13. Act of Feb. 4, 1887, *supra* note 9, § 11, 24 Stat. at 383.

14. *Id.*, § 18, 24 Stat. at 386.

15. WILLIAM E. NELSON, THE ROOTS OF AMERICAN BUREAUCRACY, 1830–1900, 2–3 (1982).

The goal of the "genteel reformers of the late nineteenth century"[16] tracked the ambition of the founding generation: They sought to invent a new "science of politics"[17] that, in the language of one reformer, would give "scientific expression to popular will," and thereby "place men's relations in society . . . under the control of trained human reason."[18] Professor Nelson has argued that these reformers, who are known as Progressives, "assumed that if they could successfully use neutral and scientific methods to ascertain the facts, their knowledge of those facts would guide them to proper solutions of the problems the nations faced." This "new scientific spirit" led Progressives to champion an array of "distinct," "problem-solving institutions" that, like the ICC, were designed "to deal separately with narrow, discrete, well-defined categories of problems."[19] Independent agencies were the model of choice for Progressives because they believed that social problems were best addressed by giving trained specialists the power, and the political insulation, to draw on their expertise to tackle those problems objectively and neutrally. The Progressive faith in the power of administrative expertise would become "the central rationale for administrative agencies as twentieth-century units of government."[20]

The Progressives wanted government *by* a well-educated, wise and virtuous elite, but not government *for* the elite. The moral core of their complaint about the politics of the late nineteenth century was that leaders exercised power in their own self-interest and in the interest of their political comrades, rather than in the larger public interest. It is no coincidence that the Progressive era produced, in addition to the modern administrative agency, the new science of "Public Administration." Woodrow Wilson, one of the founders of that discipline, spoke for many Progressives when he proclaimed that administration would replace politics in the task of running the government.[21] In this respect, the creation of the independent regulatory agency fit hand-in-glove with another prominent reform of the late nineteenth century, the creation of the civil service system. The old "spoils system," which had controlled federal administration since the presidency of Andrew Jackson (1829–1837), directed the hiring and firing of federal employees along political party lines. The civil service system, by contrast, was designed to create a largely apolitical federal work force. It provided

16. *Id*. at 158.

17. THE FEDERALIST NO. 9 *supra* note 3, at 48 (Alexander Hamilton).

18. E. L. Godkin, quoted in NELSON, ROOTS OF AMERICAN BUREAUCRACY, *supra* note 15, at 82.

19. NELSON, ROOTS OF AMERICAN BUREAUCRACY, *supra* note 15, at 82, 84–85, 100.

20. G. EDWARD WHITE, THE CONSTITUTION AND THE NEW DEAL 100 (2000).

21. See JOHN A. ROHR, TO RUN A CONSTITUTION: THE LEGITIMACY OF THE ADMINISTRATIVE STATE 66 (1986).

for merit selection and tenure rights of rank-and-file federal employees in order to insulate them from political control by the president and by members of Congress.

If Congress's organization of the ICC charted new territory in the relationship between the president and the agencies that execute federal law, the very act of creating an agency with the power to regulate individual behavior threw into question the traditional role of the judiciary in protecting individual rights in accordance with common law principles. The Interstate Commerce Act reflected the delicacy of this question. It gave the Commission authority to issue "cease and desist" orders and to require "reparation" when it found railroads to be in violation of the Act's prohibitions, but only after affording railroads the due process of a trial-like proceeding.[22] Moreover, the Act provided that the courts, and not the ICC, had power to enforce remedial orders against the railroads. The Act gave mixed signals concerning the weight of the Commission's decisions in judicial enforcement proceedings as well. It instructed courts to regard ICC findings as "prima facie evidence," while providing courts the "power to hear and determine the matter."[23] Congress effectively passed to the courts the crucial question of whether judges should defer to the commissioners' remedial decisions or make their own independent judgment on the questions of violation and remedy.

The courts, with the Supreme Court in the lead, resolved the ambiguity over the relationship between the Commission and the judiciary by assuming ultimate control over enforcement of the Interstate Commerce Act. They required that any ICC finding of statutory violation be fully re-litigated in enforcement proceedings. Those proceedings afforded railroads the opportunity to present new evidence to challenge the ICC's findings against them. Before long, the courts had reduced the power of the first modern regulatory agency to that of "a mere collector of data."[24] This initial judicial marking of its enforcement role, however, prompted Congress to enact a series of enabling acts that expanded the regulatory authority of the ICC. The courts received Congress's message, and they soon retreated into a more deferential posture when reviewing ICC decisions.

Congress drew on the independent agency model of the Interstate Commerce Act when it decided to address other national problems of the Progressive era through federal regulation. The most notable example was the creation of the Federal Trade Com-

---

22. Act of Feb. 4, 1887, *supra* note 9, § 15, 24 Stat. at 384.

23. *Id.*, § 16, 24 Stat. at 384–85.

24. Thomas K. McCraw, Prophets of Regulation 62 (1984).

mission ("FTC") in 1914.[25] Congress was moved to create the FTC because of the inefficacy of the Sherman Antitrust Act of 1890 in addressing the problem of industrial concentration. The Sherman Act authorized the Attorney General to challenge monopolies and certain other anticompetitive practices by filing suit in federal court.[26] The Act thus looked to the courts to develop antitrust policy on a case-by-case basis, in the common law tradition. Before long, it became clear that this regulatory strategy produced unstable antitrust policy, both because presidential administrations approached antitrust enforcement differently and because court decisions applying the Sherman Act were unpredictable. The congressional cure was the creation of an independent regulatory agency in the mold of the ICC to assume the lead in antitrust enforcement. In creating the FTC, Congress opted for "expert *administrative* regulation" over "hit-or-miss antitrust litigation" to address the problem of industrial concentration.[27]

Congress adopted similar administrative solutions to public problems throughout the Progressive era. The legislators created two new cabinet-level departments in 1902, the Departments of Commerce and of Labor, and it enacted such landmark regulatory statutes as the Food and Drug Act (1906), the Meat Inspection Act (1906), the Federal Power Act (1920), the Radio Act (1920), and the Air Commerce Act (1926). But notwithstanding its strategic retreat on the ICC, the Supreme Court remained hesitant to read the new enabling acts as generally displacing the traditional common law responsibility of judges to draw the boundaries between the power of government and individual freedom, especially in the economic arena. As had occurred with the ICC before them, the Court often refused to defer to the decisions of the new regulatory agencies and instead insisted on interpreting enabling acts to conform as closely as possible to common law principles. In the years preceding the Great Depression, legal historian G. Edward White has observed, "administrative government [had begun] to be recognized," but administrative agencies "continu[ed] to be seen as constitutional misfits."[28]

(c) The New Deal and Its Aftermath, 1933–1946

The Stock Market Crash of 1929 triggered a succession of events that culminated in the coming of age of the American administrative state. The Great Depression that followed the Crash rocked the double-default rule against federal regulation, which had

---

25. Federal Trade Commission Act, Public Law 203, 63rd Cong., 2nd Sess., ch. 311, § 5, 38 Stat. 717 (1914).

26. Act of July 2, 1890, *supra* note 11, § 4, 26 Stat. 209–10.

27. McCraw, Prophets of Regulation, *supra* note 24, at 116 (emphasis in original).

28. White, Constitution and the New Deal, *supra* note 20, at 103.

weakened during the Progressive era. The seemingly intractable economic emergency sapped the confidence of those who trusted in the self-healing properties of the economic marketplace. The national, indeed, international scale of the Depression similarly defied those who preferred state rather than federal regulation to correct market failures. A political change was in the air when voters in the election of 1932 transferred control over the national government from the Republicans to the Democrats in the hopes of reviving a moribund economy.

The new president, Franklin Roosevelt, worked with the new Congress to produce fifteen major regulatory statutes in the First Hundred Days of his Administration. The heart of the so-called "First New Deal" was the National Industrial Recovery Act of 1933 ("NIRA"),[29] which charted a course for federal regulation that deviated sharply from the Progressive model. Title I of the NIRA gave industry and trade groups authority to agree on the terms of competition among their members, and with the president's approval, to have their agreements enforced as federal law. Regulation of the Progressive era tended to be specific and reactive: Expert, specialized agencies policed particular problems within a limited jurisdiction. Title I, by contrast, established a regulatory regime that was breathtaking in its scope and activism. Suddenly, the federal government was supervising a comprehensive economic planning process for the conduct of virtually every trade and industry in the United States. In the less than two years of the NIRA's existence, the federal government signed off on over 500 industry "codes of fair competition."

The Supreme Court would hear none of it. In 1935, the justices unanimously ruled the NIRA's provision of code-setting authority unconstitutional in *A.L.A. Schechter Poultry Corp. v. United States*.[30] The justices often had signaled their unease with administrative authority during the Progressive era by trimming that authority, not by decreeing it a constitutional nonstarter. But the Court in *Schechter* found the grant of executive authority in the NIRA to be "without precedent."[31] In the Court's reading of the statute, Congress had provided the president with "unfettered discretion to make whatever laws he thinks may be needed or advisable for the rehabilitation and expansion of trade or industry."[32] The justices did not completely close the door on Congress's ambitious regulatory agenda, however. The *Schechter* opinion suggested that the Court took constitutional comfort in the Progressive

29. Act of June 16, 1933, 73rd Cong., 1st Sess., ch. 90, 48 Stat. 195.

30. 295 U.S. 495 (1935); see also Panama Refining Co. v. Ryan, 293 U.S. 388 (1935).

31. *Schechter*, 295 U.S. at 541.

32. *Id.* at 537–38.

model of regulation, and that Congress had best pursue its regulatory program within that model.[33]

Congress immediately responded to the Court's cue, enacting a series of regulatory statutes that constituted a "Second New Deal." Unlike the NIRA, these statutes fit the Progressive mold. For example, the National Labor Relations Act of 1935 scrupulously followed the policing model of the FTC's organic act. It established the National Labor Relations Board as an independent agency to regulate labor-management relations by resort to a trial-like, adjudicatory process.[34] The ambitious public benefits scheme of the Social Security Act of 1935 pushed further beyond the Progressive model of governmental policing, but Congress located the authority for administering the program in a specialized, expert agency, the Social Security Board.[35] After a decent interval, Congress bridged the gap between the policing model of Progressive regulation and the NIRA in the Agricultural Adjustment Act of 1938, by authorizing active government planning in the form of price regulations and crop restrictions, but also by providing that authority to a specialized, expert agency (the Department of Agriculture) with reference to a particular, and particularly problematic, industry.[36]

The Court accepted the constitutionality of the enabling acts of the Second New Deal. And before long, the justices relaxed the close and skeptical review that had characterized much of their approach to agency action during the Progressive era. Bowing to the Progressive and New Deal justifications of administrative agencies based on their neutrality and expertise, the Court now tended to defer to agency decisions within the scope of the authority that Congress had provided them. The Court also renounced any intention to hold agencies to traditional common law principles when pursuing their statutory missions,[37] thereby allowing agencies the policymaking flexibility that Progressives and New Dealers believed to be essential to good administration. "[I]f one took inventory of the state of regulation in the late 1930s," Robert Rabin has written, "it was undeniable that the federal administrative system had been entirely transformed in the short space of a generation."[38]

But all was not quiet on the regulatory front. The growth of the administrative state during the New Deal era proceeded in step with the emergence of a determined opposition to administrative

33. *Schechter* is discussed in detail in § 2.3(a).

34. Act of July 5, 1935, 74th Cong., 1st Sess., ch. 372, 49 Stat. 449.

35. Act of Aug. 14, 1935, 74th Cong., 1st Sess., ch. 531, 49 Stat. 620.

36. Act of Feb. 16, 1938, 75th Cong., 3rd Sess., ch. 30, 52 Stat. 31.

37. See, e.g., SEC v. Chenery Corp., 332 U.S. 194 (1947); NLRB v. Hearst Publications, 322 U.S. 111 (1944).

38. Rabin, *Federal Regulation in Historical Perspective, supra* note 1, at 1262.

government. The Court's acceptance of administrative government after the Second New Deal only intensified the deep discomfort that lodging government power in federal agencies had always caused many observers. The concerns of these opponents of the administrative state were interrelated and mutually reinforcing. As a result of the New Deal settlement, it appeared to many opponents that Congress now possessed free rein in conveying government power to administrative agencies; that many agencies exercised that power without the procedural safeguards that were necessary to ensure the fairness of their decisions; and that the courts had defaulted in their responsibility to protect individual rights by adopting an overly deferential posture when reviewing agency action. The result of this series of institutional breakdowns, according to these opponents, was an "administrative absolutism"[39] that threatened individual rights intolerably.

The first bill designed to curb agency discretion was introduced in Congress in 1929, the year of the great stock market crash. That reform effort was picked up again in 1933, even as Congress passed the NIRA and the remainder of the enabling acts of the First New Deal. Congress adopted its first administrative reform measure in 1935, the year of the Second New Deal, when it authorized the creation of a daily publication of the federal government, the *Federal Register*, and required that agencies publish their documents having "general applicability and legal effect," as well as their documents "prescrib[ing] a penalty."[40] The high-water mark of the congressional effort to curb the expansion of administrative government occurred in 1940, when the House came within a few dozen votes of overriding President Roosevelt's veto of the Walter–Logan Act, a statute that would have ratcheted up the procedural requirements for agency decisionmaking as it intensified judicial review over agency decisions. Reform efforts simmered on the back burner during the Second World War, but a public consensus for reform took shape almost immediately thereafter.

(d) The Maturation of the Modern Administrative State, 1946

The administrative reform movement culminated, and modern administrative law came of age, with Congress's unanimous adoption of the Administrative Procedure Act ("APA") in 1946.[41] Robert Rabin has described the APA as "a highly conventional lawyer's view of how to tame potentially unruly administrators."[42] The Act

39. American Bar Association Special Committee on Administrative Law (1938), quoted in WHITE, CONSTITUTION AND THE NEW DEAL, *supra* note 20, at 117.

40. The Federal Register Act of 1935, 44 U.S.C. §§ 1501–1511.

41. 5 U.S.C. §§ 551, 553–559. 701–706.

42. Rabin, *Federal Regulation in Historical Perspective*, *supra* note 1, at 1265.

also represented a hard-won compromise between those of the Progressive and New Deal faith who believed that independent and expert administrators provided the best government and those opponents of the administrative state who believed that agencies were constitutional anomalies unfit to govern with legitimacy. Justice Robert H. Jackson, writing for the Supreme Court in 1950, captured this understanding of the APA. "The Act," he wrote, "represents a long period of study and strife; it settles long-continued and hard-fought contentions, and enacts a formula upon which opposing social and political forces have come to rest. It contains many compromises and generalities and, no doubt, some ambiguities."[43]

The ambiguities to which Justice Jackson referred were intentional. They also were necessary. The contending forces that disagreed fundamentally over the location of the proper balancing point between administrative effectiveness and the protection of individual rights often were unable to agree on specific statutory language. In effect, the APA's studied ambiguity framed these disagreements and passed them along to the courts to resolve when applying the Act to real-world agency actions. As we shall see throughout this book, the difficult task of calibrating the need for effective administration with a proper regard for individual rights has remained a constant theme—and tension—in modern administrative law.

If many of the APA's provisions are unclear, the general terms of the deal that produced the Act are fairly apparent. The APA settled that federal agencies would continue to exercise governing authority under broad statutory mandates, but that they now would do so according to "a formal articulation of agency due process."[44] The APA tracked, but softened, the approach of the Walter–Logan Act by providing, as Justice Jackson put it, "a new, basic and comprehensive regulation of [agency] procedures."[45] The Act, among other things, required federal agencies to separate their investigative and prosecutorial functions from their adjudicatory functions; extended to interested parties a right to participate in agency decisionmaking affecting their rights; delineated default procedural requirements for agency rulemaking and formal adjudication; and provided for the availability and scope of judicial review of agency action. The essential terms of the APA compromise have held, for the statute has been amended only sparingly since its enactment.

43. Wong Yang Sung v. McGrath, 339 U.S. 33, 40 (1950).

44. Rabin, *Federal Regulation in Historical Perspective, supra* note 1, at 1266.

45. *Wong Yang Sung,* 339 U.S. at 36.

The adoption of the APA brought unaccustomed regulatory peace as all of the primary institutions of the federal government—Congress, the president, and the courts—settled into the post-New Deal consensus on government administration. But with the velocity of economic and social change and the volatility of American politics in the second half of the twentieth century, the administrative state would not remain at peace for long.

(e) The Activism of the Public Interest Era, 1964–1977

While the principal (although by no means only) preoccupation of New Deal reformers was to enlist federal agencies in the service of stimulating and controlling the national economy, the economic prosperity of the post-War years afforded policy makers the luxury of taking on an agenda of broader social reform. Beginning in 1964 with the Civil Rights Act and the "War on Poverty," the 1960s witnessed unprecedented efforts by the federal government to assist those members of American society who had become marginalized by economic disadvantage or by racial, ethnic, religious, or gender discrimination. During the 1970s, the federal government added the protection of the environment, consumers, and workers to the regulatory agenda. This ambitious undertaking prompted Congress to create a new generation of administration agencies. A sampling of the agencies created between 1964 and 1977 evokes the preoccupations of what commentators often describe as the "public interest era": the Equal Employment Opportunity Commission (1964); the Department of Housing and Urban Development (1965); the National Highway Traffic Safety Administration (1966); the Environmental Protection Agency (1970); the Occupational Safety and Health Administration (1970); the Consumer Product Safety Commission (1972); the Nuclear Regulatory Commission (1975); the National Transportation Safety Board (1976); the Federal Mine Safety and Health Review Commission (1977); the Office of Surface Mining (1977); and the Department of Energy (1977).

The public interest era reflects both continuity with and change from the reform movements of the Progressive and New Deal periods. The continuity that links the three is obvious: the creation of administrative agencies to ameliorate perceived market failures. The discontinuity that distinguishes the public interest era from the earlier two reform movements is subtle, but important. Progressives and New Dealers created agencies because of their faith in the competence, neutrality and expertise of administrators in identifying and solving public problems. That faith was forever shaken during the public interest era. The jarring public unrest that has come to define the 1960s—the controversies over civil rights for African–Americans and other racial and ethnic minority groups, equal rights for women, and perhaps above all, the Vietnam

War—carried over into the 1970s. The Watergate scandal, the first resignation by an American president, and the defeat of American forces in Vietnam all contributed to the general mood of public distrust that hovered about government leaders.

It is little wonder that the post-New Deal consensus justifying broad agency authority on the basis of a special, institutional expertise withered in this corrosive environment. Indeed, government administrators became especially vulnerable to challenge because a theory of agency "capture" had taken hold, in which it was claimed that agencies over time tended to become controlled by the very interests they had been created to regulate. In response to this diagnosis of regulatory failure, individuals formed self-styled "public interest groups" to protect interests, such as environmental and consumer protection, that they believed government administrators routinely ignored.

There was in all of these developments a fundamental contradiction that haunted the public interest era: Although lawmakers created administrative agencies at a feverish rate to address a broad range of social problems, those very agencies were not trusted to regulate in the public interest, at least not without considerable prodding. And indeed, Congress engaged in such prodding during this period. While many enabling acts of the Progressive and (especially) the New Deal eras essentially charged administrators to regulate as they saw fit in their areas of jurisdiction, Congress more carefully circumscribed the scope of governing authority it conferred on agencies during the public interest era. In addition to providing more precise policy direction for agencies, some of the new enabling acts added to the rulemaking procedures required by the APA. Some statutes took the more pointed approach of adopting such "action-forcing" techniques as establishing firm deadlines for agencies to carry out particular responsibilities. And finally, in something of a symbol of the public interest era, the National Environmental Policy Act of 1970 ("NEPA") merged procedure and substance by requiring, "to the fullest extent possible," that "all agencies of the Federal government" prepare and issue an environmental impact statement in connection with all "major Federal actions significantly affecting the quality of the human environment."[46] Thus, while Congress continued the Progressive/New Deal preference for active government, lawmakers were active in another sense as well. They were intent, as one observer noted, on establishing "legislative primacy in the regulatory process."[47]

---

46. 42 U.S.C. § 4332 (2) (c).

47. CASS R. SUNSTEIN, AFTER THE RIGHTS REVOLUTION: RECONCEIVING THE REGULATORY STATE 29–30 (1990).

The new congressional activism of the public interest era was more than matched by a renewed judicial activism. And just as the enabling acts of the public interest era were a departure from the past, so too was the new judicial activism. In the Progressive era, reviewing courts closely reviewed agency action in an effort to maintain the supremacy of common law norms, as well as the courts' traditional role as principal guarantor of individual rights, in the nascent administrative state. In the post-New Deal era, the courts backed off because they had come to accept that Congress wished for federal agencies, and not the courts, to exercise the primary decisionmaking authority in the mature administrative state. Judges believed that they facilitated the fulfillment of congressional mandates best by deferring to the regulatory and enforcement decisions of the responsible agencies. During the public interest era, the courts stepped up their review of agency action because they now believed that a strong judicial check was necessary to ensure that agencies remain true to their statutory mission. As the influential D.C. Circuit explained, "Our duty, in short, is to see that important legislative purposes, heralded in the halls of Congress, are not lost or misdirected in the vast hallways of the federal bureaucracy."[48] Judges thus responded to concerns over agency capture by themselves capturing more control over agency decisionmaking.

The public interest era thus witnessed a thorough re-definition of the role and scope of judicial review in the administrative state. The Supreme Court early on endorsed a "basic presumption of judicial review"[49] as it lowered several of the traditional barriers that had hindered the general availability of court review of agency action.[50] With more agency decisions opened to judicial review, courts, led by the U.S. Court of Appeals for the District of Columbia Circuit, proceeded to check agency decisionmaking in two primary ways—one procedural and the other substantive. In the procedural approach, reviewing courts ensured that all affected individuals and groups, and especially public interest groups, were allowed full and fair representation in administrative proceedings before upholding agency decisions. The leading exemplar of this procedural approach became known as "hybrid rulemaking" (see § 6.1). In the substantive approach, reviewing courts took a "hard look" at agency decisions in order to ensure that the agencies themselves had taken a "hard look" at policy problems before acting on them. Skeptical judges insisted that agencies explain the basis of their decisions

48. Calvert Cliffs' Coordinating Committee, Inc. v. United States Atomic Energy Commission, 449 F.2d 1109, 1111 (D.C.Cir. 1971).

49. Abbott Laboratories v. Gardner, 387 U.S. 136, 140 (1967).

50. See, e.g., Association of Data Processing Serv. Org. v. Camp, 397 U.S. 150 (1970) (standing); Abbott Laboratories v. Gardner, 387 U.S. 136 (1967) (ripeness).

sufficiently to demonstrate that they had engaged in "reasoned decision-making" that was faithful to their statutory mandate.[51] This substantive approach became known as "hard look review" (see § 8.7(b)).

The vigorous activism of Congress and the courts to ensure that regulation serve the public interest did not succeed in quelling the overwhelming public skepticism toward government administration that characterized the period. In many ways, this activism, especially that of the courts, seemed to exacerbate rather than ameliorate a growing sense of regulatory dysfunction. Thus the public interest era, which originated in doubts about the competence of agencies to regulate in the public interest, concluded amid uncertainty over the efficacy of regulation itself.

(f) The Retrenchment of the Deregulation Era, 1978– Present

The skepticism of government administration that shaped the public interest era has dominated the contemporary administrative state. The Progressive/New Deal vision of administrators as neutral experts who, if insulated from political control, will correct market failures in the public interest seems especially distant. Administrative agencies are now widely seen as political actors, for better and for worse. The central division between the public interest era and the contemporary administrative state lies in their differing responses to the debunking of the scientific vision of government administration. The reaction of the public interest era centered on the activism of Congress and the courts to keep agency regulatory decisions aligned with the public interest. The repercussions of the contemporary skepticism of administration are still playing out, but it is already clear that the predominant response has been a process of deregulation.

The deregulatory movement began in 1978, when Congress provided for the phased withdrawal of economic regulation of the domestic airline industry.[52] Congress followed with statutes that abolished, or at least sharply curbed, economic regulation of the surface transportation industries (trucking and railroads), long distance telecommunications, banking, and the production of natural gas. The symbolic highpoint of the legislative push for deregulation came in 1995, when Congress abolished the Interstate Commerce Commission, the first modern administrative agency and an erstwhile model for administrative growth.[53]

51. See Greater Boston Television Corp. v. FCC, 444 F.2d 841, 851, 852 (D.C. Cir 1970), cert. denied, 403 U.S. 923 (1971).

52. Airline Deregulation Act, Pub. L. No. 95–504, 95th Cong., 2d Sess., 92 Stat. 1705.

53. ICC Termination Act of 1995, Pub. L. 104–88, 104th Cong., 1st Sess., 109 Stat. 803.

The administration of President Ronald Reagan (1981–1989) broadened Congress's initiative by encouraging deregulation beyond the economic regulation that Congress had targeted, and indeed, throughout the federal government. President Reagan introduced his central deregulatory initiative less than one month after taking office in 1981, issuing an executive order (Executive Order No. 12,291) that positioned the White House's Office of Management and Budget ("OMB") as the dominant, central clearinghouse for agency rulemaking. As far back as the Nixon administration (1969–1974), presidents had enlisted OMB in an effort to gain some measure of political control over administrative policymaking, but none had done so as aggressively as President Reagan. His executive order prohibited executive agencies (but not independent agencies) from issuing major rules unless the agency could convince OMB that "the potential benefits to society [from] the regulation outweigh the potential costs to society."[54] The executive order thus provided OMB considerable clout, acting on behalf of the president, to pressure agencies into toning down or abandoning major rulemaking initiatives. The presidents who have succeeded Presided Reagan have tweaked, but have continued, the central requirement that executive agencies clear major rules with OMB on the basis of a cost-benefit analysis (see § 2.4(c)).

A second, contemporary effort to reorient government administration in a deregulatory direction has been the replacement of traditional, "command-and-control" regulations with "market-based" alternatives. Under the command-and-control model, agencies enforce their statutory mandates by requiring individuals to take (or not to take) certain actions, under penalty of law. Critics have charged that command-and-control regulations often impose substantial and unnecessary compliance costs on regulated entities, as well as on the government regulators who police those entities. These critics also contend that command-and-control regulations often are misdirected, requiring (or preventing) actions by regulated entities that are not as beneficial (or as harmful) as government administrators believe them to be. As an alternative to the command-and-control model, these critics have encouraged "market-based" strategies that offer economic incentives to encourage individuals to take socially desirable actions, without requiring them to take (or not to take) specific actions. They also have advocated regulatory approaches that would have agencies set public policy goals and allow individuals the freedom to devise the most cost-effective means of meeting those goals. Advocates of such market-based alternatives to traditional command-and-control regulation claim that this regulatory strategy produces better regulation at less cost.

---

54. Executive Order No. 12,291, § 2(b), 46 Fed. Reg. 13,193 (1981).

The movement toward market-based regulation reflects a profound shift in attitude concerning government administration. Command-and-control regulations followed from the Progressive/New Deal assumption that expert government administrators know best how to achieve the goals that Congress establishes in enabling acts. Market-based regulations follow from the current skepticism about any such expertise. Market-based regulatory strategies extend to regulated entities the kind of flexibility in achieving statutory agenda that formerly resided in government administrators. Congress endorsed the market-based alternative to command-and-control regulation in the 1990 Amendments to the Clean Air Act,[55] and incentive-based systems have become especially prominent in contemporary environmental regulation.

President Reagan's executive order providing for OMB review of agency rulemaking did not simply fuel the momentum toward deregulation in the contemporary administrative state. It also reflected, as it reinforced, the politicization of government administration that has come to characterize the current era. If government administration is regarded as primarily a matter of politics rather than as an exercise of some special expertise, it makes sense for the president, as the chief elected official in the Executive Branch, to control the actions of administrators. President Reagan's executive order, in this sense, reflects an extension of the skepticism of the public interest era. If government administrators lack sufficient credibility to justify judicial deference to their decisions, why then should the president, who has the ultimate constitutional responsibility for executing the laws, be expected to defer?

The trend toward political control over administrative decisionmaking has accelerated in recent years. President Reagan himself followed up his executive order requiring OMB review of major rulemaking with another executive order (Executive Order 12,498) that strengthened OMB's role in shaping the regulatory planning process of agencies. Subsequent presidents have followed President Reagan's lead by maintaining political control of agency policymaking. Congress also has gotten into the act by imposing its own set of reporting requirements as preconditions on agency rulemaking. Most notably, in 1996 Congress adapted President Reagan's model for OMB review by providing for fast track, legislative review of agency rulemaking. In this scheme, agencies are required to submit various analyses of their major rules, including a cost-benefit analysis, to Congress before those rules take effect. The act imposes a 60–day waiting period during which Congress can pass a statute prohibiting the agency from issuing the rule (see § 2.3(c)).[56]

55. 42 U.S.C. §§ 7651j–7661d.   **56.** 5 U.S.C. §§ 801–808.

The reporting-and-review requirements established by recent presidents and Congress have had a direct as well as an indirect effect on agency rulemaking. The direct effect has been to enhance the political accountability of agency rulemaking by structuring a role for the principal political actors in the administrative process. The indirect effect of these requirements has been to increase the cost and delay of agency rulemaking to such an extent that it discourages agencies from undertaking major rulemaking initiatives. The presidential and congressional review initiatives of the contemporary era remain experimental and controversial. But the political consensus that lies at the core of these initiatives was made clear when President William Clinton, the first Democratic president since the Reagan Administration, pronounced early in his tenure, "The era of big government is over." The regulatory retrenchment initiated by Congress and the president since 1978 has returned the early American double-default rule against federal regulation to its strongest position since before the New Deal.

The themes of deregulation and politicization of administrative government have shaped not only congressional and presidential initiatives in the contemporary administrative state, but also have encouraged courts to rethink yet again their approach to reviewing agency decisions. During the public interest era, federal judges took an active role in keeping agencies true to their regulatory mission, but that stance seems out of place in an era that is skeptical of the efficacy of regulation, and in any event, conceives of agencies as political actors. It is not surprising, then, that federal courts in the contemporary era have retreated from the aggressive review that characterized the public interest era. Contemporary judicial review now occupies a position between the activism of that period and the wholesale deference of the post-New Deal era.

The judicial retreat began in 1978, the very year Congress initiated its push toward deregulation. In *Vermont Yankee Nuclear Power Corp. v. National Resources Defense Council, Inc.,*[57] the Supreme Court advised lower courts that they lacked authority to impose procedural requirements on agency decisionmaking beyond those established by Congress or by the agencies themselves. Then-Justice William H. Rehnquist, writing for the Court without dissent, admonished reviewing courts that they were "to play only a limited role" in a "reasonable review process." Justice Rehnquist added, "The fundamental policy questions appropriately resolved in Congress and in the state legislatures are *not* subject to reexamination in the federal courts under the guise of judicial review of agency action.... [C]ourts should perform their appointed function.... Administrative decisions should be set aside in this con-

57.   435 U.S. 519 (1978).

text, as in every other, only for substantial procedural or substantive reasons as mandated by statute, not simply because the court is unhappy with the result reached."[58] In other words, judges must stick to the law when they review agency actions, and not second-guess the policy decisions of Congress and the agencies.

The Court extended *Vermont Yankee*'s message of judicial restraint to the substantive review of agency decisionmaking in *Chevron U.S.A. v. Natural Resources Defense Council, Inc.*[59] *Chevron* instructed reviewing courts to defer to agency interpretations of ambiguities in their enabling acts. The *Chevron* decision revolutionized the traditional understanding of judicial review, which had held that it was primarily the role of reviewing courts, and not agencies, to provide authoritative statutory interpretations. In *Chevron*, the justices seemed not only to accept, but also to celebrate, a highly politicized conception of agency decisionmaking. Here is Justice John Paul Stevens, writing for the Court without dissent:

> Judges are not experts in the field, and are not part of either political branch of the Government. Courts must, in some cases, reconcile competing political interests, but not on the basis of the judges' personal policy preferences. In contrast, an agency to which Congress has delegated policy-making responsibilities may, within the limits of that delegation, properly rely upon the incumbent administration's views of wise policy to inform its judgments. While agencies are not directly accountable to the people, the Chief Executive is, and it is entirely appropriate for this political branch of the Government to make such policy choices—resolving the competing interests which Congress itself either inadvertently did not resolve, or intentionally left to be resolved by the agency charged with the administration of the statute in light of everyday realities.[60]

Chevron represented the highpoint of judicial restraint in contemporary administrative law, but as we shall see, the justices recently have retreated somewhat from the *Chevron* position.[61]

* * *

Reflecting on the regulatory history of the United States, Thomas McCraw commented, "The single constant in the American experience with regulation has been controversy."[62] The same might be said of the history of American administrative law. The

---

58. *Id*. at 558 (emphasis added) (citation omitted).

59. 467 U.S. 837 (1984).

60. *Id*. at 865–66.

61. See United States v. Mead Corp., 533 U.S. 218 (2001). *Chevron* and its progeny are discussed in § 8.5(b)-(d).

62. McCraw, Prophets of Regulation, *supra* note 24, at 301.

reasons for this controversy are fairly clear. Government administration raises fundamental issues on which Americans have always divided. But there would be controversy even without such divisions. The tasks of government regulation and of administrative law are extremely difficult. Congress has typically turned to administrative regulation only after other institutions have failed to resolve public problems. As for administrative law, the challenge of devising a legal framework that both legitimates and controls the authority of administrative agencies is not to be underestimated. But if the tasks of administrative agencies and of administrative law are difficult, they also are crucial. Americans have relied on agencies to run their government, to see them through economic depression and world wars, and to protect their health, wealth, and safety during quieter times. Americans have relied on administrative law to ensure that agencies perform these functions with due regard for the rule of law, a proper respect for individual rights, and a sense of fidelity to our deepest constitutional commitments.

Finally, and perhaps most importantly, a review of the history of the American administrative state and of American administrative law shows that our understanding of each has changed over time. If controversy has been a constant of government administration, so has change. And there is no reason to believe that controversy and change will ever cease being part of the American administrative experience. Every generation's understanding of the role of government administration, and therefore of the role of administrative law, is but a snapshot of a moving target. It is to the development of that picture that we now turn.

Chapter 2

ADMINISTRATIVE AGENCIES IN AMERICAN CONSTITUTIONAL GOVERNMENT

Administrative law provides the legal framework within which government officials affect individual rights. So does the Constitution. It should not be surprising, then, that administrative law contains a substantial constitutional component. Two constitutional doctrines play an especially significant role in administrative law—procedural due process and separation of powers. The former doctrine is considered in Chapter 3. Separation of powers is the subject of this chapter.

§ 2.1   An Introduction to Separation of Powers and Checks and Balances in the United States Constitution

The theory of separated powers is easy to state, but often is difficult to apply. It is a two-part doctrine that begins with a descriptive statement. The theory posits that all governments possess three, and only three, broad categories of power. These are (1) the legislative power (the power to make law), (2) the executive power (the power to carry out those laws), and (3) the judicial power (the power to adjudicate cases that arise from either the making or execution of the law). It is an axiom of separation of powers theory that every governmental action is to be classified into one, and only one, of these three categories. This descriptive statement is followed by a normative claim. Separation of powers theory holds that good governance is obtainable only if each of the three powers of government is assigned to a distinct power holder.

Separation of powers promises to serve two values that are indispensable to good government. First, as James Madison argued, separating the powers of government is an "essential precaution in favor of liberty."[1] This power dispersal, the argument goes, is necessary to prevent tyranny, which Madison defined as "[t]he accumulation of all powers, legislative, executive, and judiciary, in the same hands."[2] In addition to securing individual liberty, separation of powers increases governmental effectiveness. On this claim, dispersing the powers of government makes possible a division of labor that enhances institutional competence.[3] Separation of powers thus was essential to the framers' constitutional aspiration of creating "that happy mean which ... combines the energy of government with the security of private rights."[4] In other words, the framers believed that separation of powers was an indispensable condition for a government that was both effective and safe.

One would expect a government that is constituted in accordance with separation of powers theory to consist of three institutions, each of which is assigned at least primary responsibility over one of the three governmental powers. This, of course, describes the government of the United States. The first three articles of the Constitution constitute the three branches of the federal government. Article I is the legislative article. It begins by "vest[ing]" "[a]ll legislative powers" granted by the Constitution to "a Congress of the United States which shall consist of a Senate and House of Representatives" (§ 1). Article II is the executive article, and it begins with a similar Vesting Clause that assigns "[t]he executive Power ... [to] a President of the United States of America" (§ 1, cl. 1). The judicial article, Article III, follows the

§ 2.1

1. See THE FEDERALIST No. 47, at 312 (James Madison) (Modern Library ed., 1941). For development of the link between separation of powers and individual liberty, see Rebecca L. Brown, *Separated Powers and Ordered Liberty*, 139 U. PA. L. REV. 1513 (1991).

2. See THE FEDERALIST No. 47, *supra* note 1, at 312.

3. For development of the link between separation of powers and governmental effectiveness, see Louis Fisher, *The Efficiency Side of Separated Powers*, 5 J. AM. STUD. 113 (1971).

4. THE FEDERALIST No. 26, *supra* note 1, at 159 (Alexander Hamilton).

same track. It vests "[t]he judicial Power of the United States . . . in one Supreme Court, and in such inferior Courts as the Congress may from time to time ordain and establish" (§ 1). After naming each of the principal institutions of the federal government, and vesting them with their assigned power, the three articles follow a similar pattern. They delineate the specific powers that each of the branches possess within the general categories of authority that have been vested in them, outline the basic institutional structure of each branch, and finally, prescribe the method for selecting the members of each branch.

The first three articles of the Constitution provide not only for three *distinct* branches of the federal government, but also for three *distinctive* institutions that the framers specifically designed to handle their assigned powers. Congress is the framers' optimal lawmaker. It is the largest, most representative, and thus most democratic of the three branches. At the same time, its bicameral organization tempers democratic responsiveness by fostering deliberation, compromise, and thus moderation, in the legislative process. The president is the framers' optimal CEO. Because the president is selected by a national election, he or she is accountable to all of the people of the United States for administration of the federal government. The framers reinforced that accountability by placing the executive power in a unitary office, which discourages buck-passing for decisions that go awry. They also believed, that a unitary executive would foster strength, energy, and decisiveness in the execution of federal law and in government administration. Finally, an unelected, life-tenured judiciary promises an independent and principled exercise of the judicial power, which the framers believed was necessary for protecting individual rights and for holding government officials within the rule of law.

The seeming simplicity of the framers' embrace of separation of powers in the government of the United States is compromised by a profound constitutional silence, however. Although the Constitution embodies separation of powers in the structure of the document and incorporates the theory in the organization of the government it creates, there is no "Separation of Powers Clause," as such. Indeed, the text of the Constitution does not mention the phrase "separation of powers." There is thus no constitutional provision that expressly requires the institutions of government to conform their actions to a stated principle of separation of powers. Perhaps more importantly, there is no provision of the Constitution that authoritatively defines the understanding of separation of powers that guided the framers' handiwork. This is a striking omission because such provisions were common in the state constitutions of the time. Why the silence?

There are three possible explanations. The absence of an explicit separation of powers norm in the Constitution may have reflected the framers' skepticism that "parchment barriers" requiring separated powers would effectively control "the encroaching spirit of power."[5] This skepticism was fed by the experience in many states, which had stated strict separation norms in their constitutions only to violate them in practice. The framers' belief that prescribing a constitutional principle would have been similarly ineffective may have led them to favor a strategy of institutionalizing separation of powers doctrine by writing it into the nature and operations of the three federal branches. But although this explanation might account for the framers' decision to embody the doctrine in their governmental design, it does not justify their failure to illuminate that design by prescribing a separation principle to govern the actions of the new government.

That failure might better be explained by a lack of confidence on the part of the framers that they could articulate a principle of separated powers with the degree of specificity necessary to serve as a constitutional standard of governance. As Madison explained, "Experience has instructed us that no skill in the science of government has yet been able to discriminate and define, with sufficient certainty, its three great provinces—the legislative, executive, and judiciary."[6] This modesty might account for the peculiarity of the vesting clauses of the first three articles allocating the "legislative," "executive," and "judicial" powers to Congress, the president, and the courts, respectively, without defining the meaning of those terms.

An alternative account of the framers' reticence suggests that a lack of consensus, rather than an inability to articulate a separation principle, may have been at work. The framers compromised many of their disagreements by agreeing to disagree, leaving the Constitution silent on the contested issue, and trusting in the constitutional operations of the government they created to address the issue in due course. Although there was consensus within the founding generation expressing allegiance to the "political maxim" of separated powers,[7] there were multiple meanings of the theory in competition at the time. The principal disagreement was between those who adopted a pure theory of separated powers, and those who blended separation theory with the related, but distinct, doc-

---

5. THE FEDERALIST No. 48, *supra* note 1, at 321 (James Madison); see THE FEDERALIST No. 48, *supra* note 1, at 326 (J. Madison) ("a mere demarcation on parchment of the constitutional limits of the several departments, is not a sufficient guard against those encroachments which lead to a tyrannical concentration of all powers of government in the same hands").

6. See THE FEDERALIST No. 37, *supra* note 1, at 229 (James Madison).

7. See THE FEDERALIST No. 47, *supra* note 1, at 312 (James Madison).

trine of checks and balances. This disagreement ultimately spilled over into opposition to the Constitution: A prominent theme of the Anti-federalist attack was the objection that the proposed government violated separation of powers requirements. The framers may have thought that writing an explicit separation principle into the document would exacerbate this tension and provide a focal point of attack by the opponents of ratification.

A pure theory of separated powers demands the *complete* separation of governmental institutions. Each branch is confined strictly to the exercise of its assigned power. Separation purists believe that complete separation is necessary for each branch to possess the independence and power to check the others, and ultimately, to prevent any one branch from controlling the government.[8]

The framers rejected such a purist approach in favor of a strategy that prescribed only a *partial* separation of powers among the branches of the federal government. According to Madison, separation of powers meant "no more" than that "the *whole* power of one department [may not be] exercised by the same hands which possess the *whole* power of another department."[9] The framers' separation theory thus allowed the three departments to have "*partial agency* in, [and some] *control* over, the acts of each other."[10]

The partial separation of powers embodied in the Constitution resulted from a combination of separated powers theory with the theory of checks and balances. In a system of checks and balances, each branch of government is assigned some role in the exercise of the other branches' functions. The framers combined the theory of checks and balances with separation theory because of their belief, paradoxically, that in order to maintain "the degree of separation ... essential to a free government," the three departments must be "connected and blended as to give to each a constitutional control over the others."[11]

The overarching strategy of interweaving checks and balances throughout a government of largely separated powers is reflected throughout the Constitution. For example, Congress's lawmaking authority is subject to the president's veto power (art. I, § 7, cls. 2, 3). The president, as chief executive, has the power to appoint the

---

8. See M.J.C. VILE, CONSTITUTIONALISM AND THE SEPARATION OF POWERS 13 (1967).

9. THE FEDERALIST NO. 47, *supra* note 1, at 314 (James Madison) (emphasis in original).

10. *Id.* at 313 (James Madison); see THE FEDERALIST NO. 66, *supra* note 1, at

429 (Alexander Hamilton) (separation of powers is "entirely compatible with a partial intermixture of [the] departments for special purposes, preserving them, in the main, distinct and unconnected").

11. THE FEDERALIST NO. 48, *supra* note 1, at 321 (James Madison).

senior officials of his or her administration, but only with the "Advice and Consent of the Senate" (art. II, § 2, cl. 2). In addition, those officials, as well as the president and vice president, are subject to impeachment and removal from office by Congress (art. I, § 2, cl. 5; *id.*, § 3, cl. 6; art. II, § 4). Even the tenure of federal judges, the most independent of government actors, depends on decisions by the other branches of government. Judges are appointed by the president with Senate approval (art. II, § 2, cl. 2) and are subject to impeachment and removal by Congress (art. II, § 4). The judiciary, for its part, holds the trump card of judicial review, empowering federal judges to set aside the actions of the other branches for infidelity to the Constitution or other governing laws.[12] These and other combinations of power-separation and power-sharing arrangements in the day-to-day operations of the federal government create an intricate web of institutional relationships that, the framers hoped, would prevent any of the three branches from emerging as a tyrant.

The disagreement within the founding generation between those who insisted on a pure separation of powers and those who believed it necessary to compromise complete institutional separation in the interest of enhancing checks and balances remains vigorous today. It takes the form of the equally intense debate among judges and legal scholars over the relative merits of formal and functional approaches to separation of powers issues. The typical formal approach deduces from the three vesting clauses a constitutional acceptance of a pure version of separated powers theory. While separation formalists concede that the Constitution did not "hermetically" seal the three branches of the federal government from each other,[13] they resist deviations from the model of pure separation that are not explicitly authorized by the Constitution.[14] Formalist judges favor a categorical analysis that inquires whether a branch's actions are within the scope of authority vested in it by the Constitution.[15]

The linkage between separation formalism and separation purism is apparent in the Supreme Court's classic statement of the formal approach to separation of powers in *Immigration and Naturalization Service v. Chadha*,[16] which ruled legislative vetoes unconstitutional (see § 2.3(b)). In his opinion for the Court, Chief Justice Warren E. Burger wrote:

12. See THE FEDERALIST No. 78, *supra* note 1, at 505–09 (Alexander Hamilton).

13. Buckley v. Valeo, 424 U.S. 1, 121 (1976).

14. See, e.g., INS v. Chadha, 462 U.S. 919, 955–56 (1983); Myers v. United States, 272 U.S. 52, 116 (1926).

15. See, e.g., Morrison v. Olson, 487 U.S. 654, 697 (1988) (Scalia, J., dissenting); Bowsher v. Synar, 478 U.S. 714 (1986): INS v. Chadha, 462 U.S. 919 (1983); Youngstown Sheet & Tube Co. v. Sawyer, 343 U.S. 579 (1952); Myers v. United States, 272 U.S. 52 (1926).

16. 462 U.S. 919 (1983).

The Constitution sought to divide the delegated powers of the new federal government into three defined categories, legislative, executive and judicial, to assure, as nearly as possible, that each Branch of government would confine itself to its assigned responsibility. The hydraulic pressure inherent within each of the separate Branches to exceed the outer limits of its power, even to accomplish desirable objectives, must be resisted.[17]

The Chief Justice, like other separation formalists, believed that the courts are constitutionally obligated to resist any such overreaching by the political branches.

Separation functionalists reject the ideal of pure separation as fundamentally mistaken, claiming that balanced governance requires more blending of the three governmental powers than formalists would allow. The linkage between separation functionalism and the rejection of separation purism comes through clearly in Justice Robert H. Jackson's classic statement in the *Steel Seizure* case:

The actual art of governing under our Constitution does not and cannot conform to judicial definitions of the power of any of its branches based on isolated clauses or even single Articles torn from context. While the Constitution diffuses power the better to secure liberty, it also contemplates that practice will integrate the dispersed powers into a workable government. It enjoins upon its branches separateness but interdependence, autonomy but reciprocity.[18]

As Justice Jackson's statement illustrates, separation functionalists tend to emphasize the necessary coordination of the branches, rather than their independence.

Separation functionalists also champion a "pragmatic, flexible approach" to separation of powers issues,[19] in opposition to the categorical analysis favored by separation formalists.[20] For a functionalist, the crucial inquiry is not whether a government actor has strayed beyond a constitutionally fixed sphere of authority, but rather whether the action has disrupted the "proper balance" of powers among the branches.[21] Functionalist judges thus are especially on guard against efforts by one branch to "aggrandize"

17. *Id*. at 919.

18. Youngstown Sheet & Tube Co. v. Sawyer, 343 U.S. 579, 635 (1952) (Jackson, J., concurring).

19. See Nixon v. Administrator of General Services, 433 U.S. 425, 442 (1977).

20. See, e.g., Commodity Futures Trading Commission v. Schor, 478 U.S. 833, 847–48 (1986).

21. See *Nixon*, 433 U.S. at 443.

its power at the expense of the others,[22] as well as against a branch's actions that "encroach" on the authority of another branch.[23] Separation functionalists typically seek to preserve a properly balanced government by balancing the relevant interests, asking first whether one branch has prevented another branch from "accomplishing its constitutionally assigned functions."[24] If so, the functionalist asks the decisive question, "whether that impact is justified by an overriding need to promote objectives within the constitutional authority" of the acting branch.[25] Deploying such a balancing analysis, functionalist courts typically uphold "statutory provisions that to some degree commingle the functions of the Branches, but that pose no danger of either aggrandizement or encroachment."[26]

The battle between separation formalists and separation functionalists has yet to produce a clear winner.[27] The Supreme Court decisions that have shaped the separation of powers component of administrative law sometimes have reflected a formalistic approach,[28] and at other times a functional approach.[29] Notwithstanding this ongoing debate, or perhaps because of it, the Constitution's separation of powers might best be understood neither as a definitional allocation of authority nor as a balancing scale, but rather, at least with respect to domestic affairs, as a constitutionally prescribed *process* of decisionmaking by which the government as a whole may legitimately take action that creates or extinguishes individual rights. (See Figure 2–1.)

---

22. See, e.g., Morrison v. Olson, 487 U.S. 654, 694 (1988); *Schor*, 478 U.S. at 856.

23. See, e.g., Mistretta v. United States, 488 U.S. 361, 382 (1989).

24. *Nixon*, 433 U.S. at 443.

25. *Id.*, 433 U.S. at 443.

26. *Mistretta*, 488 U.S. at 382.

27. For accounts of the formalism-functionalism debate, see Brown, *Separated Powers*, supra note 1, at 1522–31;

Thomas W. Merrill, *The Constitutional Principle of Separation of Powers*, 1991 SUP. CT. REV. 225, 229–35 (1991); Keith Werhan, *Toward an Eclectic Approach to Separation of Powers:* Morrison v. Olson *Examined*, 16 HAST. CONST. L.Q. 393, 425–29 (1989).

28. See, e.g., INS v. Chadha, 462 U.S. 919 (1983).

29. See, e.g., *Schor*, 478 U.S. at 851.

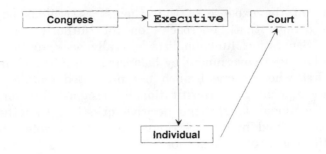

Figure 2-1: The Separation of Powers Process

According to this process-based conception of the separation of powers, individual rights are altered only as a result of a three-stage process of decisionmaking whereby (1) Congress enacts a law that authorizes (2) an executive official to take an action, (3) subject to judicial review.[30] This process-based orientation makes vivid the essential connection between the separation of powers and the rule of law, under which the government may affect individual rights only pursuant to acts of Congress and in accordance with the Constitution.

The crucial feature of the separation of powers process is that each governmental actor lacks the authority to alter individual rights unilaterally, and thus, is blocked by the ordinary operation of government from acquiring tyrannical power, as Madison understood it. Accordingly, Congress cannot administer the laws it enacts. The executive must trace the authority for its administration back to an act of Congress. And at the request of an injured party, courts ensure that each branch has acted lawfully and within constitutional bounds. Ultimately, then, the government alters individual rights authoritatively, and legitimately, only as a whole, and only with the alignment of each of the three branches of the government.

§ 2.2   An Introduction to the Place of Administrative Agencies in the Separation of Powers

Administrative agencies pose a double-barrel challenge to the constitutional assumption that each of three distinct branches

---

30. For an elaboration of this process-based approach to separation of powers, see Keith Werhan, *Normalizing* *the Separation of Powers*, 70 Tul. L. Rev. 2681 (1996).

would handle one, and only one, of the three powers of the federal government. First, administrative agencies appear to embody the evil of tyranny that separation of powers was designed to avoid. Agencies typically have authority to make legally binding rules (which resembles the legislative power of Congress), to enforce statutes and administer programs (which is executive in nature), and to adjudicate disputes (which resembles the judicial power of the federal courts). On this description, do not agencies fit Madison's definition of tyranny as "[t]he accumulation of all powers, legislative, executive, and judiciary, in the same hands?"[1] The combination of the three powers of government in administrative agencies poses a second, related problem. If each of the three branches of government is authorized to handle only one of the three powers, can these multi-powered agencies fit within any one branch? Justice Robert H. Jackson became so flustered by this problem that he memorably described agencies as constitutional abominations that occupied "a veritable fourth branch of the Government [that] . . . deranged our three-branch legal theories much as the concept of a fourth dimension unsettles our three-dimensional thinking."[2]

The challenges agencies pose to separation of powers theory are real, and they caused considerable controversy and confusion during the early development of the administrative state. Some defenders of administrative government during the New Deal brazenly argued that separation of powers was an eighteenth-century anachronism that was not up to the task of organizing modern governments. These New Dealers claimed that "the administrative process [had sprung] from the inadequacy of a simple tripartite form of government to deal with modern problems."[3] This "defense" conceded the unconstitutionality of the administrative state instead of defending its legitimacy.

The best (yet not completely satisfying) response to the challenges that agencies pose to the constitutional requirement of separated powers lies in the so-called traditional model of administrative law (see § 1.4). The traditional model begins with Congress passing an organic (or enabling) act that creates administrative agencies and gives them their authority. Agencies only have the powers given them by statute. If they exceed those powers, courts invalidate their actions upon judicial review. Viewed through the

§ 2.2

1. THE FEDERALIST No. 47, at 312 (James Madison) (Modern Library ed., 1941).

2. Federal Trade Commission v. Ruberoid Co., 343 U.S. 470, 487 (1952) (Jackson, J., concurring). For an across-the-board attack on the constitutionality of the modern administrative state, see Gary Lawson, *The Rise and Rise of the Administrative State*, 107 HARV. L. REV. 1231 (1994).

3. JAMES M. LANDIS, THE ADMINISTRATIVE PROCESS 1 (1938).

lens of the traditional model, it can be seen that even when agency actions "resemble"[4] lawmaking (i.e., rulemaking) or judicial decisions (i.e., adjudication), they always are taken in administration of statutory authority, and thus are executive in nature.[5] And because administrative agencies can be said to exercise only the executive power, they can be situated within the executive branch.[6] (See Figure 2–2.)

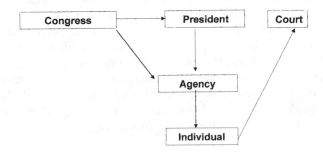

Figure 2-2: Place of Adminstrative Agencies in Separation of Powers

As Justice Stephen G. Breyer observed, "This constitutional understanding explains why both commentators and courts have often attached the prefix 'quasi' to descriptions of an agency's rulemaking or adjudicative functions.... The terms 'quasi legislative' and 'quasi adjudicative' indicate that the agency uses legislative *like* or court *like* procedures but that it is not, constitutionally speaking, either a legislature or a court."[7]

The traditional model also offers a measure of comfort to those who are concerned that the concentration of authority in administrative agencies is incompatible with the framers' acceptance of the doctrine of checks and balances. Even though agencies appear to concentrate all of the powers of government within their corridors,

4. See INS v. Chadha, 462 U.S. 919, 953 n.16 (1983).

5. See FMC v. South Carolina State Ports Authority, 535 U.S. 743, 773–74 (2002) (Breyer, J., dissenting); Bowsher v. Synar, 478 U.S. 714, 726 (1986).

6. See *South Carolina State Ports Authority*, 535 U.S. at 773–74 (Breyer, J., dissenting); Freytag v. Commissioner

of Internal Revenue, 501 U.S. 868, 910 (Scalia, J., concurring in part and concurring in the judgment); *Bowsher*, 478 U.S. at 726.

7. *South Carolina State Ports Authority*, 535 U.S. at 774 (Breyer, J., dissenting).

the traditional model reveals that they are far from the governmental tyrant that Madison had feared. The key insight here is that agencies act under the supervisory authority of each of the three principal constitutional institutions.[8] At the outset, Congress retains the legislative power to define the scope of agency authority by statute. When agencies exercise their statutory authority, they do so subject to the overriding power of the president to "take Care that the Laws be faithfully executed" (Art. II, § 3). And finally, the courts exercise their power of judicial review to ensure the lawfulness of agency action.

The traditional model of administrative law thus helps to legitimate agency authority under the Constitution by aligning the administrative process with the process of governmental decision-making prescribed by the separation of powers: Congress enacts a law authorizing executive action that is subject to judicial review. But this alignment, as is often the case with the American Constitution, is a double-edged sword. While it provides constitutional legitimacy for the exercise of administrative power, it also imposes constitutional limits on the role that each governmental actor—Congress, the president, the courts, and the agencies themselves—can play in the administrative process.

§ 2.3   Administrative Agencies and Congress

Congress plays an instrumental role in the administrative process, but the separation of powers restricts its participation to activities that are consistent with its constitutional status as national lawmaker. Legislators engage in the administrative process in two basic ways. First, they launch the administrative process by creating agencies, by defining the scope of agency authority, and by funding agency activities. Congress performs each of these tasks by enacting statutes. Congress also provides an oversight function, with the aim of ensuring that agencies exercise their authority and spend their money in a manner that is consistent with evolving legislative policy goals.

The constitutional status of Congress as national lawmaker also prescribes the limits of the legislative role in the administrative process. At the outset, Congress must ensure that enabling acts creating administrative agencies and authorizing them to act do not amount to a delegation of its legislative power. And later, when overseeing agency action, Congress must take care not to venture beyond its legislative role by attempting to administer the enabling acts they have passed. In other words, separation of powers re-

---

8. See Harold H. Bruff, *On the Constitutional Status of the Administrative Agencies*, 36 Am. U. L. Rev. 491, 511 (1987); Peter L. Strauss, *The Place of Agencies in Government: Separation of Powers and the Fourth Branch*, 84 Colum. L. Rev. 573, 577–80 (1984).

quires that legislators avoid the extremes of either ceding or exceeding their role as the nation's lawmakers.

(a) The Nondelegation Doctrine

The nondelegation principle states the formal proposition that Congress cannot delegate its legislative power to any other institution.[1] Paraphrasing John Locke, whose writings deeply influenced the founding generation, the nondelegation principle limits Congress to making laws, rather than lawmakers.[2] The nondelegation principle is rooted to some degree in the "well-known maxim" of the common law of agency, *delegata potestas non potest delegari* (a delegated power cannot be delegated),[3] but in recent years, the Supreme Court has stressed the Lockean linkage between the prohibition against legislative delegations and separation of powers.[4]

Although the Constitution does not explicitly bar Congress from ceding its legislative power, the nondelegation principle finds textual support in the Vesting Clause of Article I, which vests *"[a]ll* legislative Powers ... in ... Congress"* (§ 1 (emphasis added)). Read through the lens of the principle of popular sovereignty, the Vesting Clause of Article I constitutes a delegation of the entire legislative power of the federal government by "the people of the United States" (U.S.CONST., preamble) to Congress, and for that reason, Congress is powerless to abdicate its lawmaking responsibility by delegating it to others.[5] John Locke anticipated this fundamental principle of American constitutionalism in his *Second Treatise of Government*:

> The People alone can appoint the Form of the Commonwealth, which is by Constituting the Legislative, and appointing in whose hands that shall be. And when the People have said, We will submit to rules, and be govern'd by *Laws* made by such Men, and in such Forms, no Body else can say other Men shall make *Laws* for them; nor can the people be bound by any *Laws* but such as Enacted by those, whom they have Chosen, and Authorized to make *Laws* for them.[6]

The nondelegation principle also reinforces the constitutional commitment to representative democracy. Congress possesses the

---

§ 2.3

1. See Field v. Clark, 143 U.S. 649, 692 (1892).

2. John Locke, *The Second Treatise of Government* § 141, lines 13–16 (1690), in JOHN LOCKE, TWO TREATISES OF GOVERNMENT 363 (1988).

3. See J.W. Hampton, Jr. & Co., 276 U.S. 394, 405–06 (1928).

4. Mistretta v. United States, 488 U.S. 361, 371–72 (1989).

5. See Whitman v. American Trucking Associations, Inc., 531 U.S. 457, 472 (2001).

6. Locke, *Second Treatise of Government*, *supra* note 2, at § 141, lines 3–11, pp. 362–63.

lawmaking power because it is the most democratic of the three branches of government. It thus would subvert the political accountability hardwired into the legislative process for Congress to farm out its lawmaking authority to institutions that are less democratic, and therefore less accountable, in their decisionmaking.[7]

Although some have questioned the constitutional pedigree of the nondelegation principle,[8] such questioning has been rare among the justices of the Supreme Court. The Court has steadily maintained the essential position of the nondelegation principle, that Congress cannot delegate its legislate power. The enduring doctrinal difficulty associated with the nondelegation principle has been defining what it means for Congress to delegate its legislative power. The nondelegation principle has always appeared puzzling in light of the day-to-day practice of government administration. Beginning with its very first session, when Congress gave officials in the brand new Treasury Department the power to "estimate the duties payable" on imports,[9] as well as to adjudicate claims for veterans' pensions for "invalids who were wounded and disabled during the [Revolutionary War],"[10] Congress, drawing on its necessary and proper power, has vested government administrators with considerable discretion to take actions with the force of law. In the modern era, the challenge of squaring the nondelegation principle with the reality of agency power has become all the more acute, not only because of the growth of the administrative state, but also because of the increased use of agency rulemaking, which produces the functional equivalent of laws.[11]

Chief Justice John Marshall, characteristically, spotted the separation of powers puzzle that Congress creates when it enacts a

7. See JOHN H. ELY, DEMOCRACY AND DISTRUST: A THEORY OF JUDICIAL REVIEW 131–34 (1980); DAVID SCHOENBROD, POWER WITHOUT RESPONSIBILITY: HOW CONGRESS ABUSES THE PEOPLE THROUGH DELEGATION 99–106 (1993)

8. See, e.g., SOTIRIOS A. BARBER, THE CONSTITUTION AND THE DELEGATION OF CONGRESSIONAL POWER 12 (1975).

9. Act of July 31, 1789, 1st Cong., 1st Sess., ch. 5, 1 Stat. 29.

10. Act of Sept. 29, 1789, 1st Cong., 1st Sess., ch. 24, 1 Stat. 95.

11. In a rare exception to the nearly universal judicial endorsement of the constitutional imperative of the nondelegation doctrine, Justice John Paul Stevens, in a recent opinion joined by Justice David H. Souter, encouraged his colleagues to acknowledge that Congress has delegated "legislative power" whenever a statute authorizes an agency to engage in rulemaking. To Justice Stevens, this acknowledgement was not constitutionally fatal, because the text of Article I's Vesting Clause "do[es] not purport to limit the authority of [Congress] to delegate authority to others." Justice Stevens's skepticism of a constitutional ban on congressional delegations of the legislative power, however, did not mean that he would sanction all such delegations without limit. Instead, consistently with contemporary nondelegation doctrine, Justice Stevens only would uphold legislative delegations when they provide "a sufficiently intelligible principle." *American Trucking*, 531 U.S. at 488–90 (Stevens, J., concurring in part and concurring in the judgment).

law that vests government administrators with discretion to act with the force of law. Marshall wrote, "The difference between the departments undoubtedly is, that the legislature makes, the executive executes, and the judiciary construes the law; but the maker of the law may commit something to the discretion of the other departments, and the precise boundary of this power is a subject of delicate and difficult inquiry, into which a Court will not enter unnecessarily."[12] Marshall's tentative statement charted the future direction of the nondelegation doctrine. The basic judicial strategy for squaring the nondelegation principle with the pervasive exercise of administrative discretion in American government has been to stake out a position somewhere between the extremes of holding either that Congress must make all decisions that entail policy discretion or that Congress may delegate all such policy decisions to other institutions. For the most part, the Court has followed Marshall's advice in giving Congress wide berth in deciding which policy decisions to make and which to pass on to others.

The Early Nondelegation Doctrine. Chief Justice Marshall's cautionary statement that the justices would not "enter unnecessarily" into Congress's prerogative to "commit something to the discretion of the other departments" set the tone for the early development of the nondelegation doctrine. Marshall's suggested approach to fashioning a nondelegation doctrine was only partially successful, however. In *Wayman v. Southard*,[13] Marshall experimented with a formalistic, categorical approach that would prohibit Congress from delegating "important subjects" that are "strictly and exclusively legislative." With respect to legislative subjects that are of "less interest," Congress would be free to make "general provision" and then entrust to others the power "to fill up the details."[14] Chief Justice Marshall offered no examples of the Article I powers that he believed could and could not be delegated. His reticence is understandable, for as the Court has noted in a different context, it is difficult to envision a "principled basis" upon which to create such a hierarchy of constitutional provisions.[15] It is hardly surprising, then, that the modern Supreme Court has rebuffed efforts to raise special constitutional barriers to the delegation of certain of Congress's legislative powers.[16]

---

12. Wayman v. Southard, 23 U.S. (10 Wheat.) 1, 46 (1825).

13. 23 U.S. (10 Wheat.) 1 (1825).

14. *Id*. at 42–43.

15. See Valley Forge Christian College v. Americans United for Separation of Church and State, Inc., 454 U.S. 464, 484 (1982).

16. See Touby v. United States, 500 U.S. 160, 165–66 (1991) (crimes); Skinner v. Mid–America Pipeline Co., 490 U.S. 212, 222–23 (1989) (taxes); J.W. Hampton & Co. v. United States, 276 U.S. 394, 409 (1928) (taxes and customs duties).

The Marshall Court's acceptance in *Wayman* of the lawmakers' prerogative to charge others with the task of fleshing out "general" statutory provisions did gain a foothold in constitutional jurisprudence, however. The early Court's essential position was that Congress could "commit something to the discretion" of executive officers as long as the lawmakers fulfilled their legislative duty by enacting a statute that provided sufficient policy direction to those officers. Although the justices manifested their acceptance of such congressional delegations as early as 1813,[17] they did not lay the doctrinal groundwork for their permissiveness until the final decade of the nineteenth century.

In *Field v. Clark*,[18] the Court upheld an enabling act that authorized the president to suspend the duty-free status of specified articles if the president found that the exporting nation imposed "reciprocally unequal and unreasonable" import restrictions on American goods. Adopting a decidedly functional and "practical construction of the constitution," the justices found that the statute did not, "in any real sense, invest the president with the power of legislation." The Court was content that Congress had exercised the legislative power by establishing the duty-free status of the articles, by authorizing the president to suspend that status "upon a named contingency," and by specifying the duties to be charged on the articles that the president suspended. As the *Field* Court saw it, the president's suspension power was executive rather than legislative in nature because it "related only to the enforcement of the policy established by congress." When the president suspended the duty-free status of imported articles, he did so as "the mere agent of the law-making department to ascertain and declare the event upon which its expressed will was to take effect." The Court in *Field* recognized that the president enjoyed "large discretion" in determining whether any particular nation had imposed "reciprocally unequal and unreasonable" import restrictions on American products.[19]

Not long after deciding *Field*, the Court upheld the power of Congress to give administrative agencies the discretionary authority to issue rules with the force of law. This is a significant step beyond *Field*, where the enabling act had simply created presidential discretion, "upon a named contingency," to replace one statutory provision (duty-free status) with another (a specified duty). The Court took this step in *Buttfield v. Stranahan*.[20] The justices in *Buttfield* upheld the Tea Inspection Act, which authorized the Secretary of the Treasury to "establish uniform standards of puri-

---

17. The Cargo of the Brig Aurora v. United States, 11 U.S. (7 Cranch) 382 (1813).

18.   143 U.S. 649 (1892).

19.   See *id.* at 691–93.

20.   192 U.S. 470 (1904).

ty, quality, and fitness for consumption of all kinds of teas imported into the United States." The Act made it illegal to import tea that did not meet the Secretary's standards. The challengers claimed that the Act unconstitutionally delegated Congress's "legislative power" by committing "the determination of what teas may be imported" to the "arbitrary discretion" of the Secretary. The justices read the Act as "express[ing] the purpose to exclude the lowest grades of tea." They therefore were satisfied that Congress had set the "primary standard" and had charged the Secretary with "the mere executive duty to effectuate the legislative policy declared in the statute." The Court thus found the Tea Act to be "within the principle of [*Field*]," explaining, "Congress legislated on the subject as far as was reasonably practicable, and from the necessities of the case was compelled to leave to executive officials the duty of bringing about the result pointed out by the statute. To deny the power of Congress to delegate such a duty would, in effect, amount but to declaring that the plenary power vested in Congress to regulate foreign commerce could not be efficaciously exerted."[21]

The Court reinforced *Buttfield* in *United States v. Grimaud*, upholding a more expansive enabling act that authorized the Secretary of Agriculture generally to issue rules "for the protection against destruction by fire and depredations upon . . . public forests and forest reservations."[22] The Act, moreover, made violation of the Secretary's regulations a federal crime. Invoking *Field*'s "practical construction of the constitution," the Court began with the recognition that it was "impracticable" for Congress itself to regulate the numerous uses that might be made of the many national forests, which varied in their features and thus posed differing managerial challenges. With that functional orientation, the justices manifested little difficulty in aligning Congress's grant of broad discretionary authority to the Agriculture Secretary with the delegations they had upheld in *Field* and *Buttfield*:

> [I]n authorizing the Secretary of Agriculture to meet . . . local conditions [in the national forests], Congress was merely conferring administrative functions upon an agent, and not delegating to him legislative power. . . . From the beginning of the government, various acts have been passed conferring upon executive officers power to make rules and regulations—not [only] for the government of their departments, but [also] for administering the laws which did govern. None of these statutes could confer legislative power. . . . [W]hen Congress had legislated and indicated its will, it could give to those who were to act under such general provisions "power to fill up the details" by the establishment of administrative rules and regu-

---

21. *Id*. at 471–72 n.1, 496.   **22.** 220 U.S. 506, 509 (1911).

lations, the violation of which could be punished by fine or imprisonment fixed by Congress, or by penalties fixed by Congress, or measured by the injury done.[23]

Grimaud, along with *Field* and *Buttfield*, demonstrate the latent potency of Chief Justice Marshall's early conception of the congressional prerogative to authorize administrators "to fill up the details" of "general [statutory] provision[s]," especially when shorn of the caveat that such a prerogative existed only for legislative subjects of "less interest."[24]

This early judicial understanding of the nondelegation principle crystallized into constitutional doctrine on the eve of the Stock Market Crash of 1929. In *J.W. Hampton, Jr., & Co. v. United States*,[25] the justices upheld a tariff law that gave the president broader discretion than had the statute at issue in *Field*. The enabling act before the Court in *J.W. Hampton* authorized the president to "increase or decrease ... any rate of duty" that Congress had provided in the act as "necessary to equalize ... differences in [the] costs of production" between the United States and the exporting nation. Once again echoing *Field*'s endorsement of a "practical construction of the constitution" in evaluating congressional delegations, the Court in *J.W. Hampton* observed, "In determining what [Congress] may do in seeking assistance from another branch, the extent and character of that assistance must be fixed according to common sense and the inherent necessities of the governmental co-ordination." The Court continued, "The field of Congress involves all and many varieties of legislative action, and Congress has found it frequently necessary to use officers of the executive branch, within defined limits, to secure the exact effect intended by its acts of legislation, by vesting discretion in such officers to make public regulations interpreting a statute and directing the details of its execution, even to the extent of providing for penalizing a breach of such regulations."[26]

The justices in *J.W. Hampton* finally prescribed a constitutional test to enforce the nondelegation principle, a test that has since become authoritative: "If Congress shall lay down by legislative act an *intelligible principle* to which the person or body authorized to [act] is directed to conform, such legislative action is not a forbidden delegation of legislative power." In the *J.W. Hampton* framework, Congress exercises the legislative power by enacting a statute with an "intelligible principle." The "person or body" that exercises discretion pursuant to such a principle acts not as a legislator, but "merely in execution" of an act of Congress.[27]

---

23. *Id*. at 516–17.

24. See *Wayman*, 23 U.S. at 42–43.

25. 276 U.S. 394 (1928).

26. *Id*. at 401, 406.

27. *Id*. at 409–11 (emphasis added).

In these early cases, the Supreme Court acknowledged the formal nondelegation principle (i.e., Congress cannot delegate its legislative power) even as it devised a functional nondelegation doctrine that readily legitimated congressional conferrals of broad discretionary authority to the president and to federal agencies to issue rules with the force of law. Although their written opinions suggest that the justices took nondelegation claims seriously, they did not invalidate a single enabling act on that ground. This pattern abruptly changed, however, in the wake of the Great Depression that followed on the heels of *J.W. Hampton*'s apparent, and apparently permissive, settlement of the nondelegation doctrine.

The New Deal Cases. Within the first five months of 1935, the Supreme Court invalidated two statutory grants of administrative authority on nondelegation grounds.[28] Both of these delegations were "emergency" provisions of Title I of the National Industrial Recovery Act of 1933 ("NIRA"),[29] which was the centerpiece of the "New Deal" program "to halt the downward spiral of the depression and reinvigorate the national economy."[30] (See § 1.5(c).) In the light of the 100–year history of judicial acceptance of legislative delegations, these decisions of 1935 stand out in sharp relief. What makes them truly remarkable, however, is that the Court thereafter returned to its old pattern of rejecting nondelegation challenges to congressional grants of administrative authority.

The pressing question arising from the NIRA decisions of 1935 is, why are they the only two instances in which the Supreme Court has found a violation of the nondelegation principle? Did the decisions rectify a congressional mistake, that is, did Congress neglect to include an "intelligible principle" in the NIRA to guide administrative discretion, as *J.W. Hampton* required? Or did they represent a judicial mistake, that is, did the justices overstep their authority by "enter[ing] unnecessarily" into Congress's prerogative to "commit something to the discretion of the other departments,"

---

28. A.L.A. Schechter Poultry Corp. v. United States, 295 U.S. 495 (1935); Panama Refining Co. v. Ryan, 293 U.S. 388 (1935). The year following these two decisions, the Court invoked the rule against legislative delegations to invalidate another New Deal statute in *Carter v. Carter Coal Co.*, 298 U.S. 238 (1936). But *Carter*, unlike the two previous decisions, involved delegations of lawmaking power to "private persons" rather than to executive officials, which the Court regarded as "legislative delegation in its most odious form." *Id.* at 311. The leading commentary on legislative delegations to nongovernmental entities is Louis Jaffe, *Law Making by Private*

Groups, 51 HARV. L. REV. 201 (1937). For more recent commentary, see Harold J. Krent, *Legal Theory: Fragmenting the Unitary Executive*, 85 NW. U. L. REV. 62 (1990); David M. Lawrence, *Private Exercise of Governmental Power*, 61 IND. L.J. 647 (1986).

29. Act of June 16, 1933, 73rd Cong., 1st Sess., ch. 90, §§ 3, 9, 48 Stat. 195, 196, 200.

30. Robert L. Stern, *The Commerce Clause and the National Economy, 1933–1946*, 59 HARV. L. REV. 645, 653 (1946).

against Chief Justice Marshall's admonition?[31] The two NIRA decisions are aberrational, but they are worthy of careful attention for the same reason that airline accidents are closely studied: Understanding what went wrong in these cases enriches one's understanding of the proper operation of the nondelegation doctrine.

The first section of the NIRA declared a "national emergency of widespread unemployment and disorganization of industry." Section 1 also delineated Congress's long list of policy objectives in passing the Act. These objectives were (1) to "remove obstructions to the free flow of interstate and foreign commerce," (2) to promote the "organization of industry for the purpose of cooperative action among trade groups," (3) to promote "united action of labor and management," (4) to "eliminate unfair competitive practices," (5) to "promote the fullest possible utilization of the present productive capacities of industries," (6) to "avoid undue restriction on production," (7) to "increase the consumption of industrial and agricultural products by increasing purchasing power," (8) to "reduce and relieve unemployment," (9) to "improve standards of labor," and (10) generally to "rehabilitate industry and ... conserve natural resources."[32] In order to effectuate these policies, Title I of the NIRA authorized the president, or the president's designee, to approve "codes of fair competition" for the many trades and industries operating throughout the United States.[33] Underscoring the emergency nature of this code-setting authority, Congress included a sunset provision that provided for the termination of Title I in two years, or sooner if the president (by proclamation) and Congress (by joint resolution) "declare that the emergency recognized by section 1 has ended."[34]

The Court's first blow against Title I did not involve the president's code-setting authority, however. In *Panama Refining Co. v. Ryan*,[35] the justices invalidated an "almost overlooked"[36] provision that Congress had included near the end of Title I to address the especially acute depression of oil prices. Section 9(c) of the NIRA "authorized [the president] to prohibit the transportation in interstate and foreign commerce" of so-called "hot oil," that is, petroleum and petroleum products that had been produced in excess of quotas established by state law.[37] The president issued an executive order prohibiting the interstate or foreign shipment of hot oil less than a month after the NIRA took effect. Section 9(c) made violations of the president's order a federal crime.

---

31. See *Wayman*, 23 U.S. at 46.

32. Act of June 16, 1933, *supra* note 29, § 1, 48 Stat. at 195.

33. *Id.*, §§ 2(b), 3(a), 48 Stat. at 195, 196.

34. *Id.*, § 2(c), 48 Stat. at 196.

35. 293 U.S. 388 (1935).

36. Stern, *Commerce Clause, supra* note 30, at 658.

37. Act of June 16, 1933, *supra* note 29, § 9(c), 48 Stat. at 200.

The Court in *Panama Refining* invalidated section 9(c) of the NIRA as "an unconstitutional delegation of legislative power." All of the justices agreed that section 9(c) defined *what* Congress had authorized the president to do (halt the shipment of hot oil out of state). They also agreed that section 9(c), read in isolation, contained no language guiding or limiting the president's discretion in deciding whether or not to take the authorized action. As the Court put it, the "brief and unambiguous" provision appeared to give the president "an unlimited authority to determine the policy and to lay down the prohibition, or not to lay it down, as he may see fit."[38] The key question in *Panama Refining* was whether Congress's declaration of policy in section 1 of the NIRA supplied the "intelligible principle" that section 9(c) so obviously lacked.

Only one member of the Court thought so. Justice Benjamin N. Cardozo, writing in dissent, argued that "the whole structure" of the NIRA suggested, "by reasonable implication," that "the President is to forbid the transportation of [hot] oil when he believes, in the light of the conditions of the industry as disclosed from time to time, that the prohibition will tend to effectuate the declared policies ... announced by section 1." The congressional policies delineated in section 1, moreover, provided "sufficient definition of a standard to make [section 9(c)] valid." Justice Cardozo supported his acceptance of section 9(c) by invoking the theme of constitutional pragmatism that had been a prominent feature of the Court's nondelegation precedent from the beginning. Because of the "host of unforeseen contingencies" that clouded the "intricate" task of determining on an on-going basis whether prohibiting the shipment of hot oil furthered Congress's policy objectives, Cardozo argued, the legislators had no choice but "to declare the act to be done and the policies to be promoted, leaving to the delegate of its power the ascertainment of the shifting facts that would determine the relation between the doing of the act and the attainment of the stated ends."[39] To Justice Cardozo, section 9(c) was no different than the delegations that the Court had upheld from *Field* to *J.W. Hampton*.

Justice Cardozo failed to persuade any of his colleagues that the congressional policy statement in section 1 of the NIRA supplied an intelligible principle which ensured that a presidential order halting the shipment of hot oil would be an executive rather than a legislative act. The majority of the Court read section 1 to be "simply an introduction of the act," including a "general outline of policy" which provided "nothing ... [that] limits or controls the authority conferred by section 9(c)." The majority in *Panama Refining* therefore concluded that Congress had "abdicate[d]" its "essential legislative function" by providing a standardless "trans-

38. *Panama Refining*, 293 U.S. at 414–15.

39. *Id*. at 435–43 (Cardozo, J., dissenting).

fer" of legislative authority to the president to enforce state oil-production quotas.[40]

The disagreement among the justices in *Panama Refining* was on the application rather than the meaning of the nondelegation principle. Although Justice Cardozo disagreed with the majority's assessment of the inadequacy of the section 1 policy statement to legitimate the exercise of presidential authority pursuant to section 9(c), he accepted the constitutional "need to discover in the terms of the act a standard reasonably clear whereby [the president's] discretion must be governed."[41] And the majority shared Cardozo's functional understanding of a nondelegation principle that possesses sufficient flexibility to allow Congress to exercise its constitutional powers effectively. The majority wrote, in language that Justice Cardozo, as well as earlier Courts, could have endorsed:

> Undoubtedly legislation must often be adapted to complex conditions involving a host of details with which the national Legislature cannot deal directly. The Constitution has never been regarded as denying to the Congress the necessary resources of flexibility and practicality, which will enable it to perform its function in laying down policies and establishing standards, while leaving to selected instrumentalities the making of subordinate rules within prescribed limits and the determination of facts to which the policy as declared by the Legislature is to apply. Without capacity to give authorizations of that sort we should have the anomaly of a legislative power which in many circumstances calling for its exertion would be but a futility.[42]

The rhetoric of the *Panama Refining* majority evidenced no intention to re-define the nondelegation principle. Rather, the Court viewed section 9(c) of the NIRA as a departure from its nondelegation precedent. And perhaps in response to the hyperactivity that characterized the New Deal Congress, the justices might have seen *Panama Refining* as providing an opportunity to underscore a constitutional boundary that they had often declared, but that they had never enforced to invalidate a congressional grant of administrative authority.

Congress's response to *Panama Refining* was swift and instructive. In less than two months, the legislators replaced section 9(c) of the NIRA with the Connolly Hot Oil Act.[43] The Act banned the interstate shipment of hot oil, but authorized the president to lift the ban upon a finding (1) that supply was insufficient to meet

40. *Id.* at 418–21.

41. *Id.* at 434 (Cardozo, J., dissenting).

42. *Id.* at 421.

43. Act of Feb. 22, 1935, 74th Cong., 1st Sess., ch. 18, 49 Stat. 30.

demand, and (2) that such disparity caused "an undue burden on or restriction of interstate commerce in petroleum and petroleum products." The Act also empowered the president to replace the statutory ban upon a finding that those conditions ceased to exist.[44] The Connolly Act provided the flexibility of section 9(c), allowing the president to lift and impose the ban on hot oil shipments according to the "host of unforeseen circumstances" that had concerned Justice Cardozo. At the same time, however, the act returned to the delegation model that had passed judicial scrutiny in *Field* and *J.W. Hampton*, with Congress enacting a rule that was subject to change upon an executive finding that certain specified conditions existed. The Connolly Act remains on the statute books today.[45]

The Court moved from the periphery of Title I of the NIRA to the statute's core—Congress's delegation in section 3 of code-setting authority to the president—in *A.L.A. Schechter Poultry Corp. v. United States*.[46] *Schechter* involved a constitutional challenge to a code of fair competition that the president had approved for the live poultry industry in the metropolitan New York area. As was typical of the NIRA codes, the Live Poultry Code included a set of fair labor standards, which among other things, prohibited child labor, created a right of collective bargaining, and established the minimum number of workers that slaughterhouses were required to employ. The code also regulated the trade practices within New York's live poultry industry by, among other things, fixing prices and prohibiting "unfair methods of competition."[47]

Section 3 of the NIRA, unlike section 9(c), provided some limitation on the president's code-setting authority. Before approving a code of fair competition, Congress required the president to find that the proposed code did not "promote monopolies" or "eliminate," "oppress," or "discriminate against" "small enterprises." Section 3 required more generally that the president approve only those codes which would "tend to effectuate the policy" of Title I, as stated in section 1 of the Act. For codes that had been proposed by "trade or industrial associations or groups," the president also was required to find that the proponents "impose[d] no inequitable restrictions" on membership and were "truly representative" of their trades or industries.[48]

Despite the limiting language of section 3, the Court, this time unanimously, ruled that the code-setting authority that Congress had provided to the president crossed the constitutional line because it had bestowed on him "virtually unfettered" discretion to

44. *Id.*, §§ 3–4, 49 Stat. at 31.

45. 15 U.S.C. §§ 715–715m.

46. 295 U.S. 495 (1935).

47. *Id.* at 523–25.

48. Act of June 16, 1933, *supra* note 29, § 3(a), 48 Stat. at 196.

govern American industry. Section 3's limits on the president's code-setting authority, the Court held, were too "few" and too "broad" to satisfy constitutional requirements. And the delineation of congressional policies in section 1, the Court found, was no more helpful in confining presidential discretion to issue codes of fair competition than they had been to guide the president's decision to ban the shipment of hot oil. In the Court's reading, section 1 simply "embraced a broad range of objectives" that "point[ed] toward a single goal—the rehabilitation of industry and the industrial recovery which unquestionably was the major policy of Congress in adopting the National Industrial Recovery Act." The statutory policy statement fell short because it did not express "standards of legal obligation," which the Constitution required Congress to establish in order to "perform its essential legislative function."[49]

Nor did the statutory modifier "fair competition" provide the necessary "standard of legal obligation" to cabin the president's code-setting authority. The legislators had provided no definition of what they meant by "fair competition," and the term lacked any established legal meaning. To the justices, "fair competition" was simply "a convenient designation for whatever set of laws ... the President may approve ... as being wise and beneficent [sic] provisions for the government of [a] trade or industry in order to accomplish the broad purposes of rehabilitation, correction, and expansion which are stated in the first section of title 1."[50]

And finally, the weakness of the limitations Congress had included in the NIRA was compounded by the "sweeping" breadth of authority the statute had delegated. The NIRA left the president free to fashion codes for "a host of different trades and industries" and thereby to control "the vast array of commercial and industrial activities throughout the country." The Court in *Schechter* found this combination of an exceedingly vague and extraordinarily broad delegation to have been "without precedent."[51]

Justice Cardozo, who in *Panama Refining* had found Congress's declaration of policies in section 1 of the NIRA sufficient to uphold the president's authority in section 9(c) to halt the shipment of hot oil, wrote a concurring opinion in *Schechter* to explain why those same policies were insufficient to justify the president's code-setting authority in section 3. His explanation is revealing. The difference in the two cases for Justice Cardozo was the differing scope of presidential authority that Congress had created in the two sections. Whereas the section 9(c) delegation was "confined to [a] single act" (prohibiting shipment of hot oil), section 3's code-setting authority provided the president "a roving commission to

---

49. *Schechter*, 295 U.S. at 530, 534, 536, 541–42.

50. *Id.* at 531.

51. *Id.* at 539, 541.

inquire into evils and upon discovery correct them." Justice Cardozo would not have been troubled had Congress simply conveyed to the president a "negative" authority to "eliminate[e] ... business practices that would be characterized by general acceptation as oppressive or unfair." Section 3, however, provided the president the "positive" authority "to include whatever ordinances may be desirable or helpful for the well-being or prosperity of the industry affected." That "extension" of presidential authority, Justice Cardozo believed, was "as wide as the field of industrial regulation." It amounted to "delegation running riot."[52]

Although *Panama Refining* and *Schechter Poultry* will be forever linked, the Supreme Court recently distinguished between the lessons taught by the two NIRA decisions. In *Whitman v. American Trucking Associations, Inc.*,[53] the Court described *Panama Refining* as rejecting a delegation (section 9(c)) that "provided literally no guidance for the exercise of discretion."[54] The Court's decision in *Panama Refining* thus can be seen as addressing a "defect in draftsmanship" that Congress "easily cured" by enacting the Connally Hot Oil Act.[55] By contrast, the justices in *Whitman* described *Schechter* more broadly as invalidating a delegation (section 3) that "conferred authority to regulate the entire economy on the basis of no more precise a standard than stimulating the economy by assuring 'fair competition.'" Section 3's conferral of code-setting authority was not standardless, but the vagueness of the standards combined with the breadth of delegated power to microregulate all trades and industries throughout the United States economy proved to be a constitutionally toxic combination. As the Court in *Whitman* explained, *Schechter* teaches the functional lesson that "the degree of agency discretion that is acceptable varies according to the scope of the power congressionally conferred."[56] The extraordinary breadth of the president's code-setting authority conveyed by section 3 demanded more determinacy in the statutory standards, and the simple phrase "fair competition" and the list of general policies that introduced the NIRA were not up to that task. Without firm limits, the *Schechter* Court was concerned that the president could roam the national economy as something of a Frankenstein's monster, uncontrollably regulating the four corners of the national economy as he saw fit.

The Contemporary Doctrine. The Court's decisions in *Panama Refining* and *Schechter Poultry* came amidst the justices' broader rejection of the early New Deal effort to stimulate a

52. *Id*. at 551–53 (Cardozo, J., concurring).

53. 531 U.S. 457 (2001).

54. Id. at 474.

55. Stern, *Commerce Clause, supra* note 30, at 658.

56. *American Trucking*, 531 U.S. at 474–75.

national recovery from the Great Depression. In a series of decisions between 1937 and 1942, the justices reinterpreted Congress's commerce power to expand considerably the range of economic controls that the federal government might institute.[57] Soon after the Court loosened constitutional constraints on congressional authority to regulate interstate commerce, the justices returned to the nondelegation doctrine that they had revitalized in *Panama* and *Schechter*. Although the Court has overruled neither decision, the justices have never wielded *Panama* or *Schechter* to invalidate another enabling act on nondelegation grounds.[58]

The justices retreated from the restrictive potential of *Panama* and *Schechter* just two years after they had completed their recognition of Congress's plenary power to regulate interstate commerce. In *Yakus v. United States*,[59] the Court upheld the Emergency Price Control Act of 1942, an enabling act that resembled the NIRA in its delegation of broad, but temporary, regulatory authority to administrative officials in perilous times. The Act created the federal Office of Price Administration and empowered the new agency to establish a "comprehensive scheme" for controlling prices and rents in the face of inflationary pressures and profiteering during World War II. The act directed the Price Administrator, among other things, to establish maximum prices of commodities that "in his judgment will be generally fair and equitable and will effectuate the purposes of [the] Act" when, again in the Administrator's judgment, such prices "have risen or threaten to rise to an extent or in a manner inconsistent with the purposes of this Act."[60] The language of this delegation resembled that of section 3 of the NIRA, which the Court had invalidated in *Schechter*. The modifier "fair and equitable" was hardly more determinate than "fair competition." And in both instances, Congress tried to provide some content, and thus some limit, on administrative authority by tying those standards to the stated purposes of the enabling act.

The Court in *Yakus* nevertheless upheld Congress's delegation of price-control authority because the legislators had "marked" the

---

57. See Wickard v. Filburn, 317 U.S. 111 (1942); United States v. Darby, 312 U.S. 100 (1941); NLRB v. Jones & Laughlin Steel Corp., 301 U.S. 1 (1937).

58. Lower federal courts have done so on rare occasion, however. See South Dakota v. United States Dep't of Interior, 69 F.3d 878 (8th Cir. 1995), vacated and remanded, 519 U.S. 919 (1996) (invalidating an enabling act authorizing the Secretary of the Interior "in his discretion, to acquire . . . any interest in lands . . . for the purpose of providing land for Indians" as lacking "intelligible

principles"); Massieu v. Reno, 915 F.Supp. 681, 707–11 (D.N.J. 1996), reversed on other grounds, 91 F.3d 416 (3rd Cir. 1996) (invalidating an enabling act authorizing the deportation of "an alien whose presence or activities in the United States the Secretary of State has reasonable ground to believe would have potentially serious adverse foreign policy consequences for the United States" as "virtually standardless").

59. 321 U.S. 414 (1944).

60. *Id.* at 419–21.

"boundaries of the field of the Administrator's permissible action."
The justices discerned sufficient content in the Price Control Act's
directions to the Price Administrator, as well as in the statutory
purposes which glossed those standards, purposes that the justices
found to be more focused than those of the NIRA. In short, the
Price Control Act gave the Administrator more guidance than the
NIRA had provided to the president. For example, when setting
price ceilings, the Act instructed the Administrator, "[s]o far as
practicable, [to] ascertain and give due consideration" to market
prices during a specified two-week base period. The Act also listed
several "relevant factors" for the Administrator to consider when
adjusting the base price for a commodity, and it required the
Administrator to provide a "statement of considerations involved"
in setting any maximum price. In the end, the justices were
satisfied that the Price Control Act was a proper "exercise by
Congress of its legislative power" because "Congress ha[d] stated
the legislative objective, ha[d] prescribed the method of achieving
that objective—maximum price fixing—and ha[d] laid down standards to guide the administrative determination of both the occasions for the exercise of the price-fixing power, and the particular
prices to be established."[61]

Although the Court was correct in observing that the statutory
delegation in *Yakus* was more directive than that of the NIRA, it is
difficult to define a clear constitutional distinction between the two
delegations. Importantly, the Court in *Yakus* made little effort to do
so. Instead, the justices used *Yakus* to integrate the NIRA decisions
into the permissive approach to the nondelegation doctrine that
had prevailed before the New Deal. They began by reviving the pre-
New Deal theme of constitutional pragmatism, reminding that the
nondelegation principle did not require "the impossible or the
impracticable" from Congress. They then incorporated the lesson of
Panama Refining and *Schechter Poultry*, which the justices explained as requiring only that enabling acts satisfy "the essentials
of the legislative function," which included, first, "the determination of the legislative policy," and second, the provision of "a
defined and binding rule of conduct." So long as Congress observes
those two "essentials" of legislation, *Yakus* reestablished that the
legislators are free to decide, in their policymaking discretion,
whether to grant administrators "a narrow or broad" authority to
administer the statutory rule of conduct. "Congress is not con-

---

61. *Id.* at 423. The Court's decision
in *Yakus* was consistent with other similarly strong rejections of nondelegation
challenges to congressional enabling acts
after 1937. See, e.g., Lichter v. United
States, 334 U.S. 742 (1948); Fahey v.
Mallonee, 332 U.S. 245 (1947); American
Power & Light Co. v. SEC, 329 U.S. 90
(1946); FPC v. Hope Natural Gas Co.,
320 U.S. 591 (1944); National Broadcasting Co. v. United States, 319 U.S.
190 (1943); United States v. Rock Royal
Co-op, 307 U.S. 533 (1939).

fined," the Court advised, "to that method of executing its policy which involves the least possible delegation of discretion to administrative officers."[62]

The Court's final move in *Yakus* was to reformulate the intelligible principle test of *J.W. Hampton* in light of the holdings of *Panama Refining* and *Schechter*. The Court wrote, "Only if we could say that there is an *absence of standards* for the guidance of the Administrator's action, so that it would be *impossible* in a proper proceeding to ascertain whether the will of Congress has been obeyed, would we be justified in overriding [Congress's] choice of means for effecting [public policy]."[63] There is something new in *Yakus*'s nondelegation test. Instead of stressing the necessity of adequate standards in an enabling act to separate Congress's exercise of the legislative power from the administrator's exercise of the executive power, the Court emphasized the need of a statutory standard that is sufficient to allow judges to engage in *ultra vires* review of the administrator's action. This reorientation of the nondelegation doctrine ties this constitutional principle to the traditional model of administrative law (see § 1.4). In *Yakus*, the Court suggested that if an enabling act lacks standards that permit a reviewing court to ensure the legality of an agency's actions, the model breaks down and the delegation is invalid. If on the other hand, Congress includes in the act "standards" that make it "[]possible" for a reviewing court "to ascertain whether the will of Congress has been obeyed," that is, an intelligible principle, the legislators have provided at least the bare minimum necessary for the traditional model to operate, and the statute must stand.

The Court's most important expression of the contemporary approach to the nondelegation doctrine is to be found in *Mistretta v. United States*.[64] In *Mistretta*, the justices upheld the Sentencing Reform Act of 1984, which authorized the United States Sentencing Commission to issue guidelines limiting the discretion of federal judges when sentencing defendants who have been convicted of committing a federal crime.[65] The Court affirmed the pedigree of the nondelegation doctrine as "rooted in the principle of separation of powers," and returned to the language of *J. W. Hampton*'s

---

62. *Yakus*, 321 U.S. at 424–26.

63. *Id.* at 426 (emphasis added).

64. 488 U.S. 361 (1989).

65. The Supreme Court more recently has held that the federal sentencing guidelines violated criminal defendants' Sixth Amendment right to a jury trial because they required sentencing judges to vary sentences based on facts that had not been found by a jury. United States v. Booker, 543 U.S. 220 (2005).

The Court remedied that infirmity by severing the provisions of the Sentencing Reform Act that made the sentencing guidelines mandatory rather than advisory. The Court explicitly held that its decision in *Booker* did not affect *Mistretta*'s acceptance of the validity of the Act's delegation of authority to the Sentencing Commission to formulate sentencing guidelines. *Id.* at 242–43.

intelligible principle test for determining whether Congress has crossed the constitutional line when enabling administrative authority. That test simply requires that an enabling act "lay down . . . an intelligible principle to which [an administrator] is directed to conform." The justices endorsed as well the long-standing pragmatic approach to the nondelegation principle, advising that they intended to apply the test with "a practical understanding that in our increasingly complex society, replete with ever changing and more technical problems, Congress simply cannot do its job absent an ability to delegate power under broad general directives." So long as Congress provides intelligible principles as guidance, *Mistretta* settled, the nondelegation doctrine imposes no constitutional barrier to enabling acts that vest administrators with "significant discretion" to decide "matters of policy."[66]

Although *Mistretta*'s adoption of *J. W. Hampton*'s intelligible principle test, as well as the functional approach to nondelegation doctrine associated with the *Hampton* test, tracked the *Yakus* reformulation of nondelegation doctrine, the Court in *Mistretta* also noted a more recent innovation. On those occasions since *Panama* and *Schechter* when the justices have worried that Congress had dangerously approached the outer limits of what the nondelegation doctrine permits, they have responded by "giving narrow constructions to statutory delegations" rather than by invalidating them.[67]

The most prominent example of this post-*Schechter* judicial technique for addressing nondelegation problems is *Industrial Union Department, AFL–CIO v. American Petroleum Institute* (the *Benzene* decision),[68] in which the Court invalidated an occupational safety and health standard issued by the Occupational Safety and Health Administration ("OSHA") that strictly limited the presence of benzene in the workplace. Section 3(8) of the Occupational Safety and Health Act of 1970 defined "occupational safety and health standard" as a rule that is "reasonably necessary or appropriate to provide safe or healthful employment and places of employment."[69] But because benzene is a carcinogen, OSHA believed that a different section of the Act concerning "toxic materials or harmful physical agents" was controlling. That section required

66. *Mistretta*, 488 U.S. at 371–72, 379, 378; see *J. W. Hampton*, 276 U.S. at 409.

67. *Mistretta*, 488 U.S. at 373 n.7.

68. 448 U.S. 607 (1980). Other examples include National Cable Television Ass'n v. United States, 415 U.S. 336 (1974) (narrowly interpreting enabling act providing administrative fee-setting authority in response to nondelegation concern); Kent v. Dulles, 357 U.S. 116 (1958) (narrowly interpreting an enabling act in order to deny the Secretary of State "unbridled discretion" in deciding whether to issue a passport). For a discussion of the role of nondelegation concerns in the interpretation of enabling acts, see Cass R. Sunstein, *Nondelegation Canons*, 67 U. CHI. L. REV. 315 (2000).

69. 29 U.S.C. § 652(8).

OSHA to "set the standard which most adequately assures, to the extent feasible, on the basis of the best available evidence, that no employee will suffer material impairment of health or functional capacity"[70] In OSHA's reading, the section regarding toxic materials required the agency to limit workplace exposure to the higher of two levels: the level that guaranteed the health and safety of every worker exposed to benzene or the level that reduced workplace exposures as much as was feasible.[71] Because OSHA was unable to determine a safe level of exposure to benzene, the agency set the exposure limit at the lowest level that was both technologically feasible and economically viable.[72]

In a plurality opinion, Justice John Paul Stevens rejected OSHA's position that section 3(8) of the Act does not apply when the agency regulates exposure to toxic materials. Justice Stevens concluded instead that section 3(8) "*implies* that, before promulgating any standard, [OSHA] must make a finding that the workplaces in question are not safe," a condition that exists, according to Stevens, when workers are threatened "with a significant risk of harm." The use of the word "implies" is telling, because although Justice Stevens offered textual justifications for his more restrictive interpretation of the Act, he made clear his concern with "the unprecedented power over American industry" that would have followed from OSHA's approach to carcinogens. The echoes of *Schechter* came through clearly in Stevens's analysis. Because "there are literally thousands of substances used in the workplace that have been identified as carcinogens or suspect carcinogens," he wrote, "the Government's theory would give OSHA power to impose enormous costs that might produce little, if any, discernible benefit." The existence of such broad administrative power, Justice Stevens continued, raised the question whether the Act had made "such a 'sweeping delegation of legislative power' that it might be unconstitutional under the Court's reasoning in [*Schechter* and *Panama*]. A construction of the statute that avoids this kind of open-ended grant should certainly be favored."[73]

70. *Id.*, § 655(b)(5).

71. *Benzene*, 448 U.S. at 639 (plurality opinion).

72. *Id.* at 613.

73. *Id.* at 642, 645–46 (emphasis added). In *Whitman v. American Trucking Associations, Inc.*, 531 U.S. 457 (2001), the Court disallowed agencies the interpretative latitude that the Stevens plurality exercised in the *Benzene* decision in order to avoid nondelegation problems, explaining:

The idea that an agency can cure an unconstitutionally standardless delegation of power by declining to exercise some of that power seems to us internally contradictory. The very choice of which portion of the power to exercise—that is to say, the prescription of the standard that Congress had omitted—would *itself* be an exercise of the forbidden legislative authority. Whether the statute delegates legislative power is a question for the courts, and an agency's voluntary self-denial has no bearing upon the answer.

Id. at 473.

The Court's decision in *Mistretta* and Justice Stevens's plurality opinion in *Benzene* outline the contemporary Court's settled approach to the nondelegation doctrine. Both cases reflect the Court's continuation of Chief Justice Marshall's deep unease over invalidating statutory delegations of administrative authority. The intelligible principle test of *J.W. Hampton* and *Mistretta* prescribes what may well be the most lenient constitutional standard short of simply requiring that Congress create administrative authority by enacting a procedurally proper statute. Requiring that statutory standards be "intelligible," according to the dictionary definition of the term, demands only that standards be "comprehensible" or "capable of being understood."[74] As *Yakus* would have it, this states the minimum standard necessary for courts to engage in *ultra vires* review of agency action, but no more. The *Benzene* decision, moreover, illustrates how courts tweak questionable statutory standards in order to make them constitutionally palatable. The contemporary approach to the nondelegation doctrine thus enables courts to exercise their Article III role of judicial review over agency action, while at the same time allowing Congress the broadest legislative discretion under Article I, short of *carte blanche*, to define the contours of administrative power. It was hardly surprising, then, when the justices in the recent decision of *Whitman v. American Trucking Associations, Inc.*, summarily rejected an effort by the D.C. Circuit court of appeals to tighten the nondelegation standard by requiring that enabling acts provide a "determinate criterion" to guide agency action.[75]

The Continuing Controversy over the Soundness of the Nondelegation Doctrine. Although the essential elements of the contemporary nondelegation doctrine have long been in place, the doctrine continues to generate considerable controversy. The lingering question is whether the doctrine's legitimation of significant administrative discretion to act with the force of law is consistent with American constitutional norms and values, as well as with the public good. The central criticism is that such a permissive nondelegation doctrine undermines democracy because it allows elected representatives to avoid public accountability by passing "important policy choices" to unelected administrators.[76] "That legislators often find it convenient to escape accountability," Dean John Hart Ely has argued, "is precisely the reason *for* a nondelegation doctrine."[77] Another, related criticism of contemporary nondelegation

---

74. The American Heritage Dictionary of the English Language 682 (1969).

75. 531 U.S. 457, 475 (2001).

76. Ely, Democracy and Distrust, *supra* note 7, at 131–34. Other leading statements of this view include Schoenbrod, Power Without Responsibility, *supra* note 7, at 99–106; Peter H. Aronson, Ernest Gelhorn, & Glen O. Robinson, *A Theory of Legislative Delegation*, 68 Cornell L. Rev. 1 (1982).

77. Ely, Democracy and Distrust, *supra* note 7, at 133.

doctrine is that broad legislative delegations threaten individual liberty. On this argument, allowing such delegations makes it too easy for Congress to enact statutes; entrusts lawmaking power to institutions—the presidency and administrative agencies—that are not designed to handle that power safely; and not least, concentrates in the executive the powers both to make and enforce laws, two powers that the framers had taken great pains to separate.[78]

Some critics of the permissiveness of the contemporary nondelegation doctrine take a somewhat different tack. They argue that broad legislative delegations undermine the rule of law, which requires that government officials act only pursuant to preexisting legal authority. The argument here is that only determinate statutory standards which make clear the scope and limits of agency power satisfy the rule of law.[79] The lack of legislative direction provided by broad delegations also may undermine the public good by leading to dysfunctional administration. On this argument, agencies are typically designed to provide "highly rationalized administration," and indeterminate legislative standards undermine that ideal by unduly opening the administrative process to "political factors."[80]

These criticisms often have been met by a two-pronged, pragmatic response. The first response views the critics' demand for determinate legal standards as an unrealistic aspiration for modern regulatory legislation. As we have seen, this has been a consistent theme of the Court's nondelegation jurisprudence. In this view, a permissive nondelegation doctrine that accepts broad legislative conferrals of administrative authority is a necessary, although perhaps regrettable, feature of modern government.[81] On this argument, Congress simply lacks the time, the information, the expertise, and the prescience to settle determinatively each and every policy question associated with government regulation. To demand such determinacy, these defenders argue, would be to make effective administrative government impossible.

Some proponents of contemporary nondelegation doctrine complement the claim of limited congressional competence with a deep

---

78. See SCHOENBROD, POWER WITHOUT RESPONSIBILITY, *supra* note 7, at 107–18; Marci A. Hamilton, *Representation and Delegation: Back to Basics*, 20 CARDOZO L. REV. 795 (1999); Nadine Strossen, *Delegation as a Danger to Liberty*, 20 CARDOZO L. REV. 861 (1999).

79. The leading statement of this view is THEODORE LOWI, THE END OF LIBERALISM: THE SECOND REPUBLIC OF THE UNITED STATES 92–107, 300–01 (2d ed. 1979). For a commentary on this view, see

Thomas O. Sargentich, *The Delegation Debate and Competing Ideals of the Administrative Process*, 36 AM. U. L REV. 419, 423–27 (1987).

80. See Louis L. Jaffe, *The Illusion of the Ideal Administrator*, 86 HARV. L. REV. 1183, 1188–91 (1973).

81. See Richard J. Pierce, Jr., *Political Accountability and Delegated Power: A Response to Professor Lowi*, 36 AM. U. L REV. 391, 403–07 (1987).

skepticism about the ability of judges to satisfactorily enforce a restrictive nondelegation doctrine. In this view, the enforcement authority of the courts is compromised by the absence of judicially manageable standards to distinguish between constitutional and unconstitutional delegations.[82] As one commentator put it, "The nondelegation doctrine utterly lacks the intelligible standards that it demands of legislation."[83] Because of the absence of acceptable standards of review, judicial decisions evaluating legislative delegations "will almost inevitably appear partisan, and might often be so."[84] Justice Antonin Scalia has elaborated on this concern:

> [W]hile the doctrine of unconstitutional delegation is unquestionably a fundamental element of our constitutional system, it is not an element readily enforceable by the courts. Once it is conceded, as it must be, that no statute can be entirely precise, and that some judgments, even some judgments involving policy considerations, must be left to the officers executing the law and to the judges applying it, the debate over unconstitutional delegation becomes a debate not over a point of principle but over a question of degree.... Since Congress is no less endowed with common sense than we are, and better equipped to inform itself of the "necessities" of government; and since the factors bearing upon those necessities are both multifarious and (in the nonpartisan sense) highly political, ... it is small wonder that we have almost never felt qualified to second-guess Congress regarding the permissible degree of policy judgment that can be left to those executing or applying the law.[85]

In this view, while judges are willing to determine whether Congress has provided an intelligible limit on administrative discretion, as the contemporary doctrine requires, they are far less comfortable deciding whether any such intelligible limit affords administrators "too much" discretion.

While some defenders of contemporary nondelegation doctrine simply have criticized the critics' demand for determinate standards, others have attempted a positive case for enabling Congress to delegate broad policymaking discretion to administrative officials. These proponents take the critics head on, suggesting that vague and broad delegations may be superior to narrow and determinate delegations. One claim, for example, holds that broad dele-

82. See Pierce, *Political Accountability, supra* note 81, at 393–403; Richard B. Stewart, *Beyond Delegation Doctrine,* 36 Am. U. L Rev. 323, 324–28 (1987).

83. Peter H. Schuck, *Delegation and Democracy: Comments on David Schoenbrod,* 20 Cardozo L. Rev. 775, 793 (1999).

84. Richard B. Stewart, *The Reformation of American Administrative Law,* 88 Harv. L Rev. 1669, 1697 (1975); see Sunstein, *Nondelegation Canons, supra* note 68, at 321, 326–28.

85. Mistretta v. United States, 488 U.S. 361, 415–16 (1989) (Scalia, J., dissenting on other grounds).

gations may enhance the public good by providing the flexibility necessary for effective government.[86] Another claim posits that, "[s]trangely enough," "vague delegations to administrative agencies" may foster rather than frustrate democracy. While statutory provisions tend to become entrenched, administrative policies can keep pace with evolving public preferences by shifting in response to presidential elections. On these claims, insisting on determinate statutory standards would "result in wonderfully wooden behavior."[87]

(b) The Legislative Veto

The contemporary state of the nondelegation doctrine represents something of a Pyrrhic victory for Congress. The legislators have won recognition of their prerogative to vest administrative agencies with the authority to make and to enforce public policy subject only to minimal statutory guidance. But in the wake of that victory, legislators must cope with the result of the nondelegation doctrine's permissiveness—namely, the transfer of considerable policymaking discretion from Congress to the agencies. Administrative discretion often is sufficiently robust to enable agencies to adopt policies and to take actions that many in Congress do not support. Thus, to the extent legislators have provided government administrators with decisionmaking discretion, they have jeopardized their ability to control public policy.

Congress, like the rest of us, often wants to have it both ways. Legislators at times wish to define the boundaries of agency authority broadly, in the interest of administrative flexibility, and at the same time control how agencies exercise their authority, in the interest of administrative accountability. But while the separation-of-powers principle (in the form of the nondelegation doctrine) gives Congress considerable leeway in creating agency authority, it provides sharper limits on the power of legislators to control agency actions taken pursuant to that authority. Congress learned that lesson when the Supreme Court invalidated the "legislative veto," which was the most powerful device for controlling agency actions that Congress has ever exercised.

Statutory provisions authorizing legislative vetoes have assumed a variety of forms, but they all share the common characteristic of empowering Congress, or some unit of Congress, to invalidate agency action on its own. Provisions authorizing legislative

86. Sunstein, *Nondelegation Canons*, *supra* note 68, at 324–26.

87. Jerry L. Mashaw, *Prodelegation: Why Administrators Should Make Political Decisions*, 1 J. L. ECON. & ORG. 81, 95–99 (1985). For similar arguments, see Pierce, *Political Accountability*, *supra* note 81, 407–08; David B. Spence & Frank Cross, *A Public Choice Case for the Administrative State*, 89 GEO. L.J. 97 (2000).

vetoes often appear in enabling acts, which may thus be seen as providing contingent delegations of administrative authority, by which Congress permits agencies to act subject to a process of legislative review and override. So viewed, legislative veto provisions serve as a hedge against the broad discretionary power that Congress often finds it necessary to vest in agencies to fulfill their policy missions.

At the height of the legislative veto's popularity, at least within Congress, the Supreme Court decided *Immigration & Naturalization Service v. Chadha*,[88] which used a formalistic approach to invalidate the practice in all of its forms. The Court in *Chadha* held that every exercise of a legislative veto over agency action violates the procedural requirements for lawmaking prescribed by Article I of the Constitution. The crucial premise here is that a legislative veto is a "law" in the constitutional sense. In *Chadha*, the Court held that legislative vetoes so qualified because they had "the purpose and effect of altering the legal rights, duties, and relations of persons ... outside the Legislative Branch." If this premise is accepted, the constitutional violation is clear. As the Court reasoned in *Chadha*, because a legislative veto is a law, it is subject to the procedural requirements that the Constitution imposes on congressional lawmaking.[89] Article I of the Constitution provides that before a bill "become[s] a law," it must (1) pass both the House of Representatives and the Senate (the bicameralism requirement) and (2) be presented to the president for signature or veto (the presentment requirement) (§ 7, cl. 2). Some legislative veto provisions satisfy the first requirement of bicameralism by requiring the concurrence of both the House and the Senate to invalidate agency action. But even such a "two-house veto," by definition, violates Article I's presentment requirement. The whole point of a legislative veto is to provide an *exclusively* legislative check on executive power.[90]

In a strong but solitary dissent, Justice Byron R. White fashioned a functional defense of the legislative veto as a device providing an appropriate counterweight to the exercise of broad agency discretion that characterizes the contemporary administrative state. Justice White challenged the majority's premise that legislative vetoes should be regarded as laws. He observed that the exercise of a legislative veto is always authorized by statute, which

88.   462 U.S. 919 (1983).

89.   *Id.* at 952, 954–58. The Court in *Chadha* described these procedural requirements as "integral parts of the constitutional design for the separation of powers." *Id.* at 946.

90.   Within weeks of deciding *Chadha*, the Supreme Court summarily af-

firmed a decision by the D.C. Circuit that invalidated a statutory provision authorizing a two-house legislative veto. United States Senate v. FTC, 463 U.S. 1216 (1983), aff'g., 691 F.2d 575 (D.C.Cir. 1982).

counts as a law that satisfies the bicameralism and presentment requirements of Article I. White coupled that observation with the irony that while the nondelegation doctrine allows Congress to empower agencies to act with the force of law, the ban on legislative vetoes prohibits the legislators from delegating to themselves the power to invalidate agency actions pursuant to the very authority that they have granted.[91]

This irony results from the separation of powers, however. The power to administer statutes is an executive power, and executive officers can act with the force of law only when they assume that administrative role.[92] Legislators, by contrast, can act with the force of law only when they act within their legislative role by passing statutes. For Congress to enact a statute that authorizes itself to administer the statute's provisions violates the separation between lawmaker and law-administrator that the framers constituted when they separated Article I and Article II of the Constitution. Thus, even if one accepts Justice White's premise that a legislative veto is better viewed as an action authorized by statute rather than as a putative law, the veto nevertheless violates separation of powers by permitting Congress to execute the laws.[93] When legislators override an action taken by an agency pursuant to its enabling act, they are executing the enabling act as they think best. On this argument, a legislative veto is unconstitutional not (or not only) because it is a procedurally defective law, but rather (or also) because it constitutes a "congressional usurpation of Executive Branch functions."[94]

The legislative veto thus was stymied by a constitutional checkmate. Congress could not justify the assertion of a veto power over executive action as a legislative act because it did not satisfy the procedural requirements for such acts set by the Constitution. Nor could Congress justify the veto as the exercise of statutory authority because the power to implement statutes is an executive power, which is off limits to Congress. After *Chadha*, Congress can invalidate an agency action "in only one way"—by enacting a statute.[95]

(c) The "Report and Wait" Process

The Small Business Regulatory Enforcement Fairness Act of 1996[96] provides that no administrative rule "can take effect" unless

91. *Chadha*, 462 U.S. at 986–97 (White, J., dissenting).

92. *Id.* at 953 n.16.

93. See Bowsher v. Synar,478 U.S. 714, 726–27 (1986) (holding that Congress cannot exercise removal power over any individual who engages in executive functions).

94. See *id*. at 727.

95. *Chadha*, 462 U.S. at 954–55.

96. 5 U.S.C. §§ 801–808. For an analysis of the legislative review process established by the Small Business Act, see Daniel Cohen & Peter L. Strauss, *Congressional Review of Agency Regulations*, 49 ADMIN. L. REV. 95 (1997).

the agency issuing the rule first submits it, together with a report and other information, to each House of Congress.[97] If the rule qualifies as a "major rule,"[98] the act imposes a default waiting period of 60 legislative days,[99] during which Congress has the opportunity to enact a "joint resolution of disapproval" pursuant to a special "fast-track" legislative procedure delineated in the act.[100] Such a joint resolution is the functional equivalent of a statute. It requires majority votes in the House and the Senate (satisfying the bicameralism requirement), as well as the president's signature (satisfying the presentment requirement). If the president vetoes the joint resolution, the usual constitutional requirement of a two-thirds vote in each House of Congress applies in order to override the veto (U.S.Const. art. I, § 7, cl. 3). If Congress enacts a joint resolution of disapproval, the agency rule does not take effect (or continue in effect, if it has already become effective), and the agency is precluded from re-issuing "substantially the same" rule in the future, unless it is "specifically authorized" by a later federal statute.[101]

Congress waited five years before invalidating an agency rule pursuant to the report-and-wait procedure of the Small Business Act.[102] Did Congress's "veto" of the rule offend *Chadha*? The Supreme Court has not considered the constitutionality of report–and–wait procedures since *Chadha*, but in a pre-*Chadha* decision, *Sibbach v. Wilson & Co.*, the justices noted with apparent approval the report-and-wait feature of the act of Congress enabling the Court to approve rules of civil procedure for the federal judiciary.[103] In *Sibbach*, the justices recognized the "value" of report-and-wait provisions: They provide Congress an opportunity to ensure that agency action pursuant to a statutory delegation is consistent with the legislative purpose.[104] It seems clear, moreover, that the Small

---

97. 5 U.S.C. § 801(a)(1) (A)-(B). The act adopts the definition of "agency" provided by the Administrative Procedure Act, 5 U.S.C. § 551(1). 5 U.S.C. § 804 (1). For a discussion of the APA definition of "agency," see § 1.2.

98. The Act defines major rules primarily according to their economic impact. See 5 U.S.C. § 804 (2).

99. *Id.*, § 801(a)(2)(B)-(3). The president can eliminate the waiting period for rules that fall within several statutory exceptions. *Id.*, § 801(c).

100. *Id.*, § 802.

101. *Id.*, § 801(b). If a rule is invalidated by a joint resolution of disapproval, the Act provides that the rule "shall be treated as though [it] had never tak-

en effect." *Id.*, § 801(f). The Act also provides that "no court or agency may infer any intent of the Congress" if the legislators do not enact a joint resolution of disapproval. § 801(g).

102. Pub. L. No. 107–5, 107th Cong., 1st Sess., 115 Stat. 7 (2001). The victim of Congress's ire was "a ten-year effort [by the Occupational Safety and Health Administration (OSHA)] to establish ergonomics standards to reduce the number and severity of musculoskeletal disorders (MSDs) experienced by U.S. workers." Jerry L. Mashaw, et al., Administrative Law: The American Public Law System 111 (2003). For a brief account of this episode, see *id.* at 111–12.

103. 312 U.S. 1, 14–15 (1941).

104. *Id.* at 15.

Business Act cured the procedural defect of the legislative veto because a joint resolution of disapproval satisfies the bicameralism and presentment requirements of Article I. The Court in *Chadha* suggested as much when it noted that its excision of the legislative veto provision in the INS's enabling act left in place a "report and wait" provision along the lines "approved by the Court in *Sibbach*."[105] At bottom, the legal effect of the Small Business Act is to extend for major rules the general 30-day waiting period for rules established by the Administrative Procedure Act (see § 553(d)). Such an effect should not pose a constitutional problem.

(d) Other Congressional Controls on Administrative Agencies

Chadha underscores the separation of powers principle that Congress can act to control agency decisions only to the extent its actions conform to its constitutional role as a legislative rather than an executive body. That constitutional limit noted, Congress's legislative powers provide it a variety of means to exert considerable influence over an agency's execution of its enabling acts. This section provides a glimpse at the opportunities these means offer to Congress.

Statutory Controls. As demonstrated by the Small Business Regulatory Enforcement Act of 1996, discussed in the previous section, Congress can pass, and often has passed, statutes that impose generally applicable requirements on agency decisionmaking. In fact, much of administrative law is the product of just such an enactment, the Administrative Procedure Act. Another prominent example of a generally applicable statute that has had a profound effect on the administrative process is the National Environmental Policy Act of 1969 ("NEPA"),[106] which requires, among other things, that federal agencies prepare an "environmental impact" statement in connection with "major Federal actions significantly affecting the quality of the human environment."[107]

Congress also has an opportunity when drafting an enabling act to provide specific controls on any administrative authority that it creates. Enabling acts do not simply define the substantive power of an agency. They frequently include provisions specifically tailored to foster the optimal decisionmaking environment for a particular agency.[108] For example, Congress may choose to create either

---

105. See *Chadha*, 462 U.S. at 935 n.9, 959; see also City of Alexandria v. United States, 737 F.2d 1022, 1025 (Fed. Cir. 1984) (severability ruling in *Chadha* indicates that "clearly in the Supreme Court's eyes, 'report and wait' is a legitimate and constitutional means by which Congress can check and review executive action").

106. 42 U.S.C. § 4331 et seq.

107. *Id.*, § 4332(C).

108. See Matthew McCubbins, Roger G. Noll & Barry Weingast (McNollgast), *Structure and Process, Politics and Poli-*

an executive or an independent agency, depending on a legislative judgment whether the agency will fulfill its policy mission better with or without some insulation from political control by the president (see § 1.2). In addition, Congress may design a decision-making process that best suits an agency's mandate by including special procedural provisions in an enabling act. Congress also may introduce so-called "action forcing" provisions in an enabling act, requiring, for example, that the agency issue rules by a fixed deadline. And finally, Congress may include in an enabling act a "sunset" provision that fixes an expiration date for the administrative authority it provides. Such a provision enables the legislators to reassess the agency's performance before renewing its statutory authority.

Advice-and-Consent Power. The Senate's power of "Advice and Consent" concerning the appointment of agency heads and other senior administrative officials opens a source of legislative influence over the policy direction of agencies (U.S. CONST. art. II, § 2, cl. 2). True, the Appointments Clause makes the president "the principal agent" in appointing senior government officials (see § 2.4(a)).[109] And although the constitutional text provides the Senate a veto power over the appointment of agency policymakers, senators only rarely have rejected a presidential nominee for administrative office. Still, the Senate's advice-and-consent role provides an important check on the president's discretion to select government policymakers. As Alexander Hamilton explained, "the necessity of [the Senate's] concurrence" hovers in the shadow of every major executive appointment, and thus exerts a "powerful," though usually "silent," "restraint" on presidential prerogative.[110] In addition, confirmation hearings offer senators the ideal setting for soliciting policy commitments from senior administrative officials as part of the political dialogue over their confirmation.[111]

Power of the Purse. The legislative power to appropriate funds for the "Common Defence and general Welfare of the United States" provides Congress with authority to fine-tune agency discretion on an annual basis (U.S. CONST. art. I., § 8, cl. 1). Because the Constitution reinforces Congress's "power of the purse" by disallowing any "Money [to] be drawn from the Treasury, but in Consequence of the Appropriations made by Law" (art. I., § 9, cl.

cy: *Administrative Arrangements and the Political Control of Agencies*, 75 VA. L. REV. 431 (1989).

109. THE FEDERALIST No. 65, at 423 (Alexander Hamilton) (Modern Library ed., 1941).

110. THE FEDERALIST No. 76, *supra* note 109, at 493–96 (Alexander Hamilton).

111. For a thorough review of the Senate's advice-and-consent power, see William G. Ross, *The Senate's Constitutional Role in Confirming Cabinet Nominees and other Executive Officers*, 48 SYRACUSE L. REV. 1123 (1998).

7), each year every agency must convince legislators to fund their initiatives.[112] As a practical matter, an agency's "activities are authorized only to the extent of their appropriations."[113] Notwithstanding the authority that Congress grants to administrators in enabling acts, legislators can halt a federal program in its tracks simply by declining to fund the program in an annual appropriations law. Alternatively, Congress can redirect agency priorities by specially earmarking funds for a particular program. Congress also has used appropriations laws to tweak enabling acts, at least during a fiscal year, by including "riders" that impose special conditions on an agency's expenditures to implement one or more of its programs. The scope of Congress's power to enact such appropriation riders remains an open constitutional question.[114] But wherever the outer limit of that authority lay, it remains clear that the appropriations power offers Congress "a low-cost vehicle for effective legislative control over executive activity."[115]

Legislative Oversight. Congress's legislative authority supports a general oversight role regarding agency performance because administrative enforcement of federal statutes is relevant to legislative decisions of whether to amend current statutes or to enact new ones.[116] Legislative oversight of government administration takes a variety of forms, ranging from public congressional hearings (coupled with Congress's subpoena power) to private communications between legislators (and their staff) and executive officials, including the president. Congress's oversight role allows legislators to signal their policy preferences to, as well as to secure policy commitments from, agency officials. As a result of Congress's oversight powers, agency officials often exercise their policymaking discretion in anticipation of the likely legislative reaction.

Courts of appeals decisions have established varying rules governing legislative attempts to influence agency decisionmaking in pending proceedings. Legislators may intercede in an informal rulemaking proceeding, provided they limit their "pressure" to "factors … made relevant by Congress in the applicable stat-

---

112. For discussion of, as well as disagreement over, the question whether the president or other government officers possess authority to spend some federal money without congressional authorization, see J. Gregory Sidak, *The President's Power of the Purse*, 1989 DUKE L.J. 1162 (answering, "yes"); Kate Stith, *Congress' Power of the Purse*, 97 YALE L.J. 1343 (1988) (answering, "no").

113. Stith, *Congress' Power of the Purse*, *supra* note 112, at 1356.

114. For a useful discussion, see Jacques B. Leboeuf, *Limitations on the*

Use of Appropriations Riders by Congress to Effectuate Substantive Policy Changes, 19 HASTINGS CONST. L.Q. 457 (1992).

115. Stith, *Congress' Power of the Purse*, *supra* note 112, at 1360.

116. See, e.g., Eastland v. United States Servicemen's Fund, 421 U.S. 491, 504 (1975). The "subject" of a legislative investigation must be one on which Congress has power to legislate. *Id.* at 504 n.15.

ute."[117] The D.C. Circuit has explained, "[I]t is entirely proper for Congressional representatives vigorously to represent the interests of their constituents before administrative agencies engaged in informal, general policy rulemaking, so long as individual Congressmen do not frustrate the intent of Congress as a whole as expressed in statute, nor undermine applicable rules of procedure." The courts expect agencies "to balance Congressional pressure with the pressures emanating from all other sources."[118] Reviewing courts have not allowed legislative attempts to influence the outcome of agency adjudications, however. Such legislative pressure has been held to violate the procedural due process rights of the parties to those proceedings.[119] In addition, the Administrative Procedure Act broadly prohibits ex parte communications between legislative officials and agency decisionmakers in formal administrative proceedings (see § 5.6).

§ 2.4   Administrative Agencies and the President

Article II of the Constitution vests the "executive Power ... in a President of the United States of America" (§ 1). Entrusting the executive power to a single official marked a profound departure from most state constitutions at the time, which had tended to opt for chief executive offices that were both weak and plural. The Constitutional Convention concluded, however, that creation of a strong, unitary executive office should be an important feature of the new federal government. Alexander Hamilton, writing in *The Federalist*, argued that a unitary presidency strengthened public accountability by making it clear who holds the ultimate responsibility for executive action. Hamilton also believed that a unitary executive fostered the energy that was "essential to the steady administration of the laws."[1]

The primary constitutional function of the president, at least with respect to domestic affairs, is to enforce acts of Congress. Article II makes the president the Nation's chief law enforcement officer by giving him or her the power, as well as the duty, to "take Care that the Laws be faithfully executed" (§ 3). The framers understood, of course, that the president would not personally administer the vast majority of the laws that the Constitution had placed under her or his care. They fully anticipated that Congress, drawing on its necessary and proper power, would create the

117. Sierra Club v. Costle, 657 F.2d 298, 447 (D.C.Cir. 1981); see D.C. Federation of Civic Associations v. Volpe, 459 F.2d 1231, 1246 (D.C.Cir. 1971), cert. denied, 405 U.S. 1030 (1972).

118. *Sierra Club*, 657 F.2d at 447–48.

119. See Pillsbury Co. v. FTC, 354 F.2d 952 (5th Cir. 1966).

§ 2.4

1. THE FEDERALIST NO. 70, at 454, 457–61 (Alexander Hamilton) (Modern Library ed., 1941).

administrative "departments" that actually would run the federal government. True to that constitutional design, Congress most often has vested the authority to administer statutory programs in a federal agency or in an agency official, rather than in the president. In the administrative state, agency officials, not the president, primarily exercise the executive power. The president largely fulfills the constitutional obligation to "take care" that the laws are "faithfully executed" by overseeing the manner in which administrative agencies carry out their statutory authority.

The president, of course, has many means at his or her disposal for overseeing agency action. This section focuses on three such means that have created constitutional controversy over the years. These are the president's power (1) to appoint government administrators, (2) to remove government administrators, and (3) to direct the actions of government administrators.

(a) The Appointment of Administrative Officials

The pragmatic politicians attending the Constitutional Convention approached the assignment of the appointments power warily because they regarded the authority to select government officials as "the most insidious and powerful weapon of eighteenth-century despotism."[2] Their experience provided two warnings. English constitutional law at the time classified the appointment of magistrates as a prerogative right of the Crown. The framers believed that the King had used the power of appointment to spread his influence over the English government to such a degree that the balance of power tilted unhealthily toward the Crown. Many state constitutions had overcompensated for that imbalance by entrusting legislators with the appointment of administrators. The result, in the framers' view, was a degree of legislative control over the executive that simply swung the balance of power in the opposite direction. The lesson of the English and state experiences seemed clear: The Convention was determined to work out an appropriate balance between legislative and executive authority in staffing the executive branch.[3]

Rather than providing one method, or authority, for appointing all executive personnel, the Constitution arranges all those who occupy executive positions into a four-layer pyramid and prescribes different selection rules for each layer. (See Figure 2–3.)

---

2. GORDON WOOD, THE CREATION OF THE AMERICAN REPUBLIC, 1776–1787, at 143 (1969).

3. For an examination of the historical forces, as well as the political compromises, that helped shape the Constitution's allocation of the appointments power, see Theodore Y. Blumoff, *Separation of Powers and the Origins of the Appointment Clause*, 37 SYRACUSE L. REV. 1037 (1987).

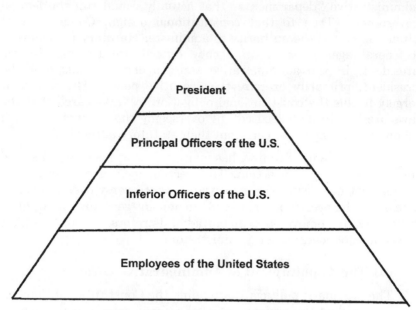

Figure 2 – 3: The Executive Pyramid

At the top of the pyramid, of course, is the president, who with the vice president, hold the only executive offices created by the Constitution. These also are the only executive officials who are selected by popular election, albeit indirectly through the Electoral College (U.S.CONST. art. II, § 1).

The Appointments Clause of the Constitution (art. II, § 2, cl. 2) controls the selection of the "Officers of the United States," who are divided into two groups—"principal officers" and "inferior officers."[4] Principal officers occupy the level of the executive pyramid directly below the president; inferior offers reside directly below principal officers.

The selection of principal officers is the only administrative appointment that requires interbranch agreement. The Appointments Clause requires that the president select principal officers "by and with the Advice and Consent of the Senate." The justices have described this unique sharing of the appointments power as designed "to preserve political accountability relative to important Government assignments."[5] Alexander Hamilton, writing on the presidency in *The Federalist*, explained the thinking behind the

---

4. Although the term "principal officer" does not appear in the Appointments Clause, it is used in the preceding clause (art. II, § 2, cl. 1).

5. Edmond v. United States, 520 U.S. 651, 663 (1997).

split authority. On one hand, Hamilton argued that the president should take the lead in the appointments process because important executive officials should be the choice, although not necessarily the first choice, of the president. He also believed that the president was best positioned to select these senior executives based on their "intrinsic merit" for a particular office.[6] Somewhat paradoxically, Hamilton saw the counterpoint of Senate confirmation as "an excellent check" against the president's "appointment of unfit characters" to federal office. This check, Hamilton believed, typically would operate silently by providing the president an incentive to nominate only individuals who would merit Senate confirmation.[7]

The Appointments Clause establishes presidential nomination and Senate confirmation—the selection method that is *required* for principal officers—as only the "default" method for selecting inferior officers.[8] Congress may override that default mode whenever the legislators "think proper" by enacting a law vesting the power to appoint inferior officers "in the President alone, in the Courts of Law, or in the Heads of Departments" (art. II, § 2, cl. 2). The conspicuous absence from that list of appointing authorities, of course, is Congress.[9] In the scheme of the Appointments Clause, Congress is confined to its legislative role of enacting statutes, with the single exception of the Senate's power to confirm or to reject the president's nomination of principal officers. That legislative role is nevertheless crucial in the appointments process. Only Congress has power to create federal offices, principal and inferior, and with respect to inferior officers, it has "significant discretion" in assigning the power of appointment.[10] As a corollary to its power to create federal offices, Congress also has some leeway in specifying the qualifications for officeholders. But just as Congress cannot execute the statutes that it enacts, it may not appoint the incumbents of the offices it creates.[11]

Finally, at the base of the federal executive pyramid, reside the many "employees of the United States" who do not qualify as officers of the United States.[12] Drawing on the Necessary and

---

6. THE FEDERALIST NO. 76, *supra* note 1, at 492–94 (Alexander Hamilton). At the Constitutional Convention, the influential James Wilson remarked, "A principal reason for unity in the Executive was that officers might be appointed by a single, responsible person." I MAX FARRAND, THE RECORDS OF THE FEDERAL CONVENTION OF 1787, at 119 (1911).

7. THE FEDERALIST NO. 76, *supra* note 1, at 494–95 (Alexander Hamilton).

8. *Edmond*, 520 U.S. at 660.

9. The denial of a legislative appointments power tracks the constitutional

prohibition against sitting Members of Congress "holding any Office under the United States" (art. I, § 6, cl. 2).

10. Morrison v. Olson, 487 U.S. 654, 673 (1988).

11. See Buckley v. Valeo, 424 U.S. 1, 127–31 (1976); Springer v. Government of the Philippine Islands, 277 U.S. 189, 202 (1928).

12. See Freytag v. Commissioner of Internal Revenue, 501 U.S. 868, 880 (1991); *Buckley*, 424 U.S. at 126 n.162.

Proper Clause, Congress is free to devise any method for selecting federal employees who do not rise to the status of officer of the United States, so long as that selection method otherwise satisfies constitutional requirements.[13]

Although the selection rules of the Appointments Clause seem clear enough, the Convention's failure to define key terms has created several lingering uncertainties. For example, just who are the "Officers of the United States" that must be appointed in compliance with the Appointments Clause? And what distinguishes inferior officers, for whom Congress may vary the default selection rule of presidential nomination and Senate confirmation, from principal officers, on whose selection the president and the Senate must always agree? It even has proven difficult to pin down the identity of the "Heads of Departments" whom Congress may authorize to appoint inferior officers. The case law is too sparse to unravel these mysteries fully, but recent decisions by the Supreme Court have begun to provide content to the hardly self-defining language of the Appointments Clause.

The Definition of "Officers of the United States." The Appointments Clause governs only the selection of "Officers of the United States." Although the Constitution does not define the meaning of that term, the framers signaled that this would be a rather select group of officials by requiring that the president "Commission all the Officers of the United States" (art. II, § 3). It would make little sense to require presidential commissions for all federal employees, even circa 1789. The Supreme Court accordingly has defined "Officers of the United States" somewhat restrictively, limiting the designation to those who exercise "significant authority pursuant to the laws of the United States."[14] This definition guides the justices in making two important distinctions that control the application of the Appointments Clause. The first is the distinction between officers of the United States and legislative officers, whom Congress is free to appoint on its own without regard to the Appointments Clause. The second distinction is between officers of the United States and government employees, whose hiring flies beneath the radar of the Appointment Clause.

The Distinction between Officers of the United States and Legislative Officers. In *Buckley v. Valeo*,[15] the Court's leading Appointments Clause decision, the justices described officers of the United States as having a significant role in "the administration and enforcement of the public law." Legislative officers, by

---

13.   See *Buckley*, 424 U.S. at 134–35.

14.   See *id.*, at 126; see also *id.* at 141 (Officers of the United States perform "a significant governmental duty . . .

pursuant to a public law"); *Freytag,* 501 U.S. at 880 (quoting *Buckley*).

15.   424 U.S. 1 (1976).

contrast, "carry out appropriate legislative functions." In *Buckley*, the justices evaluated the constitutional status of the Federal Election Commission, which Congress had created in the wake of the Watergate scandals to regulate federal elections. In light of the sensitivity of the Commission's mandate, Congress had provided for an unusual method of selecting the six voting members of the new agency: The president selected two of the Commissioners, the president pro tempore of the Senate selected another two, and the Speaker of the House selected the remaining two Commissioners. Because these selection methods did not comply with the Appointments Clause, the Court barred the Commission from exercising its "substantial powers" to "flesh out" or to enforce the statutes under its jurisdiction. Such significant executive powers, the Court held, could only be exercised by officers of the United States who had been selected according to the terms of the Appointments Clause. The Court cleared the Commission, as then constituted, only to exercise those of its statutory powers that were "essentially of an investigative and informative nature," because Congress could have delegated such powers to one of its committees.[16] After *Buckley*, Congress quickly amended the Commission's organic act to provide for the selection of Commissioners in compliance with the Appointments Clause, and thus to allow the Commission fully to exercise it statutory authority.

The Distinction between Officers and Employees of the United States. The Court's limitation of the selection rules of the Appointments Clause to those officers who are entrusted with significant authority to administer and to enforce federal law recognizes Congress's broad authority under the Necessary and Proper Clause to provide for the hiring of federal employees who are "lesser functionaries subordinate to officers of the United States."[17] Instead of wielding the substantial discretionary authority that is the marker of the officers of the United States, federal employees tend to perform "ministerial tasks."[18]

The Supreme Court's most important application to date of the distinction between officers and employees was in *Freytag v. Commissioner of Internal Revenue*.[19] In *Freytag*, the Court considered the status of the "special trial judges" of the United States Tax Court. The chief judge of that court assigned these special judges to decide several types of cases. In other cases, the chief judge assigned special trial judges to assist the full-fledged judges of the Tax Court by conducting hearings and proposing decisions. The justices found the special trial judges to be officers of the United States rather than federal employees. The officer status of the special

---

16. *Id*. at 128, 137, 139.

17. *Id*. at 126 n.162.

18. *Freytag*, 501 U.S. at 881.

19. 501 U.S. 868 (1991).

judges came through clearly for the Court in their "independent authority" to decide some cases in lieu of the Tax Court judges, who quite clearly qualified as officers of the United States.[20]

The justices in *Freytag* also held, however, that the supporting role which the special trial judges played for the Tax Court judges itself was sufficient to require that their selection satisfy the requirements of the Appointments Clause. Even though the special trial judges in their supporting role lacked authority to make final decisions, they still exercised significant "duties and discretion," such as presiding over trials, ruling on the admissibility of evidence, and enforcing compliance with discovery orders. The Court also pointed to certain features of the office of special trial judge which suggested that it possessed a somewhat special status in the eyes of Congress. The legislators had established the office "by law," as the Appointments Clause requires for officers of the United States, and again by law, Congress had specified "the duties, salary, and means of appointment for that office."[21]

The Distinction Between Principal and Inferior Officers of the United States. Distinguishing a principal from an inferior officer is important, recall, because the Appointments Clause requires that principal officers be selected by the president with Senate confirmation, but allows Congress some flexibility in providing for the appointment of inferior officers. Yet neither the Appointments Clause nor the Supreme Court's interpretation of the Clause's selection rules has firmly established an "exclusive criterion" to apply the distinction.[22] In *Edmond v. United States*,[23] however, the justices took a significant step in clarifying the distinction between principal and inferior officers by identifying the criterion that provides at least the starting point for analysis—whether the officer in question is subordinate to "some higher ranking officer or officers below the President." In determining the subordinate status of an officer, *Edmond* made clear that it was not sufficient simply to find other officers "who formally maintain a higher rank, or possess responsibilities of a greater magnitude." Rather, the Court explained, inferior officers are "officers whose work is *directed and supervised* at some level by others who were appointed by Presidential nomination with the advice and consent of the Senate."[24]

Justice David H. Souter wrote a concurring opinion in *Edmond* to hold open the possibility that officers who are supervised by

20. *Id.* at 881–82.

21. *Id.*

22. Edmond v. United States, 520 U.S. 651, 661 (1997); see Morrison v. Olson, 487 U.S. 654, 671 (1988) ("The line between 'inferior' and 'principal' officers is one that is far from clear, and the Framers provided little guidance into where it should be drawn.").

23. 520 U.S. 651 (1997).

24. *Id.* at 662–63 (emphasis added).

principal officers might nevertheless be regarded as principal officers themselves. Justice Souter agreed with the *Edmond* majority that an officer could not qualify as inferior if he or she had no superior other than the president. But Souter regarded the subordinate status of an officer as a necessary but insufficient determinant of inferior status. For officers with superiors, Justice Souter advocated "a detailed look at [their] powers and duties" in order to settle whether they are principal or inferior officers within the meaning of the Appointments Clause.[25]

Edmond places in question the Court's controversial holding in *Morrison v. Olson* that the office of independent counsel, formerly known as the office of special prosecutor, was of inferior rather than principal status.[26] Independent counsel possessed complete power and independent authority to investigate and prosecute allegations of criminal wrongdoing by senior executive officials, including the president. In *Morrison*, the justices relied on several considerations in evaluating that unusual federal office. At the outset, they considered it important that the Attorney General could remove an independent counsel, albeit only for cause. Although the Attorney General lacked authority to direct and supervise an independent counsel, as *Edmond* now seems to require for inferior status, this removal power suggested to the *Morrison* Court that an independent counsel was "to some degree 'inferior' in rank and authority." But the justices did not rest their conclusion of the inferior status of the office of independent counsel solely on the removal authority of the Attorney General. A check of the powers and duties of an independent counsel convinced them that the office did not rise to the principal level. The justices emphasized that "an independent counsel is appointed essentially to accomplish a single task, and when that task is over the office is terminated."[27]

The Court's formal and categorical approach to the distinction between principal and inferior officers in *Edmond* is in considerable tension with its more functional and multi-factored analysis in *Morrison*. It is possible to square the two decisions by concluding that an independent counsel was subordinate to the Attorney General because of the latter's removal authority.[28] But such an alignment would require the justices to broaden the *Edmond* definition of subordinate status beyond those "whose work is directed and supervised" by principal officers. In light of the tension between *Edmond* and *Morrison*, and the Court's caveat in *Edmond* that there is no "exclusive criterion" for distinguishing a principal from an inferior officer, it might be best to heed Justice Souter's

25. *Id*. at 667, 668 (Souter, J., concurring).

26. 487 U.S. 654, 670–73 (1988).

27. *Id*. at 671–72.

28. See Bowsher v. Synar, 478 U.S. 714 (1986).

advisory that the Court's approach to this distinction remains unsettled "at this stage of the Court's thinking."[29]

Heads of Departments. The Appointments Clause provides Congress with discretion to authorize the president, the courts, or "the Heads of Departments" to appoint inferior officers of the United States. The clause, however, does not identify the department heads whom Congress can entrust with this appointment authority. The Constitution refers to "Departments" on several occasions, but it neither constituted nor defined those entities. The various constitutional references hint, however, that the "Heads of Departments" the framers may have had in mind when drafting the Appointments Clause were "the principal Officer[s] in each of the executive Departments" mentioned in the Opinions Clause, which appears in the preceding paragraph (art. II, § 2, cl. 1).[30] But what are the "executive Departments"?

It is tempting to equate the "Heads of Departments" mentioned in the Appointments Clause with the heads of federal agencies, so that Congress may authorize any agency head to appoint the inferior officers of that agency. But in *Freytag v. Commissioner of Internal Revenue*, the justices narrowly rejected that translation.[31] The Court in *Freytag* instead "[c]onfin[ed] the term 'Heads of Departments' in the Appointments Clause to executive divisions like the Cabinet-level departments." The Court justified using cabinet-level departments as the benchmark for the Appointments Clause because they are "limited in number and easily identified." "[A] holding that every organ in the Executive Branch is a department," the Court worried, "would multiply indefinitely the number of actors eligible to appoint" inferior officers. The justices also believed that this limitation fostered political accountability, because the heads of the cabinet departments are "subject to the exercise of political oversight" by the president.[32]

The important unanswered question following *Freytag* concerns how broadly or narrowly the Court will apply the phrase "executive divisions *like* the Cabinet-level departments" to include agencies that are not in the president's cabinet. *Freytag* sent conflicting signals on that question. On one hand, the Court's insistence on limiting the number of eligible appointment authorities, as well as its emphasis on maintaining the political accountability of appointing officials, suggest that the justices will hesitate

---

29. *Edmond*, 520 U.S. at 668 (Souter, J., concurring).

30. *Freytag*, 501 U.S. at 886; *Buckley*, 424 U.S. at 127; United States v. Germaine, 99 U.S. 508, 511 (1879).

31. 501 U.S. 868, 885 (1991). Four justices in *Freytag* were willing to ex-

tend the meaning of "Departments" in the Appointments Clause to include "all independent executive establishments." *Id.* at 919 (Scalia, J., concurring in part and concurring in the judgment).

32. *Id.* at 885–86.

before stretching beyond the cabinet departments. On the other hand, the Court in *Freytag* expressly reserved "any question involving an appointment of an inferior officer by the head of one of the principal agencies, such as the Federal Trade Commission."[33] This reservation is puzzling, because the FTC is a prototypical independent agency that is at least somewhat insulated from the political control of the president.

(b) The Removal of Administrative Officials

The Constitution created a process of impeachment to enable Congress to remove the president, the vice president, and "all Civil Officers of the United States" who are found guilty of "Treason, Bribery, or other high Crimes and Misdemeanors" (art. II, § 4). Impeachment is solely a legislative power, and it gives Congress an important check against executive officials who abuse their authority. The Constitution, however, did not indicate whether impeachment provides the only means of removing executive officers. There apparently was no recorded debate on this question during the Constitutional Convention.[34] Yet few have interpreted the Constitution to foreclose the removal of executive officers other than by impeachment. The controversy has centered on devising the constitutional rules to govern such removals.

The Decision of 1789. One of the most pressing obligations of the First Congress was to flesh out the federal executive beyond the offices of the president and vice president, the only executive offices established by the Constitution (see § 1.5(a)). The legislators took up that challenge by creating the Departments of Foreign Affairs, Treasury, and War as the first agencies of the United States Government. The members of the First Congress recognized that the heads of these new departments would be principal officers of the United States who must be nominated by the president and confirmed by the Senate. The problem that gave the legislators pause was formulating a provision for the removal of the department heads from office. The extended debate in the House of Representatives over the removal provision in the organic act of the Department of Foreign Affairs (now the Department of State) generated no less than four competing interpretations of the Constitution's allocation of the power to remove the heads of the executive departments.[35]

33. *Id.* at 887 n.4.

34. See Myers v. United States, 272 U.S. 52, 109 (1926).

35. This account of the Decision of 1789 is taken from CHARLES C. THACH, JR., THE CREATION OF THE PRESIDENCY, 1775–1789: A STUDY IN CONSTITUTIONAL HISTORY 143–52 (1969) (originally published, 1922); Edward S. Corwin, *Tenure of Office and the Removal Power under the Constitution*, 27 COLUM. L. REV. 353, 361–69 (1927); David P. Currie, *The Constitution in Congress: The First Congress and the Structure of Government, 1789–*

The first interpretation held that significant executive officers were removable only by impeachment. All but a few members of the First Congress rejected this interpretation on pragmatic grounds: It made the removal of incompetent or corrupt administrators too difficult. There also was textual support for distinguishing between the tenure of federal judges, who are removable only by impeachment, and executive officers. The Constitution suggests that impeachment is the exclusive means of removing federal judges by providing that judges "shall hold their Office during good Behavior" (art. III, § 1). There is no parallel provision safeguarding the tenure of non-judicial officers of the United States. The First Congress thus accepted that its impeachment power supplemented rather than displaced the authority to remove government officials by less arduous means. The disagreement in 1789 lay in defining those alternative means.

The search for the constitutional location of the removal power split the House into three roughly equal groups. One of these groups held that the power to remove an executive official should mirror the power to appoint that official, and thus that the president could remove principal officers like department heads only with the consent of the Senate. This interpretation followed the position that Alexander Hamilton had taken in *The Federalist*. Hamilton believed that such a power-sharing arrangement would promote "a steady administration" by disallowing a new president from unilaterally removing the officials appointed by her or his predecessor.[36]

Another group of representatives read the Constitution to vest in the president alone the power to remove the heads of executive departments. Some proponents of this third interpretation, led by Hamilton's co-author of *The Federalist*, James Madison, relied on Article II's creation of a unitary executive. Because the Constitution prescribed presidential control over the administration of government, Madison's group argued, the president alone should possess removal authority. Others in this group would assign the president the removal power because the president possessed the power of appointment. Still others who adopted this interpretation simply believed that it made functional sense for the president to be able to remove executive officers.

The final group of House members argued that the power of removal from executive office should parallel the constitutional power to create the office. Because Congress, under its necessary and proper power, decided whether to create an office, this interpretation held, the legislators could also decide the tenure of the

1791, 2 U. OF CHI. L. SCH. ROUNDTABLE 161, 195–201 (1993).

36. THE FEDERALIST No. 77, *supra* note 1, at 497 (Alexander Hamilton).

incumbent of that office. Every House member who held this view, however, believed it best, as a matter of policy, for Congress to authorize the president alone to remove the heads of the new departments.

In the end, the proponents of the third and fourth interpretations prevailed in the House, which approved provisions authorizing the president alone to remove the Secretaries of Foreign Affairs, Treasury, and War from office. But because the members of the winning coalition advanced different opinions on the constitutional location of the removal power, it is unclear whether the removal provisions reflected a judgment by House members that the Constitution mandated an exclusive presidential power of removal, or simply that presidential removal represented the best policy option. The senators, who did not record their debate, split evenly on whether to provide the president an unencumbered power to remove the first executive department heads. The Senate adopted the House provision only on the tie-breaking vote of Vice President John Adams. Thus, the best interpretation of the so-called "Decision of 1789" might well be that the First Congress was unable to settle the vexing separation of powers questions surrounding the constitutional placement of the power to remove the heads of executive departments other than by impeachment.

The Supreme Court's Jurisprudence. Although Congress took up the question of the Constitution's allocation of the power to remove executive officers as one of its first orders of business, the Supreme Court did not immediately weigh in on the question. Indeed, the Court's first extensive consideration of the removal power did not come until the twentieth century, when the Court decided *Myers v. United States*.[37] *Myers* involved an order by President Woodrow Wilson to his Postmaster General to fire a postmaster. The firing violated a statute providing that the president could remove postmasters only "with the advice and consent of the Senate." A divided Court, led by Chief Justice (and former President) William Howard Taft, upheld the postmaster's removal, holding that the Constitution vests the president with the "exclusive" and "unrestricted" power to remove "executive officers of the United States whom he has appointed with the advice and consent of the Senate."[38]

Chief Justice Taft relied on the Decision of 1789 as precedent for finding an "exclusive and illimitable power"[39] in the president

---

37.   272 U.S. 52 (1926).

38.   *Id.* at 106–07, 134; see *id.* at 176. In an earlier decision, *United States v. Perkins*, 116 U.S. 483 (1886), the Court, in a brief treatment, made clear that Congress possessed broad authority to

dictate the terms for removing inferior officers, and by extension, federal employees as well.

39.   Humphrey's Executor v. United States, 295 U.S. 602, 627 (1935).

to remove principal executive officers. He interpreted the decision of the First Congress to authorize the president to remove the heads of the first executive departments as flowing from a constitutional imperative rather than from a mere policy preference. The Chief Justice followed the Madison group of House members by grounding the exclusivity of the president's removal power on Article II's creation of a unitary executive. As had Madison, the Chief Justice believed that the president could fulfill his constitutional mandate to "take Care that the Laws be faithfully executed" (art. II, § 3) only if he possessed unilateral power to remove senior executive officials.[40]

Chief Justice Taft took on the Hamiltonian position that the power to remove principal officers should reflect the interbranch sharing of the appointment power prescribed by the Constitution. Perhaps drawing on his experience in the White House, Taft believed that the presidential stakes were higher for the removal of executive officers than for their appointment. Senate rejection of a nominee for executive office would not necessarily undermine the president's ability to control administration because the president could always nominate another candidate in whom he or she had confidence. Requiring Senate confirmation for removals from office, however, would run the risk of saddling the president with "subordinate executive officers, ... who by their inefficient service under him, by their lack of loyalty to the service, or by their different views of policy might make his taking care that the laws be faithfully executed most difficult or impossible." Taft thus worried that Senate involvement in removal decisions would impose "a much greater limitation upon the executive branch" than the advice-and-consent power that the Constitution provided for the appointment of principal officers.[41]

Chief Justice Taft's opinion for the Court in *Myers* represents perhaps the strongest endorsement of presidential autonomy in American constitutional jurisprudence. The justices have stood by *Myers*'s ruling that the separation of powers bars legislators from taking any part in the decision to remove officials who exercise the executive power, other than by impeachment. Indeed, the Court has solidified that ruling in recent years by equating congressional involvement in removal decisions with the legislative veto. To the justices, both actions threaten "congressional usurpation" of the executive power.[42]

Within ten years of deciding *Myers*, however, the Court began to rethink whether it made constitutional sense to disable Congress from restricting in any way the president's power to remove admin-

40. *Myers*, 272 U.S. at 117.
41. *Id.* at 121, 131.

42. See Bowsher v. Synar, 478 U.S. 714, 723, 726–27 (1986).

istrative officials who, unlike *Myers*'s postmaster, lead modern regulatory agencies. *Humphrey's Executor v. United States*[43] involved President Franklin Roosevelt's removal of a member of the Federal Trade Commission whom Roosevelt's predecessor, President Herbert Hoover, had appointed to office. Following the logic of *Myers*, President Roosevelt explained his decision to fire the Commissioner as an effort to align "the work of the Commission" with his "aims and purposes." The ousted Commissioner, however, claimed that the president's desire for like-minded Federal Trade Commissioners was not a lawful basis for his termination because the agency's organic act limited the grounds for removing Trade Commissioners to "inefficiency, neglect of duty, or malfeasance in office." Roosevelt naturally responded that under *Myers*, Congress's for-cause restriction on his removal authority was unconstitutional.[44]

The Court in *Humphrey's Executor* upheld the removal restriction. Henceforth, the justices held, *Myers*'s acceptance of an "exclusive and illimitable power of removal" in the president would be limited to "purely executive officers." The "character of the office" at issue in *Myers* so qualified because postmasters were "restricted to the performance of executive functions." The office of postmaster was "merely one of the units in the executive department," and postmasters thus served as "subordinate[s]" and "aid[s]" of the president.[45]

The justices viewed the office of Federal Trade Commissioner differently. In the Court's description, "The Federal Trade Commission is an administrative body created by Congress to carry into effect legislative policies embodied in the statute in accordance with the legislative standard therein prescribed, and to perform other specified duties as a legislative or as a judicial aid." The actions of such a law-enforcement agency, the justices believed, could not "be characterized as an arm or an eye of the executive." The FTC served functions that the Court described as either "quasi legislative" (referring to the authority to conduct investigations and to submit reports to Congress) and "quasi judicial" (referring to the Commission's adjudicative authority). An agency with an amalgam of such powers, the Court concluded, "occupie[d] no place in the executive department and ... exercise[d] no part of the executive power vested by the Constitution in the President." Because regulatory agencies such as the FTC operated outside the executive domain, *Humphrey's Executor* held, Congress could allow them to

43. 295 U.S. 602 (1935).   **45.** *Id*. at 626–28, 631.
44. *Id*. at 618, 621–26.

"act in discharge of their duties independently of executive control."[46]

The Court's trimming of *Myers* in *Humphrey's Executor* resulted from the justices' belief that Chief Justice Taft's insistence on an untouchable removal power in the president was incompatible with the emergence of the modern regulatory agency, which extended government administration far beyond the original executive departments that the First Congress had created in 1789. The justices accepted the legitimacy of Congress's policy choice to structure regulatory agencies as law-enforcement bodies that are politically independent and "nonpartisan." But their rationale for distinguishing *Humphrey's Executor* from *Myers* was itself incompatible with the principle of separation of powers. If regulatory agencies with "quasi legislative" and "quasi judicial" powers had "no place in the executive department," what was their place in a government divided into three, and only three, branches? Moreover, the Court's description of a law-enforcement agency like the FTC—an "administrative body" that "carr[ies] into effect legislative policies embodied in [a] statute in accordance with the legislative standard therein prescribed"—hardly describes an entity that "exercises no part of the executive power vested by the Constitution in the President."[47] Indeed, the Court's description captures the core meaning of the executive power, namely, the enforcement of acts of Congress.

The evolution of administrative law undermined the rationale, but not the result, in *Humphrey's Executor*. Regulatory agencies like the FTC are now understood to exercise the executive power (because they enforce their enabling acts), even when their actions resemble Congress's exercises of the legislative power (as in rule-making) or of the courts' exercise of the judicial power (as in adjudication) (see § 2.2). The contemporary Court accordingly has found it necessary to revise the distinction between *Myers* and *Humphrey's Executor* to fit this new understanding.

The revision occurred in *Morrison v. Olson*.[48] In *Morrison*, the Court evaluated the organic act creating the office of independent counsel, which had authority to investigate, and if warranted, to prosecute senior executive officials, including the president, for violations of federal law. As had been true of the FTC Commissioners before the Court in *Humphrey's Executor*, Congress designed the office of independent counsel to enable the incumbent to fulfill this sensitive law-enforcement mission independently. The act thus provided that the Attorney General could remove an independent counsel "only for good cause, physical disability, mental incapacity,

---

46. *Id*. at 624, 628–29.   **48.** 487 U.S. 654 (1988).

47. *Id*. at 624–26, 628.

or any other condition that substantially impairs the performance of [the] independent counsel's duties."[49]

This good-cause restriction resembled the removal restriction that the Court had upheld in *Humphrey's Executor*. But whereas *Humphrey's Executor* rested on the rationale that FTC Commissioners "exercise[d] no part of the executive power," the Court in *Morrison* freely acknowledged that "the law enforcement functions" performed by the independent counsel were executive in nature. Under the *Myers/Humphrey's Executor* distinction, the *Morrison* Court's acknowledgement would have triggered the *Myers* rule of "illimitable power" in the president to remove an independent counsel from office. The justices instead used *Morrison* to further marginalize *Myers*. "[O]ur present considered view," the *Morrison* Court declared, "is that the determination of whether the Constitution allows Congress to impose a 'good cause'-type restriction on the President's power to remove an official cannot be made to turn on whether or not that official is classified as 'purely executive.' "[50]

The Court in *Morrison* replaced *Myers*'s formalistic approach to the president's removal power with a more functional orientation. "The analysis contained in our removal cases is designed not to define rigid categories of those officials who may or may not be removed at will by the President," the Court explained, "but to ensure that Congress does not interfere with the President's exercise of the 'executive power' and his constitutionally appointed duty to 'take care that the laws be faithfully executed' under Article II." Having switched from a formal to a functional approach, the Court in *Morrison* reaffirmed as "undoubtedly correct" the *Myers* rule prohibiting Congress from aggrandizing its power by "involv[ing] itself in the removal of an executive official." But the justices broadened congressional authority to restrict the president's power to remove executive officers. After *Morrison*, the president has illimitable power to remove only those " 'purely executive' officials who must be removable by the President at will if he is to be able to accomplish his constitutional role."[51]

Morrison's ruling that the president is constitutionally entitled to remove only some, rather than all, "purely executive" officials at will left the identity of those officials unclear. The Court in *Morrison* advised that it would make that assessment on an ad hoc basis, determining for each office whether "the President's need to control the exercise of [a particular official's] *discretion* is ... central to the functioning of the Executive Branch."[52] The heads of the

---

49. *Id*. at 663.

50. *Id*. at 689, 691.

51. *Id*. at 686, 689–90.

52. *Id*. at 691 (emphasis added).

executive departments who occupy a seat in the president's cabinet are likely candidates for the exercise of such presidential control. Because of their close proximity to the president and the political nature of their service, the president may well have a special need to dismiss cabinet members in whose discretion he no longer trusts.

Yet *Morrison* suggests, as a general matter, that Congress may protect the tenure, and thus the independence, of the heads of administrative agencies by requiring that the president have good cause for removing them from office. In the usual case, *Morrison* implies, the president need not control the discretion of executive officers in order to fulfill her or his constitutional function of ensuring that they faithfully execute the laws. A good-cause restriction on the president's removal power, the Court in *Morrison* ruled, leaves "ample authority to assure that [an officer] is competently performing his or her statutory responsibilities in a manner that comports with the provisions of [an enabling act]." What Congress likely cannot do, the Court suggested in *Morrison*, was to "completely" deny the president the power to remove an official who exercises executive power. Without the authority to remove such an official for good cause, the president would be left without the "means . . . to ensure the 'faithful execution' of the laws."[53]

If Congress possesses authority to restrict the president's power to remove a particular officer, the legislators can enforce that restriction by providing for judicial review of the president's removal decision to ensure that it satisfies the statutory criteria. Because the purpose of judicial review is to ensure that an officer is removed only in accordance with statute, a provision for judicial review does not "put any additional burden on the President's exercise of executive authority."[54]

(c) Presidential Oversight of Government Administration

The Constitution vests the legislative and judicial powers of the federal government in two distinctive institutions—Congress and the federal courts, respectively. By contrast, the Constitution entrusts the executive power to a single individual, the president. This difference in the Vesting Clause of Article II signals the establishment of what is often described as the "unitary executive." It seems clear that the president's unique status as the ultimate caretaker of the executive power provides him or her at least some measure of control over the actions of government officials who perform executive functions. Defining the scope and limits of presidential control over executive officers has proven to be exceedingly difficult, however.

---

53. *Id*. at 691–92.   **54.** *Id*. at 693 n.33.

Alexander Hamilton, writing in *The Federalist*, described the president as a kind of Chief Executive Officer of the federal government with administrators serving under her or his supervisory control. "The persons ... to whose immediate management [the administration of government is] committed," Hamilton wrote, "ought to be considered as the assistants or deputies of the chief magistrate, ... and ought to be subject to his superintendence."[55] Several provisions of Article II support Hamilton's conception of the president's supervisory authority over executive officers. Most prominently, the Take Care Clause obligates the president to "take Care that the Laws be faithfully executed" (§ 3). The idea of the president as CEO of the federal government also is supported by the Opinions Clause, which provides that the president may "require" the heads of the executive departments to provide him or her with written opinions "upon any Subject relating to the Duties of their respective Offices" (§ 2, cl. 1).

A closer reading of the Constitution blurs Hamilton's vision of the president as CEO, however. The framers delicately designed the presidency to be "suitably energetic but safely republican,"[56] and the specific power grants of Article II often are double-edged swords. Thus, although the president has the power (and obligation) to see that the laws are faithfully executed, the text stops short of giving the president power to *personally* execute those laws. Similarly, the Opinions Clause, by its terms, simply allows the president to demand reports from the executive department heads with respect to the execution of *their* duties, and not to take over those duties and make them her or his own.[57] And of course, the Constitution's vesting in Congress of the power "[t]o make all Laws which shall be necessary and proper for carrying into Execution ... all other Powers vested by [the] Constitution in the Government of the United States, or in any Department or Officer thereof" (art. I, § 8, cl. 18), suggests that the legislators have at least some say in the administration of the federal government.[58] After all, the president's authority to "take Care that the Laws be faithfully executed" obligates him or her to deploy the executive power in accordance with all valid acts of Congress, and not simply with her or his preferences.[59]

55. THE FEDERALIST NO. 72, *supra* note 1, at 469 (Alexander Hamilton).

56. JACK N. RAKOVE, ORIGINAL MEANINGS: POLITICS AND IDEAS IN THE MAKING OF THE CONSTITUTION 82 (1996).

57. See Peter L. Strauss, *Presidential Rulemaking*, 72 CHI.-KENT L. REV. 965, 979–80 (1997).

58. See William Van Alstyne, *The Role of Congress in Determining Inci-* *dental Powers of the President and of the Federal Courts: A Comment on the Horizontal Effect of "The Sweeping Clause,"* 36 OHIO ST. L.J. 788 (1975).

59. See Chrysler Corp. v. Brown, 441 U.S. 281, 302–03 (1979); Youngstown Sheet & Tube Co. v. Sawyer, 343 U.S. 579, 587–88 (1952).

Given these constitutional crosscurrents, it is hardly surprising that the Court has found it difficult to define the proper constitutional role of the president concerning the execution of statutes that Congress has placed in the hands of other government administrators. We know from our earlier discussion that the Constitution provides the president a means of controlling administration by vesting in him or her the power to appoint agency heads, albeit subject to Senate confirmation. Congress can limit the president's appointment discretion somewhat by specifying the qualifications of the offices that it creates. We also have seen that the president has the power to fire agency heads, although Congress may require that the president demonstrate "good cause" for most removals. The ultimate, as well as the most difficult, question triggered by the unitary presidency created by Article II concerns the extent of the president's constitutional authority to direct the decisionmaking of officials who perform executive functions.

The Supreme Court, and the federal courts generally, have had surprisingly little to say on this question. But early in the nineteenth century, the justices established the important starting point for defining the scope of the president's supervisory power over executive officers when they decided *Kendall v. United States*.[60] *Kendall* arose from a claim by a group of individuals that the Postmaster General had refused to compensate them for services rendered on a contract to transport the mail. Congress passed a law authorizing the Solicitor of the Treasury Department to arbitrate the claim and directing the Postmaster General to pay any award ordered by the Solicitor. When the Postmaster General refused to honor the Solicitor's award in favor of the individuals, the individuals filed suit.

The Postmaster General believed that only the president could direct him to pay the award. He therefore claimed that a judicial order enforcing the Solicitor's award pursuant to the statute would constitute "an infringement upon the executive department of the government." But the justices would have none of it. They rejected the idea that "every officer in every branch of [the executive] department is under the exclusive direction of the President." The Court continued, Congress by law can "impose upon any executive officer any duty [it thinks] proper," provided the statute does not otherwise violate the Constitution, and the president cannot direct any officer to violate such a statutory duty. Thus, because Congress had passed a statute requiring the Postmaster General to honor the Solicitor's arbitration award, the president had no power to direct otherwise. When Congress imposes a duty on an executive officer, the Court in *Kendall* explained, "the duty and responsibility [of

---

60.   37 U.S. (12 Pet.) 524 (1838).

that officer] grow out of and are subject to the control of the law, and not to the direction of the President."[61]

The Court in *Kendall* established the fundamental principle that the president cannot relieve executive officers of their obligation to comply with valid acts of Congress. But *Kendall* did not settle the scope of presidential authority to direct government administrators to make decisions that do not violate a statutory duty. As the Court noted in *Kendall*, the statute there clearly had directed the Postmaster General to pay the Solicitor's arbitration award and thus had left him with no discretion to refuse.[62] But what if, as is often the case, a statute is unclear or gives an administrator the discretion to choose among several lawful options? May the president direct the administrator to choose a particular interpretation or option, or must the president permit the administrator's preference to stand?

The Court addressed this more difficult question in *Myers v. United States*,[63] a decision that stands as perhaps the strongest judicial endorsement of a robust executive power to control government administration. In his lengthy opinion for the Court, Chief Justice William Howard Taft ranged beyond the president's power to remove executive officials, which was at issue in the case. In dicta, he addressed as well what he saw as the intimately related question of the scope of presidential power to direct the decision-making of executive officials. Drawing on the premise of the unitary executive, the Chief Justice recognized broad authority in the president to control the decisions that executive officers make pursuant to their statutory authority. Taft explained, "The ordinary duties of officers prescribed by statute come under the general administrative control of the President by virtue of the general grant to him of the executive power, and he may properly supervise and guide their construction of the statutes under which they act in order to secure that unitary and uniform execution of the laws which article 2 of the Constitution evidently contemplated in vesting general executive power in the President alone." In the *Myers* dicta, Chief Justice Taft acknowledged that the exercise of such presidential control was nevertheless subject to constitutional limits. For example, he questioned the power of the president to intervene in agency adjudications, where due process values are at stake.[64] And Taft observed more generally, "Of course there may be duties so peculiarly and specifically committed to the discretion of a

61. *Id.* at 610.

62. *Id.* at 611.

63. 272 U.S. 52 (1926).

64. *Id.* at 135; see also Portland Audubon Soc'y v. Endangered Species Committee, 984 F.2d 1534, 1543–48 (9th Cir. 1993) (provision of the Administrative Procedure Act prohibiting ex parte communications during formal agency adjudications applies to the president and the White House staff).

particular officer as to raise a question whether the President may overrule or revise the officer's interpretation of his statutory duty in a particular instance."[65]

As recounted in the preceding section, the Court in *Humphrey's Executor* and in *Morrison* retreated from the holding in *Myers* that Congress cannot provide for independent administration of statutory authority by forbidding the president to remove administrative officials because of policy disagreements. It would seem to follow from these decisions that the president also lacks authority to undermine the statutory independence of such officials more directly by requiring them to exercise their statutory discretion in accordance with his or her wishes. But what of administrative officials who exercise statutory authority without the protective cloak of a good-cause limitation on their removal? Because *Myers* allows the president to fire such officials at will, it is clear that he or she may do so if they refuse to obey policy directions. Does it also follow that the president may require these executive officials to adopt *his* or *her* policy directives in exercising *their* statutory discretion?

The Supreme Court has yet to resolve this question, but the decision by the influential D.C. Circuit court of appeals in *Sierra Club v. Costle*[66] suggests a likely answer, at least with respect to informal administrative rulemaking.[67] *Sierra Club* involved a challenge by environmental groups to an important set of emission standards issued by the Environmental Protection Agency, which is an executive rather than an independent agency. The groups alleged, among other things, that the agency's rulemaking was tainted by a series of closed meetings between EPA officials and the president, along with White House staff and other senior executive officials. The court of appeals upheld the legality of the meeting. At least with respect to executive agencies like the EPA, the court of appeals "recognize[d] the basic need of the President and his White House staff to monitor the consistency of executive agency regulations with Administration policy. He and his White House advisers surely must be briefed fully and frequently about rules in the making, and *their contributions to policymaking considered*."[68]

The italicized language suggests that the D.C. Circuit's decision in *Sierra Club* limits as well as supports the involvement of the president and White House staff in rulemaking decisions by executive agencies. In the *Sierra Club* framework, Article II enables the president, together with members of the White House staff, to

---

65. *Myers*, 52 U.S. at 135.

66. 657 F.2d 298 (D.C.Cir. 1981).

67. See *Portland Audubon Soc'y*, 984 F.2d at 1545 (limiting *Sierra Club* to informal rulemaking proceedings).

68. *Id*. at 404–08 (emphasis added).

review and to express their views regarding administrative regulatory decisions. But while executive agencies are obligated to consider those views, they need not follow them. The distinction between presidential cajoling and binding direction observes the fine line the framers walked in the Take Care and the Opinions Clauses. It also is true to *Kendall*. For the president to direct, and thus to take over, the decisionmaking of an agency pursuant to its statutory authority threatens to undermine Congress's decision to vest that authority in the agency rather than in the president. In such an event, the president might be seen as violating, rather than executing, the law.[69]

White House Planning and Review of Agency Rulemaking. "From the point of view of administration," writes historian Forrest McDonald, "the history of the presidency in the twentieth century has been the history of presidents' attempts to gain control of the sprawling federal bureaucracy."[70] At the beginning of the last century, presidents largely relied on their appointments power to guide government administration. Early twentieth-century efforts by presidents to reorganize the government in order to enhance their control over administration typically met with stiff congressional resistance. But the legislators gradually relented. The first breakthrough occurred in 1921, when Congress authorized the president to prepare a unified budget proposal on an annual basis for legislative consideration.[71] The budget act provided the president a measure of fiscal control over administrative action. In 1932, Congress passed the first of a series of statutes permitting the president to reorganize the government, albeit subject to a legislative veto.[72] President Franklin Roosevelt used the authority provided by a later reorganization act in 1939 to establish the Executive Office of the President, an important advance that created an institutional base for the exercise of presidential power.[73] As the

69. See Robert V. Percival, *Presidential Management of the Administrative State: The Not–So–Unitary Executive*, 51 Duke L.J. 963, 971–72 (2001). There has been considerable recent scholarship on the scope of presidential power to control the discretionary decisionmaking of administrative agencies. See, e.g., Steven G. Calabresi & Saikrishna Prakash, *The President's Power to Execute the Laws*, 104 Yale L.J. 541, 593–99 (1994); Steven G. Calabresi & Kevin H. Rhodes, *The Structural Constitution: Unitary Executive, Plural Judiciary*, 105 Harv. L. Rev. 1153, 1166 (1992); Lawrence Lessig & Cass R. Sunstein, *The President and the Administration*, 94 Colum. L. Rev. 1 (1994).

70. Forrest McDonald, The American Presidency: An Intellectual History 329 (1994).

71. Act of June 10, 1921, 67th Cong., 1st Sess., ch.18, §§ 201–17, 42 Stat. 20, 20–23.

72. Act of June 30, 1932, 72nd Cong., 1st Sess., ch. 314, §§ 401–408, 47 Stat. 382, 413–15. This act marked the first appearance of a legislative veto provision in an act of Congress. See INS v. Chadha, 462 U.S. 919, 968–69 (1983) (White, J., dissenting). The Supreme Court in *Chadha* ruled that legislative vetoes are unconstitutional (see § 2.3(b)).

73. See E.O. 8,248, 4 Fed. Reg. 3,864 (1939).

Nation coped with the successive twentieth-century traumas of the Great Depression, World War II, and the Cold War, there eventually emerged a public "perception of presidential responsibility" for the operations of the federal government.[74]

There existed a significant gap, however, between the perception and the reality of presidential control over the post-War government. This gap took on special urgency when Congress greatly expanded the regulatory role of federal agencies in the late 1960s and early 1970s (see § 1.5(e)). It is hardly coincidence that since 1971, every president has enlisted the Office of Management and Budget, a unit of the Executive Office of the President, in an effort to exert centralized control over federal regulation.[75] President Ronald Reagan made the decisive move in 1981. Within weeks of his taking office, President Reagan issued Executive Order 12,291, which authorized the Office of Information and Regulatory Affairs ("OIRA") within OMB to review all major rulemaking initiatives by the executive agencies in order to guarantee that the expected benefits of the regulation outweighed the projected costs.[76] President Reagan reinforced the status of OMB as regulatory clearinghouse four years later when he issued Executive Order 12,498. The new executive order established an annual "regulatory planning process," managed by OMB, to make agency rulemaking initiatives consistent with administration policy.[77]

President William Clinton substituted his own Executive Order 12,866 for the Reagan orders in 1993.[78] President Clinton's executive order retained, and expanded upon, the basic outline of President Reagan's regulatory planning and review process. President George W. Bush tweaked the Clinton order in 2002,[79] and Executive Order 12,866, as amended by President Bush's Executive Order 13,258, remains in effect. A presidential planning and review process for agency regulation, operated by OIRA, seemingly has become a permanent fixture of the administrative process.

The stated purpose of Executive Order 12,866 is to "reform and make efficient the regulatory process."[80] The executive order begins with a statement of "regulatory philosophy," together with a delineation of twelve "principles of regulation" that the president expects agency rulemaking to honor, "to the extent permitted by

---

74. McDONALD, AMERICAN PRESIDENCY, *supra* note 70, at 330–34.

75. For a brief review of the regulatory control efforts of Presidents Richard Nixon and Jimmy Carter, see Harold Bruff, *Presidential Management of Agency Rulemaking*, 57 GEO. WASH. L. REV. 533, 546–49 (1989).

76. E.O. 12,291, 46 Fed. Reg. 13,193 (1981).

77. E.O. 12,498, 50 Fed. Reg. 1,036 (1985).

78. 58 Fed. Reg. 51,737 (1993).

79. E.O. 13,258, 67 Fed. Reg. 9,385 (2003).

80. E.O. 12,866, as amended by E.O. 13,258, preamble, *supra* notes 78 and 79.

law."[81] The executive order authorizes OMB to secure administrative compliance with the president's priorities by managing processes for planning and reviewing agency regulation.

Executive Order 12,866 centralizes an early leadership role in the White House for shaping the regulatory agenda of federal agencies. The executive order requires each agency to submit to OMB an annual "regulatory plan," which describes and justifies "the most important . . . regulatory actions" under consideration for the coming year. OMB then organizes a comprehensive review of each of the agency's regulatory plans by White House officials and by affected agencies. The final regulatory plan of each agency is compiled in an annual publication, called the *Unified Regulatory Agenda*. Unlike President Reagan's Executive Order 12,498, Executive Order 12,866 *requires* that independent agencies as well as executive agencies participate in the annual planning process.[82] By contrast, President Reagan had *requested*, and received, the voluntary participation of independent agencies in his regulatory planning process.

Executive Order 12,866 followed President Reagan's Executive Order 12,291 in exempting independent agencies from the regulatory review process, however. The Clinton executive order also left in place the essentials of the White House review process established by Executive Order 12,291. Executive agencies remain obliged to vet their "significant" rulemaking initiatives with OMB. The focal point of OMB review is still a cost-benefit justification of the rule. OMB may block the issuance of an agency rule by returning it to the agency "for further consideration."[83]

Just as President Clinton expanded the regulatory planning process by requiring the participation of independent agencies, he created the potential for greater White House involvement in the agencies' final rulemaking decisions. Executive Order 12,291 had left the final decision with the agency, which was obligated only to respond to OMB's views. Clinton's executive order is more ambiguous about where the final decisionmaking authority rests. Executive Order 12,866 includes a dispute resolution provision that appears to give the president the final say when OMB and an agency are unable to resolve a conflict that arises during regulatory review.[84] But another section of the order provides, "Nothing in this order shall be construed as displacing the agencies' authority

81. E.O. 12,866, as amended by E.O. 13,258, § 1, § 2(a), *supra* notes 78 and 79.

82. E.O. 12,866, as amended by E.O. 13,258, § 4, *supra* notes 78 and 79.

83. E.O. 12,866, as amended by E.O. 13,258, § 6, *supra* notes 78 and 79 . . .

84. E.O. 12,866, as amended by E.O. 13,258, § 7(d), *supra* notes 78 and 79 . . .

or responsibilities, as authorized by law."[85] As far as is publicly known, Executive Order 12,866's presidential dispute resolution process has been invoked only on "rare" occasions.[86] According to Dean Elena Kagan, who served in the White House during the Clinton Administration, "the dispute resolution provision of the Clinton executive order did not change the essential way that OMB regulatory review operated [under Executive Order 12,291]."[87]

The regulatory review process that President Reagan initiated in 1981 has remained controversial on both policy and constitutional grounds. As to policy, there are both substantive and procedural criticisms of OMB's entry into the regulatory process. The substantive controversy is over the centrality of cost-benefit analysis to agency regulation. To some observers, a cost-benefit requirement is an essential safeguard for rational and efficient government regulation.[88] Others are troubled by the difficulty of assigning economic values to many of the social benefits produced by regulation.[89] Still others complain that imposition of a general cost-benefit requirement unjustifiably privileges economic efficiency over other social values, such as promoting the health and safety of the public.[90]

The procedural controversy centers on the wisdom of providing a role for OMB in the agency rulemaking process. The division here is often between those who believe that government regulation is (or should be) a product of agency specialization and expertise, and those who are convinced that politics trumps expertise in driving regulatory actions by agencies.[91] Supporters of the White House review process tend to have a political vision of government regulation.[92] They claim that the president, and only the president, can bring the coordination and political accountability that is necessary for legitimate and effective government regulation.[93] Critics of

---

85. E.O. 12,866, as amended by E.O. 13,258, § 9, *supra* notes 78 and 79.

86. JEFFREY S. LUBBERS, A GUIDE TO AGENCY RULEMAKING 253 n.52 (4th ed. 2006).

87. Elena Kagan, *Presidential Administration*, 114 HARV. L. REV. 2245, 2289 (2001).

88. See, e.g., Christopher C. DeMuth & Douglas H. Ginsburg, *White House Review of Agency Rulemaking*, 99 HARV. L. REV. 1075, 1081–82 (1986).

89. See, e.g., Thomas O. McGarity, *Regulatory Analysis and Regulatory Reform*, 65 TEX. L. REV. 1243, 1293–95 (1987).

90. Alan B. Morrison, *OMB Interference with Agency Rulemaking: The Wrong Way to Write a Regulation*, 99 HARV. L. REV. 1059, 1065 (1986).

91. For an argument that the distinction between expertise and politics is blurred in the White House's process of regulatory review, see Kagan, *Presidential Administration*, supra note 87, at 2352–58.

92. See, e.g., DeMuth & Ginsburg, *White House Review of Agency Rulemaking*, supra note 88, at 1081; Peter L. Strauss & Cass R. Sunstein, *The Role of the President and OMB in Informal Rulemaking*, 38 ADMIN. L. REV. 181, 187 (1986).

93. See, e.g., DeMuth & Ginsburg, *White House Review of Agency Rulemaking*, supra note 88, at 1081; Kagan, *Presidential Administration*, supra note 87, at 2331–46; Strauss & Sunstein, *Role of the President and OMB in Informal Rulemaking*, supra note 92, at 187.

centralized review tend to value agencies for their programmatic expertise. They complain that the quality of regulation will suffer if the balance of regulatory power shifts to non-experts in OMB who lack the institutional resources and technical competence to review rules across the vast domain of federal regulation.[94] Some of these critics also worry that White House review itself unduly politicizes regulatory decisions by administrative agencies,[95] and in any event, blurs the accountability of government regulation as between the White House and the agencies.[96]

The constitutional controversy over White House regulatory review has ignited the deeper disagreement over the scope of presidential power to direct agency decisionmaking, discussed in the preceding part of this section. Supporters of White House regulatory review tend to rely on a strong view of the unitary presidency, which envisions the president as a hands-on Chief Executive Officer of the federal government.[97] As expressed in one commentary, "Agency heads exercise their statutory authority at the president's pleasure" because "it is his constitutional responsibility, not theirs, to take care that the laws are faithfully executed."[98]

Constitutional challengers of White House regulatory review typically begin with the premise that the executive orders are fundamentally inconsistent with the enabling acts that authorize agency rulemaking.[99] Enabling acts delegate authority to a particular agency to issue rules in accordance with statutory standards. The executive orders undermine that congressional scheme, the challengers argue, by imposing a centralized rulemaking superstructure requiring agencies to make their regulatory decisions in accordance with the president's standards.[100] To these challengers,

94. See, e.g., Bruff, *Presidential Management of Agency Rulemaking, supra* note 75, at 545; Morrison, *OMB Interference with Agency Rulemaking, supra* note 90, at 1066–67; Robert V. Percival, *Presidential Management of the Administrative State, supra* note 69, at 1006–07.

95. See Cynthia R. Farina, *Undoing the New Deal Through the New Presidentialism*, 22 Harv. J. L. Pub. Pol'y 227, 233–34; Percival, *Management of the Administrative State, supra* note 69, at 1010.

96. Percival, *Management of the Administrative State, supra* note 69, at 1009.

97. See, e.g., James F. Blumstein, *Regulatory Review by the Executive Office of the President: An Overview and Policy Analysis of Current Issues*, 51

Duke L.J. 851, 851–53 (2001); DeMuth & Ginsburg, *White House Review of Agency Rulemaking, supra* note ___, at 1082–83; Thomas O. Sargentich, *The Administrative Process in Crisis—The Example of Presidential Oversight of Agency Rulemaking*, 6 Admin. L.J. Am. U. 710, 715 (1993).

98. DeMuth & Ginsburg, *White House Review of Agency Rulemaking, supra* note 88, at 1083.

99. See Morrison, *OMB Interference with Agency Rulemaking, supra* note 90, at 1062–63.

100. For an argument that congressional delegations of rulemaking authority to executive agencies usually should be interpreted to authorize the president to direct the agencies' rulemaking decisions, see Kagan, *Presidential Adminis-*

the executive orders place substantive (cost-benefit balancing) and procedural (OMB clearance) obstacles to agency rulemaking against the wishes of Congress.[101] On this argument, White House review of agency regulation may be depicted as violating *Kendall*'s foundational principle that the president lacks the power to direct agencies to act in violation of acts of Congress.

Supporters of the White House regulatory review process respond to this constitutional challenge by emphasizing that Executive Order 12,866 requires agencies to follow presidential direction only "to the extent permitted by law."[102] With that caveat, it might be argued that the executive order observes the *Kendall* limit on presidential authority: The president declaims any authority to direct agencies to violate any statutory duties that Congress has placed on them. And reviewing courts have held statutory requirements to trump those of the executive order when they have come into conflict.[103]

Executive Order 12,866 also threatens the boundary on presidential authority marked by the D.C. Circuit in *Sierra Club v. Costle*,[104] which allows the president to consult with agencies concerning their rulemaking, but not to direct the content of agency rulemaking. If the Supreme Court adopts the *Sierra Club* limit (which it has not done to date), the president would be unable to resolve disputes between OMB and federal agencies with respect to rulemaking content, as Executive Order 12,866 seems to provide. Rather, the agencies would be required to consider the views of the White House, but they would remain free to make all final decisions on the content of their rules.[105]

---

tration, supra note 87, at 2319–31. For an argument that the broad spectrum of congressional legislation concerning the administrative process reflects an intention to deny the president a policymaking role, see Morton Rosenberg, *Beyond the Limits of Executive Power: Presidential Control of Agency Rulemaking Under Executive Order 12,291*, 80 MICH. L. REV. 193, 221–34 (1981).

101. See Morrison, *OMB Interference with Agency Rulemaking, supra* note 90, at 1062–63; Rosenberg, *Beyond the Limits of Executive Power, supra* note 100, at 213.

102. E.O. 12,866, as amended by E.O. 13,258, § 1(b), *supra* notes 78 and 79; see Strauss & Sunstein, *Role of the President and OMB in Informal Rulemaking, supra* note 92, at 192.

103. The case law thus far has been limited to district court decisions holding that OMB review does not justify an

agency's failure to meet a statutory deadline for promulgating regulations. See American Lung Association v. Browner, 884 F.Supp. 345, 349 (D.Ariz. 1994); Natural Resources Defense Council v. EPA, 797 F.Supp. 194, 198 (E.D.N.Y. 1992); Environmental Defense Fund v. Thomas, 627 F.Supp. 566, 570–72 (D.D.C. 1986).

104. 657 F.2d 298, 404–08 (D.C. Cir. 1981).

105. Strauss & Sunstein, *Role of the President and OMB in Informal Rulemaking, supra* note 92, at 192. In *National Grain and Feed Association v. OSHA*, 866 F.2d 717, 729 n.22 (5th Cir. 1989), the Fifth Circuit summarily rejected a claim that OMB review had unlawfully "displaced the [agency's] congressionally-authorized role in formulating [rules]." The court of appeals held that the facts did not support the claim because "OMB's recommendations did not become part of the final rule."

§ 2.5 Administrative Agencies and the Courts

Article III of the Constitution vests the "judicial Power of the United States ... in one Supreme Court, and in such inferior Courts as the Congress may from time to time ordain and establish" (§ 1). The distinguishing quality of the federal judiciary, at the time of the framing as well as today, has been its relative political independence. Alexander Hamilton reflected the mindset of many members of the founding generation when he wrote that an "independent spirit in the judges" was "essential to the faithful performance of [their] arduous duty."[1] The contemporary Supreme Court has emphasized two values that are served by an independent judiciary. Judicial independence fosters the ideal of impartial adjudication. The federal judiciary's independence also helps to secure its position of equality in a government of separated powers and checks and balances.[2]

Article III secures judicial independence primarily through its provisions governing the selection, salary, and tenure of federal judges. The federal judiciary is unelected. Federal judges are selected in the same manner as are principal officers of the United States: They are appointed by the president, subject to Senate confirmation (art. II, § 2, cl. 2). But unlike other principal officers, a federal judge's pay cannot be decreased (art. III, § 1). And most importantly, federal judges hold office "during good Behavior" (art. III, § 1). Although federal judges, together with all other "civil Officers of the United States," are subject to impeachment (art. II, § 4), congressional removals have been rare. As Alexander Hamilton predicted, the good-behavior standard has provided judges with "permanency in office."[3]

From the beginning, the Supreme Court has regarded the adjudication of "cases" and "controversies" as the essence of the judicial power.[4] But although the authority of federal judges is largely limited to resolving cases and controversies within the federal judicial power,[5] Congress has never provided that all such disputes must be adjudicated exclusively in the federal courts provided for in Article III. Drawing on its legislative powers,

---

§ 2.5

1. THE FEDERALIST NO. 78, at 508 (Alexander Hamilton) (Modern Library ed., 1941).

2. See Commodity Futures Trading Comm'n v. Schor, 478 U.S. 833, 848, 850 (1986); Thomas v. Union Carbide Agricultural Products Co., 473 U.S. 568, 582–83 (1985).

3. THE FEDERALIST NO. 78, *supra* note 1, at 505 (Alexander Hamilton).

4. See Muskrat v. United States, 219 U.S. 346, 356 (1911); Hayburn's Case, 2 U.S. (2 Dall.) 409 (1796).

5. Federal judges are not completely limited to resolving cases, however. See, e.g., Mistretta v. United States, 488 U.S. 361 (1989) (upholding the service of federal judges on the U.S. Sentencing Commission); Morrison v. Olson, 487 U.S. 654 (1988) (upholding judicial appointments of independent counsel).

Congress has created a number of "legislative courts" (also called, "Article I courts") to resolve cases that fall within the purview of "constitutional courts" (also called, "Article III courts"). The judges of a legislative court do not enjoy the salary and tenure protections afforded by Article III of the Constitution. Moreover, because Congress draws on its Article I legislative powers to create legislative courts, it is free to direct those courts to resolve disputes without regard to the limits on the judicial power delineated in Article III.[6]

The Supreme Court consistently has held that Congress can assign to legislative courts some—but not all—of the cases or controversies that are included within the federal judicial power.[7] But the justices have struggled mightily in their attempts to define the nature of the constitutional limits on the adjudicatory authority of legislative courts, and this intersection of administrative law and the law governing federal courts remains uncommonly obscure. The treatment here is basic.

(a) Administrative Agencies as Adjudicative Alternatives to Federal Courts

Since its very first session, Congress has authorized administrative agencies to adjudicate disputes that the legislators might have assigned to federal courts as "Cases ... arising under ... the Laws of the United States" (art. III, § 2, cl. 1). The First Congress authorized executive officials to adjudicate customs matters, as well as claims for military pensions.[8] Later Congresses have felt equally free to create administrative tribunals to adjudicate controversies falling within the federal judicial power when the legislators have found it "necessary and proper" to do so. When Congress draws on its Article I powers to provide administrative adjudicatory authori-

---

6. See Glidden Co. v. Zdanok, 370 U.S. 530, 544 (1962) (plurality op.).

7. The Court first upheld the authority of a legislative court to adjudicate a dispute falling within the federal judicial power in *Murray's Lessee v. Hoboken Land & Improvement Co.*, 59 U.S. (18 How.) 272 (1856). See also Williams v. United States, 289 U.S. 553 (1933) (upholding the constitutionality of the Court of Claims as a legislative court); Ex parte Bakelite, 279 U.S. 438 (1929) (upholding the constitutionality of the Court of Customs Appeals as a legislative court). For academic commentary considering whether, and to what extent, Article III should be interpreted to permit the creation of legislative courts to handle cases within the federal judicial power, see Paul Bator, *The Constitu-*tion as Architecture: Legislative Courts under Article III*, 65 IND. L.J. 233 (1990); David P, Currie, *Bankruptcy Judges and the Independent Judiciary*, 16 CREIGHTON L. REV. 441 (1983); Richard Fallon, *Of Legislative Courts, Administrative Agencies and Article III*, 101 HARV. L. REV. 916, 918–26 (1988); Martin H. Redish, *Legislative Courts, Administrative Agencies, and the* Northern Pipeline *Decision*, 1983 DUKE L.J. 197 (1983); Craig A. Stern, *What's a Constitution Among Friends: Unbalancing Article III*, 146 U. PA. L. REV. 1043 (1998).

8. See Act of July 31, 1789, 1st Cong., 1st Sess., ch. 5, 1 Stat. 29 (1989) (customs); Act of Sept. 29, 1789, 1st Cong., 1st Sess., ch. 24, 1 Stat. 95 (1789) (military pensions).

ty, it triggers the same Article III concerns that are raised by the creation of legislative courts.

There are many reasons why Congress on occasion might opt for administrative adjudication over judicial proceedings. One motivation may be to protect the federal judiciary: The sheer number of adjudications necessitated by the modern administrative state would overwhelm the courts.[9] In some instances, administrative agencies may provide a more attractive forum than the federal courts. Administrative adjudication offers the potential benefits of relative speed, efficiency, and expertise in comparison with federal courts.[10] And sometimes, the legislators select administrative adjudication over judicial proceedings with the hope that agencies will interpret and apply acts of Congress with a greater sense of commitment to their legislative policy goals.

The Supreme Court generally has upheld congressional conferrals of adjudicatory authority to administrative agencies, although the justices consistently have recognized that Article III places limits on Congress's discretion to opt for administrative adjudication over judicial proceedings. The precise nature of those limits remains frustratingly unclear, however. Traditionally, the principal fault line in the Article III jurisprudence governing the adjudicatory power of administrative agencies has been the distinction between "public rights" and "private rights." The justices recognize broad congressional authority to choose as between administrative tribunals (and legislative courts) and constitutional courts for adjudicating public rights,[11] but they engage in a "searching" review of statutory schemes authorizing agencies to adjudicate private rights.[12]

Notwithstanding the centrality of the distinction between public rights and private rights in marking the Article III boundaries on Congress's power to assign adjudicatory authority to administrative agencies, the justices have not clearly defined either type of right. The essential examples of each right are fairly clear, however. Residing at the "core" of the "inherently" judicial power over disputes involving private rights are common law claims brought by a private party against another private party.[13] In the administrative setting, the core public rights proceeding is a statutory enforcement action by the government in its sovereign capacity.[14]

---

9. See Atlas Roofing Co. v. Occupational Safety and Health Review Comm'n, 430 U.S. 442, 455 (1977); Crowell v. Benson, 285 U.S. 22, 54 (1932).

10. See *Schor*, 478 U.S. at 855–56.

11. See *Crowell*, 285 U.S. at 50–51; *Murray's Lessee*, 59 U.S. at 284.

12. *Schor*, 478 U.S. at 851, 853–54.

13. *Id*. at 853–54; see Northern Pipeline Constr. Co. v. Marathon Pipe Line Co., 458 U.S. 50, 68 (1982) (plurality op.); Ex parte Bakelite Corp., 279 U.S. 438 (1929).

14. See *Atlas Roofing*, 430 U.S. at 450 (defining public rights disputes as "cases in which the Government sues in

The difference in treatment between public rights and private rights arises from their differing natures. Public rights involve "matters that could be conclusively determined by the Executive and Legislative Branches," as well as by the Judicial Branch. Allowing administrative agencies (or legislative courts) to resolve disputes involving such rights therefore poses little "danger of encroaching on the judicial powers."[15] By contrast, the adjudication of disputes over private rights is "normally within the purview of the judiciary," and their removal to administrative agencies (or legislative courts) heightens the risk of congressional encroachment.[16] Article III does not bar Congress from giving administrative officials *complete* authority to resolve public rights disputes.[17] But when the legislators authorize agencies to adjudicate private rights, they must take care to "maintain the essential attributes of the judicial power."[18]

Although the distinction between public and private rights is important in determining the constitutionality of administrative adjudicative power, it is not "determinative."[19] The Court's decision in *Community Futures Trading Commission v. Schor*[20] demonstrates that Congress may enable agencies to adjudicate private rights, provided it preserves "the essential attributes of the judicial power."[21] *Schor* involved an enabling act that gave the Community Futures Trading Commission broad authority to adjudicate claims for reparations brought by disgruntled customers against commodity brokers for alleged violations of either the act or the Commission's regulations. Upon the filing of a reparations claim, the Commission's regulations permitted (but did not require) the broker to file a counterclaim against the customer for any claim "aris[ing] out of the transaction or occurrence or series of transactions or occurrences set forth in the complaint."[22] *Schor* held that Article III did not bar the Commission from hearing such a counterclaim based on state common law.

The justices acknowledged that state common law claims reside at the "core" of the private rights "normally reserved to Article III courts." But that acknowledgement launched rather than conclud-

its sovereign capacity to enforce public rights created by statutes within the power of Congress to enact"); *Crowell*, 285 U.S. at 50 (describing public rights disputes as "cases ... which arise between the government and persons subject to its authority in connection with the performance of the constitutional functions of the executive or legislative departments"). The public rights category is not limited to disputes in which the government is a party, however. See *Thomas*, 473 U.S. at 586.

15. *Thomas*, 473 U.S. at 589.

16. *Schor*, 478 U.S. at 853.

17. See *Crowell*, 285 U.S. at 50–51.

18. See *id*. at 51–54.

19. *Schor*, 478 U.S. at 853.

20. 478 U.S. 833 (1986)

21. See *Crowell*, 285 U.S. at 51–54.

22. *Schor*, 478 U.S. at 836–37.

ed the Court's inquiry. In upholding the Commission's jurisdiction over state-law counterclaims in reparations proceedings, the justices took a decidedly functional approach, "weigh[ing] a number of factors, . . . with an eye to the practical effect that the congressional action will have on the constitutionally assigned role of the federal judiciary." Several features of the administrative scheme convinced the Court that the "the magnitude of any intrusion on the Judicial Branch" by the Commission's jurisdiction over state-law counterclaims could "only be termed *de minimis*." It was important in *Schor* that the counterclaims were permissive rather than mandatory, and thus that the brokers were free to file their claims against a customer in court rather than in a CFTC reparations proceeding. The justices also emphasized that the enabling act did not reflect an effort by Congress to broadly displace judicial authority over state-law claims. Rather, the act simply provided adjudicative authority over "a narrow class of common law claims as an incident to the CFTC's primary, and unchallenged, adjudicative [authority over reparations claims]" solely "to ensure the effectiveness" of the reparations process. And perhaps most importantly, the enabling act gave Article III courts an important role in reviewing and enforcing the Commission's orders. Article III courts determined whether the weight of the evidence supported the Commission's factual findings and reviewed the legal determinations of the Commission *de novo*. Moreover, the Commission lacked power to enforce its orders: Only an Article III court could do so. For this combination of reasons, the Court held, the administrative adjudicatory process at issue in *Schor* preserved rather than usurped "the essential attributes of the judicial power."[23]

Schor signals that the distinction between public rights and private rights may be somewhat muted when agencies, as is typical, adjudicate matters subject to meaningful judicial review. The Court's decision in *Thomas v. Union Carbide Agricultural Products Co.*[24] illustrates how the distinction itself at times can be difficult to discern in an administrative setting. In *Thomas*, the Court held that Congress, in the exercise of its Article I powers, could "create a seemingly 'private' right that is so closely integrated into a public regulatory scheme as to be a matter appropriate for agency resolution with limited involvement by the Article III judiciary."[25] *Thomas* involved a complex and comprehensive scheme administered by the Environmental Protection Agency for the regulation of pesticides. The enabling act required manufacturers of pesticides under certain circumstances to share information with other pesticide manufacturers, in return for compensation. The act provided for binding arbitration by EPA when manufacturers could not agree on

23. *Id*. at 851–57.   **25.** *Id*. at 593–94.
24. 473 U.S. 568 (1985).

the amount of compensation for the shared information. The rub in *Thomas* was that the act provided only for very limited judicial review of EPA's arbitral awards. Article III courts could set aside an award only on a finding of fraud, misconduct, or misrepresentation in connection with an award.

The Court nevertheless upheld the statutory scheme as "a pragmatic solution to the difficult problem of spreading the costs of generating adequate information regarding the safety, health, and environmental impact of a potentially dangerous product." The justices characterized the rights at issue in the EPA arbitration proceedings as something of a hybrid. They were neither purely public nor purely private. The key for the Court seemed to be that the data-sharing for which compensation was owed "serve[d] a public purpose as an integral part of a program safeguarding the public health." Because of the public dimension of the private right to compensation at issue in *Thomas*, the Court was satisfied that the judicial review authorized by the act, although extremely limited, was nevertheless sufficient to "protect against arbitrators who abuse or exceed their powers or willfully misconstrue their mandate under the governing law."[26]

Although *Schor* and *Thomas* make clear that the justices are open to administrative adjudication of private rights that are linked to public regulatory schemes, the distinction between public rights and private rights remains the Court's central focus in determining the scope of congressional authority to prefer administrative tribunals over federal courts for the resolution of disputes that are within the federal judicial power.[27]

(b) Administrative Adjudication and the Right of Trial by Jury

The Seventh Amendment to the United State Constitution guarantees "the right of trial by jury" in "Suits at common law," at least when the amount in controversy exceeds the princely sum of twenty dollars. The key question here, of course, concerns the meaning of a common law suit. The Supreme Court has approached that question against the background of the division between law and equity that had organized the English judicial system at the time of the American Revolution.[28] The justices have required jury trials in cases that would have been decided by the English law courts of the late eighteenth century, but not in suits that would have been assigned to the equity or admiralty courts of that era.

26. *Id.* at 589–92.

27. See Granfinanciera, S.A. v. Nordberg, 492 U.S. 33 (1989).

28. See *id.* at 41–42; Curtis v. Loether, 415 U.S. 189, 193 (1974).

This does not mean, however, that the Seventh Amendment right to jury trial is limited to common law forms of action, circa 1776. The Court has interpreted the phrase "Suits at common law" to embrace *statutory claims* in which "legal rights" rather than "equitable rights" are in dispute.[29] In distinguishing between law and equity, the justices often have looked to the nature of the remedy at stake in the litigation. If a claim is for a money judgment, it typically (although not necessarily) is one of law rather than of equity.[30] But although the justices have not hesitated to apply the Seventh Amendment right to jury trial in *judicial* proceedings involving statutory claims for monetary relief, they have resisted Seventh Amendment challenges to *administrative* proceedings involving similar claims.[31] According to the Court, "[J]ury trials would be incompatible with the whole concept of administrative adjudication and would substantially interfere with [an agency's] role in [a] statutory scheme."[32]

The Supreme Court's leading decision on the applicability of the Seventh Amendment right to jury trial in administrative proceedings is *Atlas Roofing Co. v. Occupational Safety and Health Review Commission.*[33] There the Court ruled that the Seventh Amendment did not bar Congress from authorizing administrative adjudication leading to the imposition of civil penalties without a jury trial. The Commission possessed the statutory authority to impose civil penalties against any employer for maintaining an unsafe working condition in violation of the Occupational Safety and Health Act of 1970. The challengers argued that such an enforcement proceeding amounted to "a suit for a money judgment which is classically a suit at common law," and thus that the Seventh Amendment required "a jury determination of all issues of fact in such a case." The justices rejected the challenge, "[a]t least in cases in which 'public rights' are being litigated."[34]

As evidenced by the Court's reliance on the distinction between public and private rights, the justices in *Atlas Roofing* relied on the Article III precedent upholding public rights schemes that "created new statutory obligations, provided for civil penalties for their violation, and committed exclusively to an administrative agency the function of deciding whether a violation has in fact occurred."[35]

---

29. *Granfinanciera*, 492 U.S. at 42; Parsons v. Bedford, 28 U.S. (3 Pet.) 433, 447 (1830); see Tull v. United States, 481 U.S. 412 (1987); Curtis v. Loether, 415 U.S. 189 (1974).

30. See *Granfinanciera*, 492 U.S. at 47–48; *Curtis*, 415 U.S. at 196–97.

31. See Atlas Roofing Co. v. Occupational Safety and Health Review Commission, 430 U.S. 442 (1977) (civil penalties); National Labor Relations Board v. Jones & Laughlin Steel Corp., 301 U.S. 1, 48–49 (1937) (back pay).

32. *Curtis*, 415 U.S. at 194.

33. 430 U.S. 442 (1977).

34. *Id.* at 449–50.

35. *Id.* at 450; see *id.* at 450–52; *Granfinanciera*, 492 U.S. at 54.

The Court, in other words, has refused to interpret the Seventh Amendment to prohibit agency adjudications that do not violate Article III's vesting of the judicial power in the federal courts.[36]

36. *Atlas Roofing*, 430 U.S. at 460; see *Granfinanciera*, 492 U.S. at 53–54. The Supreme Court has not applied the Sixth Amendment's right to trial "by an impartial jury" in "all criminal prosecutions" to administrative proceedings that result in the imposition of civil penalties. The justices have accepted the congressional characterization of such impositions as civil and remedial rather than criminal and punitive in nature. See Helvering v. Mitchell, 303 U.S. 391, 402 (1938); Lloyd Sabaudo S.A. v. Elting, 287 U.S. 329, 334 (1932). The Court has drawn a constitutional line at imprisonment, however, reserving the sentencing power for constitutional courts. See Wong Wing v. United States, 163 U.S. 228 (1896).

Chapter 3
DUE PROCESS IN THE ADMINISTRATIVE STATE

As reviewed in the previous chapter, the constitutional principles of separation of powers and checks and balances not only provide a source of legal rules governing the administrative process, but also, as we shall see in later chapters, they influence the development and application of many statutory and judicial requirements for agency decisionmaking and judicial review. The same is true of the constitutional principle of due process.

The Fifth and Fourteenth Amendments to the United States Constitution prohibit the federal government and the states, respectively, from depriving anyone of "life, liberty, or property, without due process of law." In each amendment, the phrase "due process of law" has both a substantive and a procedural meaning. "Substantive due process," as a general matter, prohibits the government from depriving individuals of their interests in liberty or property unless the government's action is rationally related to a legitimate public purpose.[1] The constitutional requirement that

1. See, e.g., Lingle v. Chevron, U.S.A., 544 U.S. 528, 542 (2005); County of Sacramento v. Lewis, 523 U.S. 833, 846 (1998); Williamson v. Lee Optical

such governmental deprivations be rational and legitimate is easily met,[2] and accordingly, substantive due process review is not a significant component of administrative law. Its principal service has been to provide a background principle underlying the authority of reviewing courts under section 706(2)(A) of the Administrative Procedure Act to "hold unlawful and set aside agency action" that is "arbitrary, capricious, an abuse of discretion, or otherwise not in accordance with law" (see § 8.7).

"Procedural due process," on the other hand, has always been a central component of American administrative law. Indeed, this guarantee has been called the oldest American civil right. The phrase "due process of law" first appeared in England in 1354, when Parliament adopted a statute providing, "[N]o man of what Estate or Condition that he be, shall be put out of land or Tenement, nor taken, nor imprisoned, nor disinherited, nor put to death, without being brought in answer by due process of law."[3] The influential seventeenth-century jurist Sir Edward Coke tied the meaning of "due process of law" to Magna Carta (1215), which had obligated King John to proceed "by the law of the land" when depriving English freemen of their life, liberty, or property.[4]

While Coke's equation of "due process of law" with the Great Charter's "law of the land" convinced neither his contemporaries in England nor many historians of later generations, it found a ready home in America. The Supreme Court adopted Coke's position as its own in the justices' first interpretation of the Fifth Amendment's due process clause.[5] Although the original meanings of "due process of law" and "law of the land" in England are a matter of scholarly dispute, the central understanding of procedural due process in American constitutional jurisprudence has long been clear: Government officials may deprive an individual of life, liberty, or property only pursuant to a process of decisionmaking that is "fundamentally fair."[6] The essential elements of a constitutionally fair process demand that an individual receive notice and opportunity to be heard before being "finally deprived of a protected . . .

Co., 348 U.S. 483, 487–88 (1955). The courts impose a higher burden on the government to justify deprivations of fundamental liberty interests. See, e.g., Washington v. Glucksberg, 521 U.S. 702, 719–20 (1997). Governmental deprivations of life—that is, the death penalty— are not within the province of administrative law.

2. See *County of Sacramento*, 523 U.S. at 846 ("cases dealing with abusive executive action have repeatedly emphasized that only the most egregious official conduct can be said to be arbitrary in the constitutional sense").

3. 28 Ed. III, ch.3 (1354).

4. Article XXXIX of Magna Carta provided, "No freeman shall be taken and imprisoned or disseized or exiled or in any way destroyed, nor will we go upon him nor send upon him, except by the lawful judgment of his peers and by the law of the land."

5. Murray's Lessee v. Hoboken Land & Improvement Co., 59 U.S. 272, 276 (1855).

6. *County of Sacramento*, 523 U.S. at 845–46.

interest."[7] The paradigmatic example of procedural due process is a judicial trial.

Although it is important analytically to distinguish between the substantive and procedural meanings of due process, it also is useful to observe their connection. The dual meaning of due process provides complimentary means of protecting individuals against the arbitrary exercise of government power.[8] Substantive due process serves this goal by demanding that government officials support their actions with a "reasonable justification in the service of a legitimate governmental objective."[9] Procedural due process safeguards against official arbitrariness by providing affected individuals "an opportunity to speak up in [their] own defense" and by requiring the government to "listen to what [they have] to say."[10] Moreover, in practice if not in theory, procedural due process protections influence the substance of governmental action. Restraining *how* the government may act inevitably affects *what* the government may do. As legal historian John Orth has written, "Procedural due process, far from being a mere requirement of technical fastidiousness, retains the potential to unsettle the powerful."[11]

§ 3.1   The Rulemaking–Adjudication Distinction

As a threshold matter, the Constitution's guarantee of procedural due process applies to administrative agencies only when they adjudicate. The procedural due process rights of individuals do not constrain agency rulemaking. The classic exposition of this central principle of administrative law is to be found in two decisions by the Supreme Court early in the twentieth century—*Londoner v. City and County of Denver*[1] and *Bi-Metallic Investment Co. v. State Board of Equalization*.[2] Curiously, both decisions arose from taxing disputes in Denver, Colorado.

Londoner involved the assessment of a tax by Denver on property owners for their share of the costs of certain road improvements. The city charter permitted Denver to allocate those

---

7. Logan v. Zimmerman Brush Co., 455 U.S. 422, 433 (1982); see United States v. James Daniel Good Real Property, 510 U.S. 43, 48 (1993); Mathews v. Eldridge, 424 U.S. 319, 333 (1976); Board of Regents of State Colleges v. Roth, 408 U.S. 564, 569–70 (1972). The procedural due process protections of the Fifth and Fourteenth Amendments are identical in application. See Paul v. Davis, 424 U.S. 693, 702 n.3 (1976).

8. See *County of Sacramento*, 523 U.S. at 845; Daniels v. Williams, 474 U.S. 327, 331 (1986); Hurtado v. California, 110 U.S. 516, 527 (1884).

9. *County of Sacramento*, 523 U.S. at 846.

10. Fuentes v. Shevin, 407 U.S. 67, 81 (1972); see *Daniels*, 474 U.S. at 331.

11. John V. Orth, Due Process of Law: A Brief History 88 (2003).

§ 3.1

1. 210 U.S. 373 (1908).

2. 239 U.S. 441 (1915).

costs among the properties benefiting from the improvements. The property owners claimed, however, that due process required the city to hold a hearing before setting the tax. Denver had only permitted the property owners to state their objections to the planned tax in writing. The Court agreed that the property owners were constitutionally entitled to the oral hearing they demanded. "[W]here the legislature of a state ... commits to some subordinate body the duty of determining whether, in what amount, and upon whom [a tax] shall be levied," explained the justices, "due process of law requires that, at some stage of the proceedings, before the tax becomes irrevocably fixed, the taxpayer shall have an opportunity to be heard, of which he must have notice." Although the Court in *Londoner* did not expect Denver to provide every element of a judicial trial, the justices demanded that the city create the opportunity for some kind of oral, evidentiary hearing, "however informal."[3]

Bi-Metallic involved an order by state agencies requiring the assessor of Denver to increase the valuation of all taxable property in the county by 40 percent. A property owner in Denver claimed that the order, if carried out by the assessor, would deprive him of property without due process of law because he had been provided no opportunity for a hearing to challenge the increased valuation of his property. The Court rejected the claim, explaining, "Where a rule of conduct applies to more than a few people, it is impracticable that everyone should have a direct voice in its adoption.... There must be a limit to individual argument in such matters if government is to go on." The Court distinguished *Londoner* as involving "[a] relatively small number of persons ... who were exceptionally affected, in each case upon individual grounds." *Bi-Metallic*, by contrast, involved "a rule of conduct" that applied to "more than a few people," "all" of whom were "equally concerned."[4] In short, the tax assessment in *Londoner* triggered procedural due process requirements because it was adjudicatory. The property-valuation increase in *Bi-Metallic* avoided due process requirements because it was rulemaking.

Bi-Metallic's handling of *Londoner* suggests that the justices identified three distinctions between the adjudication in *Londoner* that had triggered procedural due process protections and the rulemaking in *Bi-Metallic* that did not. One distinction concerned the nature of the two types of agency decisions (a decision "in each case upon individual grounds" v. "a general determination"). Another difference related to the effect of the two types of decisions on individuals (each individual "exceptionally affected" v. "all" individuals "equally" affected). And finally, the third distinction cited

---

3. *Londoner*, 210 U.S. at 385–86.   4. *Bi-Metallic*, 239 U.S. at 445–46.

the number of individuals affected by the two types of decisions ("[a] relatively small number of persons" v. "more than a few people"). Each of these distinctions is discussed in turn.

(a) Nature of the Decisions

The tax assessment in *Londoner* was adjudication because it was an *individualized* determination: The agency there had "the duty of determining whether, in what amount, and upon whom [a tax] would be levied."[5] The agency in *Londoner* apportioned the cost of the road improvements according to its estimation of each property owner's benefit.

The increase in property valuation in *Bi-Metallic* was rulemaking because it was a *generalized* determination: The increase reflected "a general determination dealing only with the principle upon which all the assessments in a county had been laid."[6] The agency in *Bi-Metallic* determined that the Denver assessor had "adopted a system of undervaluation throughout a county," and it therefore ordered an across-the-board increase in property valuation that applied "equally" to everyone who owned property in Denver.[7]

The Court's constitutional frame of reference in *Londoner* was the judiciary. When an agency adjudicates, it, like a court, establishes the rights and duties of individuals on "individual grounds."[8] The Anglo–American legal system traditionally has relied on judicial trials to make such determinations. Because the Constitution prescribes due process for judicial decisionmaking, the Court in *Londoner* seemed to reason, such a requirement should attach when agencies act like a court, that is, when they adjudicate.

The Court's frame of reference in *Bi-Metallic* was the legislature. When an agency issues a "rule of conduct," it, like a legislature, establishes the rights and duties of individuals on "general" grounds. If the state legislature had increased the property taxes of Denver residents by increasing the rate of taxation, the Court in *Bi-Metallic* observed, "no one would suggest that [due process] was violated unless every person affected had been allowed an opportunity to raise his voice against it."[9] Because the Constitution does not prescribe due process for legislative decisionmaking, the Court in *Bi-Metallic* seemed to reason, no such requirement should attach when agencies act like a legislature, that is, when they make rules. Judicial trials are designed for the adjudication of individual rights,

5. *Londoner*, 210 U.S. at 385.

6. *Bi-Metallic*, 239 U.S. at 443.

7. *Id.* at 445.

8. *Id.* at 446.

9. *Id.* at 445–46; see also Minnesota State Bd. For Community Colleges v.

Minnesota Community College Faculty Ass'n,, 465 U.S. 271, 284 (1984) ("To recognize a constitutional right to participate directly in government policymaking would work a revolution in existing government practices.").

and not for the more policy-oriented task of formulating legislative rules.

Professor Kenneth Culp Davis, an influential administrative law scholar, has distinguished the nature of agency decisionmaking in adjudication and in rulemaking by emphasizing the different types of factfinding involved in the two types of actions. In Professor Davis's scheme, "adjudicative facts" are particular to the parties to a proceeding. They "usually answer the question of who did what, where, when, how, why, with what motive or intent." "Legislative facts," by contrast, are general in nature rather than specific to a particular party. They help decisionmakers "decide questions of law and policy and discretion."[10]

In Professor Davis's account of the *Londoner-Bi-Metallic* distinction, procedural due process applies to administrative adjudication because the agency decisionmaker "ordinarily" cannot accurately find facts without giving the parties notice and "an opportunity for trial." This is because the "the parties know more about the facts concerning themselves and their activities than anyone else is likely to know." According to Davis, procedural due process does not apply to administrative rulemaking because affording each affected party an evidentiary hearing often would not improve agency decisionmaking. Because legislative facts are general in nature, the affected parties "may often have little or nothing to contribute to [their] development."[11]

Professor Davis's explanation of the differing natures of agency decisionmaking in rulemaking and in adjudication provides a functional justification for the *Londoner-Bi-Metallic* distinction. An evidentiary hearing might have been necessary to make the individualized tax assessment at issue in *Londoner*. Because assessing the actual value of an individual's property might well have required evidence possessed only by the property owner, the owner's participation likely had been essential to a sound decision. Affording each property owner in Denver a similar hearing opportunity might have been thought unnecessary (and perhaps counterproductive) to the *Bi-Metallic* agency's determination that property in Denver generally had been undervalued by about 40 percent. Individual property owners could have spoken to the assessment of their homes, of course, but they had no special access to evidence concerning the assessments of property county-wide.

(b) Nature of the Effect on Individuals

The Court in *Bi-Metallic* also distinguished *Londoner* in part because *Londoner*'s tax assessment "exceptionally affected" several

10. KENNETH CULP DAVIS, 1 ADMINISTRATIVE LAW TREATISE § 7.02, at 413–12 (1958).

11. *Id.*

property owners in Denver, whereas the 40 percent increase in property valuation at issue in *Bi-Metallic* "equally" affected all of Denver's property owners. One must take care, however, in evaluating whether an agency action equally affects individuals, and thus is rulemaking, or exceptionally affects individuals, and thus is adjudication. The *Bi-Metallic* Court acknowledged that statutes may have a profound effect on individuals, "sometimes to the point of ruin." The same is true of administrative rules. And although the across-the-board increase in property valuation in *Bi-Metallic* equally affected all of Denver's property owners by raising each of their valuations by 40 per cent, in another sense the effect of the state agency's order on individual property owners varied depending on the degree to which each property owner's prior assessment had reflected an undervaluation of his or her property.[12]

Such variability in the effect of "equally applicable" legislation and administrative rulemaking is common. Even though a "rule of conduct" applies equally to a group of persons, its effect on each person within the group depends on his or her circumstances. For example, a government agency may require that all applicants for a particular job possess a college degree. That requirement is a rule because it applies equally to all job applicants. But its effect on each job applicant depends on whether or not the applicant has a degree.

The subtlety required for analyzing the effect of agency action on individuals when applying the rulemaking-adjudication distinction is illustrated by the Second Circuit's decision in *Air Line Pilots Association v. Quesada*.[13] The Federal Aviation Administration had issued a regulation establishing a mandatory retirement age of 60 for all air line pilots. As in *Londoner*, the agency had provided interested parties only an opportunity to submit written comments before it had issued the regulation. And also as in *Londoner*, the challengers (here, a number of pilots) claimed that due process owed each of them an oral, evidentiary hearing before the agency required their retirement. Such a due process hearing would have allowed each pilot to demonstrate that he or she was able to continue flying.

The Second Circuit rejected the pilots' due process claim. The key in *Air Line Pilots Association* was that the 60–year-old mandatory retirement age applied equally to all pilots, just as in *Bi-Metallic*, the 40–percent property-valuation increase had applied equally to all Denver property owners. The equal application of the new mandatory retirement age held true even though the regula-

---

12. *Bi-Metallic*, 239 U.S. at 444–46 ("it is obvious that injustice may be suffered if some property in the county already has been valued at its full worth").

13. 276 F.2d 892 (2nd Cir. 1960), cert.denied, 366 U.S. 962 (1961).

tion would severely affect the livelihood of air line pilots, especially those who were near or over the age of 60. It also held true even though application of the regulation might be considered unfair to those pilots over the age of 60 who remained able to do the job. But these pilots were no different than the property owners in *Bi-Metallic* whose property had not been undervalued by 40 percent.[14] The lesson of *Bi-Metallic* and of *Air Line Pilots Association* is that the alleged unfairness of a generally applicable rule does not give rise to a procedural due process claim.

(c) Number of Individuals Affected

The first factor the *Bi-Metallic* Court cited in distinguishing *Londoner* was the "relatively small number of persons" who were affected by the tax assessment in the earlier decision. By contrast, the Court noted, "Where a rule of conduct applies to more than a few people, it is impracticable that everyone should have a direct voice in its adoption."[15] The difference in the number of affected individuals provides two justifications for requiring individual hearings in adjudication but not in rulemaking.

The first justification is the obvious one of practicality. Providing oral, evidentiary hearings for the relatively few people affected by the assessment in *Londoner* is one thing; guaranteeing such a hearing to each property owner in Denver (or to each of the 18,000 air line pilots affected by the mandatory retirement regulation in *Air Line Pilots Association*) is quite another. As the Court more recently explained, "Government makes so many policy decisions affecting so many people that it would likely grind to a halt were policymaking constrained by constitutional requirements on whose voices must be heard."[16] Requiring individual hearings for everyone affected by administrative rules, as a practical matter, would deny rulemaking power to agencies.

The difference in numbers usually affected by agency rulemaking and adjudication is important for a second reason. In *Bi-Metallic*, the Court reminded that the absence of procedural due process rights left intact the political influence that Denver property owners, as a group, possessed "over those who make the rule."[17]

---

14. *Id.* at 896–97; see also Interport Pilots Agency, Inc. v. Sammis, 14 F.3d 133, 142–44 (2nd Cir. 1994) (agency decision denying all ship pilots licensed in Connecticut the right to pilot vessels in a New York harbor "was essentially legislative rather adjudicative"; procedural due process requirements therefore did not apply); McMurtray v. Holladay, 11 F.3d 499 (5th Cir. 1993) (state law that eliminated the jobs of a category of state employees did not trigger procedural due process rights of those employees).

15. *Bi-Metallic*, 239 U.S. at 445–46.

16. *Minnesota Bd. for Community Colleges*, 465 U.S. at 285; see also *Bi-Metallic*, 239 U.S. at 445 ("There must be a limit to individual argument in such matters if government is to go on.").

17. *Bi-Metallic*, 239 U.S. at 445; see also *Minnesota Bd. for Community Col-*

This political check arises from the collective voting power of affected individuals, and thus it is directly related to "the sweep of governmental action."[18] Surely the property owners of Denver had sufficient numbers to make their voices heard by their elected political leaders, and through those leaders, by the administrators who had increased their property valuations.

The potential political check in the background of *Bi-Metallic* is nowhere to be found in *Londoner*. When the government proceeds against an individual property owner, it is unrealistic to expect all property owners in Denver to rally to his or her defense. In such circumstances, the individual property owner's right to notice and hearing substitutes for the absence of a political check on agency decisionmakers. The oral, evidentiary hearing required by *Londoner* is an equalizer that helps balance power between an individual and the government. It literally gives the individual a voice that the government otherwise would not hear, or respond to, before acting to deprive her or him of liberty or property. *Bi-Metallic*'s limiting of procedural due process protections to individuals involved in agency adjudication reinforces those protections by husbanding this powerful constitutional resource for the type of governmental decisionmaking where it is most needed.

Although the difference in numbers provided the *Bi-Metallic* Court powerful justifications for applying procedural due process requirements to adjudication and not to rulemaking, the number of people affected by an agency decision does not determine whether administrative action is rulemaking or adjudication. The decision by the Tenth Circuit in *Anaconda Co. v. Ruckelshaus*[19] provides a vivid illustration that numbers can be an unreliable guide to the rulemaking-adjudication distinction. Anaconda filed suit to enjoin the Environmental Protection Agency from issuing a regulation limiting the emissions of sulfur oxide in a Montana county. Anaconda was the only entity affected by the regulation because it was the only significant source of sulfur oxide emissions in the county. Anaconda claimed that it had been denied due process because EPA had rejected its request for an evidentiary hearing. The court of appeals rejected the claim, finding that the regulation's exclusive effect on Anaconda did not make EPA's decision individualized, and

---

leges, 465 U.S. at 285 ("It is inherent in a republican form of government that direct public participation in government policymaking is limited. . . . Disagreement with public policy and disapproval of officials' responsiveness . . . is to be registered principally at the polls.").

18. O'Bannon v. Town Court Nursing Center, 447 U.S. 773, 800 (1980) (Blackmun, J., concurring in the judgment) ("as the sweep of governmental action broadens, so too does the power of the affected group to protect its interests outside rigid constitutionally imposed procedures").

19. 482 F.2d 1301 (10th Cir. 1973).

therefore adjudicatory.[20] EPA had written the regulation in general terms, and thus the regulation would apply to any future source of sulfur-oxide emissions in the county. *Anaconda* teaches that it is the generalized nature of an agency's decision, and the general applicability of that decision, rather than the number of individuals actually affected, that govern the rulemaking-adjudication distinction.[21]

* * *

Viewed in isolation, the rulemaking-adjudication distinction may seem to have a disturbing, all-or-nothing quality. Even if the judicial-type procedures prescribed by procedural due process do not fit the legislative-type decsionmaking that characterizes agency rulemaking, it does not necessarily follow that there should be *no* due process of administrative rulemaking.[22] For many, the Court's assurance of a political check to control agency rulemaking provides cold comfort. After all, the people affected by federal regulation do not elect their rulemakers. Federal administrators, at best, are only indirectly accountable to the regulated public through the capacity of Congress and the president to oversee agency rulemaking (see §§ 2.3, 2.4).

Yet it is important to recognize the limits of *Bi-Metallic*. That decision did not free agency rulemaking from all constitutional

---

20. *Id*. at 1306.

21. See also Pro–Eco, Inc. v. Board of Commissioners of Jay County, 57 F.3d 505, 513 (7th Cir. 1995) ("We do not believe that generally applicable prophylactic legislation provoked by the fear of one particular actor converts an elected body's legislative act into a quasi-judicial or administrative act that would [trigger procedural due process]."); Interport Pilots Agency, Inc. v. Sammis, 14 F.3d 133, 144 (2nd Cir. 1994) (the fact that an "agency rule . . . announc[ing] the scope of what it considers to be its jurisdiction . . . had a predictable impact on identifiable individuals did not convert its legislative action into an adjudication"); McMurtray v. Hollady, 11 F.3d 499, 504 (5th Cir. 1993) (29 state employees who were equally affected by a rule "qualif[y] as a general class of people"); Quivira Mining Co. v. NRC, 866 F.2d 1246, 1261–62 (10th Cir. 1989) ("[c]ourts uniformly have rejected" the assertion that a rule that "potentially will apply only to one site" is adjudication rather than rulemaking); Hercules, Inc. v. EPA, 598 F.2d 91, 118 (D.C.Cir. 1978) ("fact that [an entity] is the sole domestic manufactur-

er . . . affected by the [agency action] . . . does not, ipso facto," mean the action is adjudication and not rulemaking). Some judges have expressed suspicion that an administrative rule which applies only to a few persons might reflect adjudication on the sly and thus have encouraged courts to review such actions carefully to ensure that the agency's decision truly was general rather than individualized in nature. See, e.g., *O'Bannon*, 447 U.S. at 800–01 (Blackmun, J., concurring in the judgment); Richardson v. Town of Eastover, 922 F.2d 1152, 1158 (4th Cir. 1991).

22. For arguments that courts should devise some form of procedural due process for legislative-type decisionmaking in order to foster lawmaking that is both deliberative and democratically accountable, see Peter M. Shane, *Back to the Future of the American State: Overruling Buckley v. Valeo and Other Madisonian Steps*, 57 U. Pitt. L. Rev. 443, 455–58 (1996); Hans A. Linde, *Due Process of Lawmaking*, 55 Neb. L. Rev. 197, 235–55 (1976).

limitations.[23] It simply held that one constitutional right—that of procedural due process—did not apply to administrative rulemaking. Nor did *Bi-Metallic* free rulemaking from all procedural constraints. Congress is free to fill the constitutional void by enacting statutes imposing procedural requirements for agency rulemaking. And Congress has done so, in general statutes such as the Administrative Procedure Act, as well as in particular enabling acts.

Just as *Bi-Metallic* should not be over-read to free administrative rulemaking from all legal constraints, *Londoner* should not be over-read to require that agencies provide evidentiary hearings in all adjudications. Were this the case, administrative government would grind to a halt, and *Londoner* would be subject to the same practicality concerns that discouraged the justices from applying procedural due process to administrative rulemaking.

Read in conjunction with *Bi-Metallic*, *Londoner* means that determining agency action to be adjudication rather than rulemaking is a necessary but insufficient condition for triggering procedural due process protections. *Londoner* does not identify the additional elements necessary for the application of procedural due process to agency adjudication, and the selection of that "trigger" has proven to be a continuing source of controversy.

§ 3.2　The Early Understanding of Procedural Due Process: The Right–Privilege Distinction

It says much about the differences between the early and modern government of the United States that the Supreme Court's first interpretation of the due process clauses arrived as late as 1855. When the justices finally began to chart the constitutional meaning of procedural due process in *Murray's Lessee v. Hoboken Land & Improvement Co.*,[1] they used the traditional common law of England as their frame of reference. The Court's nod toward the common law had two important implications for the justices' early approach to procedural due process. First, as illustrated by *Londoner*, the Court tended to define due process in relation to the common law model of the judicial trial. The early jurisprudence seemed to assume that procedural due process required the "fundamentals of a trial."[2]

The second implication of the common law orientation of procedural due process doctrine was the Court's tendency to re-

---

23. See Collins v. Harker Heights, 503 U.S. 115, 125 (1992) (substantive due process "protects individual liberty against certain government actions regardless of the fairness of the procedures used to implement them").

§ 3.2

1. 59 U.S. 272 (1855).

2. See Ohio Bell Telephone Co. v. Public Utilities Commission of Ohio, 301 U.S. 292, 300 (1937).

serve constitutional safeguards for governmental deprivations of individual interests that traditionally had been actionable at common law. The Court translated common law understandings into the language of procedural due process by distinguishing between "rights" and "privileges." According to this distinction, the government was held to have "deprived" an individual of "liberty" or "property" only if it had infringed a "right" that was recognized at common law. In early administrative practice, such deprivations principally included the imposition of fines and taxes, as well as the confiscation of tangible property. The distinctive quality of these common law rights was not simply their traditional pedigree, but also their character as "inherent" individual rights. English jurisprudence before the American Revolution understood common law as a kind of settled, albeit unwritten, constitution that defined and protected individual rights. English courts discovered and enforced common law rights; they did not create them.

By contrast, no one had a right at common law to government largess. Individual entitlements created by statute were regarded as government-created "privileges," and not as inherent individual rights. The government, as gift giver, had complete control over the terms and conditions of its gift. And because individuals had no pre-existing claim to these statutory privileges, the government could withdraw them at will. Procedural due process, along with other constitutional rights, simply did not apply.

The judicial mindset underlying the right-privilege distinction was on display in an early free speech opinion written by Justice Oliver Wendell Holmes, Jr., when he was a member of the Supreme Judicial Court of Massachusetts. In *McAuliffe v. Mayor of City of New Bedford*,[3] a police officer challenged his dismissal for engaging in political activity that the officer claimed was constitutionally protected as free expression. Justice Holmes, who later wrote one of the most eloquent defenses of a strong individual right to freedom of speech,[4] brushed off the challenge. Holmes wrote, "The petitioner may have a constitutional right to talk politics, but he has no constitutional right to be a policeman. . . . The servant cannot complain, as he takes the employment on the terms which are offered him."[5] The police officer's employment was a privilege, not a right, and thus the government could withdraw it at will.

Notwithstanding the traditional pedigree and seductive logic of the right-privilege distinction, the doctrine always had an unsettling quality. The essential problem was that the privileges the

3. 155 Mass. 216, 29 N.E. 517 (1892).

4. Abrams v. United States, 250 U.S. 616, 630–31 (1919) (Holmes, J., dissenting).

5. *McAuliffe*, 29 N.E. at 517.

doctrine insulated from constitutional protection included a wide range of government activity that profoundly affected people's lives. The right-privilege distinction left government officials free of procedural constraints when they fired employees, terminated benefits, and took countless other actions on which individuals depended for their livelihood, as well as for their standing in their communities. The absence of procedural due process constraints on such governmental actions became increasingly untenable as the scope of American administrative government expanded during the twentieth century. Many became concerned that adherence to the right-privilege distinction in the modern administrative state licensed the kind of wholesale arbitrariness by government officials that the due process clauses were supposed to prevent.

A paradox of the right-privilege regime is that the very starkness of the distinction, with its all-or-nothing quality, made procedural due process jurisprudence inherently unstable. Just as England long ago had found it necessary to create a system of equity courts to ameliorate the unforgiving application of the common law in the law courts, so too American judges tweaked, and at times evaded, the right-privilege distinction to prevent injustice. By 1970, the right-privilege distinction remained "nominally intact," in the language of an influential critique at the time, but its normative power had been "gradually eroded."[6]

§ 3.3   The Due Process Revolution

The Supreme Court finally stepped out from under the right-privilege distinction in *Goldberg v. Kelly*,[1] and in doing so, ignited a revolution in procedural due process jurisprudence. The Court in *Goldberg* conducted a due process audit of New York City's procedures for terminating welfare benefits of individuals whom city officials believed had become ineligible. Those procedures provided that a caseworker meet informally with a recipient before an "initial termination" of benefits. The recipient could contest that termination at an administrative trial-type hearing. A recipient who prevailed at the hearing was reinstated on the welfare rolls and received the benefits that had been wrongfully withheld since the initial termination. If after the hearing the agency issued a "final termination" of welfare benefits, the recipient could seek judicial review.

---

6. William W. Van Alstyne, *The Demise of the Right–Privilege Distinction in Constitutional Law*, 81 HARV. L. REV. 1439, 1442 (1968). Professor Van Alstyne's leading study of the right-privilege distinction documented "[n]early a dozen means" that courts used "to circumvent," without repudiating, "the harsh consequences" of the doctrine. *Id.* at 1445.

§ 3.3

1. 397 U.S. 254 (1970).

The Court in *Goldberg* held as a threshold matter that welfare beneficiaries were entitled to the protections of procedural due process before New York could initially terminate their benefits. In so holding, the justices served notice that they no longer would deny procedural due process protections on the ground that "public assistance benefits are a 'privilege' and not a 'right.' "[2] But having clearly removed the right-privilege distinction as constitutional gatekeeper, the Court failed to make clear its choice of a replacement "trigger" for procedural due process protections. The *Goldberg* opinion is susceptible to two interpretations on that score. The first posits an "entitlement" trigger; the second focuses on whether the recipient had suffered a "grievous loss."

The key for the Court in *Goldberg* might have been that welfare benefits were "a matter of *statutory entitlement* for persons qualified to receive them." Because of that statutory entitlement, the city's termination of welfare benefits "involve[d] state action that adjudicates important rights." If this "entitlement" reading is correct, the Court in *Goldberg* tweaked rather than abandoned the right-privilege distinction. In essence, the justices added the deprivation of rights created by statute to the deprivation of rights recognized at common law to define the category of government deprivations triggering procedural due process protections. This expansion would have reflected the justices' recognition that "[m]uch of the existing wealth in this country takes the form of rights that do not fall within traditional common-law concepts of property." In this entitlement interpretation of *Goldberg*, the Court protected "welfare entitlements" because they constituted part of the "new property" created by the government since the heyday of the common law.[3]

The *Goldberg* opinion contains language that extends beyond the entitlement interpretation, suggesting that the justices may have abandoned the idea that only the denial of rights, whatever their source, could constitute the deprivation of property or liberty necessary to trigger procedural due process protections. In the section of the opinion analyzing whether the denial of welfare benefits triggered procedural due process protection (and indeed, almost immediately following the observation that New York's welfare benefits were statutory entitlements), the justices introduced a functional balancing test. The justices wrote, "The extent to which procedural due process must be afforded the recipient is influenced by the extent to which he may be condemned to suffer *grievous loss*, and depends upon whether the recipient's interest in avoiding that loss outweighs the governmental interest in summary

---

2. *Id*. at 262.   **3.** *Id*. at 262 & n.8 (emphasis added).

adjudication.''[4] The Court in *Goldberg* concluded that the beneficiaries were entitled to due process before the initial termination of their welfare payments only after engaging in that balancing analysis. The justices did not engage in any comparable entitlement analysis. The "grievous loss" interpretation thus might well provide a better account of *Goldberg*'s due process trigger than the "entitlement" interpretation.

It was the balancing of the private and public interests at stake in the termination of welfare benefits that appeared to convince the justices that "only a pre-termination evidentiary hearing provides the recipient with procedural due process." The justices in *Goldberg* considered the beneficiaries' interest in the uninterrupted flow of welfare benefits to be uniquely compelling. The Court wrote, "[T]he crucial factor in this context—a factor not present in the case of . . . virtually anyone else whose governmental entitlements are ended—is that termination of aid pending resolution of a controversy over eligibility may deprive an eligible recipient of the very means by which to live while he waits." By contrast, the justices found that the public interests at stake in welfare terminations cut both ways. Appropriate notice and hearing contributed to the public interest, the Court held, because the government, like the beneficiaries, had an interest in ensuring that welfare benefits not be "erroneously terminated." On the other hand, the justices recognized the legitimacy of the public interest "in conserving fiscal and administrative resources" by minimizing administrative procedures. In the end, though, the Court in *Goldberg* concluded that the city's interest in a cost-efficient, summary termination process was "not overriding in the welfare context."[5]

The *Goldberg* Court, like the Court in *Londoner*, held that the pre-termination due process hearing "need not take the form of a judicial or quasi-judicial trial." And indeed, because the city granted welfare beneficiaries a full, trial-type hearing after the initial termination of benefits, the justices determined that pre-termination hearings need only provide "minimum procedural safeguards, adapted to the particular characteristics of welfare recipients," and sufficient to "to protect a recipient against an erroneous termination of his benefits." But by the time the justices had completed their list of the "minimum procedural safeguards" required by due process, the mandated pre-termination hearing included the essentials of a judicial trial. *Goldberg* required the city (1) to provide welfare beneficiaries "timely and adequate notice detailing the reasons for a proposed termination"; (2) to provide an

4. *Id.* at 262–63 (emphasis added). This balancing test followed an earlier deviation from the right-privilege distinction. See Cafeteria and Restaurant Workers Union, Local 473 v. McElroy, 367 U.S. 886, 894–95 (1961).

5. *Goldberg*, 397 U.S. at 264–66.

oral, adversarial, evidentiary hearing; (3) to allow beneficiaries to retain an attorney; (4) to provide "an impartial decision maker"; (5) to base its termination decision on the record, that is, "solely on the legal rules and evidence adduced at the hearing"; and (6) to explain and justify its termination decision in writing. The Court in *Goldberg* explained the overriding need for oral, evidentiary hearings in the welfare context by emphasizing that "written submissions are a wholly unsatisfactory basis for decision" when "credibility and veracity are at issue, as they must be in many termination proceedings.... In almost every setting where important decisions turn on questions of fact, due process requires an opportunity to confront and cross-examine adverse witnesses."[6]

The Supreme Court's decision in *Goldberg* reflects a curious ambivalence toward the relationship between procedural due process and its common law heritage. On one hand, whether one adopts the "entitlement" interpretation or the "grievous loss" interpretation of *Goldberg*'s due process trigger, the justices left behind the traditional common law limits on the kinds of governmental deprivation that required due process protections. On the other hand, the justices seemed to continue, and perhaps, to harden, the traditional view that trial-type evidentiary hearings typically were necessary to satisfy procedural due process.

The Court intensified this disconnect the term following *Goldberg* in *Wisconsin v. Constantineau*,[7] which reinforced the "grievous loss" approach to triggering procedural due process. In *Constantineau*, the justices invalidated a state statute that allowed certain individuals to prevent anyone in a municipality from providing alcoholic beverages "to any person given to the excessive use of such ... beverages." The Court held that the statute violated due process because it did not provide individuals notice and opportunity for a hearing before they were barred from purchasing alcoholic beverages. Such a prohibition, the Court held, attached "a stigma or badge of infamy" on the targeted individual, and this was sufficient to trigger procedural due process protections. The justices explained, "Where a person's good name, reputation, honor, or integrity is at stake because of what the government is doing to him, notice and an opportunity to be heard are essential."[8]

Goldberg and *Constantineau* were transformative decisions which ignited a "due process explosion" that carried the potential of requiring evidentiary administrative hearings whenever the government threatened an individual with "an adjudication of important interests."[9] According to Judge Henry J. Friendly of the

6. *Id.* at 266–71.

7. 400 U.S. 433 (1971).

8. *Id.* at 436–37.

9. See Bell v. Burson, 402 U.S. 535, 539 (1971).

Second Circuit, a leading jurist at the time, the protective umbrella of procedural due process expanded more in the "five years [since *Goldberg*] than in the entire period since ratification of the Constitution."[10]

§ 3.4 The Due Process Counterrevolution and the Contemporary Approach

It did not take long for the justices to rethink the due process revolution they had provoked in *Goldberg*. Just one term after *Constantineau* had reinforced *Goldberg*'s suggestion that an individual's "grievous loss" was sufficient to trigger procedural due process protections, the Court stepped back in the companion cases of *Board of Regents of State Colleges v. Roth*[1] and *Perry v. Sindermann*.[2] *Roth* and *Sindermann* redirected the due process "trigger" back toward the text of the Fifth and Fourteenth Amendments, requiring claimants to demonstrate that government officials had "deprived" them of an interest in "liberty" or "property" before receiving procedural due process protections. Several years later, the Court followed up on its retrenchment regarding the types of deprivations necessary to trigger procedural due process protections by cutting back on the scope of those protections. In *Mathews v. Eldridge*,[3] the Court flipped *Goldberg*'s suggestion that trial-type hearings ordinarily were necessary to satisfy due process. After *Mathews*, the adversarial, evidentiary hearings prescribed by *Goldberg* became the exception rather than the rule for due process.

The cumulative effect of the Court's post-*Goldberg* retrenchment has been to reformulate the methodology for analyzing procedural due process problems (see Figure 3–1).

10. Henry J. Friendly, *Some Kind of Hearing*, 123 U. Pa. L. Rev. 1267, 1273 (1975).

§ 3.4

1. 408 U.S. 564 (1972).

2. 408 U.S. 593 (1972).

3. 424 U.S. 319 (1976).

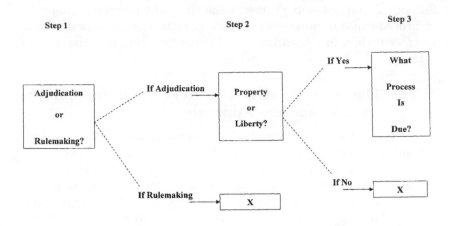

Figure 3-1: Procedural Due Process Methodology

Contemporary procedural due process methodology proceeds according to a three-step analysis. Courts begin with the *Londoner-Bi-Metallic* distinction to determine whether the relevant agency action is adjudication or rulemaking (see § 3.1). If the action qualifies as adjudication, courts ask whether the agency action "triggers" the due process clause of the Fifth or Fourteenth Amendment. In order to trigger due process, the government must "deprive" (see § 3.4(c)) an individual of an interest in "property" (see § 3.4(a)) or "liberty" (see § 3.4(b)). (Deprivations of "life," i.e., the death penalty, are adjudicated in the courts, not in administrative agencies.) If—but only if—agency adjudication deprives an individual of property or liberty within the meaning of the due process clauses, courts will determine the process that is due for such a deprivation (see § 3.4(d)).[4]

(a) Deprivation of Property

Roth **and** *Sindermann.* The contemporary approach to procedural due process begins with the Court's decisions in the companion cases of *Roth* and *Sindermann*. Both cases involved

---

4. I have organized the discussion of contemporary procedural due process doctrine by separating cases involving deprivations of property from cases involving deprivations of liberty. Another fruitful way to organize these cases is by their programmatic subject matter. See, e.g., JERRY L. MASHAW, ET. AL, ADMINISTRATIVE LAW: THE AMERICAN PUBLIC LAW SYSTEM 380–86 (5th ed. 2003) (distinguishing among cases based on the subject matter of the administrative decision at issue).

procedural due process challenges by faculty members who were terminated by their respective state colleges at the expiration of a one-year employment contract. In each case, college administrators gave the faculty members no explanation for declining to renew the contract. Nor did either college provide a hearing to allow the faculty members to contest the grounds for their dismissal. Lower courts in both cases applied *Goldberg*'s balancing test and found that the faculty members, like the welfare beneficiaries in *Goldberg*, were entitled to a due process hearing before their termination. The Supreme Court, however, used *Roth* and *Sindermann* to clarify (or perhaps, to revise) *Goldberg*'s due process trigger.

The Court in *Roth* emphasized the "boundaries" of the due process clauses by reconnecting their coverage to the constitutional text. The justices reminded, "The requirements of procedural due process apply only to the deprivation of interests encompassed by the [due process clauses'] protection of liberty and property." And in assessing whether the government had deprived an individual of an interest in liberty or property, the justices announced that they would now look at the "nature" rather than the "weight" of the threatened individual interest. The Court reserved the interest balancing associated with the grievous loss interpretation of *Goldberg* to the "determination of the form of hearing required" *after* it has been established that the government has deprived an individual of a protected property or liberty interest.[5]

Having shifted focus from the weight to the nature of the individual interests at stake in an administrative adjudication, the justices in *Roth* embraced the "entitlement" interpretation of the *Goldberg* trigger over the "grievous loss" interpretation for claimed deprivations of property. The Court wrote, in language that has been quoted in scores of procedural due process decisions after *Roth*, "To have a property interest in a benefit, a person clearly must have more than an abstract need or desire for it. He must have more than a unilateral expectation of it. He must, instead, have a *legitimate claim of entitlement* to it."[6] Such entitlements, the Court held, "are not created by the Constitution. Rather they are created and their dimensions are defined by existing rules or understandings that stem from an independent source such as state law—rules or understandings that secure certain benefits and that support claims of entitlement to those benefits."[7]

---

5. *Roth*, 408 U.S. at 569, 571–72, 577.

6. *Id.* at 577 (emphasis added). According to the Court in *Roth*, due process had been triggered in *Goldberg* because the beneficiaries "had a claim of entitlement to welfare payments that was grounded in the statute defining eligibility for them." *Id.*

7. *Id.* Where a claimed entitlement is created by state law, federal courts should defer to authoritative interpreta-

According to *Roth*, the function of procedural due process, at least with respect to property deprivations, is to secure benefits to which an individual is entitled by some law other than the Constitution. The existence of a legal right to a benefit provides external validation, and thus legal legitimacy, to an individual's expectation that government officials may not withdraw the benefit at will. The primary purpose of a due process hearing in the *Roth* regime is to allow individuals to demonstrate their right to possess some benefit that the government seeks to take away.[8]

Roth's requirement that individuals prove "a legitimate claim of entitlement" to establish a property interest protected by due process has been roundly criticized by a number of legal scholars. One criticism is that by making application of procedural due process contingent upon the terms of positive law, the entitlement approach empowers the legislative and executive branches, rather than the courts, to control the application of constitutional norms.[9] Providing majoritarian control over the incidence of due process requirements, this criticism goes, is inconsistent with the general tenor of constitutional rights, which contemplates a robust judicial role in protecting individuals and minorities against hostile governmental actions.[10] Indeed, it has been observed that *Roth* creates "perverse incentives" for the government to eliminate legal entitlements and thereby roll back procedural due process protections.[11]

But the central charge against *Roth* is that the entitlement requirement suffers from the same formalism that the justices decried when abandoning the right-privilege distinction.[12] Because the entitlement approach explicitly disregards the weight of an individual's interest in a benefit, it cannot distinguish between interests that are of more or less value to individuals.[13] According to this criticism, *Roth*'s entitlement trigger is simultaneously over- and underinclusive.[14] It is overinclusive because positive law at times entitles individuals to benefits that are not sufficiently impor-

tions of that law by the state courts. See Bishop v. Wood, 426 U.S. 341, 345 (1976).

8. *Roth*, 408 U.S. at 576, 577.

9. See, e.g., Sidney A. Shapiro & Richard E. Levy, *Government Benefits and the Rule of Law: Toward a Standards-Based Theory of Due Process*, 57 ADMIN. L. REV. 107, 108, 113–18 (2005); Rodney A. Smolla, *The Reemergence of the Right–Privilege Distinction in Constitutional Law: The Price of Protesting Too Much*, 35 STAN. L REV. 69, 75 (1982).

10. See Cynthia R. Farina, *Conceiving Due Process*, 3 YALE J. L. & FEMINISM 189, 200 (1991).

11. Stephen F. Williams, *Liberty and Process: The Problem of Government Benefits*, 12 J. LEGAL STUDIES 3, 13–14 (1983).

12. See, e.g., Smolla, *Reemergence of the Right–Privilege Distinction*, *supra* note 9, at 69.

13. Williams, *Liberty and Process*, *supra* note 11, at 13.

14. William Van Alstyne, *Cracks in "The New Property": Adjudicative Due Process in the Administrative State*, 62 CORNELL L. REV. 445, 484 (1977).

tant to warrant a due process hearing before their withdrawal.[15] It is underinclusive because not every interest that is important to individuals is secured by a legal entitlement. On this criticism, *Roth* frustrates a central purpose of the due process clauses by permitting the government to arbitrarily deprive individuals of their important interests.[16]

Notwithstanding these criticisms, the justices have shown no inclination to rethink *Roth*. The Court's adoption of and adherence to the entitlement trigger is best understood as a compromise between two positions that the justices found unattractive—the traditional right-privilege distinction rejected in *Goldberg* and *Goldberg*'s seeming embrace of the "grievous loss" approach as a replacement. As the justices saw it, *Roth*'s entitlement trigger promises to fix meaningful "boundaries" on the otherwise "infinite" range of interests that the grievous loss approach opens to procedural due process requirements.[17] The entitlement approach also has been defended as fostering democratic values by transferring the decision to create property interests from the courts to more politically accountable decisionmakers in the legislative and executive branches.[18] These perceived benefits almost certainly became dominant on the Court with the benefit of hindsight. The experience of the "due process revolution" following *Goldberg* likely encouraged the justices to embrace the entitlement trigger in order to establish a firm limiting principle restricting the burgeoning efforts to constitutionalize administrative adjudicatory processes. Indeed, one influential commentator has argued that *Roth* secured rather than undermined *Goldberg*'s due process revolution by making it "appear more law-like."[19]

The primary advantage of the entitlement approach over the right-privilege distinction was its flexibility and capacity for growth. By opening the meaning of "property" beyond the limits of the traditional common law, the Court was able to accommodate the "new property" that the right-privilege-distinction had frozen out. *Roth* was emphatic in its rejection of the traditional gatekeeper to procedural due process protections: "[T]he Court has fully and

---

15. See Sandin v. Conner, 515 U.S. 472, 480–82 (1995); Thomas W. Merrill, *The Landscape of Constitutional Property*, 86 VA. L. REV. 885, 931–34 (2000) (arguing that the Court has addressed the problem of overinclusion by lessening or eliminating the procedural requirements of due process rather than by redefining property).

16. See Henry P. Monaghan, *Of "Liberty" and "Property,"* 62 CORN. L. REV. 405, 409 (1977); Shapiro & Levy, *Government Benefits*, supra note 9, at 108.

17. *Roth*, 408 U.S. at 570, 572.

18. Susan N. Herman, *The New Liberty: The Procedural Due Process Rights of Prisoners and Others under the Burger Court*, 59 N.Y.U. L. Rev. 482, 527 (1984); Merrill, *Constitutional Landscape of Property*, *supra* note 15, at 920–21.

19. Merrill, *Constitutional Landscape of Property*, *supra* note 15, at 918.

finally rejected the wooden distinction between 'rights' and 'privileges' that once seemed to govern the applicability of procedural due process rights."[20] While *Roth* represents a strategic judicial retreat from the boldness of the due process vision of the administrative state on display in *Goldberg*, the justices stopped well short of a full retreat back to the traditional common law.

The Court's analysis of the procedural due process claims in *Roth* and *Sindermann* illustrate the restrictiveness, as well as the flexibility, of the new understanding of property-as-entitlement. *Roth* made manifest the restrictiveness of the new understanding. "Just as [*Goldberg's*] welfare recipients' 'property' interest in welfare payments was created and defined by statutory terms," the Court wrote, Roth's " 'property' interest in employment ... was created and defined by the terms of his appointment." Unfortunately for Roth, the Court continued, the terms of his one-year faculty appointment "secured absolutely no interest in re-employment for the next year. They supported absolutely no possible claim of entitlement to re-employment. Nor, significantly, was there any state statute or University rule or policy that secured his interest in re-employment or that created any legitimate claim to it." Without any legitimate claim of entitlement, Roth "did not have a property interest sufficient to require the University authorities to give him a hearing when they declined to renew his contract of employment."[21]

If *Roth* showed the formality and restrictiveness of the Court's entitlement definition of property, *Sindermann* created the potential for flexibility in the new approach. Sindermann, like Roth, had been terminated at the end of a one-year faculty appointment. But unlike Roth, who was let go after his first year, Sinderman had been renewed routinely for ten years in the state–college system before his termination. Based on those ten contract renewals, Sinderman alleged that he had become tenured through his college's "de facto tenure program." Under that program, Sinderman alleged further, a faculty member who, like he, had been employed in the state-college system for seven years or more, possessed tenure. According to Sinderman, his tenured status guaranteed his retention "unless adequate cause for dismissal is demonstrated in a fair hearing, following established procedures of due process."[22]

If Sindermann could prove these allegations, the Court held, he would have "a legitimate claim of entitlement to job tenure," and thus the right to a due process hearing to challenge whether college administrators had sufficient cause to terminate his employment. The justices explained, "A person's interest in a benefit is a

---

20. *Roth*, 408 U.S. at 571.

21. *Id*. at 578.

22. *Sindermann*, 408 U.S. at 599–600 & n.6.

'property' interest for due process purposes if there are such rules or mutually explicit understandings that support his claim of entitlement to the benefit and that he may invoke at a hearing." An "unwritten 'common law' in a particular university that certain employees shall have the equivalent of tenure," the Court concluded, was sufficient to establish such a rule or understanding creating a legitimate claim of entitlement for procedural due process purposes.[23] As *Roth* made clear, however, proving the existence of such a common law is not easy. Merely showing that the college had rehired "most teachers" employed on an annual basis was insufficient to establish an unwritten tenure program.[24]

An Additional Monetary Value Requirement? In *Roth* and later decisions, the justices have focused their entitlement analysis on the *source* of the putative property right at issue, rather than the *content* of that right. This focus squares with *Roth*, where the justices served notice that henceforth they would look at the "nature" rather than the "weight" of the threatened individual interest when determining whether to apply the due process clauses.[25] Recently, however, the Court suggested that an entitlement by itself may not be sufficient to establish a property interest. In *Town of Castle Rock v. Gonzales*,[26] the Court noted that it was at least relevant to consider whether an entitlement "resemble[ed] any traditional conception of property" before deciding whether a property interest was at stake. The Court in *Castle Rock* suggested more pointedly that an entitlement should have monetary value in order to qualify as "property" protected by due process.[27] This suggestion awaits future development by the Court.[28]

Substance v. Process: The "Bitter-with-the-Sweet" Principle. In *Goldberg v. Kelly*,[29] the Court separated its analysis into two parts. The Court held first that the termination of welfare

23. *Id.* at 602–03.

24. *Roth*, 408 U.S. at 578 n.16.

25. *Id.* at 571.

26. 545 U.S. 748 (2005).

27. *Id.* at 766; see Merrill, *Landscape of Constitutional Property, supra* note 15, at 893, 960–68 (defining "property" for procedural due process purposes as a legal entitlement "having a monetary value that can be terminated upon a finding that a specific condition has been satisfied"). Professor Merrill observed that including a monetary-value requirement would distinguish government-created property interests from government-created liberty interests (see § 3.4(b)), which "typically do not have a readily ascertainable monetary value." Merrill, *Landscape of Constitu-*

tional Property, supra note 15, at 964–65.

28. At least one federal court of appeals has suggested that deprivations of property do not trigger procedural due process protections "unless they are atypical and significant in relation to the inevitable 'deprivations' that people suffer as a result of contractual disputes and the other ordinary frictions of life." Baerwald v. City of Milwaukee, 131 F.3d 681, 683 (7th Cir. 1997) (fire department's application of a rule that firefighter may not be reinstated after injury leave or sick leave without a release from treating physician did not deprive firefighter of property right protected by procedural due process).

29. 397 U.S. 254 (1970).

benefits had triggered the protections of procedural due process. This was a *substantive* determination. The Court then concluded that the state's pre-termination procedures did not measure up to the requirements of due process (see § 3.3).[30] This, of course, was a *procedural* determination. The justices maintained this substantive-procedural dichotomy in *Roth*. The Court in *Roth* determined the substantive question—that is, whether procedural due process was applicable—by asking whether the individual interest at stake was supported by a legitimate claim of entitlement. The justices also announced in *Roth* that they would approach the procedural determination—that is, whether the agency's "form of hearing" satisfied due process—through a "weighing process."[31]

Just a couple of years after *Roth*, however, several justices in *Arnett v. Kennedy*[32] suggested that the entitlement approach to defining protected property interests essentially collapsed the substantive and procedural determinations of procedural due process analysis into one inquiry. *Arnett*, like *Roth*, involved the dismissal of a public employee. But Arnett, unlike Roth, enjoyed job tenure. An act of Congress provided that Arnett, as a federal employee in the competitive civil service, could be fired "only for such cause as will promote the efficiency of the service." Federal regulations afforded tenured employees an opportunity for a hearing to contest their firing after, but not before, their initial termination. Arnett, relying on *Roth*, argued that the civil service statute gave him a legitimate claim of entitlement to hold his job absent sufficient cause for his dismissal. He also argued, relying on *Goldberg*, that due process required the government to give him "a full adversarial hearing" before the initial job termination.[33] A narrow majority of the Court upheld Arnett's dismissal.

Then-Justice William H. Rehnquist, writing for a three-justice plurality, reached the surprising conclusion that the procedures the government had made available to Arnett to challenge his dismissal were part and parcel of any entitlement to job tenure that he had enjoyed, and thus that they were not subject to a due process challenge. Justice Rehnquist conceded that Arnett had a statutory entitlement that he not be fired without sufficient cause, but the statute creating that right, Rehnquist argued, also defined "the procedure by which 'cause' was to be determined." In other words, Arnett possessed the "substantive right" to his job subject to "the procedural limitations which Congress attached to it." This Catch–22 has become known as the "bitter-with-the-sweet" principle. The Rehnquist plurality explained, "[W]here the grant of a substantive right is inextricably intertwined with the limitations on the proce-

---

30. *Id.* at 261–71.

31. *Roth*, 408 U.S. at 570–71.

32. 416 U.S. 134 (1974).

33. *Id.* at 151.

dures which are to be employed in determining that right, a litigant in the position of [Arnett] must take the bitter with the sweet."[34]

There is logic to the "bitter-with-the-sweet" principle. As Justice Rehnquist observed, from Congress's perspective, the substance and procedure of job termination may well have been a package deal. The legislators had granted tenure on the understanding that federal employees would not be allowed a trial-type hearing before their termination. It therefore struck the Rehnquist plurality as unseemly for a federal employee to complain about the conditions on which Congress had bestowed the gift of job security.[35] This logic, however, is the logic of the right-privilege distinction, which the Court had renounced in *Goldberg* and had renounced again in *Roth*.[36]

The "bitter-with-the-sweet" principle not only shared the logic of the right-benefit distinction, it reproduced the same stifling effect on procedural due process protections. Under both approaches, the legislators or government officials who create a legal entitlement have free rein to determine the procedural protections, if any, to secure that entitlement.[37] By eliminating the *Goldberg-Roth* distinction between the substance of a right and the procedures for enforcing that right, the *Arnett* plurality would deny courts authority under the due process clauses to require *any* procedural protection beyond that which legislators or government officials wish to provide. In each approach, the recipient of government largess must accept the "bitter with the sweet."[38]

Justice Lewis F. Powell, writing for himself and one other, concurred in the judgment that due process did not guarantee Arnett a trial-type hearing before his termination. But Justice Powell rejected the plurality's "bitter-with-the-sweet" innovation as "incompatible with the principles laid down in *Roth* and *Sindermann.*" Justice Powell explained, "[T]he right to procedural due process ... is conferred, not by legislative grace, but by constitutional guarantee. While the legislature may elect not to confer a property interest in federal employment, it may not constitutionally authorize the deprivation of such an interest, once conferred, without appropriate procedural safeguards.... [T]he adequacy of

34. *Id.* at 151–54.

35. *Id.* at 152–53.

36. See *id.* at 210 (Marshall, J., dissenting).

37. See *id.* at 177–78 (White, J., concurring in part and dissenting in part).

38. For criticism of the "bitter-with-the-sweet" principle, see Cynthia R. Farina, *On Misusing "Revolution" and*

"*Reform": Procedural Due Process and the New Welfare Act*, 50 ADMIN. L. REV. 591, 617 (1998); Martin H. Redish & Lawrence C. Marshall, *Adjudicatory Independence and the Value of Procedural Due Process*, 95 YALE L.J. 455, 468 (1986). For a defense of the "bitter-with-the-sweet" principle, see Frank Easterbrook, *Substance and Due Process*, 1982 SUP. CT. REV. 85, 112–14; Williams, *Liberty and Process, supra* note 11, at 6–7.

statutory procedures for deprivation of a statutorily created property interest must be analyzed in constitutional terms."[39]

Even though the "bitter-with-the-sweet" principle swayed only three justices in *Arnett*, and met with outright rejection by the Court on at least a couple of occasions after *Arnett*,[40] the allure of the idea occasionally captivated state courts and lower federal courts. The final straw came in *Cleveland Board of Education v. Loudermill*,[41] which was yet another job-termination case. In *Loudermill*, an impatient Court wrote, "[I]t is settled that the 'bitter with the sweet' approach misconceives the constitutional guarantee. If a clearer holding is needed, we provide it today. The point is straightforward: the Due Process Clause provides that certain substantive rights—life, liberty, and property—cannot be deprived except pursuant to constitutionally adequate procedures. The categories of substance and procedure are distinct. Were the rule otherwise, the Clause would be reduced to a mere tautology. 'Property' cannot be defined by the procedures provided for its deprivation any more than can life or liberty."[42]

What is "a Legitimate Claim of Entitlement"? In the years since *Roth* and *Sindermann*, the "hallmark of property" has been "an individual entitlement grounded in law, which cannot be removed except 'for cause.' "[43] To be grounded in law, "[a] claim of entitlement . . . must be derived from [1] statute or [2] legal rule or [3] through a mutually explicit understanding."[44]

Although the test for defining the property interests protected by procedural due process is often described casually as requiring an entitlement to a benefit, it is important to remember that *Roth* required only that the individual demonstrate a *"legitimate claim of entitlement"* to support a property interest.[45] An individual need not prove that she or he is legally entitled to receive a benefit in order to establish a legitimate claim of entitlement. To possess a legitimate claim of entitlement, an individual need only demonstrate that he or she would have a right to a benefit *if* the

---

39. *Arnett*, 416 U.S. at 166–67 (Powell, J., concurring in part and concurring in the result in part). Justice Powell ultimately decided that the pre-termination process afforded Arnett satisfied the requirements of procedural due process. *Id*. at 167–71 (Powell, J., concurring in part and concurring in the result in part).

40. See Logan v. Zimmerman Brush Co., 455 U.S. 422, 431–32 (1982); Vitek v. Jones, 445 U.S. 480, 491 & n.6 (1980).

41. 470 U.S. 532 (1985).

42. *Id*. at 541. The distinction between substance and procedure in proce-

dural due process analysis cuts both ways. Just as the absence of procedural protections in an enactment of positive law cannot eliminate a due process right to such protections, the inclusion of procedural protections cannot create a legitimate claim of entitlement to a government benefit. See Bishop v. Wood, 426 U.S. 341, 345–47 (1976).

43. *Logan*, 455 U.S. at 430.

44. Leis v. Flynt, 439 U.S. 438, 442 (1979).

45. *Roth*, 408 U.S. at 577 (emphasis added).

individual satisfies the eligibility criteria specified by the applicable law. A dispute over whether an individual satisfies those criteria does not defeat a legitimate claim of entitlement.[46] The purpose of the due process hearing is to provide the claimant an opportunity to prove her or his legal entitlement to possess the benefit in dispute.[47]

In deciding whether an individual possesses a legitimate claim of entitlement that qualifies as a property interest, courts carefully parse the language of the relevant source of law. For a law to create a legitimate claim of entitlement, it must satisfy two requirements. First, the law must contain "language creating *substantive predicates* [i.e., standards] to govern official decision-making."[48] These "substantive predicates" may provide the administrative decision-maker with "significant discretion," so long as they meaningfully limit the discretion of the decisionmaker.[49] In *Cleveland Board of Education v. Loudermill*, for example, the Court held that a state statute had "plainly create[d]" an entitlement in continued public employment by prohibiting the firing of public employees "except . . . for . . . misfeasance, malfeasance, or nonfeasance in office."[50] While these standards plainly gave officials discretion in deciding whether to fire a public employee, the crucial point was that the statutory standards limited official discretion. By contrast, Roth had no legitimate claim of entitlement to his employment because, as the Court put it, "[t]here [were] no statutory or administrative *standards* defining eligibility for re-employment." State law had left the decision whether to rehire Roth "to the *unfettered* discretion of university officials."[51]

In addition to specifying "substantive predicates" that limit official discretion, the relevant law must contain "explicitly mandatory language" in order to create a legitimate claim of entitlement.[52] This requires "specific directives to the decisionmaker that if the . . . substantive predicates are present, a particular outcome *must* follow."[53] For example, the welfare beneficiaries in *Goldberg*

---

46. Memphis Light, Gas and Water Div. v. Craft, 436 U.S. 1, 11 (1978); Fuentes v. Shevin, 407 U.S. 67, 86 (1972).

47. *Roth*, 408 U.S. at 577.

48. Kentucky Department of Corrections v. Thompson, 490 U.S. 454, 462 (1989) (emphasis added); see Hewitt v. Helms, 459 U.S. 460, 472 (1983).

49. Board of Pardons v. Allen, 482 U.S. 369, 375, 380 (1987); see *Kentucky Department of Corrections*, 490 U.S. at 463.

50. 470 U.S. 532, 538–39 (1985).

51. *Roth*, 408 U.S. at 566–67 (emphasis added); see also Connecticut Bd. of Pardons v. Dumschat, 452 U.S. 458,

460–67 (1981) (prison inmate lacked entitlement to commutation of sentence because the decision was within the "unfettered discretion" of agency); *Leis*, 439 U.S. at 442–43 (out-of-state lawyer lacked entitlement to appear as counsel because court rules gave the trial judge complete discretion to disallow such appearances).

52. *Hewitt*, 459 U.S. at 472; see Town of Castle Rock v. Gonzales, 545 U.S. 748, 760 (2005); *Kentucky Department of Corrections*, 490 U.S. at 463.

53. *Kentucky Department of Corrections*, 490 U.S. at 463 (emphasis added).

possessed a legitimate claim of entitlement to continued receipt of their benefits because if they satisfied the statutory criteria for eligibility (i.e., the "substantive predicates"), the welfare statute specifically prohibited the government from terminating them. The same was true of Loudermill's employment. The civil service statute specifically provided that tenured employees could not be fired so long as they met the statutory criteria for continued employment.

A law lacks "explicitly mandatory language," and thus cannot create a legitimate claim of entitlement, if it leaves government officials with discretion to terminate a benefit even if an individual satisfies the eligibility criteria.[54] The D.C. Circuit's decision in *Washington Clinic for the Homeless v. Barry*[55] illustrates how the absence of "explicitly mandatory language" in the relevant law defeats an entitlement claim. The District of Columbia City Council enacted a law authorizing the creation of temporary shelters for eligible homeless families. The law made homeless families eligible for shelter if they satisfied several specified conditions. The court of appeals had no difficulty concluding that those conditions qualified as "substantive predicates," satisfying the first requirement for establishing a legitimate claim of entitlement. But the court ultimately found that eligible homeless families did not have an entitlement to (and thus lacked a property interest in) temporary shelter because the law did not mandate that "all families meeting [the eligibility] criteria receive shelter." The District lacked the resources to provide shelter for all eligible families, and the City Council left the task of allocating the scarce shelter accommodations among eligible families to the discretion of city officials. Due process did not require notice and hearing to determine the eligibility of these claimants for temporary because even had they established eligibility, city administrators might still have denied them shelter for any number of reasons.[56]

Administrative Practice. In *Sindermann*, *Roth*'s companion decision, the Court introduced the potential for flexibility in entitlement analysis by accepting the "unwritten 'common law' in a particular [agency]" as sufficient to establish a rule or understanding creating a legitimate claim of entitlement, and thus, a property

---

54. See *Town of Castle Rock*, 545 U.S. at 756, ("a benefit is not a protected entitlement if government officials may grant or deny it in their discretion").

55. 107 F.3d 32 (D.C. Cir. 1997).

56. *Id.* at 36–38; see also United of Omaha Life Ins. Co. v. Solomon, 960 F.2d 31 (6th Cir. 1992) (unsuccessful, lowest bidder on a public contract lacked a legitimate claim of entitlement to the contract because the contracting agency had discretionary authority to deny any bid); Eidson v. Pierce, 745 F.2d 453 (7th Cir. 1984) (eligible applicants for federally subsidized rental housing did not have a legitimate claim of entitlement to such housing because landlords had discretion to reject them as tenants).

interest.[57] In *Roth*, however, the justices made clear that proving the existence of such a common law would not be easy. Roth had demonstrated that his college had rehired "most teachers" who, like he, had been employed on an annual basis, but this, the Court held, was insufficient to establish a common law of job tenure.[58] The Court has continued to send mixed signals. Although the justices have held open the possibility of grounding a legitimate claim of entitlement on a "common law" arising from administrative practice,[59] they have never accepted such a claim.

Yet lower courts, at least on occasion, have found the common law of administrative practice sufficient to establish an entitlement. In *Furlong v. Shalala*,[60] for example, the Second Circuit held that "well over 100" decisions by an agency's administrative law judges over a period of "many months" had created a legitimate claim of entitlement to a particular reimbursement for Medicare providers. The court of appeals rejected as unduly "narrow and formalistic" the insistence of the district judge that only such "traditional" sources as statutes, regulations, and ordinances provided "an authoritative source for a property interest."[61]

Notwithstanding occasional decisions such as *Furlong*, the flexibility promised by *Sindermann*'s opening of entitlement analysis to the common law of administrative practice generally has not been realized.

The Application/Revocation Distinction. The Supreme Court's decisions examining the existence of property interests for procedural due process purposes generally have involved official decisions terminating an existing benefit. The claimants in *Goldberg*, for example, were welfare recipients whom officials believed were no longer qualified for the program. But what of individuals who *apply* for benefits under an entitlement program? Must the government give them a due process hearing before denying their applications? Individuals who apply for entitlement benefits, no less than those who already receive them, have a legal right to the benefits if they meet the eligibility criteria. But do applicants have a property interest in a benefit that they have yet to receive, and thus, do not possess? Is the applicants' legitimate claim of entitlement to the benefit sufficient to establish a property interest?

The Supreme Court has suggested that an individual entitlement must "resemble [a] traditional conception of property" to

57. *Sindermann*, 408 U.S. at 602.

58. *Roth*, 408 U.S. at 578 n.16.

59. See Jago v. Van Curen, 454 U.S. 14, 20 (1981).

60. 156 F.3d 384 (2d Cir. 1998).

61. *Id*. at 394–95.

qualify as a property interest.[62] And in *Roth*, the justices, albeit in dicta, seemed to limit the new entitlement analysis to termination cases. Procedural due process protections of property, the Court wrote, are "a safeguard of the security of interests that a person has already acquired in specific benefits." The justices seemed to use *Roth* to limit *Goldberg* to termination cases as well. They described *Goldberg* as holding, "that a person receiving welfare benefits under statutory and administrative standards defining eligibility for them has an interest in continued receipt of those benefits that is safeguarded by procedural due process."[63]

But when the issue has been squarely presented, lower federal courts have tended to conclude that applicants have a property interest in entitlement benefits, and thus that the government must observe procedural due process requirements in denying their applications.[64] Then-Justice Rehnquist, dissenting from the Court's denial of certiorari review of one such decision, argued that these holdings represented a significant expansion of *Goldberg*.[65] Yet Justice Sandra Day O'Connor, writing for herself and two others, dissented from the Court's denial of certiorari review of a state court decision that went in the opposite direction. Justice O'Connor wrote, "The conclusion ... that an applicant for general assistance does not have an interest protected by the Due Process Clause is unsettling in its implication that less fortunate persons in our society may arbitrarily be denied benefits that a State has granted as a matter of right.... One would think that where state law creates an entitlement to general assistance based on certain substantive conditions, there ... results a property interest that warrants at least some procedural safeguards."[66]

The Supreme Court has not settled whether applicants for benefits from entitlement programs are entitled to procedural due process protections.[67] The Court's opinion in *American Manufactur-*

---

62. *Town of Castle Rock*, 545 U.S. at 766.

63. *Roth*, 408 U.S. at 576.

64. See, e.g., Mallette v. Arlington County Employees' Supplemental Retirement System, 91 F.3d 630, 637–40 (4th Cir. 1996) ("As far as we can tell, every lower federal court that has considered the issue has rejected the 'application/revocation' distinction."); Midnight Sessions, Ltd. v. City of Philadelphia, 945 F.2d 667, 679 (3rd Cir. 1991); Daniels v. Woodbury County, 742 F.2d 1128, 1132 (8th Cir. 1984) ("[t]he proper inquiry" is not the application/revocation distinction; it is

whether the claimant has "a legitimate claim of entitlement to relief assistance").

65. Peer v. Griffeth, 445 U.S. 970, 970–71 (1980) (Rehnquist, J., dissenting).

66. Gregory v. Town of Pittsfield, 470 U.S. 1018, 1021 (1985) (O'Connor, J., dissenting).

67. See Lyng v. Payne, 476 U.S. 926, 942 (1986) (stating that the Court has "never held that applicants for benefits, as distinct from those already receiving them, have a legitimate claim of entitlement protected by the Due Process Clause of the Fifth or Fourteenth

ers *Mutual Insurance Co. v. Sullivan*[68] illustrates the continuing uncertainty and disagreement surrounding the issue. In a part of the majority opinion agreed to only by five justices, the Court suggested, albeit in dicta, that applicants for workers' compensation benefits did not have an entitlement to, and thus lacked a property interest in, those benefits until *after* the government had determined that they satisfied all of the eligibility criteria. But the claimants in *American Manufacturers Mutual Insurance Co.* had not argued that they possessed a property interest in their "claims for payment," so the issue of an applicant's right to procedural due process had not been formally submitted to the Court.[69] And for good measure, one member of the five-justice majority who joined the portion of the opinion that contained this dictum wrote separately to make clear, "I do not doubt ... that due process requires fair procedures for the adjudication of [the applicants'] claims for workers' compensation benefits, including medical care."[70]

(b) Deprivation of Liberty

Liberty interests protected by procedural due process may arise from two sources. First, liberty interests, like property interests, may be created by such acts of positive law as statutes and regulations. Second, liberty interests, unlike property interests, also may arise from the Constitution itself, or more specifically, from the "guarantees implicit in the word 'liberty' " in the due process clauses.[71] The Court's opinion in *Roth* underscored the expanded reach of liberty interests when the justices proclaimed, "In a Constitution for a free people, there can be no doubt that the meaning of 'liberty' must be broad indeed." That statement stands in stark contrast to the *Roth* Court's emphasis on establishing "boundaries" for the range of property interests protected by the due process clauses.[72] And while the Court in *Roth* and *Sindermann* defined "property" with considerable care, they expended very little effort in cabining the liberty interests that activate procedural due process. Within a few years, however, the justices began to restrict the definition of "liberty," bringing this due process trigger closer to the entitlement regime that has dominated the protection of property interests since *Roth*.

Amendment," but leaving question unresolved); cf. Walters v. National Ass'n of Radiation Survivors, 473 U.S. 305 (1985) (applying due process requirements to applications for veterans' death and disability benefits, but without discussing the trigger issue).

68.   526 U.S. 40 (1999).

69.   *Id.* at 60–61 & n.13.

70.   *Id.* at 62 (Ginsburg, J., concurring in part and concurring in the judgment).

71.   Wilkinson v. Austin, 545 U.S. 209, 221 (2005); see Kentucky Dep't of Corrections v. Thompson, 490 U.S. 454, 460 (1989); Hewitt v. Helms, 459 U.S. 460, 466 (1983).

72.   See *Roth*, 408 U.S. at 572.

Constitutional Rights. The many provisions of the Bill of Rights that the Court has "incorporated" into the due process clause of the Fourteenth Amendment[73] may seem the most obvious source of the constitutional content of liberty. But ironically, these fundamental rights protections have had little impact on procedural due process jurisprudence.

The major stumbling block for the usefulness of the Bill of Rights has been the Court's holding in *Roth* and *Sindermann* that merely alleging that government officials have violated one of those rights is insufficient to trigger procedural due process protections.[74] Yet an individual who succeeds in *proving* a violation of one of the Bill of Rights no longer needs procedural due process protections. Provisions such as the free speech clause of the First Amendment and the takings clause of the Fifth Amendment prohibit the government from taking particular actions (abridging freedom of speech, confiscating private property without compensation) regardless of the procedures officials used when acting.

Roth and *Sindermann* illustrate the inapplicability of the incorporated provisions of the Bill of Rights to procedural due process claims. The faculty members in those cases claimed that their nonrenewal violated their freedom of speech because it had been in retaliation for their public criticism of university administrators. As its incorporation into the Fourteenth Amendment demonstrates, an abridgment of freedom of speech constitutes a deprivation of liberty within the meaning of the due process clause. But the *allegation* of such an abridgment did not *prove* the deprivation.[75] Had the faculty members been able to convince a court that their nonrenewal violated their freedom of speech, the nonrenewal would have been unconstitutional without regard to whether their respective colleges had held a due process hearing before they acted.[76]

The lesson of *Roth* and *Sindermann* is that the constitutional liberty protected by procedural due process includes only individual interests that do *not* receive special substantive protection under the Constitution. Put another way, procedural due process comes into play only when the government possesses the substantive power to deprive an individual of a liberty interest.

There are liberty interests that the Constitution protects procedurally but not substantively, but it is not clear how many such interests exist. The best example of a procedurally protected, constitutional liberty interest is the "freedom from bodily restraint

---

73. Zinermon v. Burch, 494 U.S. 113, 125 (1990); see Duncan v. Louisiana, 391 U.S. 145 (1968).

74. *Sindermann*, 408 U.S. at 599 n.5; *Roth*, 408 U.S. at 574–75.

75. *Sindermann*, 408 U.S. at 599 n.5; *Roth*, 408 U.S. at 574–75.

76. See Ingraham v. Wright, 430 U.S. 651, 671 (1977); Paul v. Davis, 424 U.S. 693, 712–13 (1976).

and punishment."[77] The government has the substantive power to incarcerate an individual for having committed a crime, but only after affording the individual procedural due process. The most prominent example in modern procedural due process jurisprudence of a procedurally protected, constitutional liberty interest outside the context of prison administration is an individual's interest in her or his reputation.

Injury to Reputation. The protected status of an individual's reputation is grounded on two lines of legal precedent. First, the common law of defamation traditionally compensated individuals for injury to their reputation caused by false statements about their character. Second, and more specifically, the "Red Scare" following the Second World War triggered a series of legal challenges to a host of aggressive governmental efforts to bar from public employment individuals who had been found to be communists or subversives. In deciding these challenges, the justices came to appreciate that officially branding a person as "disloyal" imposed a disabling "badge of infamy ... [i]n the view of the community ... [that] inhibit[ed] individual freedom of movement."[78] This realization culminated in *Wisconsin v. Constantineau*, with the Court holding, "Where a person's good name, reputation, honor, or integrity is at stake because of what the government is doing to him, notice and an opportunity to be heard are essential."[79]

The Court in *Roth* drew on *Constantineau*, stating in dicta that the faculty member there may have had a right to a due process hearing had the state university based "the nonrenewal of his contract on a charge, for example, that he had been guilty of dishonesty, or immorality." Because such a charge "might seriously damage [an individual's] standing and associations in his community," a due process hearing may have been "essential" to allow Roth "an opportunity to clear his name." But the nonrenewal of Roth's employment contract, standing alone, had not "imposed on him a stigma or other disability that foreclosed his freedom to take advantage of other employment opportunities." While simple nonretention may have made Roth "somewhat less attractive to some other employers," the Court held, that harm fell short of "the kind of foreclosure of opportunities amounting to a deprivation of 'liberty.' "[80]

77. *Ingraham*, 430 U.S. at 673–74; see Rochin v. California, 342 U.S. 165 (1952); Meyer v. Nebraska, 262 U.S. 390, 399 (1923).

78. See Wieman v. Updegraff, 344 U.S. 183, 190–91 (1952).

79. 400 U.S. 433, 437 (1971).

80. *Roth*, 408 U.S. at 573–74 & nn.12–13; see *Sindermann*, 408 U.S. at 599.

The justices added bite to *Roth*'s embrace of *Constantineau* in *Goss v. Lopez*,[81] holding that a 10-day suspension had deprived public school students of their "liberty." In contrast to *Roth*, the *Goss* students had been suspended on "charges of misconduct," which, the Court found, "could seriously damage the students' standing with their fellow pupils and their teachers as well as interfere with later opportunities for higher education and employment."[82] *Goss* is consistent with *Roth* because it was the black mark that a suspension *for misconduct* had added to the students' record, rather than the suspension itself, that had compromised the liberty of the students.

Just one year after *Goss*, the justices abruptly shifted ground in the pivotal decision of *Paul v. Davis*.[83] The facts of *Paul* closely resembled those of *Constantineau* (*Constantineau* is summarized in § 3.3). Paul was a police chief who had circulated a flyer to local merchants in an effort to ward off shoplifting during the Christmas season. The flyer contained the names and mug shots of individuals described as "active shoplifters." Davis claimed that the inclusion of his name and photograph on the flyer had deprived him of liberty, and thus that due process had entitled him to notice and opportunity for a hearing to clear his name before the police chief released the flyer. (Davis had been charged with shoplifting when the flyer was released, but the charge was later dismissed.)

The Court used *Paul* to back off the view that "governmental defamation" of an individual, without more, constituted a deprivation of liberty. The justices recognized that circulation of the flyer had "inhibit[ed] [Davis] from entering business establishments for fear of being suspected of shoplifting and possibly apprehended, and [had] seriously impair[ed] his future employment opportunities." But these effects, the Court held, were insufficient to trigger procedural due process protections. In order to find a deprivation of liberty, the Court now held, not only must government officials impose a "stigma" on an individual's reputation, but also the individual must lose "some more tangible interest such as employment."[84]

As a result of *Paul*'s "stigma-plus" requirement, claims of harm to reputation sufficient to constitute a deprivation of liberty largely have been limited to cases involving termination of, and possibly demotion in, public employment.[85] The strictness of *Paul*'s stigma-plus requirement even in this limited context was evident

81. 419 U.S. 565 (1975).

82. *Id.* at 574–75.

83. 424 U.S. 693 (1976).

84. *Id.* at 694–97, 701–02.

85. See Mosrie v. Barry, 718 F.2d 1151, 1161–62 (D.C.Cir 1983) (demotion, but not lateral transfer, sufficient to trigger due process); cf. Gilbert v. Homar, 520 U.S. 924, 929 (1997) (reserving question of whether a job action short of termination is sufficient to trigger procedural due process).

when the justices decided *Siegert v. Gilley.*[86] Siegert, a clinical psychologist, had resigned his position at a federal mental hospital after being notified that the hospital intended to fire him for misconduct. Siegert then took a position at an Army hospital. The Army hospital asked Siegert's supervisor at the former hospital to provide information on Siegert's job performance there. Siegert's former supervisor wrote the Army hospital that he regarded Siegert as "both inept and unethical, perhaps the least trustworthy individual I have supervised." The Army hospital fired Siegert upon receipt of the former supervisor's letter. Siegert sued his former supervisor, claiming that by sending the letter to the Army hospital without first giving him an opportunity to respond, the former supervisor had deprived Siegert of liberty without due process of law. The Court held that the alleged defamation in the former supervisor's letter did not satisfy the stigma-plus requirement of *Paul* because it had been communicated *after*, rather than "incident to," the former hospital's termination of Siegert.[87] It did not matter that the letter had caused the Army to fire Siegert.

The justices have restricted claims of harm to reputation beyond *Paul*'s stigma-plus requirement. For example, the Court has ruled that a government official's defamatory statement must be made publicly in order for an individual to suffer stigmatic harm to reputation. A private, oral communication by a government official to a public employee alleging misconduct as a reason for termination does not deprive the employee of a liberty interest in his or her reputation.[88] Moreover, a due process claimant must allege that a government official's damaging statements are "substantially false." If the harmful statements are true, a due process hearing would not clear the individual's name.[89]

Liberty Entitlements. The Supreme Court recognized in a long line of prison-administration decisions that liberty interests for purposes of procedural due process may be created by acts of positive law (such as statutes and regulations) as well as by the Constitution.[90] The prison setting created a target-rich environment

---

86. 500 U.S. 226 (1991).

87. *Id.* at 227–29, 233–34; see also O'Donnell v. Barry, 148 F.3d 1126, 1140 (D.C.Cir. 1998) (defamatory statements and job demotion must occur together to trigger procedural due process).

88. Bishop v. Wood, 426 U.S. 341, 348–50 (1976). In *Goss v. Lopez*, 419 U.S. 565, 574–75 & n.7 (1975), which the Court decided before *Paul*, the Court held it sufficient that the school recorded the suspensions of students for misconduct in the schools' files, because

such files may be made available to colleges and prospective employers. It is not clear whether such a recording would be a sufficient public communication after *Bishop.*

89. Codd v. Velger, 429 U.S. 624, 627.

90. This precedent originated in *Wolff v. McDonnell*, 418 U.S. 539, 557–58 (1974). For a critique of the Court's transplanting of *Roth*'s entitlement analysis into liberty, see Herman, *The New Liberty*, *supra* note 18.

for finding such entitlements, because statutes and regulations often authorize prison administrators to punish inmates "for cause." Such disciplinary actions generated a steady stream of procedural due process claims by prisoners, and before long, federal judges found themselves mired in the day-to-day concerns of prison management.

The justices rebelled in *Sandin v. Conner*.[91] The Court held that an act of positive law providing inmates a legitimate claim of entitlement did not necessarily create a liberty interest. In order to trigger due process, the entitlement also must protect inmates against conditions of confinement that are "atypical and [impose] significant hardship ... in relation to the ordinary incidents of prison life."[92] *Sandin's* added "atypical and significant hardship" requirement is an echo of the "grievous loss" approach to triggering due process that the Court seemingly had buried in *Roth*. In *Sandin*, however, the entitlement and grievous loss approaches are complimentary rather than in competition with one another. An inmate must satisfy *both* thresholds before establishing a liberty interest sufficient to trigger procedural due process protections.

The Court in *Sandin* did not state whether the new requirement of "atypical and significant hardship" applies outside the prison-administration context, but it seems likely that the justices also will decline to require procedural due process protections for deprivations of liberty outside of prison that they regard as common or trivial. Because individuals enjoy considerably more freedom in the "ordinary incidents" of their lives than do prisoners, however, the threshold for deprivations that are "atypical and [impose] significant hardship" should be considerably lower outside of the prison setting.

At least one federal court of appeals has suggested that *Sandin* applies to claimed deprivations of property as well as of liberty. In both instances, the court stated, deprivations do not trigger procedural due process protections "unless they are atypical and significant in relation to the inevitable 'deprivations' that people suffer as a result of contractual disputes and the other ordinary frictions of life."[93]

(c) The Meaning of Deprivation

Whether governmental action constitutes a deprivation of an individual's interests protected by the due process clauses is seldom

91. 515 U.S. 472 (1995).

92. *Id*. at 483–84; see Wilkinson v. Austin, 545 U.S. 209, 221–24 (2005).

93. Baerwald v. City of Milwaukee, 131 F.3d 681, 683 (7th Cir. 1997) (fire department's application of a rule that firefighter may not be reinstated after injury leave or sick leave without a release from treating physician did not deprive firefighter of property right protected by procedural due process).

at issue. Ordinarily, any governmental action that adversely affects an individual's interest in liberty or property qualifies.[94] The Supreme Court, however, has recognized two exceptions to that general rule. This section develops those exceptions.

Direct v. Indirect Effects. An individual must be the target of the government's action in order to suffer a deprivation of liberty or property within the meaning of the due process clauses. The Supreme Court's decision in *O'Bannon v. Town Court Nursing Center*[95] nicely illustrates this principle. In *O'Bannon*, the Court held that nursing home residents had no due process right to notice and hearing before a federal agency decertified the facility in which they lived. The justices acknowledged that the decertification might cause "severe hardship" for at least some residents, because one must live in a qualified nursing home to be eligible for federal medical benefits. But that harm, the Court held, was merely "an indirect and incidental result" of the government's action against a third party, the nursing home. The nursing home residents in *O'Bannon*, the justices explained, fell on the wrong side of "[t]he simple distinction between government action that directly affects a citizen's legal rights, or imposes a direct restraint on his liberty, and action that is directed against a third party and affects the citizen only indirectly or incidentally."[96]

Negligent Actions. In *Daniels v. Williams*, the Court held that the due process clauses do not apply to "a *negligent* act of an official causing unintended loss of or injury to life, liberty, or property."[97] The justices offered two reasons for this limitation. First, they did not see in negligent actions the "abuse of power" that due process was designed to prevent. Second, and perhaps more importantly, the justices echoed *Paul v. Davis* (see § 3.4(b)) in expressing their fear that recognizing negligent deprivations of property or liberty interests would allow procedural due process norms to "supplant traditional tort law."[98]

The justices have not settled whether only *intentional* actions by government officials may constitute a deprivation of life, liberty, or property within the meaning of the due process clauses. The Court in *Daniels* suggested as much, observing, "Historically, . . . due process has been applied to *deliberate* decisions of government officials to deprive a person of life, liberty, or property." But later

---

94. Government *in*action does not trigger the due process clauses. See De-Shaney v. Winnebago County Dep't of Social Services, 489 U.S. 189 (1989). For a discussion, see David A. Strauss, *Due Process, Government Inaction, and Private Wrongs*, 1989 SUP. CT. REV. 53.

95. 447 U.S. 773 (1980).

96. *Id.* at 787–89; see Town of Castle Rock v. Gonzales, 545 U.S. 748, 764–68 (2005).

97. 474 U.S. 327, 328 (1986); see also Davidson v. Cannon, 474 U.S. 344, 347–48 (1986) (companion case).

98. *Davidson*, 474 U.S. at 347–48; see *Daniels*, 474 U.S. at 332.

in the *Daniels* opinion, the justices reserved the question, noting pointedly that they had "no occasion to consider whether something less than intentional conduct, such as recklessness or 'gross negligence,' is enough to trigger the protections of the Due Process Clause."[99]

More recently, in *County of Sacramento v. Lewis*,[100] the Court elaborated on *Daniels* in a way which suggested that something less than intentional action may be sufficient to deprive individuals of interests protected by the due process clauses. Although *County of Sacramento* involved a substantive rather than a procedural due process claim, the Court's analysis moved seamlessly between the two doctrinal lines. The justices in *County of Sacramento* began on common ground, noting that governmental "conduct intended to injure in some way unjustifiable" typically is sufficient to constitute a deprivation of protected individual interests. They narrowly described *Daniels* as "reject[ing] the lowest common denominator of customary tort liability," that is, negligence, as a constitutionally sufficient marker of due process obligations. The justices then observed that it was "a matter for closer calls" when government officials act "with culpability falling within the middle range, following from something more than negligence but less than intentional conduct, such as recklessness or gross negligence."[101]

The Court in *County of Sacramento* suggested that in order to sustain a claim of *substantive* due process against administrative action "when only midlevel fault has been shown," a claimant must prove that government officials manifested "deliberate indifference" to individual welfare in a setting where the officials enjoyed "the luxury . . . of having time to make unhurried judgments, upon the chance for repeated reflection, largely uncomplicated by the pulls of competing obligations." It is only when "such extended opportunities to do better are teamed with protracted failure even to care, indifference is truly shocking," and thus, a violation of substantive due process.[102]

It is unclear whether the Court would apply the substantive due process approach delineated in *County of Sacramento* to procedural due process claims involving "midlevel fault" by government officials.

(d) The Process That Is Due

"Once it is determined that due process applies," the Supreme Court has written in language that has frequently been quoted,

---

99. *Daniels*, 474 U.S. at 331, 334 n.3.

100. 523 U.S. 833 (1998).

101. *Id*. at 848–49.

102. *Id*. at 853.

"the question remains what process is due."[103] It is easy to forget that the due process clauses do *not* prohibit governmental deprivations of individual interests in life, liberty, and property per se. Indeed, the Constitution explicitly permits such deprivations so long as the individual is afforded "due process." The essential elements of procedural due process are clearly established: Due process obligates government officials to provide (1) notice and (2) opportunity for a hearing before finally depriving an individual of a protected interest.[104] In *Goldberg v. Kelly*, the Court strongly signaled that due process hearings must contain the core components of a judicial trial (see § 3.3). But just as *Roth* contained the explosive potential of *Goldberg* by substituting entitlement analysis for the grievous loss approach in triggering due process, *Mathews v. Eldridge*[105] reversed the *Goldberg* presumption that trial-type hearings were the due process norm.

Mathews v. Eldridge. In *Mathews*, the Court performed a due process audit of federal administrative procedures for terminating disability benefits. The enabling act entitled disabled individuals to receive benefits for the duration of their disability. Eldridge had been receiving disability benefits for nearly four years when the government made a "tentative determination" that he no longer was disabled. Regulations governing the disability-benefits program allowed Eldridge to challenge that determination, as well as to present additional information, but he could do so only in writing. After Eldridge submitted a written challenge, the agency made an "initial determination" that he no longer was disabled and terminated his benefits.

Administrative regulations permitted Eldridge to contest the agency's initial determination in a post-termination hearing before an administrative law judge. These were oral, evidentiary hearings, but they were not adversarial in nature. Agency staff was not represented by counsel, although the claimant was free to hire an attorney. Were Eldridge ultimately to prevail at the post-termination hearing by demonstrating his continuing disability, administrative regulations entitled him to retroactive benefits covering the period of his termination. But rather than challenge the termination of his disability benefits administratively, Eldridge filed suit, claiming that the government's failure to offer him a trial-type hearing before the initial termination of benefits had violated his right to procedural due process. The lower courts, relying on *Goldberg*, sustained Eldridge's claim.

103. Morrissey v. Brewer, 408 U.S. 471, 481 (1972).

104. Logan v. Zimmerman Brush Co., 455 U.S. 422, 433 (1982); see Mathews v. Eldridge, 424 U.S. 319, 333 (1976); Board of Regents of State Colleges v. Roth, 408 U.S. 564, 569–70 (1972).

105. 424 U.S. 319 (1976).

The Court in *Mathews* made clear at the outset that the justices rejected *Goldberg*'s premise that certain core elements were essential for a due process hearing. The justices embraced a contextual approach instead, emphasizing that "due process is flexible and calls for such procedural protections as the particular situation demands." The Court used *Mathews* to instruct judges to measure the constitutional adequacy of administrative due process hearings on an ad hoc basis, focusing on three "distinct factors." The first of the *Mathews* factors is "the private interest . . . affected by the official action" at issue. The second factor assesses "the risk of an erroneous deprivation" of the individual's interests "through the procedures used," together with "the probable value, if any, of additional or substitute procedural safeguards." The final *Mathews* factor evaluates "the Government's interest, including the function involved and the fiscal and administrative burdens that the additional or substitute procedural requirement would entail." The three-part *Mathews* test is best understood as an application cost-benefit balancing. In determining whether an administrative hearing satisfies due process, *Mathews* essentially directs courts to ensure that the value of procedures that a claimant demands beyond those already provided by the government justifies the cost of adding them.[106]

The three *Mathews* factors were hardly new to procedural due process jurisprudence. Indeed, the Court had invoked each of them in *Goldberg*. The innovation of *Mathews* was the justices' use of these familiar criteria to largely reverse *Goldberg*'s requirement of a trial-type hearing before the government terminates an individual's entitlement to receive public assistance.[107] The Court's analysis in *Mathews* of the three factors governing the sufficiency of administrative due process hearings illustrates the new judicial sensibility.

The Individual's Interest. The beneficiaries' interest in both *Goldberg* and *Mathews* was to continue receiving public assistance until the agency finally determined whether to terminate the benefits.[108] In *Mathews*, however, the Court found that the "potential deprivation [was] generally likely to be less" for disability recipients than it had been for the welfare beneficiaries in *Goldberg*. Welfare is a program of last resort. Had the government wrongfully terminated welfare benefits, the *Goldberg* Court had worried, a beneficiary may have been deprived "of the very means by which to live while he waits" for a final administrative determination of his

---

106. *Id.* at 333–35, 348.

107. See *id.* at 343 (establishing the "ordinary principle . . . that something less than an evidentiary hearing is suffi-

cient prior to adverse administrative action").

108. *Id.* at 334–35; *Goldberg*, 397 U.S. at 266.

eligibility. Unlike welfare benefits, disability benefits are not based on financial need. An individual who suffers a wrongful initial termination of benefits may have other sources of income sufficient to tide him or her over. Indeed, the individual may be eligible for welfare benefits.[109]

Risk of Erroneous Deprivation. The second *Mathews* factor considers "the fairness and reliability of the existing pretermination procedures, and the probable value, if any, of additional procedural safeguards."[110] In *Goldberg*, the Court had found that "written submissions [were] a wholly unsatisfactory basis" for an initial termination of an individual's welfare benefits.[111] Yet in *Mathews*, the justices were comfortable with only a "paper hearing" before an initially terminating disability benefits. This was because "[t]he potential value of an evidentiary hearing, or even oral presentation to the decisionmaker, [was] substantially less in [*Mathews*] than in *Goldberg.*"[112]

In justifying that distinction, the Court in *Mathews* relied on the differing "nature of the relevant inquiry" in the two contexts. The relevant inquiry concerning the disability benefits of *Mathews* was whether some physical or mental condition prevented an individual from holding a job. That inquiry, the Court found, usually turned on routine and unbiased medical reports by examining physicians. Such an inquiry lent itself to a paper hearing, the Court held, because it was "sharply focused and easily documented," and because medical professionals could communicate effectively in writing. By contrast, an individual's entitlement to the welfare benefits of *Goldberg* had depended on financial need. Such an inquiry required the assessment of "a wide variety of information." The justices in *Mathews* also reminded that "issues of witness credibility and veracity often [were] critical" in welfare determinations. The Court in *Goldberg* had emphasized the necessity of a trial-type hearing to resolve credibility disputes.[113]

The Government's Interest. The concluding consideration of the *Mathews* test is "the public interest," which includes "the administrative burden and other societal costs" of satisfying the claimant's demand for additional hearing requirements.[114] Whereas the justices could point to distinctions between welfare and disability programs in distinguishing between *Goldberg* and *Mathews* on the first two factors, the principal difference on the third factor arose from a profound shift in judicial outlook between the two decisions.

109. *Mathews*, 424 U.S. at 340–43; *Goldberg*, 397 U.S. at 264.

110. *Mathews*, 424 U.S. at 343.

111. *Goldberg*, 397 U.S. at 269.

112. *Mathews*, 424 U.S. at 344–45.

113. See *id.* at 343–45; *Goldberg*, 397 U.S. at 269.

114. *Mathews*, 424 U.S. at 347.

For the *Goldberg* Court, the public interest implicated by the termination of public assistance moved in opposing directions. The justices recognized the cost savings of summary decisionmaking processes. But they also understood that the wrongful termination of eligible beneficiaries compromised the public's interest, as determined by the legislature, in making public assistance available. Indeed, the Court in *Goldberg* ultimately determined that the public interest in avoiding wrongful terminations of welfare recipients outweighed the government's economic interest in summary termination processes.[115]

The Court in *Mathews*, in stark contrast to *Goldberg*, concentrated almost exclusively on the economic efficiency side of the dueling public interests at stake in entitlement programs. The justices in *Mathews* emphasized what the *Goldberg* Court had resisted, that the interest in administrative justice "[a]t some point . . . may be outweighed by the cost."[116] They also heeded Justice Hugo Black's warning, registered as the lone dissenter in *Goldberg*, that adding procedure threatened to harm beneficiaries by diverting scarce public resources from funding benefits to covering administrative costs.[117]

Mathews, like *Roth*, was a product of the chastening experience of *Goldberg*'s due process revolution, which had worried the justices that the economic cost and administrative burden of broadly "constitutionalizing" administrative procedures would become unbearable. The Court in *Mathews* was careful to note that "[f]inancial cost alone is not a controlling weight in determining whether due process requires a particular procedural safeguard prior to some administrative decision." But *Mathews* nevertheless elevated the interest of the government in "conserving scarce fiscal and administrative resources" well beyond the level it had registered in *Goldberg*.[118]

Mathews not only exhibited the justices' heightened sensitivity to the costs associated with the trial-type hearings endorsed in *Goldberg*, it also revealed a striking skepticism toward the benefits that the "judicial model of an evidentiary hearing" offered to the administrative process. Administrative agencies, the justices reminded, differed from courts in their "origin and function." It thus stood to reason that courts should not reflexively require that agencies provide trial-type hearings whenever due process applies.

Having dislodged the requirements of due process from the traditional trappings of the judicial trial, the justices in *Mathews*

---

115. *Goldberg*, 397 U.S. at 266.

116. *Mathews*, 424 U.S. at 348; see *Goldberg*, 397 U.S. at 266.

117. *Mathews*, 424 U.S. at 348; *Goldberg*, 397 U.S. at 278–79 (Black, J., dissenting).

118. *Mathews*, 424 U.S. at 347–48.

were far more willing than they had been in *Goldberg* to accord "substantial weight ... to the good-faith judgments" of government administrators in devising procedures that "assure fair consideration of the entitlement claims of individuals." All *Mathews* asked was that a due process hearing guarantee individuals "a meaningful opportunity to present their case."[119]

Mathews's skepticism of the utility of the judicial model in the administrative process has remained a prominent theme in procedural due process jurisprudence. The Court's decision in *Walters v. National Association of Radiation Survivors*[120] perhaps provides the most striking example. In *Walters*, the Court rejected a due process challenge to a statutory provision limiting to $10 the fee that veterans could pay to "an attorney or agent" for assistance with a claim for certain benefits. A veterans group complained that the fee limitation violated due process because it effectively prevented veterans from obtaining legal representation in presenting their claims for benefits. Although *Goldberg* had included the right of individuals to be represented by counsel as one of the essential elements of a due process hearing,[121] the Court in *Walters* upheld the $10–fee limitation precisely because without it, claimants would be able "freely" to retain counsel in benefits proceedings. Legal representation of claimants, warned the justices, would undermine the congressional preference for a simple and nonadversarial process of determining veterans' benefits.[122]

The Due Process Bottom Line. The three-part *Mathews* test continues to provide the framework for determining the constitutional adequacy of administrative due process hearing procedures.[123] But the ad hoc, contextual nature of *Mathews* makes it difficult to generalize about specific elements of due process hearings. This difficulty explains the lack of specificity in the Supreme Court's statements describing the bottom line of procedural due process. The justices commonly state that due process requires agencies, at minimum, to provide "*some* kind of notice" and "*some* kind of hearing," as "appropriate," given "the nature of the case," to guarantee individuals "a meaningful opportunity to present their

---

119. *Id.* at 348–49.

120. 473 U.S. 305 (1985).

121. *Goldberg*, 397 U.S. at 270–71.

122. *Walters*, 473 U.S. at 323–26.

123. *Mathews* does not apply to the notice requirement of procedural due process. See Dusenbery v. United States, 534 U.S. 161, 167–68 (2002). The Court instead applies the test formulated in *Mullane v. Central Hanover Bank & Trust Co.*, 339 U.S. 306, 319 (1950), which requires that notice be "reasonably calculated, under all the circumstances, to apprise interested parties of the pendency of the action" against them. See *Dusenbery*, 534 U.S. at 168. For a detailed analysis of the notice requirement of procedural due process, see RHONDA WASSERMAN, PROCEDURAL DUE PROCESS: A REFERENCE GUIDE TO THE UNITED STATES CONSTITUTION 129–61 (2004).

case."[124] As *Mathews*, *Walters*, and scores of other decisions make clear, informal adjudicatory processes short of a trial-type hearing generally satisfy that constitutional bottom line. Just how informal an administrative due process hearing may be, however, remains unclear.

Consultation Hearings. The Supreme Court in a variety of settings has held an "opportunity for informal consultation" with government officials to be a constitutionally acceptable due process hearing.[125] Indeed, the justices accepted informal consultations even before *Mathews*. In *Goss v. Lopez*,[126] the Court held that public school students were entitled to a due process hearing before being suspended from school on charges of misconduct. But the Court held that due process was satisfied, at least for a brief suspension, by "informal give-and-take between student and disciplinarian." More specifically, *Goss* required that school disciplinarians give a student suspected of wrongdoing "oral or written notice of the charges against him and, if he denies them, an explanation of the evidence the authorities have and an opportunity to present his side of the story." Both notice and hearing could follow immediately after the alleged misconduct.[127]

The informal, oral "consultation hearings" approved in *Goss* (sometimes called "*Goss* hearings") provide a starting point for analyzing whether the government in any particular instance has satisfied the baseline due process requirement of affording individuals a meaningful opportunity to present their case. But in cases where the Court has held a consultation hearing to satisfy procedural due process, special circumstances encouraged the justices to accept this minimal form of oral hearing. It was important in *Goss*, for example, that the students had served only a "short," 10–day suspension.[128] And in *Cleveland Board of Education v. Loudermill*,[129] the Court upheld a *Goss* hearing before the initial termination of a tenured public employee, relying "in part" on the employee's opportunity for a trial-type administrative hearing after the job termination. The Court in *Loudermill* essentially equated the pretermination process with a reasonable cause hearing.[130]

---

124. See Goss v. Lopez, 419 U.S. 565, 579 (1975); *Mathews*, 424 U.S. at 348–49; *Mullane*, 339 U.S. at 313.

125. See, e.g., Memphis Light, Gas and Water Division v. Craft, 436 U.S. 1, 16 n.17 (1978).

126. 419 U.S. 565 (1975).

127. *Id.* at 581–82, 584. See also Board of Curators v. Horowitz, 435 U.S. 78, 86 (1978) (due process requirements "far less stringent" for academic dismissal than for disciplinary suspension).

128. *Goss*, 419 U.S. at 581 (consultation hearing approved for "suspension of 10 days or less").

129. 470 U.S. 532 (1985).

130. *Id.* at 545–46 (before the initial termination, a tenured public employee was "entitled to oral or written notice of the charges against him, an explanation of the employer's evidence, and an opportunity to present his side of the story").

In situations where the individual's interest weighs more heavily than in *Goss* and *Loudermill*, or where the need for accuracy is greater, courts should require more than oral consultation to satisfy due process hearing requirements. But although expanded hearing processes likely will be required in some instances, all signs in contemporary procedural due process jurisprudence point to *Goldberg* remaining the exception to the general rule that "something less" than a full, trial-type hearing satisfies the requirements of procedural due process.[131]

Paper Hearings. If something more than an oral consultation process at times is required to satisfy procedural due process, on occasion something less than an oral process may suffice as well. *Mathews* itself provides an example of such an occasion. The Court there approved a "paper hearing" for disability terminations, at least where beneficiaries had the opportunity for a trial-type, administrative hearing after the termination of their benefits. In addition to that post-termination safeguard, it was important in *Mathews* that disability determinations lent themselves to written submissions. A paper hearing was sufficient in the disability-benefits program because the Court concluded that it adequately protected individuals against an erroneous initial termination of their benefits.[132]

The three-part test of *Mathews* leaves open the possibility that something less than an oral consultation hearing may satisfy procedural due process even in the absence of a full post-deprivation hearing. Although the Supreme Court has not considered this issue, the D.C. Circuit's decision in *Gray Panthers v. Schweiker* (*Gray Panthers II*)[133] underscores this possibility. *Gray Panthers II* involved a procedural due process challenge to administrative procedures for appeals from the denial of small claims to certain Medicare benefits. The regulations allowed claimants to challenge in writing the denial of claims under $100. The regulations also permitted these claimants to telephone an administrator familiar with their dispute. The court of appeals held that this process for handling appeals from the denial of small claims would satisfy due process if a significant number or percentage of the disputed claims did not "involve factual determinations hinging on credibility or veracity." In the absence of such a showing, the court held, due process required informal, oral consultation (*Goss*) hearings to settle the small claims.[134]

No Hearing. Because the purpose of a due process hearing is to resolve factual disputes, an individual is entitled to a hearing

---

131. *Mathews*, 424 U.S. at 343.

132. *Id.* at 343–45.

133. 716 F.2d 23 (D.C.Cir. 1983).

134. *Id.* at 36–38.

only when there is disagreement on the facts relevant to the claim.[135] This principle, of course, is consistent with the practice of federal courts, which dispose of civil actions by summary judgment when there is "no genuine issue as to any material fact" (F.R.CIV.P. 56(c)).

(e) The Timing of Due Process

Procedural due process claims require courts to decide not only *whether* an individual is entitled to a hearing and *what* procedures that hearing must include. They also require a determination of *when* the government must provide a due process hearing. As a general rule, due process demands that individuals be afforded "a meaningful opportunity to present their case" before even temporary suspensions of their interests in property or liberty.[136] The Supreme Court has described this "right to *prior* notice and a hearing" as a "central" requirement of due process.[137] The primary purpose of requiring a predeprivation hearing is to avoid "unfair or mistaken deprivations" of an individual's constitutionally protected interests.[138]

The government may argue in any particular case, however, that the public interest in a swift decision overrides an individual's right to a predeprivation hearing. The courts use the three-part test of *Mathews v. Eldridge*[139] in deciding whether to make an exception to the general rule requiring a prior hearing. For the most part, the justices have limited these exceptions to three types of cases. The first, and most solidly established, exception is reserved for "exigent circumstances."[140] Secondly, in the absence of exigent circumstances, the Court on occasion has allowed postdeprivation judicial remedies to substitute for a predeprivation administrative hearing. And finally, a postdeprivation hearing may satisfy due process when it would be "impractical to provide predeprivation process."[141]

Exigent Circumstances. In situations where the government "must act quickly," the Court has held that the availability of an adequate and reasonably prompt postdeprivation process satisfies due process.[142] In *Mathews*'s terms, the "urgency" of government

135. See Connecticut Dep't of Public Safety v. Doe, 538 U.S. 1, 4, 7–8 (2003); Gilbert v. Homar, 520 U.S. 924, 933–34 (1997).

136. See *Mathews*, 424 U.S. at 333.

137. United States v. James Daniel Good Real Property, 510 U.S. 43, 53 (1993) (emphasis added).

138. Fuentes v. Shevin, 407 U.S. 67, 81 (1972); see *James Daniel Good Real Property*, 510 U.S. at 53.

139. 424 U.S. 319, 334–35 (1976); see *James Daniel Good Real Property*, 510 U.S. at 53; Zinermon v. Burch, 494 U.S. 113, 128–30 (1990).

140. See *James Daniel Good Real Property*, 510 U.S. at 46.

141. Gilbert v. Homar, 520 U.S. 924, 930 (1997).

142. *Id.* at 924, 930 (1997); Barry v. Barchi, 443 U.S. 55 (1979) (requirement of prompt post-deprivation hearing); see also *James Daniel Good Real Property*,

action overwhelms the individual's interest in predprivation notice and hearing in these "extraordinary situations."[143]

The Court long ago established the exception for exigent circumstances in *North American Cold Storage Co. v. City of Chicago*.[144] In *North American Cold Storage*, city inspectors had attempted to seize poultry that a cold-storage company held for a wholesaler. The inspectors intended to destroy the poultry because, they claimed, it had become "unfit for human consumption." The company in turn claimed that the city's action violated due process because it had received neither notice nor opportunity for a hearing "before the seizure and destruction of the food." The Court upheld the city's summary seizure because tainted poultry created an "emergency" situation that threatened "the lives and health" of the city's residents. The justices were satisfied that the company's interests were "amply protected" by its "right" to file suit against the city after the seizure. If in that suit the court found that the company's poultry had not been tainted, the company would recover the value of the poultry that the city had wrongfully seized.[145]

The Court's decision in *Federal Deposit Insurance Corp. v. Mallen*[146] brings *North American Cold Storage* up to date. In *Mallen*, the justices upheld a federal statute authorizing the FDIC to suspend from office an indicted officer of a federally insured bank without a prior hearing. The *Mallen* Court explained the *North American Cold Storage* principle: "An important government interest, accompanied by a substantial assurance that the deprivation is not baseless or unwarranted, may in limited cases demanding prompt action justify postponing the opportunity to be heard until after the initial deprivation." Congress had found that summary suspension of indicted bank officers "may be necessary to protect the interests of depositors and to maintain public confidence in our banking institutions." Such an interest, the Court in *Mallen* held, was sufficiently important to delay due process protections until after the suspension, at least with the assurance provided by a grand jury indictment that the suspension was neither "baseless" nor "unwarranted."[147]

---

510 U.S. at 59–60 ("pressing need for prompt action" by government).

143. Boddie v. Connecticut, 401 U.S. 371, 379 (1971) ("extraordinary situations"); see also *James Daniel Good Real Property*, 510 U.S. at 59–60 ("executive urgency").

144. 211 U.S. 306 (1908).

145. *Id.* at 308–09, 314–16, 319–20.

146. 486 U.S. 230 (1988).

147. *Id.* at 231–32, 240–41. For other examples of the Court's application of the exception for exigent circumstances, see Hodel v. Virginia Surface Mining & Reclamation Ass'n, 452 U.S. 264, 298–303 (1981) (cessation of surface-mining operations); Barry v. Barchi, 443 U.S. 55 (1979) (suspension of horse trainer's license); Makey v. Montrym, 443 U.S. 1 (1979) (suspension of driver's license for refusing to take a breath-analysis test); Dixon v. Love, 431 U.S. 105, 112–15

Availability of Postdeprivation Judicial Remedies. The Supreme Court on occasion has accepted the availability of postdeprivation judicial remedies as an adequate substitute for predeprivation notice and hearing even when there was no emergency. Unlike the exigent circumstances exception, the special consideration in these cases seems not to have been any special government interest in swift action. The key to this exception lies in the remaining two *Mathews* factors. The justices sense that the deprivation does not impose a "serious loss" on the individual, and that the agency's decisionmaking procedures "are sufficiently reliable to minimize the risk of erroneous determination."[148]

The Supreme Court pioneered this exception in *Ingraham v. Wright*.[149] In *Ingraham*, the Court held that corporal punishment of public school children constituted a deprivation of liberty within the meaning of the due process clauses, but that judicial remedies were "fully adequate to afford due process." State law subjected teachers to civil actions for damages, and in extreme cases to criminal penalties, for inflicting excessive corporal punishment. Largely because of the availability of those remedies, the justices were satisfied that a predeprivation hearing was not necessary to protect students from excessive or unjustified corporal punishment. The potential civil and criminal liability, coupled with "the openness of the school environment," created a deterrent effect on school teachers and administrators that offered "significant protection" to students.[150]

The Court in *Lujan v. G & G Fire Sprinklers, Inc.*[151] again emphasized the lack of necessity for a prior hearing in holding the availability of a postdeprivation judicial remedy to satisfy due process. In *G & G Fire Sprinklers*, a state agency had withheld payments to a contractor on a public works project because the agency believed that the contractor had failed to comply with certain provisions of the contract. State law permitted the contractor to contest that withholding by suing the state agency for breach of contract. The contractor in *G & G Fire Sprinklers* instead claimed that the state's withholding violated procedural due process because it had confiscated a property interest (the contract right to full payment) without notice or opportunity for a hearing. The Court rejected the claim. The key consideration for the justices was the weakness of the contractor's property interest. The state's withholding, the Court reasoned, had denied the contractor merely

(1977) (suspension of driver's license for repeated traffic violations); Ewing v. Mytinger & Casselberry, 339 U.S. 594 (1950) (seizure of misbranded food supplements); Phillips v. Commissioner, 283 U.S. 589 (1931) (collection of federal taxes).

148. Memphis Light, Gas and Water Div. v. Craft, 436 U.S. 1, 19 (1978).

149. 430 U.S. 651 (1977).

150. *Id.* at 672, 676–78.

151. 532 U.S. 189 (2001).

of a contractual "claim for payment" instead of "any present entitlement." In the Court's judgment, the breach of contract suit "fully protected" the contractor in enforcing the claim for full payment under the contract.[152]

One must not overread *Ingraham* and *G & G Fire Sprinklers*. If the availability of postdeprivation judicial remedies *always* satisfied due process, predeprivation notice and hearing seldom would be required. The Court has recognized that judicial processes usually are inferior to a predeprivation "administrative remedy" because they typically proceed too slowly to offer "an effective safeguard against an erroneous deprivation."[153] There are thus many cases in which the justices have ruled that postdeprivation judicial remedies did not provide an "adequate substitute" for predeprivation notice and hearing.[154]

Impracticality. The Supreme Court has held that "the impracticality of providing any meaningful predeprivation process, when coupled with the availability of some meaningful means by which to assess the propriety of the [government's] action at some time after the initial [deprivation], can satisfy the requirements of procedural due process."[155] The Court created this exception in two prison cases. In *Parratt v. Taylor*,[156] a prisoner had sought compensation for the prison mail room's loss of a package that had been delivered for him. In *Hudson v. Palmer*,[157] another prisoner had sought compensation for the intentional destruction of his personal property during a search of his cell. The actions by prison employees in both cases violated prison rules. And in both cases, the Court held that the property deprivations suffered by the inmates did not violate procedural due process, provided "a meaningful postdeprivation remedy for the loss [was] available."[158] The Court justified the rulings in *Parratt* and in *Hudson* by pinning responsibility for the deprivation on the state employees rather than on the state. The prisoners had lost their property because of the "random and

---

152. *Id.* at 185–96.

153. *Memphis Light*, 436 U.S. at 20–22.

154. *Id.* at 20. For other examples of cases in which the Court has held that the availability of postdeprivation judicial remedies did not trump the requirement of predeprivation process, see North Georgia Finishing, Inc. v. Di–Chem, Inc., 419 U.S. 601 (1975); Goss v. Lopez, 419 U.S. 565, 581 (1975); Fuentes v. Shevin, 407 U.S. 67 (1972); Bell v. Burson, 402 U.S. 535, 536 (1971); Boddie v. Connecticut, 401 U.S. 371 (1971); Sniadach v. Family Finance Corp., 395 U.S. 337 (1969). For a discus-

sion of the requirement of adequate alternative remedy, see Richard H. Fallon, *Some Confusion about Due Process, Judicial Review, and Constitutional Remedies*, 93 COLUM. L. REV. 309, 356–66 (1993).

155. Parratt v. Taylor, 451 U.S. 527, 539 (1981), overruled in part on other grounds, Daniels v. Williams, 474 U.S. 327, 330–31 (1986).

156. 451 U.S. 527 (1981), overruled in part on other grounds, Daniels v. Williams, 474 U.S. 327, 330–31 (1986).

157. 468 U.S. 517 (1984).

158. See *id.* at 533.

unauthorized conduct of a state employee," rather than as a result of the faithful operation of "established state procedure." And because the employees' actions in *Parratt* and *Hudson* were unpredictable, it had been "impossible" for the state to provide "a meaningful hearing before the deprivation."[159]

The Court underscored the limited reach of *Parratt* and *Hudson* in *Zinermon v. Burch*,[160] emphasizing that the impracticality exception absolved the government of its constitutional responsibility to provide predeprivation process only when it was "impossible" for it to do so because of the unpredictability of a government employee's unauthorized action. In *Zinermon*, an individual had been voluntarily admitted into a state mental health facility even though he had not been competent to give informed consent for his admission, as state law had required. The individual claimed that because hospital employees knew, or at least should have known, that he lacked the mental competence to provide informed consent, he was entitled to the hearing that due process required before involuntary commitment to a state mental hospital. The state, relying on *Parratt* and *Hudson*, responded that the patient's admission was the result of a "random and unauthorized" action by employees of the hospital, and thus that the individual's redress was limited to the postdeprivation remedies that state law made available to him.[161]

The Court refused to apply the impracticality exception in *Zinermon* because the justices believed that the state could have devised, and thus should have devised, a process that would have reduced the risk of admitting to mental health facilities patients who are willing to sign a form for voluntary admission, but who are not competent to give their informed consent to admission. When the state authorized its employees "to deprive persons of liberty," the Court wrote, "the Constitution imposed [a] concomitant duty to see that no deprivation occur without adequate procedural protections." The nature of mental illness made it "foreseeable" that persons who were mentally ill would be unable to give informed consent to admission. The state, moreover, was "in a position to predict or avert" the voluntary admission of an incompetent patient. Thus, in contrast to *Parratt* and *Hudson*, the state in *Zinermon* bore responsibility for its employees' deprivation of the mental patient's liberty because it had "disregarded [its] duty to ensure that the proper procedures were followed."[162]

* * *

---

159. *Parratt*, 451 U.S. at 541, 543; see *Hudson*, 468 U.S. at 534. Even though the state had not authorized the employees' actions, the actions qualified as state action. *Parratt*, 451 U.S. at 541, 543.

160. 494 U.S. 113 (1990).

161. *Id.* at 136–39.

162. *Id.* at 132–39.

The ancient guarantee that government officials may deprive individuals of their liberty or property only through due process of law occupies an important doctrinal position in administrative law. But as this chapter has shown, the procedural rights that the due process clauses provide to individuals are importantly limited as well. Procedural due process applies only to administrative adjudications, and then, only when an individual's property interests or liberty interests are at risk of deprivation. And even when procedural due process applies, it often requires only informal administrative decisionmaking processes. In some instances, judicial remedies made available to individuals after an initial deprivation of a protected interest are constitutionally acceptable.

The role of procedural due process in administrative law is not limited to the constitutional rights that it affords to individuals, however. The time-honored values served by due process—such as, the fairness of governmental action and the rule of law—pervade administrative law. As the remainder of this book manifests, due process values have deeply influenced Congress and the courts in their development and enforcement of the maze of sub-constitutional rules that govern the administrative process.

Chapter 4

THE ADMINISTRATIVE PROCEDURE ACT AND THE PROCEDURAL FORMS OF AGENCY ACTION

Constitutional doctrine has an important but limited role in administrative law. While the original Constitution provided important rules guiding the creation of administrative agencies and the exercise of administrative power, the framers to a considerable degree left the decisions on these questions for the political processes they had set in motion (see Chapter 2). Similarly, the guarantee of procedural due process in the amended Constitution provided important, but limited, protections of individual rights that government administration may put at risk (see Chapter 3).

It took a while, but Congress addressed this constitutional deficit as a first order of business after the Second World War when it passed, unanimously, the Administrative Procedure Act of 1946 ("APA")(see § 1.5(d)).[1] The APA functions as a sub-constitution for administrative agencies: It provides a legal, yet flexible, framework within which virtually all federal agencies take actions affecting individual rights. The broad coverage of the Administrative Procedure Act, paradoxically, encouraged Congress to follow the example of the Constitution's framers by keeping the statute short and simple. Partly for that reason, the APA, like the Constitution, has been remarkably stable: It has been amended only sparingly since

---

1.   5 U.S.C. §§ 551, 553–559, 701–706.

its enactment over half a century ago.[2] Also like the Constitution, the long-term stability of the statutory text has been purchased, at least in part, at the price of the APA's broad provisions and strategic silences, and relatedly, of the freedom courts have felt to adjust their interpretation of the Act's requirements over time.

There are differences between the Constitution and the APA, of course. For one thing, the Constitution controls the substance of government authority as well as the procedure of governmental decisionmaking, while the focus of the APA is squarely on procedure. *What* an agency may do is governed by the agency's enabling act. The APA controls *how* agencies may exercise their substantive authority, as well as how courts may review the exercise of that authority. Yet the APA's enactment of procedural requirements governing administrative decisionmaking and its provisions for judicial review of agency action serve a critical role in checking the substantive power of federal agencies.

Another difference between the APA, which is a generally applicable statute, and the Constitution, which is the fundamental law of the land, is that Congress can override the APA. The Administrative Procedure Act did not "limit or repeal additional requirements imposed by statute or otherwise required by law," and the APA remains subject to subsequent modification by statute, at least "to the extent [Congress] does so expressly" (APA § 559). In effect, the APA provides default rules that agencies must follow unless those rules are trumped by another statute. Courts are reluctant to interpret acts of Congress to modify or to supersede the provisions of the APA, however. Recognizing that the function of the APA is to "bring uniformity to a field full of variation and diversity,"[3] statutory variance of APA requirements "must be clear."[4]

The Administrative Procedure Act is divided into two parts. The first part governs the procedures of agency decisionmaking (APA §§ 553–559). The second part governs judicial review of

2. Two significant substantive amendments to the APA supplemented, rather than changed, the original act. See the Freedom of Information Act (1966), 5 U.S.C. § 552, and the Privacy Act (1974), 5 U.S.C. § 552a. Two additional amendments tweaked the provisions of the original APA. See the Government in the Sunshine Act (1976), 5 U.S.C. § 557(d) (adding prohibition against ex parte communications in formal proceedings); Pub. L. No. 94–574, 90 Stat. 2721 (1976) (amending 5 U.S.C. §§ 702–703 to eliminate defense of sovereign immunity in suits against the federal government for relief other than

non-monetary damages). In 1978, Congress amended the APA to change the title of agency "hearing examiners" to "administrative law judges." See Pub. L. No. 95–251, 92 Stat. 183 (1978).

3. Dickinson v. Zurko, 527 U.S. 150, 155 (1999); see Wong Yang Sung v. McGrath, 339 U.S. 33, 41 (1950).

4. See *Dickinson*, 527 U.S. at 155; see also Director, Office of Workers' Compensation Programs v. Greenwich Collieries, 512 U.S. 267, 271 (1994) (the Court "do[es] not lightly presume exemptions to the APA").

agency action (APA §§ 701–706). The provisions of the APA regarding agency procedure are considered in this chapter, as well as in Chapters 5 and 6. The APA's judicial review provisions are considered in Chapters 7 and 8.

The procedural provisions of the Administrative Procedure Act, and thus the APA's procedural requirements for agency action, are in turn organized according to two distinctions. The first distinction is between rulemaking and adjudication. The second is between formal and informal proceedings. As shown in Figure 4–1, the interaction of these two distinctions yields four types of agency action—formal rulemaking, informal rulemaking, formal adjudication, and informal adjudication.[5] According to the APA, every final agency action affecting individual rights falls into one—and only one—of those four categories. For present purposes, it is sufficient to know that the APA provides a trial-type procedure for formal proceedings (whether rulemaking or adjudication), a notice-and-comment procedure for informal rulemaking, and essentially no procedure for informal adjudication.

	Formal	v.	Informal
Rulemaking	Formal Rulemaking (§§ 553, 556-557)		Informal Rulemaking (§ 553)
v.			
Adjudication	Formal Adjudication (§§ 554, 556-557)		Informal Adjudication

Figure 4-1: The Forms of Administration Action Under the APA

In determining the procedural requirements of the APA for any agency action affecting individual rights, then, one must follow a two-step analysis. One must first determine whether the action is rulemaking or adjudication within the meaning of the APA. The APA's distinction between rulemaking and adjudication is considered in § 4.1. Next, one must determine whether the APA requires the agency to adopt formal or informal proceedings. The APA's distinction between formal and informal proceedings is considered in § 4.2. The scope of agency discretion to choose between proceeding by rulemaking or adjudication is considered in § 4.3.

I draw on the *Attorney General's Manual on the Administrative Procedure Act* (*"Attorney General's Manual"*) as an interpretive guide to the APA throughout the remainder of this book.[6] The

---

5. A similar chart appears in an Appendix to *The Federal Administrative Procedure Act: Codification or Reform?*, 56 YALE L.J. 670, 705 (1947).

6. The *Attorney General's Manual* is reprinted in WILLIAM F. FUNK, et al., FEDERAL ADMINISTRATIVE PROCEDURE SOURCEBOOK 33–171 (3d ed. 2000).

United States Department of Justice prepared the *Attorney General's Manual* in 1947, just one year after Congress passed the APA, in order to advise federal agencies on the meaning of that landmark statute. As a source of statutory interpretation, the *Attorney General's Manual* has the strengths and weaknesses that one would expect from an analysis of a statute of great importance to federal agencies by the law firm for the federal government. The Supreme Court, however, has embraced the authoritativeness of the *Attorney General's Manual* from time to time,[7] and it has remained a leading source of insight for administrative lawyers.

§ 4.1 The Distinction Between Rulemaking and Adjudication Pursuant to the Administrative Procedure Act

Near the beginning of the twentieth century, the Supreme Court in *Londoner v. City and County of Denver*[1] and *Bi-Metallic Investment Co. v. State Board of Equalization*[2] distinguished between rulemaking and adjudication in defining the application of procedural due process requirements to administrative decisions. The justices noted several differences between rulemaking and adjudication in those early cases, but the key to the *Londoner-Bi-Metallic* distinction was the distinct nature of agency decisionmaking in the two types of action. According to this dichotomy, rulemaking involves a *generalized* determination by the agency, while adjudication is an *individualized* decision. When agencies engage in rulemaking, they resemble a legislature by creating "a rule of conduct" governing a group of individuals. When agencies adjudicate, they resemble a court by applying legal rules to an individual on "individual grounds" (see § 3.1).[3]

The drafters of the Administrative Procedure Act drew on the distinction between rulemaking and adjudication when they devised their procedural matrix for administrative action. The APA established two means by which administrative agencies may act with "the force of law." Agencies may use rulemaking to establish "binding" norms of conduct, or they may create "binding precedents" through adjudication.[4] The APA's drafters, however, distin-

---

7. See, e.g., Steadman v. SEC, 450 U.S. 91, 103 n.22 (1981); Chrysler Corp. v. Brown, 441 U.S. 281, 302 n.31 (1979); Vermont Yankee Nuclear Power Corp. v. Natural Resources Defense Council, Inc., 435 U.S. 519, 546 (1978).

§ 4.1

1. 210 U.S. 373 (1908).

2. 239 U.S. 441 (1915).

3. See *Bi-Metallic*, 239 U.S. at 445–46.

4. Pacific Gas & Electric Co. v. Federal Power Commission, 506 F.2d 33, 38 (D.C.Cir. 1974); see also *Attorney General's Manual on the Administrative Procedure Act* 50 (1947), reprinted in WILLIAM F. FUNK, et al., FEDERAL ADMINISTRATIVE PROCEDURE SOURCEBOOK 33–171 (3d ed. 2000) (APA "is based upon a

guished between rulemaking and adjudication on different grounds than those identified by the Supreme Court in *Londoner* and *Bi-Metallic*.

The APA's rulemaking-adjudication distinction is derived from four interrelated provisions of section 551, the act's definitional section. The key provision is section 551(4), which defines a "rule" as "an agency statement of general or particular applicability and future effect designed to implement, interpret, or prescribe law or policy." Section 551(6) labels as "orders" all final agency action that does not fit section 551(4)'s definition of a rule. Under the APA, rulemaking and adjudication are simply the processes that agencies use to produce the two forms of action at their disposal. Rulemaking is the "agency process for formulating, amending, or repealing a rule" (APA § 551(5)), while adjudication is the "agency process for the formulation of an order" (APA § 551(7)).

According to section 551(4), agency rules are distinguished by their "future effect."[5] Although it received no mention in *Londoner* and *Bi-Metallic*, the element of prospectivity has been a traditional means of distinguishing between rulemaking and adjudication. In *Prentis v. Atlantic Coast Line Co.*,[6] which the Supreme Court decided in the same year as *Londoner*, the justices observed that actions that are "legislative . . . in kind" (like rules) typically "look to the future." They apply prospectively, requiring individuals to conform their future conduct to the new rule.[7] American legal tradition discourages imposition of liability on individuals for their conduct *before* a legislative-type rule takes effect.[8] In the *Prentis* dichotomy, actions that are "judicial in kind" (like orders) look to the past. Adjudication, whether by agency or court, "investigates, declares and enforces liabilities as they stand on present or past facts and under laws supposed already to exist."[9] American legal tradition discourages adjudication that looks too far into the future by barring litigation of "premature" disputes.[10]

Despite its pedigree, the element of prospectivity is an unreliable guide to the rulemaking-adjudication distinction. Although it is

broad and logical dichotomy between rule making and adjudication").

5. See *Attorney General's Manual, supra* note 4, 14–15.

6. 211 U.S. 210 (1908).

7. *Id.* at 226.

8. See U.S. Const. art. I., § 9, cl. 3 (prohibiting enactment of ex post facto laws by Congress), § 10, cl. 1 (prohibiting enactment of ex post facto laws by state legislatures); Landgraf v. USI Film Products, 511 U.S. 244, 265 (1994) ("the presumption against retroactive legislation is deeply rooted in our jurisprudence").

9. *Prentis*, 211 U.S. at 226.

10. See Abbott Laboratories v. Gardner, 387 U.S. 136, 148 (1967). For a discussion of the ripeness doctrine in the administrative context, see § 7.3(b).

hardly the norm, legislatures can mandate the retroactive application of laws, at least outside the criminal context.[11] Agencies also may issue retroactive rules, at least when Congress expressly has granted them the authority to do so.[12] And of course, judicial decisions typically have "future effect" as precedent. In addition, it is hardly unusual for courts to grant prospective relief or to announce new rules of law when deciding cases. The APA itself legitimates the prospective potential of administrative adjudication by noting that agencies may issue "injunctive" orders (APA § 551(6)).

It should not be too surprising, then, that notwithstanding the provisions of section 551(4)-(7), courts generally fall back on the *Londoner-Bi-Metallic* distinction when determining whether agency action constitutes rulemaking or adjudication under the APA.[13] Courts sometimes invoke the element of prospectivity as well, but the key determinant of the rulemaking-adjudication distinction, in applying the APA as well as procedural due process, is whether the relevant agency action was generalized, and therefore rulemaking, or individualized, and therefore adjudication. But because of the APA's different formulation of the rulemaking-adjudication distinction, it remains possible, at least in theory, to categorize agency action differently for due process and for APA purposes. Such a disconnect may arise, for example, when an agency sets future rates for a single entity. Section 551(4) of the APA explicitly categorizes such ratemaking as rulemaking, while the *Londoner-Bi-Metallic* distinction points in the opposite direction.[14]

Another peculiarity of the APA's rulemaking-adjudication distinction is the residual, catch-all nature of adjudication within the meaning of the act. Adjudication includes final agency dispositions of all "matter[s] other than rule making" (APA § 551(6)). As noted in the *Attorney General's Manuel*, that broad definition means that the APA affixes the adjudication label to many administrative actions that bear little or no resemblance to traditional judicial functions.[15]

11. See, e.g., Immigration and Naturalization Service v. St. Cyr, 533 U.S. 289, 316 (2001).

12. Bowen v. Georgetown University Hosp., 488 U.S. 204, 208–09 (1988).

13. See SECTION OF ADMINISTRATIVE LAW AND REGULATORY PRACTICE OF AMERICAN BAR ASSOCIATION, A BLACKLETTER STATEMENT OF FEDERAL ADMINISTRATIVE LAW 21 (2004).

14. See United States v. Florida East Coast Railway Co., 410 U.S. 224, 244 (1973).

15. *Attorney General's Manual, supra* note 4, at 40. For a helpful discussion of the APA's distinction between rulemaking and adjudication, and a proposal for change, see Ronald M. Levin, *The Case for (Finally) Fixing the APA's Definition of "Rule,"* 56 ADMIN. L. REV. 1077, 1083–88 (2004).

§ 4.2 The Distinction Between Formal and Informal Proceedings Pursuant to the Administrative Procedure Act

The APA distinguishes between formal and informal proceedings in two "trigger" provisions, one controlling rulemaking (APA § 553(c)) and the other governing adjudication (APA § 554(a)). Both trigger provisions use identical language to establish a default rule favoring informal administrative proceedings. An agency is free to act by informal rulemaking or by informal adjudication unless its enabling act requires that a rule be "made" or that an adjudication be "determined" "on the record after opportunity for an agency hearing" (APA §§ 553(c), 554(a)). An agency decision is "on the record" if it is based exclusively on evidence presented at an administrative hearing, together with the parties' written submissions during the course of the proceeding (APA § 556(e)).[1] The APA's trigger provisions are diagramed in Figure 4–2.

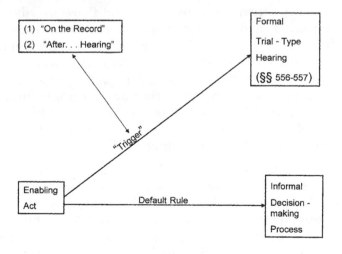

Figure 4 – 2: APA "Trigger" Provisions

Reviewing courts have been unable to agree on whether the identical language of the APA's trigger provisions for formal rulemaking and for formal adjudication have the same meaning. The unresolved issue is whether the distinction between rulemaking and adjudication requires a different interpretation of section

§ 4.2

1. See *Attorney General's Manual on the Administrative Procedure Act* 41–43 (1947), reprinted in WILLIAM F. FUNK, et al., FEDERAL ADMINISTRATIVE PROCEDURE SOURCEBOOK 33–171 (3d ed. 2000).

553(c), governing rulemaking, and section 554(a), governing adjudication.

(a) Informal Rulemaking v. Formal Rulemaking

The procedures associated with informal rulemaking are the subject of Chapter 6. For present purposes, it is enough to know that section 553 of the Administrative Procedure Act establishes a three-part process for informal rulemaking. Agencies first publish a "notice of proposed rule making" (APA § 553(b)). Members of the public interested in the rulemaking then have an opportunity to submit written comments on the agency's proposal (APA § 553(c)). After considering the public comments, the agency concludes the process by publishing a final rule, together with a "concise general statement of [its] basis and purpose" (APA § 553(c), (d)).

Formal rulemaking, like its informal counterpart, begins and ends with agency publications of a notice of proposed rulemaking and of the eventual final rule and accompanying statement of basis and purpose. The difference lies in the intervening process. Instead of requesting and reviewing written comments on the agency proposal, formal rulemaking requires an adjudicatory hearing in compliance with sections 556 and 557 of the APA. Formal adjudication is the subject of Chapter 5, but for now it is enough to know that sections 556 and 557 prescribe an agency decision based exclusively on the record produced in a trial-type proceeding.

The Administrative Procedure Act makes some allowance for the legislative character of rulemaking by tweaking its trial-type hearing procedures for formal rulemaking.[2] For example, the APA's separation-of-functions provisions that insulate the agency officials who preside over the hearing from investigative and prosecutorial staff apply to formal adjudication but not to formal rulemaking (APA § 554(d); see § 5.1). This difference in treatment reflects Congress's understanding that formal rulemaking remains a policy-making enterprise that does not require, and indeed discourages, the insulation of agency decisionmakers from other officials participating in the proceeding. And perhaps most importantly, section 556(d) of the APA allows the agency official presiding over a formal rulemaking proceeding to provide for the "submission of all or part of the evidence in written form," instead of at an oral hearing, so long as "[no] party will ... be prejudiced." In other words, section 556(d) gives agencies discretion to convert a formal rulemaking proceeding into a notice-and-comment process if they can demonstrate that no interested party would be harmed by the switch to informality. This opt-out feature stands in stark contrast to section 556(d)'s *requirement* that agencies use *oral* evidentiary hearings to

---

2.   See *id*. at 15.

resolve factual disputes on material issues in formal adjudication (APA § 556(d); § 5.3(c)).

Formal rulemaking is very much the exception to the general practice of informal (or, notice-and-comment) rulemaking. An influential study of administrative rulemaking procedures that Professor Robert Hamilton conducted in the early 1970s discovered the seemingly odd mandate of a judicial process for legislative-type rules "in a variety of different contexts which defy precise categorization." He was able to discern one "over-all pattern," however. According to Professor Hamilton, Congress for the most part has used formal rulemaking to temper delegations to agencies of "broad and largely undefined power to regulate certain aspects of specific industries." Agencies saddled with the burden of a formal hearing requirement, he found, often abandoned rulemaking.[3]

When Congress adopted the Administrative Procedure Act in 1946, hearing provisions nevertheless were common in statutes authorizing agencies to establish rates for public utilities or common carriers. Although these enabling acts typically did not specify that agencies base these rates "on the record" produced by the hearing, agencies and reviewing courts had "long assumed" that this is what Congress had in mind.[4] Formal rather than informal rulemaking was thus the traditional method of proceeding in administrative ratemaking, at least where Congress had required agencies to conduct a hearing.

The Supreme Court upset this conventional wisdom in *United States v. Florida East Coast Railway Co.*[5] *Florida East Coast* involved a challenge to rates established by the Interstate Commerce Commission to compensate railroads when other carriers borrow their freight cars. The ICC drew on its authority in section 1(14)(a) of the Interstate Commerce Act to set rates for such borrowing, "after hearing." Long before *Florida East Coast* arrived at the Court, the *Attorney General's Manual* had identified the Interstate Commerce Act as an enabling act whose hearing requirement had been consistently interpreted to require the Commission to base its rates on the record generated during a formal, trial-type proceeding.[6] Consistent with that longstanding interpretation, the ICC had commenced a formal rulemaking proceeding, but the Commission ultimately adopted the new rates without providing the trial-type hearing prescribed by sections 556 and 557 of the APA. During the proceeding, the ICC had invoked the opt-out

---

3. Robert W. Hamilton, *Procedures for the Adoption of Rules of General Applicability: The Need for Procedural Innovation in Administrative Rulemaking*, 60 CALIF. L. REV. 1276, 1311–13 (1972).

4. *Attorney General's Manual, supra* note 1, 32–33.

5. 410 U.S. 224 (1973).

6. *Attorney General's Manual, supra* note 1, 33–34.

provision of section 556(d), permitting agencies to solicit written comments on a rulemaking proposal instead of holding an oral hearing, so long as no party would be "prejudiced" by the move. Two railroad companies that considered themselves especially harmed by the rates filed separate suits, claiming that they had been prejudiced by the agency's decision not to hold a formal hearing. The lower courts in the two cases agreed and invalidated the rates.

The government in *Florida East Coast* asked the Supreme Court to review whether the railroads had been prejudiced by the ICC's invocation of the opt-out provision of section 556(d). Instead of deciding that issue, the justices invited the parties to address a more fundamental question: whether the hearing requirement of section 1(14)(a) contemplated anything more than the notice-and-comment process that the Commission had followed. The Court in *Florida East Coast* ultimately ruled that the railroads' opportunity to submit written comments on the ICC's rate proposal satisfied the statutory hearing requirement.

The Court began by holding that the hearing requirement in the ICC's enabling act did not trigger formal rulemaking under the Administrative Procedure Act. In the Court's reading, the trigger language of section 553(c) stated a two-part requirement: The enabling act must instruct an agency (1) to provide "opportunity for an agency hearing" and (2) to make its rule "on the record." A simple statutory hearing requirement, like section 1(14)(a)'s provision that the ICC set its rates "after hearing," satisfies the first, but not the second, of section 553(c)'s requirements. Before compelling an agency to follow the specific demands of sections 556 and 557 in a rulemaking proceeding, the justices insisted that the enabling act also provide that the agency make its rule "on the record," or at least that there be "other statutory language having the same meaning."[7]

The Court's decision in *Florida East Coast* that the hearing requirement of section (1)(14)(a) was insufficient to trigger formal rulemaking meant that an informal notice-and-comment procedure, which the ICC had provided, satisfied APA requirements. But as the justices recognized, satisfying the APA did not fully answer the railroads' claim to a hearing. Congress may use an enabling act to enhance the procedural requirements of the APA (see APA § 559), and the hearing provision of section (1)(14)(a) appeared to be just such an enhancement. Even if the APA did not require the ICC to follow sections 556 and 557, the railroads argued, the Interstate Commerce Act obligated the ICC to provide a "hearing."[8] The

---

7. *Florida East Coast*, 410 U.S. at 234–38.   **8.** *Id.* at 238–39.

Court concluded, however, that the hearing requirement of section (1)(14)(a) added nothing to the APA's notice-and-comment procedure for informal rulemaking.

The Court in *Florida East Coast* began with the premise that the term "hearing," standing alone, was inherently ambiguous. There are different kinds of hearings, after all. Faced with the daunting interpretive task of defining a term capable of several meanings, the justices fell back on the rulemaking-adjudication distinction. According to the Court, the best reading of an undefined "hearing" requirement turned on whether the relevant agency action was "a rulemaking-type proceeding" or "a proceeding devoted to the adjudication of particular disputed facts." Because the ICC's incentive rates "were applicable across the board," and thus were rulemaking, reasoned the justices, the hearing provision should be defined according to a legislative rather than a judicial frame of reference. They thus did not find such judicial trappings as oral testimony, cross-examination, or oral argument in section (1)(14)(a)'s hearing requirement. Instead, the justices believed that the ICC had provided a satisfactory legislative "hearing" by following a notice-and-comment process, which is the APA's default procedure for issuing legislative-type rules (see APA § 553).[9] At least in rulemaking, the Court in *Florida East Coast* seemed to conclude that an agency satisfied an undefined statutory hearing requirement simply by providing interested persons an opportunity to express their views, orally or in writing, on a rulemaking proposal.[10]

The Supreme Court's decision in *Florida East Coast* was a watershed in the judicial enforcement of statutory hearing requirements for administrative rulemaking proceedings. The federal courts of appeals generally have read the decision as "virtually establish[ing]" section 553(c)'s trigger language of "on the record" as "a touchstone test" for translating statutory hearing provisions into formal rulemaking requirements.[11] The Second Circuit, for example, relied on *Florida East Coast* in holding notice-and-comment procedures to satisfy statutory requirements that agencies provide a "full hearing"[12] and a "full opportunity for hearing"[13] in

---

9. *Id.* at 239–42, 245.

10. See *Attorney General's Manual, supra* note 1, at 34–35. For a biting criticism of *Florida East Coast*, see Nathaniel L. Nathanson, *Probing the Mind of the Administrator: Hearing Variations and Standards of Review under the Administrative Procedure Act and Other Federal Statutes*, 75 COLUM. L. REV. 721, 725–33 (1975).

11. Mobil Oil Corp. v. FPC, 483 F.2d 1238, 1250 (D.C.Cir. 1973); see, e.g.,

Farmers Union Central Exchange, Inc. v. FERC, 734 F.2d 1486, 1498–99 (D.C.Cir. 1984); Bell Telephone Co. of Pennsylvania v. FCC, 503 F.2d 1250, 1265, 1267, 1268 (3d Cir. 1974), cert. denied, 422 U.S. 1026 (1975).

12. See RCA Global Communications, Inc. v. FCC, 559 F.2d 881, 885–87 (2d Cir. 1977).

13. See American Telephone & Telegraph Co. v. FCC, 572 F.2d 17, 21–23 (2d Cir. 1978).

their rulemaking proceedings. *Florida East Coast* thus has strongly reinforced the informal notice-and-comment process of section 553 of the APA as the default method of rulemaking.

(b) Informal Adjudication v. Formal Adjudication

The Supreme Court, surprisingly, has not interpreted section 554(a) of the APA, the trigger provision for formal adjudication. The recurring question arising from section 554(a) parallels the section 553(c) issue at play in *United States v. Florida East Coast Railway Co.*[14]: whether an enabling act requiring an agency to provide a "hearing" of undefined content must also specify that the agency decide the dispute "on the record" in order to trigger the trial-type hearing procedures of sections 556 and 557. The Court's opinion in *Florida East Coast* sends conflicting signals on whether the justices' refusal to read a stand-alone hearing requirement to trigger formal rulemaking should extend to enabling acts governing administrative adjudication.

On one hand, the Court in *Florida East Coast* emphasized the importance of remaining faithful to the text of the Administrative Procedure Act. Section 554(a) states the same two-part requirement that is found in section 553(c): The enabling act must instruct an agency (1) to provide "opportunity for an agency hearing" and (2) to make its decision "on the record." As was true in the rulemaking context, a simple statutory hearing requirement regarding agency adjudication satisfies the first, but not the second, of these requirements. It is certainly possible that the justices would stick as closely to the text of section 554(a) as they did to section 553(c) in *Florida East Coast*, requiring enabling acts authorizing administrative adjudication to satisfy both requirements of section 554(a), or their equivalent, before compelling an agency to follow the specific demands of sections 556 and 557. And this may be what the drafters of the APA had intended. The Administrative Procedure Act makes informal proceedings the default process for both rulemaking and adjudication. For both types of action, the formal procedures of sections 556 and 557 are necessary only when enabling acts satisfy the identical trigger provisions of sections 554(a) and 553(c).

On the other hand, a second theme of the Court's opinion in *Florida East Coast* suggests that the justices might read the trigger provision of section 554(a) less strictly than they read section 553(c). Emphasizing the inherent ambiguity of the term "hearing," the Court in *Florida East Coast* suggested that the meaning of statutory hearing requirements varied "depending on whether

---

14.   410 U.S. 224 (1973).

[they were] used in the context of a rulemaking-type proceeding or in the context of a proceeding devoted to the adjudication of particular disputed facts."[15] The implication was that reviewing courts should read stand-alone statutory hearing provisions governing administrative rulemaking to require legislative-type hearings, but that courts should interpret such hearing provisions to require judicial-type hearings for agency adjudication. On this reading of *Florida East Coast*, the justices might be more willing to trigger formal adjudication than formal rulemaking because the formal, trial-type hearing at the heart of sections 556 and 557 of the APA fits administrative adjudication better than agency rulemaking. And this may be what the drafters of the APA had contemplated. While formal adjudication was commonplace in 1946, formal rulemaking, outside of ratemaking, was something of an aberration (as it is today).

There is another difference between rulemaking and adjudication that may distinguish *Florida East Coast* from cases involving application of the trigger provision of section 554(a). If a statutory hearing requirement in rulemaking fails to trigger the formal hearing process of 556 and 557, the informal notice-and-comment procedures of section 553 apply by default. By contrast, the APA provides no procedural fallback for informal adjudication. If a statutory hearing requirement in adjudication does not trigger sections 556 and 557, reviewing courts would have no APA procedural framework available to give shape to the "hearing" required by the enabling act.

The absence of a decisionmaking process for informal adjudication is a glaring omission of the APA. But this gap was intentional. Congress well understood that agencies conduct "the great mass of administrative routine" through informal adjudication.[16] By one estimate, between 90 and 95 percent of administrative adjudications are informal rather than formal.[17] Paradoxically, it might be the prevalence of informal adjudication throughout the administrative state that best explains why Congress concluded that it was undesirable to codify a default decisionmaking process. Informal adjudication is so ubiquitous and so varied that legislators may have felt that they could not design a single, across-the-board procedural model without compromising the ability of at least some agencies to administer at least some of their programs.

The failure of the APA to specify a set of procedures for informal adjudications does not mean that agencies are freed from

---

15. *Id.* at 239.

16. *Attorney General's Manual*, supra note 1, at 41, quoting Senate Comparative Print of June 1945, at 7 (Sen. Doc., at 22).

17. See Paul R. Verkuil, *A Study of Informal Adjudication*, 43 U. Chi. L. Rev. 739, 741 (1976).

all procedural constraints when they make such decisions. The APA provides a few procedural rights that apply to administrative action generally. For example, section 555(b) entitles parties "to appear in person or by or with counsel or other duly qualified representative in [any] agency proceeding." And section 555(e) obligates agencies to give "[p]rompt notice ... of the denial," together with "a brief statement of the grounds for denial," "of a written application, petition, or other request of an interested person made in connection with any agency proceeding." Moreover, if procedural due process is applicable, the agency must provide individuals reasonable notice and opportunity for a fair hearing (see Chapter 3). And as we shall see, agencies as a practical matter must follow a decisionmaking process that generates an administrative record and a contemporaneous explanation of their informal adjudicatory decisions sufficient to permit meaningful judicial review (see § 8.1). Finally, the presence of a hearing requirement in the enabling act must be given some content. But in the end, the absence of a generally applicable procedural safety net similar to that provided by the APA for informal rulemaking may encourage the justices to adopt a lighter trigger for formal adjudications than *Florida East Coast* established for formal rulemaking.

Because of the justices' reticence and the difficulty of the issue, it should not be surprising that the federal courts of appeals have differed in their approaches to the trigger provision of section 504(a). In one influential decision, *Seacoast Anti–Pollution League v. Costle*, the First Circuit took *Florida East Coast* head on, erecting a presumption that, "unless [an enabling act] otherwise specifies," a statutory hearing requirement for adjudication subject to judicial review triggers formal adjudication.[18] *Seacoast* involved a utility's application to the Environmental Protection Agency for an exemption from certain environmental restrictions. The enabling act authorized EPA to grant such exemptions "after opportunity for public hearing." As in *Florida East Coast*, the act did not take the additional step of requiring EPA to base its decision "on the record" produced at the hearing. The First Circuit in *Seacoast* nevertheless held that the hearing requirement in the enabling act, standing alone, satisfied the section 554(a) trigger.

The court of appeals in *Seacoast* defined its task as determining "the substantive nature of the hearing Congress intended to provide" in the enabling act. As in *Florida East Coast*, however, the legislators left no clues hinting at the kind of hearing they had in mind. Without statutory guidance, the *Seacoast* court, like the Supreme Court in *Florida East Coast*, fell back on the rulemaking-adjudication distinction as its frame of reference. But whereas the

18.   572 F.2d 872, 877 (1st Cir.), cert. denied, 439 U.S. 824 (1978).

justices in *Florida East Coast* had settled on the notice-and-comment process of section 553 as the default meaning of a rulemaking "hearing," the court of appeals in *Seacoast* concluded that the formal adjudicatory procedures of sections 556 and 557 of the APA described "exactly the kind of quasi-judicial proceeding" appropriate for administrative adjudication of "disputed facts in particular cases."[19]

Seacoast's presumption of formality for statutory hearing requirements in adjudication reversed *Florida East Coast's* presumption of informality for statutory hearing requirements in rulemaking. This reversal can be traced to the *Seacoast* court's view that the "crucial part" of the trigger language of section 554(a) was the hearing requirement, and not, as *Florida East Coast* had held for rulemaking, the specification that the agency decision be on the record. The court in *Seacoast* again drew on the rulemaking-adjudication distinction to justify this difference in emphasis. In rulemaking, the *Seacoast* court explained, the usual expectation is that the record produced at a legislative-type hearing is not the exclusive source of evidence for the agency's ultimate decision. A statutory requirement that an agency's rulemaking be based on the hearing record is therefore necessary to signal that Congress had a different expectation. By contrast, the *Seacoast* court believed that a statutory hearing requirement in connection with administrative adjudication "ordinarily implies the further requirement of decision in accordance with evidence adduced at the hearing."[20] For this reason, a statutory hearing requirement is a sufficient signal that Congress expected an agency's adjudicative decision to be on the record.

Seacoast is a mirror image of *Florida East Coast*. Both decisions addressed a stand-alone hearing requirement that only partially satisfied the APA's trigger provisions for formal proceedings. Both decisions resolved the statutory ambiguity by invoking the rulemaking-adjudication distinction. In *Florida East Coast*, the justices interpreted a statutory hearing requirement for rulemaking to require no more than notice and comment because they believed that Congress had designed that process for the typical legislative hearing. In *Seacoast*, the court of appeals interpreted a statutory hearing requirement in adjudication to require the formal, trial-type hearing prescribed by sections 556 and 557 of the APA because it was convinced that Congress had designed that process for the typical adjudicatory hearing.

Although *Seacoast* is consistent with the *Attorney General's Manual*,[21] has influenced several federal courts of appeals inter-

---

19. *Id*. at 876.
20. *Id*. at 876–78 & n.5.

21. See *Attorney General's Manual*, *supra* note 1, at 42–43.

preting section 504(a),[22] and has received at least a passing endorsement by the Supreme Court,[23] the decision has not gone unchallenged. *Seacoast* followed *Florida East Coast*'s suggestion of interpreting statutory hearing requirements through the lens of the rulemaking-adjudication distinction, but it did not harmonize with *Florida East Coast*'s theme emphasizing fidelity to the text of the APA. Section 553(c), with respect to rulemaking, and section 554(a), with respect to adjudication, contain identical trigger language. Before activating the formal procedural requirements of sections 556 and 557, an enabling act must require not only that the agency extend the "opportunity for an agency hearing," but also that the agency make the relevant decision "on the record." The parallel trigger provisions of sections 553(c) and 554(a) establish that informal proceedings are the default procedural requirements for *both* rulemaking and adjudication. Against the background of the APA, one cannot help but wonder whether *Seacoast*'s presumption of formality was the product of a judicial rather than of a congressional assessment of the appropriateness of formal, trial-type procedures for administrative adjudicatory hearings.

   Seemingly drawn by the similarity of language in the trigger provisions of sections 553(c) and 554(a), the Seventh Circuit in *City of West Chicago v. United States Nuclear Regulatory Commission*[24] applied *Florida East Coast*'s presumption of informality to statutory hearing requirements in adjudication. In *City of West Chicago*, the city complained when the Nuclear Regulatory Commission had used a written, notice-and-comment process in amending a plant's license to allow demolition of buildings and storage of contaminated soil. The NRC's enabling act had required it to provide the opportunity for a hearing before amending "any license." But the court of appeals presumed that a statutory hearing requirement, standing alone, did not trigger formal adjudication. Like the Supreme Court in *Florida East Coast*, the *City of West Chicago* court regarded the trigger language "on the record," or some similar expression of clear congressional intent, as the crucial congressional signal that a statutorily required hearing must satisfy sections 556 and 557 of the APA. The Seventh Circuit's adoption of *Florida East Coast*'s presumption of informality was so complete that it upheld the NRC's paper hearing.[25]

22. Federal courts of appeals decisions following *Seacoast* include Lane v. USDA, 120 F.3d 106 (8th Cir. 1997); Marathon Oil Co. v. EPA, 564 F.2d 1253, 1260–64 (9th Cir. 1977).

23. See Steadman v. SEC, 450 U.S. 91, 96 n.13 (1981) ("absence of the specific phrase ['on the record'] in a statu-

tory hearing requirement for agency adjudication does not remove the proceeding from the APA procedures governing formal adjudication," citing *Seacoast*).

24. 701 F.2d 632 (7th Cir. 1983).

25. *Id*. at 641, 638.

City of West Chicago stands as the polar opposite of *Seacoast*. It adopts—rather than reverses—*Florida East Coast*'s presumption of informality for statutorily required adjudicatory hearings. While *Seacoast* promoted the rulemaking-adjudication distinction as the primary guide to congressional intent for statutory hearing requirements, *City of West Chicago* seemed to regard statutory text as the only indicator of the legislative plan. For the *City of West Chicago* court, it was simply irrelevant whether the administrative decision-making at issue was legislative or judicial in nature. But is it safe to assume that Congress believes that the legislative or adjudicative nature of an agency's decision should play no role in defining the features of the hearings they require? The justices' assumption in *Florida East Coast* that legislators would be satisfied with a notice-and-comment process for legislative-type hearings is one thing. It is a more treacherous leap to assume, as did the court in *City of West Chicago*, that Congress would accept its default *rulemaking* process as adequate for the *adjudicatory* hearings it requires by statute. For example, courts generally have required some kind of *oral* hearing—albeit well short of the formal, trial-type hearing described in sections 556 and 557 of the APA—in administrative adjudications where procedural due process applies (see § 3.4(d)).

City of West Chicago has not proven to be *Seacoast*'s principal competitor, however. That distinction belongs to the D.C. Circuit's decision in *Chemical Waste Management, Inc. v. U.S. Environmental Protection Agency*.[26] *Chemical Waste* involved a challenge to the Environmental Protection Agency's procedural rules for administrative enforcement proceedings against hazardous waste facilities. The Resource Conservation and Recovery Act of 1976 ("RCRA") authorized EPA to sanction facilities that violate federal requirements governing the management and disposal of hazardous waste. These sanctions included the suspension or revocation of a facility's operating permit, as well as the imposition of civil penalties. Before imposing such sanctions, RCRA required EPA to provide the targeted facility an opportunity for a "public hearing." EPA implemented this statutory hearing requirement by providing for a formal, trial-type hearing that complied with sections 556 and 557 of the APA. Although RCRA had not required EPA to make its decision to impose sanctions "on the record," the agency concluded that this probably had been Congress's intent. EPA based that intuition on "the nature of the decision" it would make in RCRA enforcement proceedings. These would be classic, quasi-criminal adjudications, with EPA "accusing" facilities of "violating established legal standards through their past conduct," and "seeking to impose a sanction" for the violation.[27]

---

26.   873 F.2d 1477 (D.C.Cir. 1989).   **27.**   *Id.* at 1479.

Congress amended RCRA in the Hazardous and Solid Waste Amendments of 1984, adding a new provision authorizing EPA to issue corrective action orders when certain facilities release hazardous waste into the environment. Corrective action orders, as the name suggests, require facilities to take specific corrective or responsive action to address a release. The 1984 Amendments also allowed EPA to include in corrective action orders such sanctions as the suspension or revocation of a facility's right to operate and the imposition of civil penalties.

Congress's 1984 Amendments made the hearing provision in the original statute applicable to EPA proceedings for corrective action orders. EPA, however, made formal adjudicatory procedures available in corrective action order proceedings only where the agency sought to impose sanctions. EPA adopted informal hearing procedures for corrective action orders that merely required a facility to investigate or to stop a release of hazardous waste. These informal procedures allowed the facility to make both a written and an oral presentation to EPA. A facility could be represented by counsel at the oral hearing, but the rules prevented counsel from engaging in direct or cross-examination of witnesses. Only the EPA official who presided over the hearing could ask questions.

The D.C. Circuit in *Chemical Waste* held that EPA's informal procedures satisfied the statutory hearing requirement. The court began on common ground, noting that a statutory hearing provision, without more, does not clearly communicate whether Congress had intended to require agencies to use a formal, trial-type process. But unlike the Supreme Court in *Florida East Coast*, or the courts of appeals in *Seacoast* and in *City of West Chicago*, the D.C. Circuit in *Chemical Waste* did not use the inherent ambiguity of a stand-alone hearing requirement as the basis for a *judicial* presumption for or against a formal, trial-type proceeding. The *Chemical Waste* court chose instead to defer to the "expertise" of administrative officials in designing a hearing process that best fits the decision that Congress had authorized the agency to make. The court of appeals in *Chemical Waste* asked only that the agency's interpretation of a statutory hearing requirement be reasonable.[28]

---

28. *Id.* at 1480–82. The court of appeals approached the trigger issue through the lens of the Supreme Court's then-recent decision in *Chevron U.S.A. v. Natural Resources Defense Council*, 467 U.S. 837 (1984), which required judicial deference toward agency interpretations of ambiguous provisions in their enabling acts. But because *Chevron* deference applies only to "an agency's construction of the statute which it administers," *id.* at 842, and because determining whether a hearing requirement in an agency's enabling act triggers the formal procedures of the Administrative Procedure Act requires interpretation of both statutes, it is questionable whether *Chevron* applied in *Chemical Waste*. "See Metropolitan Stevedore Co. v. Rambo, 521 U.S. 121 n.9 (1997) ('The APA is not a statute that the [agency] is charged with administering.')"; § 8.5(c) The *Chemical Waste* approach to section 554(a) never-

Chemical Waste cedes primary authority to the agency when translating a stand-alone statutory hearing requirement into administrative practice. That primacy proceeds from the understanding that Congress has delegated the authority to implement its enabling acts to agencies and not to courts. On this understanding, the judicial role is not to decide how best to design a statutorily required hearing, but rather to review the legality of the agency's implementation of the hearing requirement. When Congress foregoes the opportunity in an enabling act to make clear the nature of the hearing it had in mind, *Chemical Waste* gives agencies the flexibility to devise any hearing process that is reasonable in light of the relevant agency decision.

That flexibility was on display in *Chemical Waste*. EPA's interpretation of RCRA's hearing requirement had varied according to "the particular nature of the issues" involved in its different enforcement proceedings.[29] When EPA sought sanctions against a facility for noncompliance with its legal obligations, the agency concluded that a formal adjudicative hearing was appropriate. But where agency officials sought only to direct a facility to investigate or to counteract a release of hazardous waste in the environment, EPA preferred an informal, oral hearing.

The D.C. Circuit accepted as reasonable EPA's choice of an informal, oral hearing procedure for corrective action order proceedings that did not contemplate sanctions against a hazardous waste facility. The court accepted EPA's rationale that these proceedings raised fewer factual issues than sanctions proceedings; that EPA officials could resolve the factual issues that arose in corrective action order proceedings without the need for a trial; and that informal procedures allowed agency officials to respond relatively quickly to releases of hazardous waste.[30] Time was not as crucial a factor in sanctions proceedings.

The *Chemical Waste* approach to the APA trigger provision of section 504(a) is appealing because it occupies a middle position between the *Seacoast* presumption of formality and the *City of West Chicago* presumption of informality for enabling acts that require an adjudicative hearing without specifying that the agency's decision must be on the record. But the deference to administrative interpretations of statutory hearing requirements prescribed by *Chemical Waste* is hardly trouble-free. As a general matter, the extent to which, if at all, reviewing courts should defer to adminis-

theless is defensible without resort to *Chevron*. See Vermont Yankee Nuclear Power Corp. v. Natural Resources Defense Council, Inc., 435 U.S. 519 (1978) (discussed in § 6.2); Securities and Exchange Comm'n v. Chenery Corp., 332 U.S. 194 (1947) (*Chenery II*) (discussed in § 4.3(a)).

29. *Chemical Waste*, 873 F.2d at 1481.

30. *Id.* at 1482–83.

trative interpretations of statutory provisions has long been a controversial issue in administrative law (see § 8.5). More specifically, although agencies have an especially valuable perspective in developing decisionmaking procedures for the programs they administer, they also suffer from something of a conflict of interest when defining the procedural requirements that Congress has imposed on them. Left unchecked, agencies might develop a bias in favor of informality, elevating their concerns with administrative efficiency over congressional concerns for the rights of individuals who are party to administrative adjudications. It is not clear whether the reasonableness review of *Chemical Waste* provides a sufficient check on the temptation of agency officials to make their jobs easier by streamlining statutory hearing requirements.

Each of the approaches to section 504(a) of the APA adopted in *Seacoast, City of West Chicago*, and *Chemical Waste* is defensible. But none of the approaches is incontrovertible. Indeed, the First Circuit recently abandoned its *Seacoast* decision in favor of *Chemical Waste*.[31] The disagreement among the federal courts of appeals over the application of section 554(a) to enabling acts providing stand-alone hearing requirements awaits settlement by the Supreme Court.

§ 4.3   The Power of Agencies to Choose Between Rulemaking and Adjudication

Administrative agencies may act with the force of law either by issuing rules of conduct or by resolving particular matters in adjudication.[1] The advantages and disadvantages of these regulatory options mirror each other.

The great advantage of rulemaking is its efficiency. Rules settle issues, extinguishing the need for continual re-litigation by the agency. Rulemaking also fosters coherency in administrative policymaking. Agencies can use rulemaking to establish a complete and interrelated set of norms governing public conduct within their jurisdiction. Rulemaking promotes fairness values as well, by providing advance notification to affected individuals making clear how their legal rights or obligations have changed. And because administrative rules typically govern the conduct of groups rather than of a single individual, they afford uniform treatment to all who are similarly situated.

The primary disadvantage of rulemaking is its inflexibility. Administrative rules are legally binding on agency officials as well

---

31. See Dominion Energy Brayton Point, LLC v. Johnson, 443 F.3d 12 (1st Cir. 2006).

§ 4.3

1. Pacific Gas & Electric Co. v. Federal Power Commission, 506 F.2d 33, 38 (D.C.Cir. 1974).

as on regulated parties. If agency officials decide that a change in regulatory course is necessary, they ordinarily must undertake another round of rulemaking.

The advantage of adjudication is its flexibility. Adjudication allows agencies to make regulatory decisions on an ad hoc basis, assembling administrative policy in the traditional method of the common law, one case at a time. Policymaking through adjudication is especially appropriate for programs that require agencies to make regulatory decisions that are highly fact specific, and thus not amenable to general rulemaking. Adjudication also may be attractive to an agency that is not ready to commit to hard-and-fast rules implementing a regulatory program. Adjudication allows an uncertain agency to evolve its policy over time, answering regulatory questions narrowly, as they arise. And because agencies are less bound by precedent than by rules, administrative officials have a freer hand in adjudication to make mid-course corrections of regulatory policy.

The disadvantages of adjudication are its potential for inconsistency as well as its unpredictability. When agencies engage in policymaking by individual, they often single out an unfortunate soul from among many others who are similarly situated in order to announce a new legal principle. And unlike rulemaking, in adjudication an agency's announcement and application of a new right or obligation occurs simultaneously, in the very same proceeding. Without a legally binding statement of rules to guide them, regulated parties act at their peril, predicting as best they can how an agency might decide some future dispute arising from their conduct.

Enabling acts often authorize agencies to engage in both rulemaking and adjudication. But enabling acts often fail to dictate when agencies should proceed by rulemaking or by adjudication. Nor does the Administrative Procedure Act. When Congress enables an agency to act either by rulemaking or by adjudication, the choice between those two options, by default, "lies primarily in the informed discretion of the administrative agency."[2] It thus has been left to the courts to determine what limits, if any, to place on an agency's discretion to adopt its regulatory method of choice.

(a) Agency Power to Make Policy Through Adjudication

The Supreme Court provided its leading statement on the power of agencies to choose adjudication over rulemaking as a vehicle for announcing regulatory policies just one year after Congress passed the Administrative Procedure Act. *Securities and*

---

2. See SEC v. Chenery, 332 U.S. 194, 203 (1947) (*Chenery II*).

Exchange Commission v. Chenery Corp. (Chenery II)[3] arose from the SEC's early implementation of the Public Utility Act of 1935. The act charged the SEC with responsibility to oversee the reorganization of holding companies that controlled public utilities, which had become alarmingly compromised during the Great Depression. While the SEC evaluated a proposed reorganization for Federal Water Service Corporation, a holding company subject to the act, Federal's managers busied themselves buying the company's preferred stock on the over-the-counter market. According to Federal's proposed reorganization plan, this preferred stock would convert to common stock of the new company. Although the SEC found no fraud in these purchases, Federal's management stood to acquire over ten percent of the new common stock.

The SEC would have none of it. The Commission approved Federal's reorganization plan only after denying conversion rights for the managers' preferred stock. The Commission believed that company officials managing a reorganization were fiduciaries and that they suffered from a conflict of interests when they transacted in the company's stock for personal gain during reorganization. The Commission derived this specific no-trading principle from the general standards Congress had provided in the Public Utility Act to guide its approval of reorganization plans. Section 7(d)(6) and section 7(e) of the act instructed the SEC to ensure that plans were not "detrimental to the public interest or the interest of investors or consumers." Section 11(e) of the act required that reorganization plans be "fair and equitable" to everyone concerned. Relying on these provisions, the SEC required Federal's managers to surrender their preferred stock at cost plus four percent, a rate of return calculated to reflect dividends that had accumulated since the dates of purchase.

The Federal management group cried foul. Even if the standards of the Public Utility Act supported the SEC's no-trading principle, the managers argued, the Commission could not enforce the principle against them when it adjudicated Federal's reorganization plan. The managers claimed that the SEC could establish its no-trading principle only by issuing a rule specifically prohibiting such conduct. Such a rule, they continued, must be prospective in nature and thus may govern only *future* stock transactions.[4] By contrast, the SEC had given its no-trading principle "retroactive

---

3. 332 U.S. 194 (1947).

4. See APA § 551(4) ("rule" defined as "agency statement of general or particular applicability and future effect"); Bowen v. Georgetown Univ. Hosp., 488 U.S. 204, 208 (1988) ("a statutory grant of legislative rulemaking authority will not, as a general matter, be understood to encompass the power to promulgate retroactive rules unless that power is conveyed by Congress in express terms").

effect" by applying it to transactions that had predated the Commission's adjudication of the Federal plan.[5]

The Court in *Chenery II* rejected the claim that the SEC could address management stock trading only by rulemaking. As the justices put it, "The absence of a general rule or regulation governing management trading during reorganization did not affect the Commission's duties in relation to the particular proposal before it." The Public Utility Act required the SEC to approve the holding company reorganization plans "as soon as practicable." Before approving Federal's plan, the SEC had to decide whether to allow the managers' preferred stock to convert to common stock of the new company. If the SEC "rightly felt" that allowing conversion of the reorganization managers' preferred stock would have been "inconsistent with [the] standards" of the act, the Court reasoned, the SEC would have violated its duty to faithfully administer the reorganization program had it approved the conversion "merely because there was no general rule or regulation covering the matter." The justices concluded that it would "stultify the administrative process" to require the Commission to allow the conversion even as it formulates a no-trading rule for future transactions.[6]

The Court conceded that administrative rulemaking was the preferred method for "filling in the interstices" of an enabling act. But the justices refused to impose a "rigid requirement" on agencies to flesh out the statutory standards they administer by rulemaking rather than by adjudication. Such a decree, the justices feared, "would make the administrative process inflexible and incapable of dealing with many of the specialized problems which arise" when agencies implement statutory programs. "[T]he choice made between proceeding by general rule or by individual, ad hoc litigation," Court concluded in *Chenery II*, "is one that lies primarily in the informed discretion of the administrative agency."[7]

Justice Robert H. Jackson, joined by Justice Felix Frankfurter, wrote a biting dissenting opinion in *Chenery II*, accusing the majority of ignoring the rule of law by upholding the SEC's order prohibiting Federal's management from participating in the stock conversion. For Justice Jackson, the Commission's prohibition was an exercise of "administrative authoritarianism" because it lacked a "legal basis." One might object that this criticism ignores (or discredits) the SEC's decision that allowing conversion rights to the preferred stock purchased by Federal's managers would have violated the *statutory* standards governing the Commission's approval of utility reorganization plans. But even if the Public Utility Act provided sufficient substantive support for the SEC's position,

---

5. *Chenery II*, 332 U.S. at 199–200.   **7.** *Id*. at 202–03.

6. *Id*. at 201–02.

Justice Jackson insisted that the rule of law imposed a procedural obligation on the Commission to issue a rule *specifically* outlawing management trading before rejecting such transactions.[8]

The *Chenery II* majority acknowledged that the SEC's decision had a "retroactive effect" on Federal's management group, but the justices concluded that the retroactivity "was not necessarily fatal to its validity." The majority addressed the retroactivity of the SEC's decision against Federal's managers by balancing that harm "against the mischief of producing a result which is contrary to a statutory design or to legal and equitable principles. If that mischief is greater than the ill effect of the retroactive application of a new standard," the Court concluded, "it is not the type of retroactivity which is condemned by law." The justices suggested two reasons why the retroactive effect of the *Chenery* order was tolerable. First, the SEC "had not previously been confronted with the problem of management trading during reorganization." In such a circumstance, the justices refused to deny agencies the power of using an adjudicative proceeding to announce and to apply "a new standard of conduct." The Court observed, "Every case of first impression has a retroactive effect, whether the new principle is announced by a court or by an administrative agency."[9]

The second ameliorating factor present in *Chenery II* was more implicit and more tentative than the first. The Court hinted that the retroactive effect of the SEC's order—"prevent[ing] Federal's management from securing the profits and control which were the object of the preferred stock purchases"—was not sufficient to tip the balance in the managers' favor.[10] The Court in *Chenery II* thus used the Commission's remedy to measure retroactive effect. Viewed closely, the effect of the SEC's order was *prospective* rather than retroactive in nature: The Commission had defeated the managers' expectations of enjoying future profits and future control of the new utility. By having the corporation compensate the managers with the purchase price of the stock and a modest rate of return keyed to accumulated dividends, the Commission essentially returned the managers to the *status quo ante*. Federal's managers neither gained nor lost from the stock purchase. After the SEC ruled, it was as if the purchases had never happened.

The unstated hint here is that the weight of the retroactive effect on Federal's managers would have grown, and the balance may have reversed, had the SEC gone further and penalized the managers for their stock purchases. If the Commission, for example, had imposed civil penalties, or even had the agency failed to provide for compensation to the managers for the stock they

---

8. *Id.* at 204–09, 212, 216 (Jackson, J., dissenting).

9. *Id.* at 203.

10. *Id.* at 203–04.

surrendered, the remedy would have been retroactive rather than prospective in nature. And the managers' claim that they had been punished for violating a rule that had not yet been stated would have acquired considerable potency. But in such a case, the SEC misstep would not have been opting for adjudication over rulemaking, but ordering a remedy that was "arbitrary, capricious, [or] an abuse of discretion" (APA § 706(2)(A)).

The Supreme Court made the focus on remedy explicit several decades later in *National Labor Relations Board v. Bell Aerospace Co.*[11] Unlike the management-trading issue in *Chenery II*, *Bell Aerospace* did not present the NLRB with a case of first impression. In a long line of decisions, the Board had held that buyers in a variety of industries did not enjoy collective bargaining rights under the National Labor Relations Act because they were managerial employees. The Board abruptly switched positions in *Bell Aerospace*, ruling that managerial employees (like buyers) were eligible for collective bargaining unless they were involved in labor relations. The Supreme Court invalidated the Board's order on substantive grounds, ruling that the act excluded all managers from collective bargaining, and not just those involved in labor relations. The justices remanded the case to the NLRB to determine whether Bell's buyers were managerial employees and thus ineligible for collective bargaining.[12]

The justices did not rest with a simple remand order, however. The court of appeals had ruled that the NLRB's precedent holding buyers to be managers without collective bargaining rights obligated the Board to use rulemaking to change its position. The Supreme Court disagreed, reaffirming the *Chenery II* principles that agencies may "announc[e] new principles" in adjudication and that "the choice between rulemaking and adjudication lies in the first instance within the [agency]'s discretion." The Court added that the remand proceeding in *Bell* was "especially appropriate" for adjudication. The justices explained, "The duties of buyers vary widely depending on the company or industry. It is doubtful whether any generalized standard could be framed which would have more than marginal utility. The Board thus has reason to proceed with caution, developing its standards in a case-by-case manner with attention to the specific character of the buyers' authority and duties in each company. The Board's judgment that adjudication best serves this purpose is entitled to great weight." In other words, the NLRB's decision to choose adjudication over rulemaking for determining whether Bell's buyers were managers, and thus ineligible for collective bargaining, was the type of individualized action that *Londoner* had earmarked for case-by-case decisionmak-

11.   416 U.S. 267 (1974).   **12.**   *Id.* at 274–90.

ing. The Board's power to "announc[e] new principles" was simply a byproduct of its legitimate exercise of adjudicatory authority in this case.[13]

The Court in *Bell Aerospace* rejected the company's claim that reliance on NLRB precedent in refusing to bargain with its buyers prevented the Board from retroactively applying a contrary decision to them on remand. Bell had argued that rulemaking was required in order to notify interested parties that the Board had changed its position. The Court disagreed, explaining, "the adverse consequences ensuing from [Bell's] reliance are [not] so substantial that the Board should be precluded from reconsidering the issue in an adjudicative proceeding." As in *Chenery II*, the surprise of an NLRB decision on remand that Bell's buyers were not managers would be offset by the limited nature of the Board's remedial order. The NLRB had ordered only prospective relief in its original decision finding Bell's buyers to be entitled to collective bargaining rights. Importantly, the Board had not imposed "some new liability [on Bell] for past actions which were taken in good-faith reliance on Board pronouncements. Nor [were] fines or damages involved." If the buyers prevailed on remand, the justices presumed that the NLRB again would not penalize the company for having failed to engage in collective bargaining with its buyers. The Board, as before, simply would order Bell to engage in good faith collective bargaining.[14]

The D.C. Circuit's decision in *Epilepsy Foundation of Northeast Ohio v. National Labor Relations Board*[15] illustrates the restrictive potential of *Chenery II* and of *Bell Aerospace* on administrative discretion to opt for adjudication. *Epilepsy Foundation* involved a challenge to a decision of the NLRB finding that the Foundation's discharge of an employee constituted an unfair labor practice under the National Labor Relations Act. The Supreme Court had ruled in 1975 that employees in a unionized workplace may request the presence of a union representative during an investigatory interview that the employee reasonably believes might result in disciplinary action.[16] The NLRB had extended the Supreme Court ruling in 1982 to cover employees in nonunion workplaces, but had reversed itself in 1985, once again limiting the Supreme Court ruling to unionized workplaces.

In *Epilepsy Foundation*, the Board flipped yet again, holding that employees in workplaces that were not unionized could nevertheless request the presence of a union representative at investigatory interviews. In contrast to *Chenery II* and to *Bell Aerospace*, the

---

13. *Id.* at 294.
14. *Id.* at 272, 295.
15. 268 F.3d 1095 (D.C.Cir. 2001).

16. NLRB v. J. Weingarten, Inc., 420 U.S. 251 (1975).

Board took the additional step of assessing damages against the Foundation for its failure to allow a union representative at the interview. The D.C. Circuit upheld the NLRB's substantive decision applying the Supreme Court ruling to nonunionized workplaces, but the court of appeals set aside the damages award as a "retroactive application" of the Board's decision. The court explained, "Employees and employers alike must be able to rely on clear statements of the law by the NLRB."[17] As in *Bell Aerospace*, the Board was not prevented from changing even a clearly established legal position in adjudication. The D.C. Circuit in *Epilepsy Foundation* simply deemed it an abuse of discretion for the NLRB to have imposed "some new liability" on an individual for conduct that had been consistent with the stated position of the agency at the time.[18]

Chenery II and *Bell Aerospace* thus have established two complementary principles: (1) the choice between rulemaking and adjudication lies "primarily in the informed discretion of the administrative agency"; and (2) an agency abuses that discretion if the "retroactive effect" of an adjudicatory order exceeds an agency's strong interest in administering its enabling acts as it deems proper.[19] The Supreme Court, at least to date, has not identified any factor other than the retroactive nature of an administrative remedy that would justify judicial invalidation of an agency decision to establish and enforce administrative policy in adjudication rather than rulemaking.

(b) Agency Power to Resolve Adjudicatory Issues Through Rulemaking

Chenery II and *Bell Aerospace* accept broad authority in agencies to establish principles of law through adjudication rather than through rulemaking. In this section, we ask the opposite question: To what extent may agencies use their rulemaking power to settle issues they otherwise are subject to an adjudicatory hearing requirement?

The Supreme Court first took up this question in *United States v. Storer Broadcasting Co.*[20] Congress had authorized the Federal Communications Commission to grant applications for a broadcast license when it served the "public interest, convenience, and necessity" to do so. The act had given an applicant the opportunity for "a full hearing" in order to persuade the Commission that its

17. See *Epilepsy Foundation*, 268 F.3d at 1097–1103.

18. See *Bell Aerospace*, 416 U.S. at 295; *Epilepsy Foundation*, 268 F.3d at 1102–03.

19. *Chenery II*, 332 U.S. at 203; see *Bell Aerospace*, 416 U.S. at 295. The Court has read *Chenery II* to allow agencies to announce "specific applications" of its own rules through adjudication rather than by issuing "further, more precise rules." Shalala v. Guernsey Mem. Hosp., 514 U.S. 87, 96 (1995).

20. 351 U.S. 192 (1956).

application met the statutory standard. Based on the judgment that it would further the "public interest" to avoid the over-concentration of broadcasting facilities, the FCC issued "multiple ownership rules" limiting the number of stations that license holders could own. *Storer* involved a challenge to these rules on the ground that they denied to applicants their statutory right to a hearing on the issue whether it would serve the public interest to grant a license to an applicant who owned more than the maximum number of stations allowed by the rule. In other words, the challengers claimed that the enabling act had obligated the FCC in *each* licensing proceeding to hear evidence on whether an applicant's portfolio of broadcast stations justified a finding that granting an additional license would disserve the public interest.

The justices rejected the challenge. The enabling act's hearing requirement, the Court held in *Storer*, did not prevent the Commission from using its rulemaking authority to settle recurring issues in broadcast-licensing proceedings. The multiple ownership rules established a limitation on broadcast holdings that applied to all license applicants. Such a categorical decision, of course, fits within the *Bi-Metallic* conception of administrative rulemaking. Moreover, to prevent the Commission from using rulemaking to establish this across-the-board limit would have forced administrative officials needlessly to re-litigate the multiple ownership issue in every licensing proceeding.[21]

Although the Court in *Storer* refused to block agencies from using rulemaking to refine statutory standards subject to adjudicative hearings, the justices noted approvingly that the FCC's multiple ownership rules were sufficiently flexible to preserve the kind of individualized determination that Congress had contemplated when it required a licensing hearing.[22] The Court in *Storer* found that flexibility in a provision permitting applicants to request "waivers of or exceptions to" the Commission's limit on the number of broadcast stations that license holders could own. The waiver provision allowed applicants to use a licensing hearing to show that the multiple ownership rule should not be applied to their applications.[23]

Storer established a pattern of judicial acceptance of administrative efforts to resolve recurring issues in their adjudications

---

21. *Id.* at 202–03; see FPC v. Texaco, Inc., 377 U.S. 33, 44 (1964).

22. See *Storer*, 351 U.S. at 204; see also *Texaco*, 377 U.S. at 40 ("the statutory requirement for a hearing ... does not preclude the Commission from particularizing statutory standards through the rulemaking process and barring at the threshold those who neither measure up to them nor show reasons why in the public interest the rule should be waived").

23. See *Storer*, 351 U.S. at 201–02; see also *Texaco*, 377 U.S. at 39 ("In the present case, as in *Storer*, there is a procedure provided in the regulations whereby an applicant can ask for a waiver of the rule complained of").

through rulemaking. A relatively recent entry in this line of precedent is *Heckler v. Campbell*,[24] where the Court upheld "medical-vocational guidelines" issued by the Department of Health and Human Services to help determine a claimant's right to Social Security disability benefits. The Social Security Act required HHS to hold a hearing before deciding whether a claimant is disabled and thus entitled to benefits. Before the medical-vocational rules, a disability hearing had focused on three issues. The agency had first determined whether a claimant suffered from a physical or mental impairment. If so, HHS had assessed the claimant's job qualifications, that is, his or her physical ability, age, education, and work experience. Finally, the agency had decided whether jobs existed in the national economy for a person with the claimant's impairment and job qualifications.

HHS had called on vocational experts to offer an opinion on the final element of the agency's disability determination. Although these experts often had relied on standardized guides, they had come under frequent criticism for providing inconsistent testimony concerning claimants with similar qualifications and abilities. The Department's medical-vocational guidelines eliminated the need for the testimony of vocational experts by establishing, through rulemaking, whether or not a job existed in the national economy for claimants with particular impairments and job qualifications.

Following *Storer*, the Court in *Campbell* held that HHS's use of rulemaking to determine a claimant's employment opportunities in the national market did not violate the Social Security Act's requirement that the Department base its disability determinations on evidence presented at an adjudicative hearing. Because such a determination was "not unique to each claimant," the justices concluded, HHS could resolve it "as fairly through rulemaking as by introducing the testimony of vocational experts at each disability hearing." Indeed, the justices believed that the medical-vocational guidelines would enhance HHS's performance by improving both the "uniformity and efficiency" of disability determinations.[25]

Yet the Court in *Campbell*, as in *Storer*, took care to ensure that the medical-vocational guidelines did not subvert the individualized administrative assessment that lay at the heart of the adjudicative hearing Congress had provided for disability determinations. The justices noted, for example, that the guidelines did not relieve HHS of its statutory obligation to determine each claimant's impairment and job qualifications "on the basis of evidence ad-

---

24.   461 U.S. 458 (1983).

25.   *Id.* at 461, 465–68. The Court in *Campbell* found the Department's "need for efficiency [to be] self-evident," citing an annual disability caseload of 2.3 mil-

lion claims, with over a quarter of a million of these claims receiving a hearing before an administrative law judge. *Id.* at 461 n.2.

duced at a hearing." In addition, the medical-vocational guidelines in *Campbell*, like the multiple ownership rules in *Storer*, contained a waiver provision permitting claimants to use the disability hearing to show that the guidelines should not be applied to their individual claims. The medical-vocational guidelines also cautioned that they only described "major functional and vocational patterns," and that HHS would apply them only when the guidelines accurately described a particular claimant's qualifications and limitations.[26]

Are Waiver Provisions Necessary? The Court's emphasis on the opportunity for waiver has provided consistent counterpoint to the justices' acceptance of administrative efforts to settle recurring issues in adjudication through rulemaking. The Court has made clear that providing such a safety valve allowing an individual's particular circumstances to trump the general requirements of agency rules is a desirable feature in this context. But is it *necessary* for all rules that settle issues subject to an adjudicative hearing requirement to provide for waivers or exceptions in individual cases?

The Court's decision in *Federal Communications Commission v. WNCN Listeners Guild*[27] answered, "No." The Federal Communications Act authorized the Federal Communications Commission to approve an application for the transfer or renewal of a broadcast license if the Commission determined that such an action would serve "the public interest, convenience, and necessity." The FCC issued a rule stating that the Commission would not consider changes in entertainment programming when evaluating whether license renewals or transfers would serve the public interest. A challenger claimed that because the rule provided that the FCC would *never* consider a change in entertainment programming, it violated the Commission's statutory obligation "to make a particularized public-interest determination on every application" for license renewal or transfer.[28] The problem, Justice Thurgood Marshall noted in dissent, was that the rule, unlike the regulations upheld in *Storer* and in *Campbell*, did not allow for instances in which a particular format change disserved the public interest.[29] The Court in *WNCN Listeners Guild* nevertheless upheld the rule, explaining that *Storer* and other decisions highlighting the presence of a regulatory safety valve "did not hold that [agencies] may never adopt a rule that lacks a waiver provision."[30] This enigmatic state-

---

26. *Id.* at 462 n.5, 467, 468 n.11. The Court followed *Storer* and *Campbell* in *American Hospital Ass'n v. NLRB*, 499 U.S. 606, 612 (1991) (upholding NLRB regulations defining appropriate bargaining units).

27. 450 U.S. 582 (1981).

28. *Id.* at 600.

29. *Id.* at 608–12 (Marshall, J., dissenting).

30. *Id.* at 601 n.44.

ment, however, leaves open the possibility that a waiver provision might be necessary in some circumstances.

* * *

The Supreme Court's review of an agency's choice to proceed either by rulemaking or by adjudication recognizes that this decision is a policy determination residing primarily within the discretion of an agency. An agency is largely free to use adjudication to establish the legal principles it enforces, as well as to use rulemaking to shape the issues it adjudicates. Reviewing courts step in only when an agency abuses this broad discretion by misusing a regulatory method—either by penalizing a party for conduct that had not previously been denoted as unlawful or by using rulemaking to resolve issues that require an individualized determination.

Chapter 5

FORMAL ADJUDICATION UNDER THE ADMINISTRATIVE PROCEDURE ACT

At the midpoint of the twentieth century, Justice Robert H. Jackson, writing for the Court, observed, "Multiplication of federal administrative agencies and expansion of their functions to include adjudications which have serious impact on private rights has been one of the dramatic legal developments of the past half-century."[1] By 1946, when Congress adopted the Administrative Procedure Act,

---

1. Wong Yang Sung v. McGrath, 339 U.S. 33, 36–37 (1950).

federal regulatory agencies typically used formal adjudicatory proceedings to establish and to enforce administrative policy. A central purpose of the APA, Justice Jackson emphasized, was to shield individuals from the "arbitrary and biased use" of these regulatory adjudications.[2] The provisions of the APA governing formal agency adjudication—sections 554, 556, and 557—implement that purpose.

Yet it is important to keep in mind that the APA's provisions for formal adjudication have limited scope. They apply to relatively few agency adjudications in contemporary administrative practice. By one estimate, between 90 and 95 percent of administrative adjudications are informal rather than formal.[3] An agency must conduct adjudications in compliance with the APA *only* when its enabling act requires that it do so (APA § 554(a); see § 4.2(b)). And although the APA's provisions governing formal adjudication implement the constitutional guarantee of a fair hearing for individuals facing certain hostile actions by the government, courts typically find that procedural due process is satisfied by hearings that are far less formal than those prescribed by the APA (see § 3.4(d)).

The APA's procedures for formal adjudication are best understood as an adaptation of judicial trials to the administrative setting. Figure 5–1, which diagrams the formal adjudicatory process of the APA, makes clear this relationship to judicial proceedings.

2. *Id.* at 37.

3. See Paul R. Verkuil, *A Study of Informal Adjudication*, 43 U. Chi. L. Rev. 739, 741 (1976).

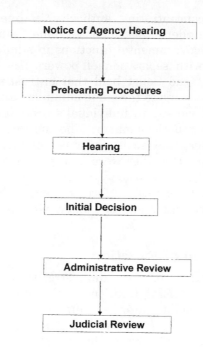

Figure 5-1: Formal Adjudication Under the APA

Understanding formal adjudication as an administrative trial highlights the persistent tension that arises when agencies with a policy mission assume "the duties of prosecutor and judge."[4] Agencies with law-enforcement responsibility often launch a proceeding by investigating possible violations of their enabling acts or of their rules. When an agency finds a probable violation, it issues and prosecutes a complaint against the party in question. These agencies close the power loop by ultimately deciding whether the party has violated the act or rule at issue. As Justice Jackson's comments illustrate, the combination of law-enforcement and law-adjudication functions in one government institution has raised lingering concerns over whether the administrative process is capable of providing individuals a fair hearing.

Although this combination of functions undoubtedly is in tension with American constitutional norms of separation of powers and procedural due process, it has become accepted as a necessity in the administrative state. After all, Congress's fundamental motivation in creating agencies is to obtain the efficiency and effectiveness

4. *Wong Yang Sung*, 339 U.S. at 41.

that result from concentrating authority in one institution to pursue a specified undertaking. The Supreme Court has accepted the combination of governmental functions in administrative agencies as consistent with separation of powers (see § 2.2). And in *Withrow v. Larkin*,[5] the Court held that entrusting investigative and adjudicative functions to the same administrative official, without more, does not violate an individual's procedural due process right to an unbiased decisionmaker. The justices in *Withrow* acknowledged, however, that such power combinations were hardly trouble-free, and thus that they were a proper subject of legislative attention.[6] The APA's provisions governing formal adjudicatory proceedings reflect Congress's effort to balance the benefits of administrative effectiveness and efficiency with the ideal of procedural fairness.

§ 5.1 Separation of Functions

The primary effort of the Administrative Procedure Act to reconcile the tension arising from the dual administrative roles of law-enforcer and law-adjudicator lies in its provisions requiring "an *internal separation of the functions* between the [agency] officials who hear and decide and those who investigate and prosecute" cases subject to formal adjudication.[1] The term "separation of functions" describes the norm that agency personnel should not participate in the decision of cases that they have helped to investigate or prosecute. The term "internal" makes clear that the APA does not require a "complete" separation of functions.[2] The act accepts a combination of law-enforcement and law-adjudication functions in a single agency, and thus it recognizes that agency heads necessarily are responsible for the exercise of both kinds of functions (APA § 554(d)(C)). The APA applies the separation norm to all agency personnel below the head(s).

(a) Institutional Separation of Functions

Section 554(d) of the APA requires the institutional separation of an agency's law-enforcement officers from its "administrative law judges" ("ALJs"), the agency officers who preside over formal adjudicatory hearings (see § 5.3(a)). Section 554(d)(2) provides that ALJs may not be "responsible to or subject to the supervision or

---

5. 421 U.S. 35 (1975); see also Richardson v. Perales, 402 U.S. 389 (1971) (approving combination of functions in Social Security disability adjudications).

6. *Withrow*, 421 U.S. at 51.

§ 5.1

1. *Attorney General's Manual on the Administrative Procedure Act* 50 (1947)

(emphasis added), reprinted in WILLIAM F. FUNK, et al., FEDERAL ADMINISTRATIVE PROCEDURE SOURCEBOOK 33–171 (3d ed. 2000); see Grolier, Inc. v. FTC, 615 F.2d 1215, 1218 (9th Cir. 1980).

2. See *Wong Yang Sung*, 339 U.S. at 46.

direction of . . . [agency personnel] engaged in the performance of investigative or prosecuting functions." Thus, although an agency's law-enforcement staff and its ALJs ultimately are responsible to the head(s) of the agency, that responsibility flows through separate channels of accountability.

In addition to the institutional separation between ALJs and agency prosecutors and investigators, section 554(d) provides restrictions on both ALJs and agency law-enforcement personnel designed to limit them to their respective roles in particular formal adjudicatory proceedings.[3]

(b) Separation-of-Functions Limitations on Administrative Law Judges in Formal Adjudicatory Proceedings

Section 554(d)(1) provides that an administrative law judge presiding over a formal adjudicatory hearing may not "consult a person or party on a fact in issue, unless on notice and opportunity for all parties to participate." The purpose of this no-consultation rule, as explained by the *Attorney General's Manual*, is to "achieve fairness and independence in the hearing process" by "assur[ing] that hearings [are] conducted by . . . officers who have not received or obtained factual information outside the record."[4]

The no-consultation rule of section 554(d)(1) applies only to the ALJ and is limited to consultation regarding "a fact in issue" in the proceeding. Section 554(d)(1) thus does not prohibit ALJs from consulting on questions of law or discretion that arise in their proceedings. (Some consultations, however, may be barred by the APA provision prohibiting ex parte communications by agency decisionmakers (see § 5.6).) With respect to the facts, however, section 554(d)(1)'s no-consultation rule is all-embracing. Not only may an ALJ not discuss the facts with a party off the record, but because section 554(d)(1) extends to consultations with any "person," an ALJ may not have such discussions with other agency personnel, regardless of their duties or lack of involvement in the case.[5]

---

3. The separation-of-functions provisions of 554(d) do not apply in certain types of proceedings concerning licensing and public utilities and carriers (APA § 554(d)(A)-(B)). The separation-of-functions provisions of section 554(d) also may be limited to formal adjudications that are prosecutorial in nature. The APA does not state such a limitation, but it may be implicit in the statute's description of agency personnel "engaged in the performance of investigative or prosecuting functions." See SECTION OF ADMINISTRATIVE LAW AND REGULATORY PRACTICE OF AMERICAN BAR ASSOCIATION, A GUIDE TO FEDERAL AGENCY ADJUDICATION 120–21 & n.75 (Michael Asimow, ed., 2003).

4. See *Attorney General's Manual, supra* note 1, at 54. Section 554(d)(1) is supplemented by section 557(d)(1)'s prohibition against ex parte communications involving agency decisionmakers in formal proceedings (see § 5.6).

5. See Butz v. Economou, 438 U.S. 478, 513–14 (1978).

Section 554(d)(1) provides a limited exception to its no-consultation rule for communications "to the extent required for the disposition of ex parte matters required by law." According to the *Attorney General's Manual*, this exception allows ALJs "to act without notice on such matters as requests for adjournments, continuances, and the filing of papers," as well as on "requests for subpenas [sic]."[6]

(c) Separation-of-Functions Limitations on Agency Law–Enforcement Personnel in Formal Adjudicatory Proceedings

Section 554(d) provides that agency personnel who prosecute or investigate a case "may not, in that or a factually related case, participate or advise in the decision, recommended decision, or agency review ... , except as witness or counsel in public proceedings." This prohibition is grounded on Congress's judgment that agency prosecutors and investigators cannot be "impartial" in a case in which they have advocated for a particular outcome (see APA § 556(b)). Based on the congressional objective of enhancing the impartiality of agency decisions in formal adjudication, the Ninth Circuit has applied the section 554(d) prohibition not only to agency personnel "with the title of 'investigator' or 'prosecutor,' but [also to] all persons who had, in that or a factually related case, been involved with ex parte information, or who had developed, by prior involvement with the case, a 'will to win.' "[7] On the other hand, section 554(d) permits an administrative law judge to obtain advice from and to consult with agency prosecutors and investigators who are not involved in that or a factually related case, at least to the extent these communications do not run afoul of section 554(d)(1) of the APA (see § 5.1(b)).

According to the *Attorney General's Manual*, the phrase "factually related case," as used in section 554(d), forbids the participation of agency investigators and prosecutors in agency decision-making when "a party is faced with two different proceedings arising out of the same or a connected set of facts." The *Attorney General's Manual* offered as illustration an agency investigation resulting in (1) a cease-and-desist proceeding and (2) a license-revocation proceeding against a party. In this example, section 554(d) would bar agency prosecutors and investigators in each proceeding from playing any role in the agency's decision whether to issue a cease-and-desist order or to revoke the party's license. By contrast, two administrative proceedings that simply share similar

---

6. *Attorney General's Manual, supra* note 1, at 55.

7. Grolier, Inc. v. FTC, 615 F.2d 1215, 1220 (9th Cir. 1980) (applying section 554(d) to the attorney-advisor of an agency head).

facts are not "factually related" within the meaning of section 554(d). For example, agency personnel who investigate or prosecute a price-fixing case against a firm may assist in the agency's decision in a similar price-fixing case against a different firm.[8]

§ 5.2   Pre-hearing Procedures

(a) Notice of Agency Hearing

Administrative agencies begin formal adjudication by issuing a complaint, which section 554(b) of the Administrative Procedure Act labels "notice of an agency hearing." Section 554(b) requires that the notice of hearing be "timely." According to the *Attorney General's Manual*, "Whether a given period of time constitutes timely notice will depend upon the circumstances, including the urgency of the situation and the complexity of the issues involved in the proceeding."[1] In enforcing the timeliness requirement, reviewing courts expect that the time period between notice and hearing be sufficient to allow the parties to prepare their case.[2]

Section 554(b) prescribes the minimum content of a hearing notice. In addition to indicating "the time, place, and nature of the hearing," the notice also must specify "the legal authority and jurisdiction" of the agency to conduct the hearing (APA § 554(b)(1)-(2)). This pleading requirement offers the parties an opportunity at the outset of the proceeding to challenge the legal authority of the agency to convene a hearing.

The only other APA requirement for a notice of hearing is that it plead "the matters of fact and law asserted" (APA § 554(b)(3)). Courts have tended to equate this requirement with the notice guarantee of procedural due process, holding that a notice of hearing must "reasonably apprise any interested person of the issues involved in the proceeding."[3] The notice of hearing must include sufficient information to allow the parties to prepare for the hearing.[4]

---

8. *Attorney General's Manual, supra* note 1, at 54 n.6.

§ 5.2

1. *Attorney General's Manual on the Administrative Procedure Act* 46 (1947), reprinted in WILLIAM F. FUNK, et al., FEDERAL ADMINISTRATIVE PROCEDURE SOURCEBOOK 33–171 (3D ED. 2000).

2. SECTION OF ADMINISTRATIVE LAW AND REGULATORY PRACTICE OF AMERICAN BAR ASSOCIATION, A GUIDE TO FEDERAL AGENCY ADJUDICATION 43 (Michael Asimow, ed., 2003).

3. North Alabama Express, Inc. v. United States, 585 F.2d 783, 787 (5th Cir. 1978); see also Rapp v. Office of Thrift Supervision, 52 F.3d 1510, 1520 (10th Cir. 1995) ("Notice [under section 554(b)(3)] is sufficient as long as the party to an administrative proceeding is reasonably apprised of the issues in controversy and is not misled.").

4. ABA GUIDE TO ADJUDICATION, *supra* note 2, at 40.

(b) Intervention

Congress drafted the Administrative Procedure Act on the assumption that agencies at times would allow interested persons to intervene as parties in their proceedings.[5] This assumption is evident in the APA's definition of "party," which includes not only persons who have been "named ... in an agency proceeding," but also those who have been "admitted as a party" or who have "properly" sought and are "entitled as of right to be admitted as a party" in an agency proceeding (APA § 551(3)). The APA's definition of "party" also contemplates that agencies either may confer full party status on intervenors or admit them "as a party for limited purposes" (APA § 551(3)).

The APA does not state the source of an interested person's right to intervene in an agency proceeding. Statutes other than the APA and agency procedural rules, of course, may entitle interested persons to intervene in a *particular* agency's proceedings. It is unlikely, however, that the APA itself provides a *general* right of intervention in administrative proceedings by interested persons. The most promising source of such a general right in the APA is section 555(b), which applies to all agency proceedings. Section 555(b) provides, in relevant part, "So far as the orderly conduct of public business permits, an interested person *may appear* before an agency ... for the presentation, adjustment, or determination of an issue, request, or controversy in a proceeding ... or in connection with an agency function" (emphasis added). It is significant that section 555(b) uses the term "appear" rather than "intervene": An appearance does not require party status in the relevant agency proceeding.[6] And even if one were to equate appearance with intervention, section 555(b)'s use of the permissive "may" instead of the mandatory "must" suggests that it permits, but does not require, agencies to allow interested persons to become parties in their proceedings.

A person's right to intervene as a party in an agency proceeding is thus generally governed by the agency's enabling act and its procedural rules. The D.C. Circuit's decision in *Office of Communications of the United Church of Christ v. Federal Communications Commission*[7] is the leading example of judicial prodding of agency officials to fully enforce the intervention rights so created. In *United Church of Christ*, the court of appeals overturned the FCC's

---

5. I use "person" here in the APA sense, thus including not only an "individual," but also a "partnership, corporation, association, or public or private organization other than an agency" (APA § 551(2)).

6. See *Attorney General's Manual, supra* note 1, at 63 (describing section

555(b) as providing interested persons an "opportunity for informal appearance," rather than for full-fledged intervention, in administrative proceedings).

7. 359 F.2d 994 (D.C.Cir. 1966).

denial of a petition to intervene filed by "representatives of the listening public" in a broadcast license renewal proceeding. The FCC's "traditional position" had confined intervention rights in license-renewal proceedings to those who could demonstrate that the renewal threatened them with economic injury or electrical interference. The Federal Communications Act, however, was not so limited. It allowed "any party in interest" to contest the renewal of a broadcast license. The D.C. Circuit thus found no statutory justification for the Commission's limitation of intervention rights to the two traditional grounds. To the contrary, the participation of listeners in license-renewal proceedings, the court explained, would serve the essential role by informing the FCC of any "programming deficiencies" of the broadcaster.[8]

An agency's decision whether to allow a person to intervene in one of its proceedings is independent of the person's standing to seek judicial review of the agency's final action. Agencies thus may permit persons to intervene in an administrative proceeding even if they would not have standing to challenge the agency's final decision.[9] And although it is unusual, agencies may deny intervention to persons who satisfy standing requirements to challenge the agency's final decision.[10]

(c) Discovery

The Administrative Procedure Act provides no right to discovery in formal adjudication (or in any other type of administrative proceeding, for that matter).[11] Enabling acts typically are silent on discovery rights as well, and only a few agencies provide for broad discovery in their procedural rules. In the absence of a statute or agency rule requiring discovery, reviewing courts invalidate administrative decisions because of the agency's denial of a discovery request only in "the most extraordinary circumstances."[12]

The absence of a general right to discovery in formal adjudication is ameliorated somewhat by several alternative means available to parties for obtaining information from their adversaries. For

---

8. *Id.* at 997–1005.

9. See Nichols v. Board of Trustees of the Asbestos Workers Local 24 Pension Plan, 835 F.2d 881, 896 n.108 (D.C.Cir. 1987).

10. See Envirocare of Utah, Inc. v. NRC, 194 F.3d 72 (D.C.Cir. 1999).

11. See, e.g., Frilette v. Kimberlin, 508 F.2d 205, 208 (3rd Cir. 1974), cert. denied, 421 U.S. 980 (1975); Moore v. Administrator, Veterans Administration, 475 F.2d 1283, 1286 (D.C.Cir. 1973). Although section 556(c)(4) authorizes

ALJs to arrange for depositions "when the ends of justice would be served," this authority contemplates the taking of depositions to preserve testimony for the hearing, and not to conduct discovery. ABA GUIDE TO ADJUDICATION, *supra* note 2, at 47.

12. See Trailways Lines v. ICC, 766 F.2d 1537, 1546 (D.C.Cir. 1985). When procedural due process applies, an agency must allow the discovery that is necessary for parties to adequately prepare for a hearing. ABA GUIDE TO ADJUDICATION, *supra* note 2, at 46.

example, although section 555(c) of the APA provides that agencies may take investigatory actions only "as authorized by law," enabling acts often provide broad investigatory powers to agencies with a law-enforcement mandate. The typical arsenal of administrative investigatory powers includes (1) reporting requirements; (2) inspection of the records and premises of regulated entities; and (3) issuance of subpoenas for testimony and for the production of documents.

The APA partially offsets these administrative investigatory powers by requiring agencies with subpoena power to issue subpoenas at the request of other parties to (and witnesses in) an agency proceeding "on a statement or showing of general relevance and reasonable scope of the evidence sought" (APA § 555(d)). According to the *Attorney General's Manual*, section 555(d) "make[s] agency subpenas [sic] available to private parties to the same extent as to agency representatives."[13]

Finally, the Freedom of Information Act ("FOIA") provides parties a potential source of information relevant to an administrative proceeding.[14] Congress enacted the FOIA in 1966 as section 552 of the APA. The act provides to members of the public a general right to obtain copies of government records, subject to several specified exceptions. Although the Supreme Court has made clear its displeasure at parties using the FOIA as a "discovery tool," the justices have recognized that an individual's status as party to an administrative proceeding neither enhances nor diminishes the individual's right under the FOIA to obtain copies of government records.[15]

(d) Settlement and Pre-hearing Conferences

It is common for agencies to enter into consent decrees before or after lodging a formal complaint against a party. Section 554(c)(1) of the Administrative Procedure Act encourages such settlements "when time, the nature of the proceeding, and the public interest permit." In order to facilitate settlement, section 556(c)(6) of the APA permits, but does not require, administrative law judges to "hold conferences for the settlement or simplification of the issues by consent of the parties or by the use of alternative means of dispute resolution."[16] ALJs also use pre-hearing confer-

---

13. *Attorney General's Manual, supra* note 1, at 67. For discussion of agency subpoena power, see ABA GUIDE TO ADJUDICATION, *supra* note 2, at 47–58.

14. For discussion of the use of the Freedom of Information Act as a means of administrative discovery, see Edward A. Tomlinson, *Use of the Freedom of Information Act for Discovery Purposes*, 43 MD. L. REV. 119 (1984).

15. NLRB v. Robbins Tire & Rubber Co., 437 U.S. 214, 242 & n.23 (1978).

16. The Administrative Dispute Resolution Act of 1990, 5 U.S.C. §§ 571–584, requires agencies to consider alternative methods of dispute resolution

ences to invite the parties to ameliorate the discovery deficit in administrative proceedings by exchanging relevant information.

In drafting section 554(c)(1), Congress "deliberately left" the "precise manner" of providing settlement opportunities to the discretion of the agencies. And the provision itself recognizes several circumstances—namely, "when time, the nature of the proceeding, and the public interest [do not] permit"—in which an agency should not be expected to provide parties an opportunity to settle. The *Attorney General's Manual* listed several examples illustrating these statutory criteria for denying (or limiting) settlement opportunities. These included cases involving "emergency" situations, proceedings pursuant to an enabling act requiring a hearing within a short time-period, cases in which the parties do not wish to settle, and situations where settlement would fail to ensure "future compliance with the law."[17]

If "the parties are unable ... to determine a controversy by consent," section 554(c)(2) of the APA instructs the agency to proceed with a hearing.

§ 5.3   The Administrative Hearing

Section 556 of the Administrative Procedure Act delineates the basic requirements of the hearing that lies at the heart of formal adjudication.[1] That hearing resembles a judicial trial: It is an adversarial, evidentiary proceeding "conducted before a trier of fact insulated from political influence."[2] As in a trial, the hearing transcript and exhibits, together with the parties' filings in the proceeding, constitute "the exclusive record" for the agency's decision (APA § 556(e)). And of course, as the Supreme Court observed, the disputes that federal agencies resolve in formal adjudication "are every bit as fractious as those which come to court."[3]

("ADR"), but leaves the nature and extent of this consideration largely to the discretion of the agency and subject to the consent of the parties, see 5 U.S.C. § 572.

17. *Attorney General's Manual, supra* note 1, at 48–50. The *Attorney General's Manual* thought it "clear" that section 554(c)(1) did not require agencies "to defer formal proceedings indefinitely while parties submit a series of proposals for the purpose of delay." *Id.* at 49.

§ 5.3

1. Because agencies typically fine tune the APA hearing requirements in their procedural rules, there is considerable variation in the manner by which each agency with formal adjudicatory authority conducts its hearings. See Citizens Awareness Network, Inc. v. United States, 391 F.3d 338, 349 (1st Cir. 2004) ("The APA lays out only the most skeletal framework for conducting [formal] agency adjudications, leaving broad discretion to the affected agencies in formulating detailed rules.").

2. See Butz v. Economou, 438 U.S. 478, 512–13 (1978).

3. *Id.* at 513.

(a) The Hearing Officer: Administrative Law Judges

The head of an agency, or one or more members of the collegial body that heads an agency, may preside over a formal adjudicatory hearing (APA § 556(b)(1)-(2)). It is rare, however, for agency heads to exercise this prerogative. In the typical case, the APA provides that "one or more [of the agency's] administrative law judges," or "ALJs," serve as hearing officer in formal proceedings (§ 556(b)(3)). There are well over a thousand ALJs serving in thirty or so federal agencies.[4]

The creation of administrative law judges as "a special class of semi-independent subordinate hearing officers"[5] was a central reform of the Administrative Procedure Act.[6] Administrative law judges are "functionally comparable" to trial judges when they preside over formal adjudicatory hearings.[7] Like a trial judge in a bench trial, an ALJ is the principal factfinder and initial decisionmaker in an administrative case.[8] The powers of administrative law judges in presiding over formal hearings track those of a trial judge. Section 556(c) of the APA empowers ALJs to "administer oaths and affirmations"; issue subpoenas; control the taking of depositions; rule on procedural matters, evidentiary questions and offers of proof; hold settlement and other prehearing conferences; and generally, "regulate the course of the hearing." Because Congress in section 556(c) vested these powers in administrative law judges, agencies cannot eliminate them.[9]

The APA requires ALJs to conduct evidentiary hearings "in an impartial manner" (APA § 556(b)). The requirement of impartiality bars ALJs from favoring the agency's representatives, or any other party, during the proceeding. Impartiality is not the equiva-

---

4. See Paul R. Verkuil, *Reflections Upon the Federal Administrative Judiciary*, 39 UCLA L. REV. 1341, 1343 (1992). There is a larger, distinct group of "Administrative Judges" ("AJs") who preside over administrative hearings that are not subject to the APA's requirements for formal adjudication. AJs enjoy considerably less independence in their decisionmaking than do ALJs. For a study of the work of AJs, see John H. Frye III, *Survey of Non–ALJ Hearing Programs in the Federal Government*, 44 ADMIN. L. REV. 261 (1992).

5. Ramspeck v. Federal Trial Examiners Conference, 345 U.S. 128, 132 (1953) (quoting from the legislative history of the APA). The original APA used the term "hearing examiner" to describe the hearing officers in formal proceed-

ings. Congress changed the name in 1978 to raise the status of hearing officers. See Pub. L. No. 95–251, 92 Stat. 183 (1978).

6. For an historical development of administrative hearing officers, see Daniel J. Gifford, *Federal Administrative Law Judges: The Relevance of Past Choices to Future Directions*, 49 ADMIN. L. REV. 1 (1997).

7. See *Butz*, 438 U.S. at 513.

8. See Association of Administrative Law Judges, Inc. v. Heckler, 594 F.Supp. 1132, 1141 (D.D.C. 1984).

9. *Attorney General's Manual on the Administrative Procedure Act* 74–75 (1947), reprinted in WILLIAM F. FUNK, et al., FEDERAL ADMINISTRATIVE PROCEDURE SOURCEBOOK 33–171 (3d ed. 2000).

lent of passivity, however. ALJs may question witnesses and may take other actions to complete a record for decision.[10]

In an effort to enhance the status of administrative law judges and to safeguard their independence, Congress has sharply limited the agencies' control over the selection and retention of their ALJs. Each agency may "appoint as many administrative law judges as are necessary" to handle its caseload,[11] but in making these appointments, agencies are limited to a list of candidates selected by the Office of Personnel Management ("OPM").[12] And although ALJs do not possess the pay and tenure protections enjoyed by Article III judges, they are more insulated from financial pressure than most agency employees.[13] Agencies do not decide the financial compensation of their ALJs. OPM instead sets the pay scales of all administrative law judges according to congressional specifications based on an ALJ's length of service.[14] Moreover, ALJs are not limited to a fixed term of office. They serve indefinitely, absent "good cause" for their removal, as determined by an independent agency (the Merit Systems Protection Board) after a formal adjudicatory hearing. Lesser, adverse personnel actions against ALJs are subject to the same "good cause" limitation.[15]

Congress has protected the independence of administrative law judges as well by limiting the agencies' supervisory authority over them. Agencies may not assign ALJs to "perform duties inconsistent with their duties and responsibilities as administrative law judges." Nor may agencies cherry pick the case assignments of their administrative law judges: "[S]o far as practicable," agencies must assign ALJs their cases "in rotation."[16]

Agencies nevertheless retain some authority to monitor and to supervise the work of their administrative law judges, provided they do not compromise an ALJ's "decisional independence."[17] For example, in *Nash v. Bowen*,[18] the Second Circuit upheld the Social Security Administration's "peer review program" of "dead" ALJ decisions in disability-benefit cases. The purpose of the program was to improve the quality of the ALJs' disability decisions, as well as to narrow the "wide disparity" among those decisions. The court

10. *Id*. at 73.

11. 5 U.S.C. § 3105.

12. For a description of the appointments process for ALJs, see Jeffrey S. Lubbers, *Federal Administrative Law Judges: A Focus on our Invisible Judiciary*, 33 ADMIN. L. REV. 109, 112–20 (1981).

13. See *Association of Administrative Law Judges*, 594 F.Supp. at 1140.

14. See 5 U.S.C. § 5372.

15. 5 U.S.C. § 7521(a). Section 7521(b) lists the types of agency personnel actions that do and do not qualify as "adverse" pursuant to section 7521(a).

16. 5 U.S.C. § 3105.

17. See Nash v. Bowen, 869 F.2d 675, 680–81 (2d Cir. 1989), cert. denied, 493 U.S. 812 (1989).

18. 869 F.2d 675 (2d Cir. 1989), cert. denied, 493 U.S. 812 (1989).

of appeals accepted the program as "legitimate agency supervision." Agency heads may use a system of "extra-appellate" review "to ensure that ALJ decisions conformed with [their] interpretation of relevant law and policy," the Second Circuit explained, provided their review did not interfere with ALJ decisions in "live" cases. The court in *Nash* also accepted the agency's establishment of monthly "production goals" that set a minimum number of decisions for each ALJ, holding that "reasonable efforts to increase the production levels of ALJs are not an infringement of decisional independence."[19]

The *Nash* court, however, found the agency's "quality assurance system" to be a "cause for concern."[20] This program attempted to limit the number of ALJ decisions reversing the denial of benefits by state agencies.[21] In the end, though, the agency satisfied the court of appeals that the program related only to the possibility that reversal rates reflect "errors in the decisionmaking of ALJs." The agency submitted statistics showing a correlation between "actual errors of law or policy in ALJ decisions and extremes in their reversal rates." It was important to the court of appeals as well that the agency only used reversal rates "as a benchmark in deciding whether there *might* be problems in the adjudicatory methods of particularly high (or low) reversal rate ALJs." Had the court found the agency's quality assurance system to have been an effort "to coerce ALJs into . . . deciding more cases against claimants," it would have invalidated the program as "a clear infringement of decisional independence."[22]

(b) Right to Counsel

Section 555(b) of the APA provides a general right to counsel to all "part[ies] . . . in [any] agency proceeding." This right is not limited to the parties. It extends to "person[s] compelled to appear in person before an agency or representative thereof." Witnesses who are required to testify during an agency hearing are thus entitled to legal representation as well.

Unlike the constitutional right to counsel in certain criminal proceedings, section 555(b) does not entitle persons to government-

---

19. *Id.* at 680.

20. *Id.* at 681.

21. State agencies made the initial determination whether claimants qualified for disability benefits. A claimant who was denied benefits by a state agency could request a *de novo* hearing before an ALJ of the federal Social Security Administration. See *Association of Administrative Law Judges*, 594 F.Supp. at 1133.

22. *Nash*, 869 F.2d at 681; see also *Association of Administrative Law Judges*, 594 F.Supp. at 1133 (earlier performance review program of the Social Security Administration with an "unremitting focus" on the rate at which ALJs allow claims for disability benefits "created an untenable atmosphere of tension and unfairness which violated the spirit of the APA, if no specific provision thereof").

appointed, publicly funded legal representation. Persons must arrange for legal representation in administrative proceedings on their own.

(c) Right to Present Evidence

The parties to a formal adjudicatory hearing are "entitled to present [their] case or defense by oral or documentary evidence" (APA § 556(d)). According to the *Attorney General's Manual*, the function of section 556(d) is to give parties a statutory right to "present their evidence orally" in addition to submitting documentary evidence.[23] But as with civil litigation, a party's right to an oral evidentiary hearing is contingent on there being material facts in dispute. If this is not the case, agencies, like courts, can enter summary judgment.[24]

(d) Right to Cross–Examination

The APA establishes the right of parties "to conduct such cross-examination as may be required for a full and true disclosure of the facts" (APA § 556(d)). As its language makes clear, section 556(d) does not grant parties an "absolute right" to cross-examination.[25] A party may pursue cross-examination only as "required for a full and true disclosure of the facts." Section 556(d) thus entitles parties to conduct "adequate," but not "unlimited," cross-examination.[26]

(e) Burden of Proof

The Administrative Procedure Act places the "burden of proof" on "the proponent of . . . [an] order," unless another statute provides otherwise (APA § 556(d)).[27] The term "burden of proof," however, is imprecise. At times, courts have equated "burden of proof" with the term "burden of persuasion," which identifies the party who must convince the decisionmaker in order to prevail on an issue. At other times, "burden of proof" simply has stood for the

23. *Attorney General's Manual, supra* note 9, at 83. For certain types of adjudications—that is, those "determining claims for money or benefits or applications for initial licenses"—agencies may allow only the submission of written evidence, provided no party is "prejudiced" by the loss of an oral hearing (see APA § 556(d)).

24. See Costle v. Pacific Legal Foundation, 445 U.S. 198, 214 (1980); Weinberger v. Hynson, Westcott & Dunning, Inc., 412 U.S. 609, 620–22 (1973).

25. Central Freight Lines, Inc. v. United States, 669 F.2d 1063, 1068 (5th Cir. 1982); Seacoast Anti–Pollution League v. Costle, 572 F.2d 872, 880 (1st Cir. 1978), overruled on other grounds, Dominion Energy Brayton Point, LLC v. Johnson, 443 F.3d 12 (1st Cir. 2006).

26. See Solis v. Schweiker, 719 F.2d 301, 302 (9th Cir. 1983); *Attorney General's Manual, supra* note 9, at 77, 78.

27. The justices "do not lightly presume" that another statute "reject[s] the APA's burden of proof provision." Director, Office of Workers' Compensation Programs v. Greenwich Collieries, 512 U.S. 267, 271 (1994).

"burden of going forward" (or the "burden of production"), which identifies the party who must first produce evidence on an issue. The drafters of the APA did not indicate which of the two meanings of "burden of proof" they had in mind for formal administrative adjudications.

The *Attorney General's Manual* read "burden of proof" in section 556(d) to mean the "burden of going forward."[28] The justices at first agreed with that interpretation,[29] but they switched course in *Director, Office of Workers' Compensation Programs v. Greenwich Collieries*,[30] defining "burden of proof" in section 556(d) to mean "burden of persuasion." The Court in *Greenwich Collieries* explained that the equation of "burden of proof" and "burden of persuasion" had become "generally accepted in the legal community" by the time Congress had enacted the APA. The justices presumed that Congress had accepted that equation as well when drafting section 556(d).[31]

(f) Standard of Proof

The APA does not specify the standard of proof that "the proponent of ... [an] order" must satisfy in order to meet the "burden of proof" imposed by section 556(d). In *Steadman v. Securities and Exchange Commission*, the Supreme Court held that the standard of proof in formal adjudication is "preponderance of the evidence," the same standard that traditionally has obtained in civil litigation.[32] This preponderance standard requires proponents to prove that "it is more likely than not that the facts they seek to establish are true."[33]

(g) Rules of Evidence

Administrative agencies do not observe the Federal Rules of Evidence. Indeed, for the most part agencies need not follow any set of formal evidence rules in their adjudicatory proceedings.[34] The Administrative Procedure Act simply instructs administrative law judges to "receive relevant evidence" (APA § 556(c)(3)). The act

---

28. See *Attorney General's Manual*, *supra* note 9, at 75.

29. See NLRB v. Transportation Management Corp., 462 U.S. 393, 404 n.7 (1983).

30. 512 U.S. 267 (1994).

31. *Id.* at 275–76.

32. 450 U.S. 91, 102 (1981).

33. SECTION OF ADMINISTRATIVE LAW AND REGULATORY PRACTICE OF AMERICAN BAR ASSOCIATION, A GUIDE TO FEDERAL AGENCY ADJUDICATION 69 (Michael Asimow, ed., 2003).

34. See Richardson v. Perales, 402 U.S. 389, 400, 407–08 (1971); FTC v. Cement Institute, 333 U.S. 683, 705–06 (1948); *Attorney General's Manual, supra* note 9, at 76 ("the technical rules of evidence [are] not ... applicable to administrative hearings"). Certain privileges, such as the attorney-client privilege, generally are available in agency adjudications. See SECTION OF ADMINISTRATIVE LAW AND REGULATORY PRACTICE OF AMERICAN BAR ASSOCIATION, A BLACKLETTER STATEMENT OF FEDERAL ADMINISTRATIVE LAW 8 (2004); Ernest Gellhorn, *Rules of Evidence and Official Notice in Formal Administrative Hearings*, 1971 DUKE L.J. 1, 28–35.

also invites agencies, "as a matter of policy," to exclude "irrelevant, immaterial, or unduly repetitious evidence" from its formal adjudicatory hearings (APA § 556(d)).

Noticeably absent from the APA's short list of excludable evidence is hearsay. Agencies generally admit hearsay evidence, unless the evidence is so attenuated as to be irrelevant. And although some states follow the "residuum rule," which prohibits administrative agencies from grounding decisions solely on hearsay evidence, there is no such prohibition in federal administrative law.[35]

Congress's relaxation of the rules of evidence in administrative proceedings follows from the conception of agency adjudication as an alternative form of dispute resolution freed from the traditional constraints of the judicial process. In this view, the specialization and expertise of agency decisionmakers eliminate the need for formal evidentiary rules, which often have been designed to protect lay jurors from evidence that might prove distracting or inflammatory.[36] A general rule of relevance provides agencies maximum flexibility to draw on the evidence they deem useful in making their decisions. Beyond the statutory instruction to admit relevant evidence, the APA therefore leaves to agencies the task of establishing rules of evidence for their proceedings, subject to the demands of procedural due process and of the enabling act governing the agency's actions (see APA § 556(c) ("[s]ubject to published rules of the agency")).[37]

(h) Official Notice

The Administrative Procedure Act permits agencies to take "official notice of a material fact not appearing in the evidence in the record" (APA § 556(e)). This permission follows judicial tradition. For example, federal courts may take judicial notice of facts that are "not subject to reasonable dispute," either because they are "generally known within the [trial court's] territorial jurisdiction," or because they are "capable of accurate and ready determination by resort to sources whose accuracy cannot reasonably be questioned" (Fed.R.Evid. 201(b)). But there are two important

---

35. See *Richardson*, 402 U.S. at 402, 407–08, 410.

36. See McDaniel v. Celebrezze, 331 F.2d 426, 429 (4th Cir. 1964); *Attorney General's Manual, supra* note 9, at 79–80. For an argument favoring broad application of the Federal Rules of Evidence to formal adjudicatory proceedings, see Michael H. Graham, *Application of the Rules of Evidence in Administrative Agency Formal Adversarial Adjudications*, 1991 U. ILL. L. REV. 353.

37. For a survey of evidentiary rules adopted by federal agencies, see Richard J. Pierce, Jr., *Use of the Federal Rules of Evidence in Federal Agency Adjudications*, 39 ADMIN. L. REV. 1, 5–6 (1987).

distinctions between judicial notice as traditionally authorized by rules of evidence and the APA's official notice.

The first distinction concerns the relative scope of authority to notice facts without supporting evidence in the hearing record. Because of the specialization and technical expertise of administrative agencies, as well as the "volume and repetition" of their caseload, the authority of agencies to take official notice of facts is far broader than the comparable judicial authority.[38] While federal judges may notice only indisputable facts, administrative law judges, in the description of the *Attorney General's Manual*, may take official notice of "all matters as to which the agency by reason of its functions is presumed to be expert, such as technical or scientific facts within its specialized knowledge."[39] As a practical matter, one commentator has noted, an administrative law judge may take official notice of "almost any information useful in deciding the adjudication."[40]

The second distinction relates to the differing effects of judicially and officially noticing a fact. When a trial judge takes judicial notice of a fact, the judge finds conclusively that the fact is true. A party may not introduce evidence at trial to disprove a judicially noticed fact.[41] When an administrative law judge officially notices a fact, the effect is simply to "transfer the burden of proof on that material fact."[42] Section 556(e) of the Administrative Procedure Act obligates the agency to provide opposing parties "an opportunity to show the contrary." To satisfy this obligation, the ALJ must "adequately inform" the parties of "the facts noticed and their source with a degree of precision and specificity" sufficient to provide opportunity for a contrary showing.[43] Thus while official notice relieves the proponent of a material fact of the usual burden of introducing a preponderance of evidence supporting a fact, it does not prevent the opponent from introducing evidence to dispute the noticed fact.[44] Nor does the doctrine relieve the agency of its obligation to determine the sufficiency of the evidence submitted in opposition to the noticed fact.

38. Castillo-Villagra v. INS, 972 F.2d 1017, 1026–27 (9th Cir. 1992); see *Attorney General's Manual*, *supra* note 9, at 79–80.

39. *Attorney General's Manual*, *supra* note 9, at 79–80. The facts that administrative hearing officers typically notice have been generated by the agency's staff or have been established in the agency's prior proceedings. See Gellhorn, *Rules of Evidence and Official Notice*, *supra* note 34, at 42.

40. See Gellhorn, *Rules of Evidence and Official Notice*, *supra* note 34, at 43.

41. F.R.Evid. 201(g) & Adv. Comm. Note.

42. See Gellhorn, *Rules of Evidence and Official Notice*, *supra* note 34, at 43–45.

43. Banks v. Schweiker, 654 F.2d 637, 642 (9th Cir. 1981).

44. Ohio Bell Telephone Co. v. Public Utilities Comm'n of Ohio, 301 U.S. 292, 300–02 (1937).

§ 5.4   The Initial Decision

Section 554(d) of the Administrative Procedure Act requires that the administrative law judge make the agency's "initial decision," unless the officer "becomes unavailable to the agency" (see also APA § 557(b)).[1] Before making an initial decision, the ALJ must give the parties a "reasonable opportunity" to submit proposed findings of fact and conclusions of law, together with "supporting reasons" (APA § 557(c)). The ALJ's initial decision is "on the record," which means, "[t]he transcript of testimony and exhibits, together with all papers and requests filed in the proceeding, constitutes the exclusive record for decision" (APA § 556(e)). The initial decision must include "findings and conclusions, and the reasons or basis therefor, on all the material issues of fact, law, or discretion presented on the record" (APA § 557(c)(A)). The ALJ's initial decision becomes the final decision of the agency "unless there is an appeal to, or review on motion of, the agency within time provided by rule" (APA § 557(b)).

§ 5.5   Administrative Review

The Administrative Procedure Act proceeds on the assumption that parties may seek review of an adverse initial decision within the agency (see APA § 557(b)), but the act itself grants no such right of appeal. Nor does due process.[1] The right to administrative appeal is thus created and largely governed by enabling acts and agency regulations.[2] Administrative appellate processes thus vary from agency to agency, and sometimes within an agency, from program to program. It nevertheless often holds true that smaller agencies with light caseloads grant parties a right to appeal adverse initial decisions directly to the head(s) of the agency, while agencies with a large caseload provide a right of appeal to an intermediate appellate body, subject to discretionary review by the agency head(s).[3]

§ 5.4

1. An agency may provide, "either in specific cases or by general rule," that "the entire record" be certified to the head(s) of the agency "for decision" (APA § 557(b)). In such a case, the ALJ issues a "recommended decision" for the agency. *Id.* On those rare occasions when the agency head(s) preside over the hearing (see APA § 556(b)(1)), the agency may announce its final decision without a prior, initial decision (APA § 557(b)).

§ 5.5

1. See SECTION OF ADMINISTRATIVE LAW AND REGULATORY PRACTICE OF AMERICAN BAR ASSOCIATION, A GUIDE TO FEDERAL AGENCY ADJUDICATION 88 (Michael Asimow, ed., 2003).

2. Even if there is no appeal, an agency may review an ALJ's initial decision on its own. By the same token, agencies can limit the issues they consider on appeal, either generally by rule or ad hoc by notifying the parties in a case (see APA § 557(b)).

3. See ABA GUIDE TO ADJUDICATION, *supra* note 1, at 88–89. For a review and assessment of the internal review processes of several federal agencies, see Russell L. Weaver, *Appellate Review in Executive Departments and Agencies,* 48 ADMIN. L. REV. 251 (1996).

On administrative review, agencies must provide the parties "a reasonable opportunity" to submit proposed findings of fact and conclusions of law, "exceptions" to the ALJ's initial decision, and "supporting reasons" for their proposed findings, conclusions, and exceptions (APA § 557(c)). The APA does not require agencies to hear oral argument.[4]

An ALJ's initial decision is not entitled to deference on administrative review, whether by the head(s) of the agency or by an intermediate appellate body.[5] Section 557(b) of the APA provides that when reviewing an initial decision, "the agency has all the powers which it would have in making the initial decision." As paraphrased by the *Attorney General's Manual*, an agency reviewing "the decision of its subordinate officer [i.e., the ALJ] ... retains complete freedom of decision—as though it had heard the evidence itself."[6] Recall that agency heads are free to preside over formal adjudicatory hearings whenever they wish (APA § 556(b)(1)). When agency heads choose instead to assign an ALJ as hearing officer, they do not relinquish their ultimate power—and responsibility—to decide the case.

But because an ALJ's initial decision becomes part of the administrative record in a case (APA § 557(c)), it may undermine a contrary decision by the agency on review. The Supreme Court explained in the leading case of *Universal Camera Corp. v. National Labor Relations Board*,[7] "[E]vidence supporting a conclusion may be less substantial when an impartial, experienced [ALJ] who has observed the witnesses and lived with the case has drawn conclusions different from the [agency's]." This is especially true, the Court emphasized in *Universal Camera*, when the case turns on the credibility of the witnesses who testified at the hearing.[8] Whenever an agency rejects an ALJ's findings of fact, it must be prepared to "explain why" to the satisfaction of an often skeptical reviewing court (see § 8.4(a)).[9]

The final agency decision, like the initial decision, must include "findings and conclusions, and the reasons or basis therefor, on all material issues of fact, law, or discretion presented on the record"

4. See *Attorney General's Manual on the Administrative Procedure Act* 85 (1947), reprinted in WILLIAM F. FUNK, et al., FEDERAL ADMINISTRATIVE PROCEDURE SOURCEBOOK 33–171 (3d ed. 2000).

5. See FCC v. Allentown Broadcasting Corp., 349 U.S. 358, 364–65 (1955); Universal Camera Corp. v. NLRB, 340 U.S. 474, 492 (1951).

6. See *Attorney General's Manual, supra* note 4, at 83.

7. 340 U.S. 474 (1951).

8. *Id.* at 496; see *Attorney General's Manual, supra* note 4, at 84; see, e.g., Penasquitos Village, Inc. v. NLRB, 565 F.2d 1074, 1078–80 (9th Cir. 1977).

9. ITT Continental Baking Co. v. FTC, 532 F.2d 207, 219 (2d Cir. 1976); see Patricia M. Wald, *Some Thoughts on Beginnings and Ends: Court of Appeals Review of Administrative Law Judges' Findings and Opinions*, 67 WASH. U.L.Q. 661, 666 (1989).

(APA § 557(c)(A)). The agency may write its final decision "in narrative or expository form," so long as the opinion states "the agency's findings and conclusions on material issues of fact, law or discretion" with sufficient specificity to inform a reviewing court of the basis of the agency's determinations in the record and in law.[10] The agency may simply adopt the ALJ's findings, conclusions, and justification, either wholly or partially, provided it does so clearly.[11] The final agency decision in formal adjudication is subject to judicial review for procedural and substantive legality. (See APA § 706(2); Chapters 7 and 8.)

Personal Decisionmaking. The officer(s) responsible for the agency's final decision on review of the ALJ's initial decision must make the decision personally. The justices established this fundamental principle of administrative adjudication in *Morgan v. United States (Morgan I)*.[12] Challengers to a decision by the Secretary of Agriculture in a formal adjudicatory proceeding charged that the Secretary had made the decision "without having heard or read any of the evidence, and without having heard the oral arguments or having read or considered the briefs which the plaintiffs submitted." According to the challengers, the Secretary had derived all of his information about the case simply by consulting with agency staff. The Court held that these allegations, if true, meant that the Secretary had denied the challengers the "full hearing" the enabling act had guaranteed them.[13]

Formal administratory proceedings, the Court reminded in *Morgan I*, are "quasi judicial character" and thus tap into "the tradition of judicial proceedings." When Congress mandated formal adjudication, the justices thus inferred that Congress necessarily incorporated the judicial "safeguard" that "the one who decides shall be bound in good conscience to consider the evidence, to be guided by that alone, and to reach his conclusion uninfluenced by extraneous considerations which in other fields might have play in determining purely executive action." The Court in *Morgan I* stressed that decisionmaking in formal adjudication was a personal obligation of the decisionmaker, "akin to that of a judge." According to the judicial ethos that informed formal administrative adjudications, "The one who decides must hear."[14]

---

10. *Attorney General's Manual, supra* note 4, at 86; see Colorado Interstate Gas Co. v. Federal Power Commission, 324 U.S. 581, 595 (1945) (the "path" of the agency's decision must be "discerned" by reviewing court); Armstrong v. CFTC, 12 F.3d 401, 404 (3rd Cir. 1993) ("No particular form of adoption is required if the agency's action permits meaningful appellate review.").

11. Cf. *Armstrong*, 12 F.3d at 403–04 (agency's summary affirmance of an ALJ's initial decision as "substantially correct" was "insufficient" because it left unclear which of the ALJ's "specific findings or conclusions" the agency had regarded as incorrect).

12. 298 U.S. 468 (1936).

13. *Id.* at 478–82.

14. *Id.* at 480–81.

The justices in *Morgan I* were quick to note, however, that the "necessary rule" of personal decisionmaking in formal adjudication "does not preclude practicable administrative procedure in obtaining the aid of assistants in the [agency]." Indeed, the APA itself prescribes one such form of assistance: Agency heads may assign ALJs to preside over the hearing (APA § 556(b)). In addition, the Court noted, agency decisionmakers may have staff members organize and analyze the evidence in the hearing record, much as judges use their law clerks. But in the end, *Morgan I* insisted that "the officer who makes the determinations must consider and appraise the evidence which justifies them."[15]

The Court decided *Morgan I* a decade before passage of the APA, and the justices' premise that agency heads are the equivalent of appellate judges when they decide a formal adjudication has not stood the test of time. Although formal administrative proceedings resemble judicial cases in many respects, the two modes of decisionmaking are not equivalent. Unlike judges, the resolution of cases is not necessarily the focal point of an agency head's responsibilities. And unlike courts, agencies house considerable nonjudicial expertise that Congress expects to inform the resolution of administrative cases. As a result if these distinctions, it is inevitable, and desirable, for agency decisions in formal adjudication to take on more of an institutional character than would be appropriate in judicial decisions.

In the years following *Morgan I*, however, the requirement of personal decisionmaking in formal adjudication has not been abandoned. It has been softened to allow more room for institutional participation in the agency's final decision. A recent restatement of administrative law summarized the contemporary understanding of the personal decisionmaking requirement as demanding no more than that the agency decisionmaker "become personally familiar with the issues in the case prior to rendering decision." According to this restatement, the decisionmaker can satisfy this softened requirement by means that the Court in *Morgan I* would not have accepted. The restatement explains, "The decisionmaker can comply with this requirement by reading portions of the transcript and briefs, hearing oral argument, reading a report of lower level decisionmakers, reading summaries prepared by staff members, or receiving a briefing by staff members."[16]

15. *Id*. at 481–82.

16. SECTION OF ADMINISTRATIVE LAW AND REGULATORY PRACTICE OF AMERICAN BAR AS-SOCIATION, A BLACKLETTER STATEMENT OF FEDERAL ADMINISTRATIVE LAW 9 (2004).

The First Circuit's decision in *Seacoast Anti–Pollution League v. Costle*[17] illustrates the type of staff assistance to agency decision-makers that is now permissible in formal adjudication. *Seacoast* involved a formal adjudication by the Environmental Protection Agency on a utility's application for a permit to discharge a pollutant into a body of water. An administrative law judge conducted the hearing and certified the record to the Regional Administrator of EPA, who denied the permit. On review, the Administrator of EPA convened a panel of in-house scientists to assist in reviewing the Regional Administrator's decision. An environmental group that had intervened in the proceeding objected that this assistance violated *Morgan I*'s rule of personal decisionmaking. The court of appeals rejected the claim. *Morgan I* does not prevent an agency head from drawing on the expertise of staff members in assessing a hearing record, the court held, so long as the head becomes personally familiar with the case before deciding it. A contrary conclusion, the court of appeals in *Seacoast* observed, would "run counter to the purposes of the administrative agencies which exist, in part, to enable government to focus broad ranges of talent on particular multi-dimensional problems."[18]

The softening of the rule of personal decisionmaking in formal administrative adjudications has been reinforced by the willingness of reviewing courts to afford a "strong presumption of agency regularity" to administrative decisions.[19] Without evidence to the contrary, judges presume that agency decisionmakers have satisfied *Morgan I* by becoming personally familiar with cases before deciding them.[20] It is not easy for parties to develop the evidence necessary to overcome this presumption. In *Morgan IV*,[21] the final installment of the *Morgan* saga, the Court held that parties generally should be denied discovery on agency decisionmakers' personal knowledge of the cases they decide. The justices explained, in language that frequently has been quoted, "It [is] not the function of the court to probe the mental processes of [agency decisionmakers]."[22]

§ 5.6   Ex Parte Communications

In the Government in the Sunshine Act of 1976,[1] Congress added section 557(d)(1) to the Administrative Procedure Act in an

17. 572 F.2d 872 (1st Cir. 1978), overruled on other grounds, Dominion Energy Brayton Point, LLC v. Johnson, 443 F.3d 12 (1st Cir. 2006).

18. *Id.* at 881.

19. Louisiana Ass'n of Indep. Producers and Royalty Owners v. FERC, 958 F.2d 1101, 1111 (D.C.Cir. 1992).

20. ABA BLACKLETTER STATEMENT, *supra* note 16, at 9–10.

21. United States v. Morgan, 313 U.S. 409 (1941).

22. *Id.* at 422, quoting Morgan v. United States, 304 U.S. 1, 18 (1938) (*Morgan II*).

§ 5.6

1. Pub.L. 94–409, § 4, 90 Stat. 1241, 1246–47 (1976).

effort "to ensure that 'agency decisions required to be made on a public record are not influenced by private, off-the-record communications from those personally interested in the outcome.' "[2] The new section 557(d)(1) complements section 554(d)(1) of the original APA, which prohibits administrative law judges from consulting with anyone regarding "a fact in issue" in a formal adjudicatory proceeding (see § 5.1(b)). Section 557(d)(1) prohibits ex parte communications between any agency official who is or who may be a decisionmaker in a formal proceeding and all interested persons who are *not* employed by the agency.[3] The APA defines "ex parte communication" as "an oral or written communication not on the public record with respect to which reasonable prior notice to all parties is not given" (APA § 551(14)). Section 557(d)(1) tracks the language of section 554(d) by allowing ex parte communications "to the extent required for the disposition of ex parte matters as authorized by law" (see § 5.1(b)).[4]

Section 557(d)(1)'s restrictions on ex parte communications begin either when the agency issues a notice of hearing, or when "the person responsible for the communication has knowledge that [a hearing] will be noticed," whichever is earlier (APA § 557(d)(1)(E)). Section 557(d)(1)(A) prohibits all "interested person[s] outside the agency" from "knowingly" making, or causing to be made, "an ex parte communication relevant to the merits of the proceeding" to "any member of the body comprising the agency, administrative law judge, or other employee who is or may reasonably be expected to be involved in the decisional process of the proceeding." Section 557(d)(1)(B) is a mirror image of section 557(d)(1)(A). It prohibits "any member of the body comprising the agency, administrative law judge, or other employee who is or may reasonably be expected to be involved in the decisional process of the proceeding" from "knowingly" making, or causing to be made, "an ex parte communication relevant to the merits of the proceeding" to "any interested person outside the agency."

Interested Persons. Section 557(d)(1) restricts ex parte communications between agency decisionmakers and persons who are not employed by the agency but who nevertheless are "interested" in the outcome of a formal administrative proceeding. The legislative history of the Government in the Sunshine Act suggests that Congress intended that the term "interested person" in section of 557(d)(1) be interpreted broadly to include any "person with an

---

2. Raz Inland Navigation Co. v. ICC, 625 F.2d 258, 260 (9th Cir. 1980) (quoting House Committee Report).

3. Because section 557 of the APA applies whenever an agency conducts a formal hearing (APA § 557(a)), the restriction on ex parte communications ap-

plies to formal rulemaking as well as to formal adjudication (APA § 557(d)(1)).

4. Similarly, the APA definition of ex parte communications explicitly excludes "requests for status reports" (APA § 551(14)).

interest in the agency proceeding that is greater than the general interest the public as a whole may have." Under this definition, a person need not be a party to a proceeding in order to be "interested" in the outcome. Nor must a person have a financial stake in the outcome of a proceeding.[5] Indeed, the Ninth Circuit has held that the president and members of the White House staff generally are "interested" in formal administrative proceedings and thus are covered by section of 557(d)(1)'s ban on ex parte communications.[6] Members of Congress and their staff,[7] as well as officials from other agencies,[8] may be regarded as "interested person[s]" within the meaning of section of 557(d)(1) as well.

Relevant to the Merits of the Proceeding. The phrase "relevant to the merits of the proceeding" in section 557(d)(1) communicates both the breadth and the limits of the APA's ban on ex parte communications with outsiders. Section 557(d)(1), unlike section 554(d)(1)'s restriction on off-the-record consultations involving administrative law judges, includes not only communications concerning the facts at issues in a proceeding, but also communications regarding relevant questions of law and the exercise of administrative discretion.[9] At the same time, courts have held that the language "relevant to the *merits* of the proceeding" permits ex parte communications regarding settlement negotiations and agency procedure.[10]

Remedies for ex parte communications. The agency decisionmaker who receives or makes a prohibited ex parte communication must fully disclose the communication "on the public record of the proceeding" (APA § 557(d)(1)(C)).[11] The D.C. Circuit has ob-

---

5. H.R.Rep. No. 880, Pt. I, 94th Cong., 2d Sess. 19–20 (1976), quoted in Professional Air Traffic Controllers Organization v. FLRA, 685 F.2d 547, 562 (D.C.Cir. 1982) (*PATCO II*).

6. See Portland Audubon Society v. Endangered Species Comm., 984 F.2d 1534, 1544–45 (9th Cir. 1993).

7. SECTION OF ADMINISTRATIVE LAW AND REGULATORY PRACTICE OF AMERICAN BAR ASSOCIATION, A BLACKLETTER STATEMENT OF FEDERAL ADMINISTRATIVE LAW 54 (2004).

8. See *PATCO II*, 685 F.2d at 568.

9. See *id.* at 563.

10. See Louisiana Association of Independent Producers and Royalty Owners v. FERC, 958 F.2d 1101, 1112 (D.C.Cir. 1992); Massman Constr. Co. v. TVA, 769 F.2d 1114, 1127 (6th Cir. 1985); *PATCO II*, 685 F.2d at 563. In addition, the APA's definition of "ex parte communication" (APA § 551(14)) makes clear that "requests for status reports" are permitted by section 557(d)(1). However, a request for a status report or a procedural inquiry that "amount[s] to an indirect or subtle effort to influence the substantive outcome of the proceedings" may be considered "relevant to the merits of the proceeding," and thus prohibited by section 557(d)(1). *PATCO II*, 685 F.2d at 563, 568 (D.C.Cir. 1982) (quoting Senate report).

11. If the prohibited ex parte communication is in writing, the agency decisionmaker simply adds it to the record. If the communication is oral, the decisionmaker must place a memorandum "stating the substance" of the communication on the record (APA § 557(d)(1)(C) (i)-(ii). The decisionmaker also must disclose "all written responses, and memoranda stating the substance of all oral responses," to the

served that publicly disclosing ex parte communications serves several therapeutic functions. Disclosure eliminates "the appearance of impropriety" that hovers over "secret communications in a proceeding that is required to be decided on the record." Disclosure also allows parties to respond to arguments that have been presented privately to an agency decisionmaker, thereby facilitating "fair decisionmaking." And finally, because ex parte communications may provide the true basis of the agency's final decision, disclosure of such communications is necessary for "meaningful judicial review."[12]

Section 557(d)(1)(D) also authorizes agencies to conduct an administrative hearing to determine whether the "claim or interest" of a party who "knowingly" was responsible for a prohibited ex parte communication "should ... be dismissed, denied, disregarded, or otherwise adversely affected." After such a hearing, the agency may impose one of the delineated sanctions "to the extent consistent with the interests of justice and the policy of the underlying statutes administered by the agency" (APA § 556(d)). Such sanctions hearings, however, are hardly a matter of course, and it is rare for an agency to dismiss a violating party's claim or interest in the underlying administrative proceeding because of ex parte communications.[13]

Section 557(d)(1) does not explicitly provide a judicial remedy for unlawful ex parte communications. The D.C. Circuit, however, in the leading case of *Professional Air Traffic Controllers Organization v. Federal Labor Relations Authority* (*PATCO II*),[14] ruled that reviewing courts should invalidate an agency decision only if the communication "irrevocably tainted ... the agency's decisionmaking process," thus making the agency's decision "unfair either to an innocent party or to the public interest that the agency was obliged to protect." The court of appeals in *PATCO* identified the following considerations to guide such a determination: (1) "the gravity of the ex parte communications"; (2) "whether the contacts may have influenced the agency's ultimate decision"; (3) "whether the party making the improper contacts benefited from the agency's ultimate decision"; (4) "whether the contents of the communications were unknown to opposing parties, who therefore had no opportunity to respond"; and (5) "whether vacation of the agency's decision and remand for new proceedings would serve a useful purpose."[15]

prohibited ex parte communication (APA § 557(d)(1)(C) (iii)).

12. *PATCO II*, 685 F.2d at 563–64 & n.32.

13. *Id.* at 564.

14. 685 F.2d 547 (D.C.Cir. 1882).

15. *Id.* at 564–65.

§ 5.7 Bias

The Administrator Procedure Act requires that administrative law judges and other administrative decisionmakers fulfill their responsibilities in formal proceedings "in an impartial manner" (APA § 556(b)). These decisionmakers may disqualify themselves "at any time" (APA § 556(b)). And the parties may seek their disqualification by "filing in good faith ... a timely and sufficient affidavit of personal bias or other disqualification" (APA § 556(b)). The agency must rule on any such affidavit, and its decision becomes "part of the record and decision in the case" (APA § 556(b)). The APA leaves undefined "the personal bias or other disqualification" that justifies removal of ALJs and other administrative decisionmakers in formal proceedings.

(a) Structural Bias

The combination of law-enforcement and law-adjudication functions in administrative agencies raises legitimate concerns about the inherent fairness of agency adjudication. The "basic requirement of due process" that individuals be afforded a "fair trial in a fair tribunal" applies to administrative adjudication as well as to judicial trials.[1] Yet in the typical administrative enforcement proceeding, the same agency investigates whether some person has engaged in unlawful conduct; prosecutes the person for that conduct; and ultimately decides whether the person's conduct was unlawful. Such a combination of functions in a trial court would be unthinkable in the American judicial tradition. It nevertheless thrives as an inherent feature of contemporary administrative government.

As we have seen throughout this chapter, the Administrative Procedure Act prescribes a process for formal adjudication that promises a considerable degree of fairness and impartiality. The act separates law-enforcement personnel from administrative adjudicators, at least in formal adjudication. It thus should not be surprising that the Supreme Court has resisted claims that "the combination of investigative and adjudicative functions *necessarily* creates an unconstitutional risk of bias in administrative adjudication."[2] Such a claim of structural bias, the Court announced *Withrow v. Larkin*, "must overcome a presumption of honesty and integrity in those serving as adjudicators." The justices promised that courts would be "alert to the possibilities of bias that may lurk in the way

---

§ 5.7

1. Withrow v. Larkin, 421 U.S. 35, 46 (1975).

2. *Id.* at 47 (1975) (emphasis added); see also Richardson v. Perales, 402 U.S. 389, 410 (1971) (rejecting a procedural due process challenge to a system authorizing a Social Security examiner both to develop the facts and to make decisions regarding disability claims).

particular procedures actually work in practice," but *Withrow* made clear that a complaining party must present "specific" evidence to establish "an unacceptable risk of bias" in an agency's adjudicative process.[3]

The Court early on registered its reluctance to indulge claims of structural bias from individuals targeted by an administrative enforcement proceeding. In *Federal Trade Commission v. Cement Institute,*[4] decided just two years after passage of the APA, the justices rejected an argument by representatives of the cement industry that the Commissioners should be disqualified by bias from adjudicating the lawfulness of the industry's pricing system. Before initiating the enforcement proceeding, the Commission had investigated the type of pricing system at issue in *Cement Institute.* As a result of that investigation, members of the Commission, both in written reports and in congressional testimony, expressed their opinion that the pricing system amounted to unlawful price fixing. These statements, the Cement Institute claimed, demonstrated that the Commissioners had "prejudged the issues" in the proceeding.[5] The Court rejected the claim.

The Commissioners' previously expressed opinions about the cement industry's pricing system, the Court held, "did not necessarily mean that the minds of its members were irrevocably closed" on the legality of that system. The investigation, the Court noted, was ex parte: Members of the cement industry had not participated. The adjudication, by contrast, was adversarial: The cement industry was "legally authorized" to fight back. In the enforcement proceeding, industry representatives presented evidence supporting their pricing system, cross-examined adverse witnesses, and fully argued their legal position before the Commission. In short, the legality of the cement industry's pricing system after the hearing might have looked different to the Commissioners than it had appeared after the investigation. It had been possible, and would hardly have been inconsistent, for the Commissioners to have concluded that while the pricing system had appeared to be illegal after their investigation, they had become convinced of its legality after the cement industry had made its case.[6]

(b) Bias in Particular Cases

Judicial resistance to claims of structural bias does not preclude reviewing courts from concluding that "the special facts and

---

3. *Withrow,* 421 U.S. at 47, 54–55 (1975).

4. 333 U.S. 683 (1948).

5. *Id.* at 700.

6. *Id.* at 701; see also *Withrow,* 421 U.S. at 57–58 ("just as there is no logical inconsistency between a finding of prob-

able cause and an acquittal in a criminal proceeding, there is no incompatibility between the agency filing a complaint based on probable cause and a subsequent decision, when all the evidence is in, that there has been no violation of the statute").

circumstances" of a particular case present a "risk of unfairness" that is "intolerably high."[7] But although procedural due process recognizes "the danger of unfairness through prejudgment,"[8] the burden of demonstrating a disqualifying prejudgment by an agency decisionmaker is considerable. A party must prove more than prior adverse rulings or a preexisting opinion on law or policy to disqualify an administrative decisionmaker.[9] A reviewing court must find that " 'a disinterested observer may conclude that [the agency decisionmaker] has in some measure adjudged the facts as well as the law of a particular case in advance of hearing it.' "[10]

In *National Labor Relations Board v. Donnelly Garment Co.*,[11] for example, the justices refused to disqualify a hearing officer from presiding over the re-hearing of a case after the officer's refusal in the first hearing to admit certain evidence had resulted in reversal. Disqualification on such grounds would have been overkill. Trial judges who are reversed on appeal are not barred from presiding over the re-trial.[12] And more generally, judges who have "expressed an opinion as to whether certain types of conduct were prohibited by law" are not disqualified from deciding cases involving such conduct.[13]

A recent restatement of the case law identified the following types of bias as sufficiently problematic to warrant removal of an agency decisionmaker: (1) "the decisionmaker has a pecuniary or other interest in the case"; (2) the agency decisionmaker "has prejudged the facts against a party"; and (3) the agency decisionmaker, before the hearing begins, has "developed personal animosity against a party, witness, or counsel or a group to which they belong."[14]

---

7. *Withrow*, 421 U.S. at 58.

8. Cinderella Career & Finishing Schools, Inc. v. FTC, 425 F.2d 583, 590 (D.C.Cir. 1970).

9. Section of Administrative Law and Regulatory Practice of American Bar Association, A Blackletter Statement of Federal Administrative Law 9 (2004).

10. *Cinderella*, 425 F.2d at 591, quoting Gilligan, Will & Co. v. SEC, 267 F.2d 461, 469 (2d Cir.), cert. denied, 361 U.S. 896 (1959).

11. 330 U.S. 219, 236 (1947).

12. *Id.* at 236–37; see also *Cement Institute*, 333 U.S. at 703 ("judges frequently try the same case more than once and decide identical issues each time").

13. *Cement Institute*, 333 U.S. at 702–03.

14. ABA Blackletter Statement, *supra* note 9, at 9.

Chapter 6

INFORMAL RULEMAKING UNDER THE ADMINISTRATIVE PROCEDURE ACT

The spare provisions of section 553 of the Administrative Procedure Act establishing a notice-and-comment process for informal rulemaking often are cited as one of the drafters' most significant innovations. Federal agencies have issued rules with the force of law since the Founding, and by the time Congress enacted the APA in 1946, rulemaking was an established feature of the administrative landscape. Yet administrative rulemaking suffered from something of an identity crisis in 1946. Agencies often used formal adjudicatory proceedings to establish administrative policy. And when setting rates, a common form of administrative rulemaking at the time, enabling acts typically directed agencies, as in formal adjudication, to base their decisions solely on evidence admitted at a trial-type evidentiary hearing. On those occasions when agencies issued rules other than rates, Congress typically left administrators free to follow any process of their choosing. The rulemaking processes agencies chose varied greatly, including informal oral hearings, conferences, consultation with interested parties, and submission of written comments.

Section 553 of the APA provided a platform for the emergence of administrative rulemaking as a dominant regulatory tool by both legitimizing and regularizing agency rulemaking processes. In section 553, Congress finally created a uniform, baseline procedure governing the issuance of agency rules with the force of law. The heart of the informal rulemaking process of section 553 is a written exchange between the agency and interested members of the public. The agency publishes a "notice of proposed rule making" and invites written comments from the public (APA § 553(b)-(c)). The agency re-evaluates its proposal in light of the comments it receives and then publishes the final rule, together with a "statement of [its] basis and purpose" (APA § 553(c)-(d)). That's it. (See Figure 6–1.)

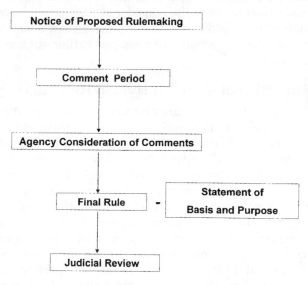

Figure 6-1 : Informal Rulemaking Under the APA

In contrast to the APA's procedures for formal agency proceedings, which adapt a judicial model of decisionmaking to the administrative process, the informal notice-and-comment procedures of section 553 prescribe a good-government, legislative model for virtually all agency rulemaking. Section 553 represents a conception of "legislative due process" that attempts (1) to enhance the quality of administrative regulation (by increasing the flow of information from the public to the agency) even as it promises (2) to ensure the fairness of administrative regulation (by allowing interested persons to protect their interests by participating in the rulemaking process).[1] In the end, the hope is that the written conversation between the regulators and the regulated structured by section 553 will promote "reasoned decisionmaking" by agencies when formulating rules with the force of law.[2]

The procedural requirements of section 553 interrelate in the service of these process values. Requiring agencies to publish a notice of proposed rulemaking enables the public to offer "meaningful and informed comment" on the proposal (APA § 553(b)).[3] The requirement that agencies consider the public comments on their proposed rules encourages administrators to adjust the final rule in response to the infusion of new information and different perspectives on their proposal (APA § 553(c)). And the "statement of basis and purpose" accompanying final rules verifies that administrative rulemakers actually considered the public's comments, even as it facilitates judicial review of the agency's rulemaking to ensure that it was the product of reasoned rather than of arbitrary decisionmaking.

§ 6.1   The Rise of Judicial Hybrid Rulemaking

Section 553(c) of the Administrative Procedure Act requires agencies, after publishing a notice of proposed rulemaking, to "give interested persons an opportunity to participate in the rule making through submissions of written data, views or arguments with or without opportunity for oral presentation." When the APA was enacted, the conventional reading of the public's "opportunity to participate" in rulemaking proceedings held that individuals possessed a *right* to submit written comments on the agency's proposal and that agencies had *discretion* to conduct some form of oral hearing as well.[1] This conventional reading of section 553(c) was shaken in the mid–1960s and early 1970s. The preference of agencies to regulate through formal adjudication, which had been so pronounced when Congress had enacted the APA, began to change. Just as administrators made the transition from adjudication to rulemaking as the procedure of choice for developing regulatory policy, Congress enacted a series of enabling acts dramatically

---

1. For a discussion of the procedural values served by the informal rulemaking process, see Cooley R. Howarth, Jr., *Informal Agency Rulemaking and the Courts: A Theory for Procedural Review*, 61 WASH. U. L.Q. 891, 896–906 (1984).

2. See Connecticut Light and Power Co. v. NRC, 673 F.2d 525, 528 (D.C.Cir 1982); Greater Boston Television Corp. v. FCC, 444 F.2d 841, 851 (D.C.Cir. 1970), cert. denied, 403 U.S. 923 (1971).

3. AMA v. Reno, 57 F.3d 1129, 1132–33 (D.C.Cir. 1995).

§ 6.1

1. See *Attorney General's Manual on the Administrative Procedure Act* 31 (1947), reprinted in WILLIAM F. FUNK, et al., FEDERAL ADMINISTRATIVE PROCEDURE SOURCEBOOK 33–171 (3d ed. 2000); James V. DeLong, *Informal Rulemaking and the Integration of Law and Policy*, 65 VA. L. REV. 257 (1979) (describing the "original APA model" of informal rulemaking).

increasing the rulemaking power of agencies to address a variety of environmental, health, safety, and social concerns (see § 1.5(e)). The simultaneous increase of administrative power and decrease in procedural formality sparked a reaction by reviewing courts, led by the D.C. Circuit, that intensified both procedural and substantive judicial review of agency rulemaking.[2]

Federal courts of appeals became convinced that section 553(c)'s opportunity to submit written comments failed to provide adequate public participation in administrative rulemaking proceedings when important and controversial issues of public health and safety were at stake.[3] They advocated a "flexible interpretation of the APA" which ensured in each case that the agency's rulemaking procedure had fulfilled its "primary objective" of acquiring the information necessary for administrators to implement their enabling acts "effectively."[4] This "flexible interpretation" untethered reviewing courts from "strict adherence to the explicit dictates of the APA,"[5] thereby freeing them to draw on "basic considerations of fairness [to] dictate procedural requirements not specified by Congress."[6]

These courts were fundamentally dissatisfied with the two procedural choices that the APA offered for administrative rulemaking. They saw the options of formal and informal rulemaking as presenting a false choice. Formal rulemaking, which required a full trial, was too formal. Yet the notice-and-comment process seemed too informal, at least for the kind of major regulatory initiatives that increasingly characterized administrative rulemaking of the era. These courts registered their dissatisfaction with the APA's limited procedural menu by prodding agencies to adopt "hybrid" procedures lying between formal and informal rulemaking, sharing elements of each. In their most aggressive form, hybrid rulemaking proceedings forced agencies to augment the notice-and-comment process by conducting an oral hearing, including a right to cross-examination if necessary to resolve "critical issues."[7]

The judicial review provisions of the Administrative Procedure Act sent mixed signals on the legitimacy of the judicial hybrid rulemaking movement. On one hand, the APA seemed to rule out the practice, instructing reviewing courts to invalidate agency action for failing to observe "procedure required by *law*" (APA

---

2. The intensified substantive judicial review, known as "hard look" review, is discussed in § 8.7(b).

3. See, e.g., O'Donnell v. Shaffer, 491 F.2d 59, 62 (D.C.Cir. 1974).

4. Mobil Oil Corp. v. FPC, 483 F.2d 1238, 1252 (D.C.Cir. 1973); see *O'Donnell*, 491 F.2d at 62.

5. *Mobil Oil Corp.*, 483 F.2d at 1252.

6. *O'Donnell*, 491 F.2d at 62.

7. *Id.* at 62; see, e.g., Appalachian Power Co. v. EPA, 477 F.2d 495, 503 (4th Cir. 1973); Walter Holm & Co. v. Hardin, 449 F.2d 1009, 1016 (D.C.Cir. 1971).

§ 706(2)(D) (emphasis added)). On the other hand, the APA's
provision describing the general scope of judicial review provided
that "reviewing court[s] *shall* ... hold unlawful and set aside
agency action ... found to be ... an abuse of discretion" (APA
§ 706(2)(A) (emphasis added)). Thus, even if the decision to adopt
rulemaking procedures beyond those "required by law" was a
matter of agency discretion, as the traditional position held, a
reviewing court still might claim APA authority to assess whether
an agency had abused its discretion in deciding not to adopt
procedures, such as an oral hearing, that extended beyond the
requirements of section 553.[8]

Chief Judge David Bazelon of the D.C. Circuit, concurring in
Ethyl Corp. v. Environmental Protection Agency,[9] wrote the leading
defense of the judicial hybrid rulemaking movement that emerged
during the late 1960s and early 1970s. Judge Bazelon urged courts
to emphasize procedural review over substantive review when assessing sophisticated administrative regulations. "[I]n cases of
great technological complexity," he argued, "the best way for
courts to guard against unreasonable or erroneous administrative
decisions is not for the judges themselves to scrutinize the technical
merits of each decision. Rather, it is to establish a decision-making
process that assures a reasoned decision that can be held up to the
scrutiny of the scientific community and the public."[10]

Judge Bazelon was deeply skeptical of the legitimacy and
competence of courts to engage in meaningful substantive review of
sophisticated scientific and technological rulemaking. Such rules,
he believed, involved legislative-type policy determinations that
were "alien to [the] true function" of courts. Moreover, "substantive review of mathematical and scientific evidence by technically
illiterate judges is dangerously unreliable." Bazelon doubted as well
the objectivity of judges when reviewing the substantive merits of
important and controversial rules. He cautioned, "The process of
making a de novo evaluation of the scientific evidence inevitably
invites judges of opposing views to make plausible-sounding, but
simplistic, judgments of the relative weight to be afforded various
pieces of technical data."[11]

Chief Judge Bazalon believed that courts could "do more to
improve administrative decision-making by concentrating [their]
efforts on strengthening administrative procedures." Judge Bazel-

---

8. See Stephen F. Williams, *"Hybrid Rulemaking" under the Administrative Procedure Act: A Legal and Empirical Analysis*, 42 U. CHI. L. REV. 401, 411–12 (1975).

9. 541 F.2d 1, 66 (D.C.Cir.), cert. denied, 426 U.S. 941 (1976) (upholding EPA regulations requiring the reduction of lead in gasoline).

10. *Id.* at 66 (Bazelon, J., concurring).

11. *Id.* at 66–67 (Bazelon, J., concurring).

on's modesty regarding substantive review of sophisticated administrative rulemaking dissipated on procedural review. The mood change came through clearly in Judge Bazalon's charge that courts "establish a decision-making process" for agencies to ensure proper rulemaking. By aggressively reviewing an agency's rulemaking procedures rather than the substance of the agency's rules, Bazelon believed that courts would encourage agencies to adopt "a framework for principled decision-making" that ultimately would "diminish the importance of judicial review by enhancing the integrity of the administrative process."[12]

§ 6.2   *Vermont Yankee* and the Demise of Judicial Hybrid Rulemaking

The Supreme Court confronted the judicial hybrid rulemaking movement in *Vermont Yankee Nuclear Power Corp. v. National Resources Defense Council*,[1] one the most significant judicial decisions in administrative law. At issue in *Vermont Yankee* was a proceeding conducted by the Atomic Energy Commission (now, the Nuclear Regulatory Commission) to promulgate a "fuel-cycle rule." This rule assigned numerical values measuring the environmental risk of reprocessing nuclear fuel and of disposing of the nuclear waste byproducts of reprocessing. The Commission intended to use the fuel-cycle rule when deciding whether to license nuclear power plants. To grant such a license, the Commission had to conclude that the anticipated benefits of a plant outweighed its projected costs. The Commission would add the values assigned by the fuel-cycle rule to its calculation of the projected costs of operating a plant. These values would add little to the cost calculation, however, because the Commission had found in its rulemaking proceeding that there was "relatively insignificant" environmental risk associated with reprocessing nuclear fuel and storing nuclear waste in connection with the operation of nuclear power plants.[2]

The fuel-cycle rule was precisely the type of significant, sophisticated and controversial regulation that had led the D.C. Circuit and other courts to require hybrid rulemaking procedures. And indeed, the Commission on its own had conducted an oral hearing during the fuel-cycle rulemaking proceeding to supplement the

12. *Id.* at 66–67 (Bazelon, J., concurring). For discussions of the judicial hybrid rulemaking precedent with varying emphases, see DeLong, *Informal Rulemaking*, *supra* note 1, at 262–76; Antonin Scalia, Vermont Yankee: *The APA, the D.C. Circuit, and the Supreme Court*, 1978 SUP. CT. REV. 345, 348–52; Paul R. Verkuil, *Judicial Review of Informal Rulemaking*, 60 VA.L.REV. 185, 234–42

(1974). For an assessment of the impact of hybrid rulemaking decisions on particular agency proceedings, see Williams, *Hybrid Rulemaking*, *supra* note 8, at 425–36.

§ 6.2

1. 435 U.S. 519 (1978).

2. *Id.* at 530.

notice-and-comment process required by section 553 of the Administrative Procedure Act. The Commission's hearing had been legislative rather than judicial in nature, however. Members of the Commission had questioned witnesses about their testimony, but interested parties could not cross-examine the witnesses.

Even though the Commission had more than complied with the requirements of section 553, an environmental group challenged the procedural sufficiency of the proceeding. The group's central complaint was that the hearing had not offered it sufficient opportunity to challenge a key staff report on which the Commission had based the low environmental risk assessment reflected in the fuel-cycle rule. The environmental group sought discovery of the information that went into preparation of the staff report, as well as an opportunity to cross-examine the author of the report.

The environmental group tapped into the hybrid rulemaking precedent by claiming that the Commission's refusal to allow discovery or cross-examination in connection with the staff report had denied the group "a meaningful opportunity to participate" in the fuel-cycle rulemaking proceeding. The D.C. Circuit, with none other than Chief Judge David Bazelon writing for the majority, had agreed that the Commission's rulemaking procedure had not been "sufficient to ventilate the issues," and accordingly, the court of appeals had invalidated the fuel-cycle rule. The court's review of the rulemaking record had convinced it that the Commission had not fostered "a real give and take . . . on the key issues." The court of appeals had stopped short of ordering the Commission to allow discovery and cross-examination concerning the staff report as demanded by the environmental group, however. Noting that there were "[m]any procedural devices for creating a genuine dialogue on these issues," the court had declined to "intrude on the agency's province by dictating to it which, if any, of these devices it must adopt to flesh out the record." The D.C. Circuit nevertheless had been firm in its conclusion that "[w]hatever techniques the Commission adopts, before it promulgates a rule limiting further consideration of waste disposal and reprocessing issues, it must in one way or another generate a record in which the factual issues are fully developed."[3]

The Supreme Court unanimously reversed the D.C. Circuit's ruling in *Vermont Yankee*, seizing on the occasion to instruct lower courts to abandon the judicial hybrid rulemaking project of "engrafting their own notions of proper procedures upon agencies." The Court in *Vermont Yankee* settled that section 553 of the

---

3. Natural Resources Defense Council, Inc. v. NRC, 547 F.2d 633, 643–54 (D.C. Cir. 1976).

Administrative Procedure Act "established the maximum procedural requirements which Congress was willing to have the courts impose upon agencies in conducting rulemaking procedures. Agencies are free to grant additional procedural rights in the exercise of their discretion, but reviewing courts are generally not free to impose them if the agencies have not chosen to grant them."[4]

The justices in *Vermont Yankee* left open the possibility that in "extremely rare" circumstances a reviewing court might be justified "in overturning agency action because of a failure to employ procedures beyond those required by the [APA]." The Court mentioned two possibilities. The first involved instances when procedural due process applies. Although courts resist such a conclusion, it is possible for an agency's action to be categorized as rulemaking under the APA, thus triggering the notice-and-comment process of section 553, and as adjudication under due process, thus triggering the requirement of an oral hearing (see §§ 3.1, 4.1). In such an instance, the agency would be obligated to satisfy the due process hearing requirement because the Constitution trumps federal statutes. The second possibility the Court identified involved an agency's "totally unjustified departure from well-settled agency procedures of long standing." In such a circumstance, the reviewing court would not order an agency to provide additional procedures that the *court* had deemed appropriate, but rather it simply would direct administrators to follow the procedures that the *agency* itself had prescribed for such proceedings.[5]

The Court in *Vermont Yankee* rejected Chief Judge Bazelon's sharp preference for procedural review over substantive review of agency rulemaking. Judge Bazelon had argued that while judges lacked the competence and legitimacy to closely examine the substance of regulatory decisions that Congress had entrusted to an agency, reviewing courts could and should ensure that an agency's rulemaking procedure delivered the best regulation possible. The justices countered that that the agencies, rather than the courts, possessed "discretion" (within statutory limits) to select the procedures that *administrators* believed best for making the "substantive judgments" that Congress had entrusted to them. The specialization and expertise of agencies not only made them better policymaking institutions than the courts, as Judge Bazalon had conceded. These attributes also placed agencies "in a better position than federal courts or even Congress itself to design proce-

---

4. *Vermont Yankee*, 435 U.S. at 524–25. *Vermont Yankee*'s disapproval of judicially created procedural requirements for agency decisionmaking applies to informal adjudication as well as to informal rulemaking. See Pension Benefit Guarantee Corp. v. LTV Corp., 496 U.S. 633 (1990).

5. *Vermont Yankee*, 435 U.S. at 524, 542.

dural rules adapted to the peculiarities of the industry and the tasks of the agency involved."[6]

The Court in *Vermont Yankee* identified several "compelling reasons" for interpreting section 553 as imposing the *maximum* rather than the *minimum* procedures that reviewing courts, absent other statutory requirements, may order agencies to follow in informal rulemaking proceedings. First, limiting courts to enforcing the notice-and-comment provisions of section 553 (as well as the requirements of other statutes) makes the procedural requirements for rulemaking predictable. Next, hybrid rulemaking review pushed agencies to judicialize their rulemaking proceedings as a hedge against judicial reversal. This judicialization ran counter to the legislative model that Congress had adopted in section 553 for administrative rulemaking. And finally, hybrid rulemaking review ignored the defining difference between informal and formal proceedings under the APA. As the justices saw it, the premise of hybrid rulemaking was that "additional procedures will automatically result in a more adequate record because it will give interested parties more of an opportunity to participate in and contribute to the proceedings." But unlike administrative decisions in formal proceedings, an agency's final rule need not be based solely on a "record" created by participants in an informal rulemaking proceeding. An agency in informal rulemaking is free to gather useful information outside that "record." The adequacy of the factual support for a final rule therefore "is not correlated directly to the type of procedural devices employed."[7]

The Supreme Court's decisive rejection of hybrid rulemaking review in *Vermont Yankee* reaffirmed the traditional model of administrative law (see § 1.4). The traditional model makes it the responsibility of Congress to establish the legal requirements for administrative action, either in a generally applicable statute such as the APA or in a particular agency's enabling act.[8] The agency has the responsibility of determining how best to fulfill its regulatory responsibilities within the legal boundaries marked by Congress. The court's role is to review administrative actions to ensure they remain within those boundaries. *Vermont Yankee* reminded reviewing courts not to trespass on the agency's domain of deciding how best to implement its enabling act.

6. *Id.* at 524–25.

7. *Id.* at 546–47.

8. *Vermont Yankee* does not prevent Congress from requiring hybrid rulemaking, and a number of enabling acts provide for such procedures. See, e.g., Federal Trade Commission Improvement Act of 1980, 15 U.S.C. § 57b–3; Clean Water Act of 1977, 33 U.S.C. § 1317; Clean Air Act Amendments of 1977, 42 U.S.C. § 7607(d); Toxic Substances Control Act of 1976, 15 U.S.C. § 2605(c); Consumer Product Safety Act of 1972, 15 U.S.C. § 2058; Occupational Safety and Health Act of 1970, 29 U.S.C. § 655.

In the end, though, the Court in *Vermont Yankee* did not uphold the fuel-cycle rule. The justices recognized that the central concern of the court of appeals had been the failure of the Commission to "generate a record in which the factual issues [concerning the rule were] fully developed."[9] Indeed, an influential commentary on judicial hybrid rulemaking at the time concluded that hybrid rulemaking decisions generally were a response to doubts that the agency had adequately explained its substantive decisions in significant rulemaking proceedings.[10] With a final jab at Judge Bazelon, the Supreme Court remanded the case to the D.C. Circuit to undertake a *substantive* rather than a *procedural* review of the fuel-cycle rule. The justices instructed the court of appeals to determine whether the "administrative record" gathered by the Commission adequately supported its conclusion that reprocessing nuclear fuel and storing nuclear waste in connection with the operation of a nuclear power plant posed only an insignificant risk to the environment. On remand, the justices emphasized, the court of appeals must limit itself to that substantive assessment, "and not stray beyond the judicial province to explore the procedural format or to impose upon the agency its own notion of which procedures are 'best' or most likely to further some vague, undefined public good."[11]

§ 6.3   Informal Rulemaking After *Vermont Yankee*

The Supreme Court cast its decision in *Vermont Yankee* as affirming "the very basic tenet of administrative law that agencies should be free to fashion their own rules of procedure."[1] And of course, after *Vermont Yankee*, courts of appeals abandoned the hybrid rulemaking precedent that had ordered agencies to adopt decisionmaking procedures, like oral hearings, that had pushed

9. *Natural Resources Defense Council*, 547 F.2d at 654; see *Vermont Yankee*, 435 U.S. at 549.

10. Stephen F. Williams, *"Hybrid Rulemaking" under the Administrative Procedure Act: A Legal and Empirical Analysis*, 42 U. CHI.L.REV. 401, 454–55 (1975).

11. *Vermont Yankee*, 435 U.S. at 549. The leading commentary on *Vermont Yankee* is Antonin Scalia, Vermont Yankee: *The APA, The D.C. Circuit, and the Supreme Court*, 1978 SUP.CT.REV. 345. For an excellent exchange on the merits of *Vermont Yankee* written on the heels of the Supreme Court's decision, see Richard B. Stewart, Vermont Yankee *and the Evolution of Administrative Pro-*

cedure, 91 HARV. L. REV. 1805 (1978) (criticizing *Vermont Yankee*); Clark Byse, Vermont Yankee *and the Evolution of Administrative Procedure: A Somewhat Different View*, 91 HARV. L. REV. 1823 (1978) (supporting *Vermont Yankee*). For analysis of *Vermont Yankee* through the lens of the difficulties agencies and reviewing courts face in fact-finding regarding scientific issues, see Thomas O. McGarity, *Substantive and Procedural Discretion in Administrative Resolution of Science Policy Questions: Regulating Carcinogens in E.P.A. and O.S.H.A.*, 67 GEO. L.J. 729 (1979).

§ 6.3

1. Vermont Yankee Nuclear Power Corp. v. National Resources Defense Council, 435 U.S. 519, 544 (1978).

agencies outside the notice-and-comment framework created by section 553 of the Administrative Procedure Act.[2] But *Vermont Yankee* has not deterred lower courts from deriving a series of *specific* procedural requirements for informal rulemaking from the *general* provisions of section 553. Although these decisions are in tension with *Vermont Yankee*'s "basic tenet" that agencies rather than reviewing courts should add to the requirements of section 553, the Supreme Court has neither embraced nor repudiated these decisions. This section reviews the case law interpreting and applying the provisions of section 553 governing informal rulemaking.

(a) Notice of Proposed Rulemaking

The first step of the rulemaking process is for agencies to provide a "[g]eneral notice of proposed rule making" ("NPRM") (APA § 553(b)). The typical method by which agencies notify the public of their rulemaking intention is by publishing an NPRM in the *Federal Register*. The *Federal Register* is a daily publication of the U.S. government (available online as well as in hard copy) that serves as the official registry of administrative actions that affect the public. Section 553(b) of the Administrative Procedure Act also allows agencies to satisfy the notice requirement by (1) naming the persons subject to the rulemaking in the notice and by personally serving the notice on those persons, or (2) otherwise providing "actual notice ... in accordance with law." These alternative methods of providing notice of a proposed rulemaking are seldom used, but they have the important, incidental effect of allowing agencies to cure an inadequate NPRM by providing actual notice to interested members of the public.[3]

Reviewing courts interpret and apply the notice requirement of section 553(b) in light of the functions that a notice of proposed rulemaking is supposed to serve in the rulemaking process. Judges generally emphasize several such functions. First, an NPRM helps to improve the quality of administrative rulemaking by exposing agency proposals to "diverse public comment."[4] The hope here is that subjecting the findings and assumptions of administrative officials to "public scrutiny" will foster "rational" and "informed" rulemaking.[5] Second, requiring public notice of an agency's rulemaking proposal furthers the values of fairness and democratic

---

2. See, e.g., Wisconsin Gas Co. v. FERC, 770 F.2d 1144, 1168 (D.C. Cir. 1985) ("to the extent that [hybrid rulemaking precedent] imposes procedural requirements not required by [an agency's enabling act] or the Administrative Procedure Act, it is no longer good law after *Vermont Yankee*").

3. See Small Refiner Lead Phase–Down Task Force v. EPA, 705 F.2d 506, 547, 549 (D.C.Cir. 1983).

4. See, e.g., *id.* at 547.

5. Weyerhaeuser Co. v. Costle, 590 F.2d 1011, 1031 (D.C.Cir. 1978); see Chocolate Manufacturers Ass'n v. Block, 755 F.2d 1098, 1103 (4th Cir. 1985).

participation by providing interested members of the public an opportunity to shape the formulation of rules that govern their conduct.[6] And third, an NPRM facilitates effective judicial review by inviting proponents and opponents of the agency's rulemaking to submit evidence supporting their positions for the administrative record.[7]

Section 553(b)(3) of the APA requires that an agency's notice of proposed rulemaking include "either [1] the terms or [2] substance of the proposed rule or [3] a description of the subjects and issues involved" in the rulemaking proceeding.[8] An NPRM usually is divided into two parts. First comes a "preamble," which describes the legal and factual basis, as well as the policy purpose, of the rulemaking proposal. It is common as well for the preamble to flag issues of special interest to the agency for commenters to discuss. The text of the agency's proposed rule follows the preamble.

Following enactment of the Administrative Procedure Act, the *Attorney General's Manual* advised agencies that their notices of proposed rulemaking "should be sufficiently informative to assure interested persons an opportunity to participate intelligently in the rule making process."[9] This statement has provided the guiding principle for reviewing courts when enforcing the public notice requirement of section 553(b).[10] To comply with this principle, an NPRM need not specify each and every provision that winds up in the agency's final rule.[11] Drawing on the legislative history of the Administrative Procedure Act,[12] reviewing courts require more gen-

---

6. See, e.g., *Small Refiners*, 705 F.2d at 547; National Ass'n of Home Health Agencies v. Schweiker, 690 F.2d 932, 949 (D.C.Cir. 1982), cert. denied, 459 U.S. 1205 (1983).

7. See, e.g., *Small Refiners*, 705 F.2d at 547; Marathon Oil Co. v. EPA, 564 F.2d 1253, 1271 n.54 (9th Cir. 1977).

8. Section 553(b) also requires that the agency's notice of proposed rulemaking include (1) "a statement of the time, place, and nature of public rule making proceedings" and (2) "reference to the legal authority under which the rule is proposed" (APA § 553(b)(1),(2)). The reference to legal authority in the NPRM "must be sufficiently precise to apprise interested persons of the agency's legal authority to issue the proposed rule." *Attorney General's Manual on the Administrative Procedure Act* 29 (1947), reprinted in WILLIAM F. FUNK, et al., FEDERAL ADMINISTRATIVE PROCEDURE SOURCEBOOK 33–171 (3d ed. 2000).

9. *Attorney General's Manual, supra* note 8, at 30.

10. See, e.g., Florida Power & Light Co. v. United States, 846 F.2d 765, 771 (D.C.Cir. 1988) (NPRM must afford interested persons "a reasonable opportunity to participate in the rulemaking process").

11. See, e.g., American Medical Ass'n v. United States, 887 F.2d 760, 767 (7th Cir. 1989); United Steelworkers of America v. Schuykill Metal Corp., 828 F.2d 314, 317 (5th Cir. 1987); Action for Children's Television v. FCC, 564 F.2d 458, 470 (D.C.Cir. 1977).

12. See S. Rep. No. 752, 77th Cong., 1st Sess. 14 (1945) (Report of the Senate Judiciary Committee on the APA) ("Agency notice must be sufficient to fairly apprise interested parties of the issues involved, so that they may present responsive data or argument relating thereto").

erally that an agency's rulemaking notice "fairly apprise interested persons of the *subjects* and *issues*" at stake in the rulemaking proceeding.[13] In order to satisfy this bottom-line requirement, the NPRM must provide enough "factual detail and rationale" concerning the rulemaking proposal to enable interested members of the public "to comment meaningfully" on the relevant issues.[14]

Agency notices of proposed rulemaking should be "clear and to the point."[15] Reviewing courts are watchful for agencies playing "a bureaucratic game of hide and seek" with the information that interested persons need to participate meaningfully in a rulemaking proceeding.[16] For example, in *MCI Telecommunications Corp. v. Federal Communications Commission*,[17] the D.C. Circuit held an agency's notice to be inadequate because officials raised the relevant issue in a footnote appended to text discussing a different issue in the "background" section of the NPRM.[18] And in *Small Refiner Lead Phase–Down Task Force v. Environmental Protection Agency*,[19] the court of appeals ruled that an NPRM raising the prospect of "unspecified changes in the definition of small refinery" was "too general" to support a final rule redefining "small refineries." The agency, held the court, fell short of the notice requirement of section 553(b) by failing to describe with "reasonable specificity . . . the range of alternatives" the agency was considering to the existing definition.[20]

Discussion of a subject or issue in the public comments provides evidence that an NPRM adequately communicated the relevance of that subject or issue in the rulemaking proceeding,[21] but such a discussion in the comments by itself cannot cure an inadequate notice.[22] Because section 553(b) requires that the *agency* notify the public of its rulemaking intentions, reviewing courts focus on the agencies' public communications when determining the adequacy of a notice of proposed rulemaking.[23] Interested mem-

---

13. Natural Resources Defense Council, Inc. v. EPA, 279 F.3d 1180, 1186 (9th Cir. 2002) (emphasis added); see *Steelworkers*, 828 F.2d at 317; *Action for Children's Television*, 564 F.2d at 470.

14. *Florida Power & Light*, 846 F.2d at 771; see *American Medical Ass'n*, 887 F.2d at 767.

15. McLouth Steel Products Corp. v. Thomas, 838 F.2d 1317, 1323 (D.C.Cir. 1988).

16. MCI Telecommunications Corp. v. FCC, 57 F.3d 1136, 1142 (D.C.Cir. 1995).

17. 57 F.3d 1136 (D.C. Cir. 1995).

18. *Id.* at 1141–43; see also *McLouth*, 838 F.2d at 1322–23 (holding a rulemak-

ing notice inadequate where the agency raised the relevant issue only in the "supplemental information" section of the NPRM and thus failed to "alert the reader to the stakes").

19. 705 F.2d 506 (D.C.Cir. 1983).

20. *Id.* at 549.

21. See, e.g., Shell Oil Co. v. EPA, 950 F.2d 741, 757 (D.C.Cir. 1991); *Steelworkers*, 828 F.2d at 318.

22. See, e.g., Horsehead Resource Development v. Browner, 16 F.3d 1246, 1268 (D.C.Cir. 1994); *Shell*, 950 F.2d at 751.

23. See, e.g., *Shell Oil Co.*, 950 F.2d at 751; *Small Refiners*, 705 F.2d at 547, 549–50; AFL–CIO v. Donovan, 757 F.2d 330, 340 (D.C.Cir. 1985).

bers of the public are not obligated to mine the public comments in order to discover the subjects and issues at play in a rulemaking proceeding.[24]

The Logical Outgrowth Rule. Perhaps the most vexing problem arising under the notice requirement of section 553(b) is determining when an agency's modification of a proposed rule requires another notice of proposed rulemaking inviting additional public comment on the change. Reviewing courts begin with the premise that agencies must remain free to make some changes to a proposed rule without having to re-start the notice-and-comment process.[25] Some difference between the proposed and final rules is a natural and desirable product of public participation in rulemaking proceedings.[26] Such differences are a healthy sign that administrators considered the public comments.[27] Indeed, a final agency rule is subject to reversal on substantive grounds if it clings to the language of a proposed rule that has been discredited by the public comments (see § 8.7(b)). But if the gap between an agency's proposal and its final rule is too wide, a second round of comments addressing the agency's change of position is necessary to permit interested members of the public to weigh in on regulatory provisions they otherwise would not have known were under consideration.[28]

In determining when an agency's shift between its proposed and final rules necessitates publication of another NPRM, reviewing courts generally ask whether the final rule is a "logical outgrowth" of the rulemaking proposal.[29] The modifier "logical" is misleading, however. Reviewing courts do not apply formal rules of logic when analyzing whether an NPRM has adequately noticed a final rule that differs from the original proposal. Rather, the logical outgrowth rule is better understood as a specific application of section 553(b)'s general requirement that the agency provide interested persons "a reasonable opportunity to participate in the rule-

---

24. See, e.g., *Small Refiners*, 705 F.2d at 547, 549–50; *AFL-CIO v. Donovan*, 757 F.2d at 340.

25. See, e.g., *Chocolate Mfgrs.*, 755 F.2d at 1103–04; International Harvester Co. v. Ruckelshaus, 478 F.2d 615, 632 n.15 (D.C.Cir. 1973).

26. See, e.g., Natural Resources Defense Council, Inc. v. Thomas, 838 F.2d 1224, 1242 (D.C.Cir. 1988).

27. See *American Medical Ass'n*, 887 F.2d at 766–69; *AFL-CIO*, 757 F.2d at 338; South Terminal Corp. v. EPA, 504 F.2d 646, 658 (1st Cir. 1974).

28. See, e.g., Natural Resources Defense Council, Inc. v. EPA, 863 F.2d

1420, 1429 (9th Cir. 1988); *Small Refiners*, 705 F.2d at 547; Connecticut Light & Power Co. v. NRC, 673 F.2d 525, 533 (D.C.Cir. 1982).

29. The First Circuit formulated the "logical outgrowth" test in *South Terminal*, 504 F.2d at 658–59. Other circuits have followed suit. See, e.g., *Natural Resources Defense Council*, 279 F.3d at 1186; *Chocolate Mfgrs.*, 755 F.2d at 1105; Taylor Diving & Salvage Co. v. Dept. of Labor, 599 F.2d 622, 626 (5th Cir. 1979); *Weyerhaeuser*, 590 F.2d at 1031.

making process"[30] by "fairly appris[ing] [them] of the subjects and issues" at stake in the proceeding.[31] New provisions of a final rule are a logical outgrowth of an agency's proposal if, but only if, interested members of the public "should have anticipated" the change.[32] Reviewing courts expect interested parties to anticipate final rule provisions that are "in character with the original scheme."[33] But when an agency "materially alters the issues involved in the rulemaking" or otherwise substantially departs from its rulemaking proposal, section 553(b) requires officials to re-notice the rule.[34]

Assume, for example, that an agency proposed a rule prescribing several specific safety standards for automobiles. An automobile manufacturer decided not to comment on the proposed rule because its cars complied with the agency's proposed standards. The final rule, however, adopted stricter standards than had the original proposal. The manufacturer could not successfully challenge the sufficiency of the agency's NPRM because the final rule (stricter safety standards) was a "logical outgrowth" of the proposed rule (lesser safety standards).[35] The agency had made it clear that the subject of its rulemaking was automobile safety, and the manufacturer should have anticipated that the stringency of those standards would be at issue. If the manufacturer objected to stricter standards than those proposed, it should have filed comments seeking to persuade the agency not to tighten the standards.[36]

Now assume that the agency, in response to one of the public comments submitted in the rulemaking proceeding on the proposed safety standards, adopted a final rule creating a new mileage standard for automobiles. In this case, a reviewing court would invalidate the mileage standard because it was not a "logical outgrowth" of the NPRM proposing new safety standards. Automobile manufacturers had no reason to anticipate that the agency

30. *Florida Power & Light*, 846 F.2d at 771.

31. *Natural Resources Defense Council*, 279 F.3d at 1186.

32. *Small Refiners*, 705 F.2d at 547; see American Water Works Ass'n v. EPA, 40 F.3d 1266, 1275 (D.C.Cir. 1994); *Horsehead Resource Development*, 16 F.3d at 1268.

33. *South Terminal*, 504 F.2d at 658; see also *American Medical Ass'n*, 887 F.2d at 767 ("generally consistent with the tenor of the original proposal").

34. *Chocolate Mfgrs.*, 755 F.2d at 1105; see *American Water Works*, 40 F.3d at 1274.

35. See, e.g., *Connecticut Light & Power*, 673 F.2d at 533 (upholding "final rules [that] were simply more stringent versions of the proposed rules"); United Steelworkers of America v. Marshall, 647 F.2d 1189, 1222 (D.C.Cir. 1980), cert. denied, 453 U.S. 913 (1981).

36. See *American Medical Ass'n*, 887 F.2d at 769 ("if interested parties favor a particular regulatory proposal, they should [submit comments] to support the approach an agency has tentatively advanced").

would issue new mileage standards.[37] The fact that the mileage rule was in response to a comment did not relieve the agency of *its* obligation to notify the public of the proposed mileage rule. In this illustration, if the agency wishes to adopt a mileage standard, it would have to issue a new notice of proposed rulemaking raising that issue.[38]

The two hypotheticals pose straightforward applications of the logical outgrowth rule. Not surprisingly, many contested cases require a more difficult determination of whether an agency's modifications to a proposed rule necessitate a new round of public comment. In approaching these closer cases, reviewing courts engage in a fact-specific analysis evaluating not only the textual differences between the proposed and final rules, but also the totality of the agency's public communications concerning the scope of its rulemaking. For example, in *South Terminal Corp. v. Environmental Protection Agency*,[39] the First Circuit upheld rules that, the court acknowledged, marked a "substantial" change from the agency's original proposal. EPA had proposed to reduce pollution from motor vehicles in the Boston area by adopting several specific motor-vehicle pollution-control measures, including parking surcharges and travel restrictions on a highway ringing the city. The agency eliminated those measures from the final rule after commenters had assailed them. EPA, however, substituted other motor-vehicle pollution-control measures in the final rule that it had not previously proposed, such as reducing parking availability and requiring more frequent automobile inspections.

The court of appeals upheld the new measures as a logical outgrowth of the rulemaking proposal because they were "in character with the original scheme." It was important to the court as well that EPA had stated in the notice of proposed rulemaking that officials would be influenced by public opposition to its proposals and that they would "consider all reasonable alternatives" for reducing automobile pollution in the Boston area. In addition, as

---

37. See, e.g., *MCI*, 57 F.3d at 1140–43 (an NPRM proposing to impose specified requirements on only one type of carrier was inadequate to support a final rule imposing those requirements on a different type of carrier).

38. See, e.g., AFL–CIO v. Donovan, 757 F.2d 330 (D.C.Cir. 1985). In *AFL-CIO*, the D.C. Circuit held that an agency had failed to comply with the notice requirement of section 553(b) when it amended an extensive set of existing regulations. The NPRM included the complete text of the regulations, flagging the changes the agency proposed in the "preamble." In response to some of the

comments, the agency changed a provision of the regulations that it had not identified as under consideration for change. The court of appeals held that the change was not a "logical outgrowth" of the NPRM. "[T]he clear impression from the notices of proposed rulemaking," the D.C. Circuit ruled, "was that only the regulations specifically identified for possible modification would be changed and that the remainder of [of the printed regulations] would be left untouched." *Id.* at 339.

39. 504 F.2d 646 (1st Cir. 1974).

part of the rulemaking proceeding, the agency had held a hearing at which a number of alternative motor-vehicle pollution-control strategies were vetted. For all of these reasons, the court concluded, interested members of the public should have anticipated that EPA would consider adopting alternative pollution-control measures for the proposed controls that had drawn strong public opposition.[40]

In *Chocolate Manufacturers Association v. Block*,[41] the Fourth Circuit concluded that a regulatory shift by the Department of Agriculture similar to that of EPA in *South Terminal* failed the logical outgrowth test. The regulations of the Agriculture Department permitted the substitution of flavored milk for fluid whole milk in a federal food program. After Congress amended the enabling act instructing USDA to ensure that the substituted foods it allowed in the program had nutritional value, the Department initiated a rulemaking proceeding. The rulemaking proposal maintained the USDA's long-standing position allowing flavored milk as a substitute for whole milk. But the NPRM, like EPA's rulemaking notice in *South Terminal*, invited the public "to make recommendations for alternatives not considered in the proposed regulations." Of the 1,000 or so comments USDA received, 78 recommended that the agency delete flavored milk from the list of approved foods. The agency's final rule adopted that position, prohibiting for the first time the use of flavored milk in the food program.

Although the court of appeals acknowledged that generally an agency's "approval of a practice in a proposed rule may properly alert interested parties that the practice may be disapproved in the final rule in the event of adverse comments," it nevertheless ruled, at least in "the specific circumstances of this case," that the provision prohibiting flavored milk as a substitute for whole milk was not a logical outgrowth of the agency's proposal. The Fourth Circuit in *Chocolate Manufacturers*, like the First Circuit in *South Terminal*, scoured the rulemaking record in reaching this conclusion. It was important to the court of appeals in *Chocolate Manufacturers* that USDA had permitted the use of flavored milk in the program since its inception. And although USDA had compiled extensive research on the nutritional value of substituted foods before issuing its proposal, the Department never suggested deleting flavored milk from its list of approved foods. Moreover, the NPRM explicitly endorsed flavored milk as an appropriate substitute for whole milk. "The total effect of the history of the use of flavored milk, the preamble discussion, and the proposed rule," the court found, "could have led interested persons only to conclude that a change in flavored milk would not be considered." Because USDA had provided no public notice that it might delete flavored

---

40. *Id*. at 656–60.   **41.** 755 F.2d 1098 (4th Cir. 1985).

milk from its list of approved foods, it could not take that action without providing interested members of the public an opportunity to comment.[42]

Disclosure of Relevant Studies, Reports, and Factual Information. Reviewing courts require that agencies disclose and make "readily available" to the public the important studies, data and information on which they rely when formulating their rule-making proposals.[43] Courts have justified the extension of the public notice requirement of section 553(b) to include disclosure of the factual material underlying rulemaking proposals as an essential step in realizing the APA's purpose of "fairly appris[ing] interested persons of the subjects and issues before the Agency" in a rulemaking proceeding.[44] Without disclosure of the studies and data underlying a proposed rule, interested members of the public would be left with "an [in]accurate picture of the [agency's] reasoning."[45] Commenters also would be denied the opportunity to engage in "the stuff of scientific debate," such as critiquing the agency's methodology or challenging the inferences administrators drew from the data.[46] For these reasons, reviewing courts have determined, in the D.C. Circuit's frequently quoted language, "It is not consonant with the purpose of a rule-making proceeding to promulgate rules on the basis of ... data that, [in] critical degree, is known only to the agency."[47]

An agency's disclosure of the key data, methodology, and studies on which it relied in preparing s rulemaking proposal must be "in a form that allows for meaningful comment."[48] In *Engine Manufacturers Association v. Environmental Protection Agency*,[49] the D.C. Circuit invalidated a rule charging engine manufacturers the cost of testing motor vehicles and engines for compliance with federal emission standards. EPA had disclosed a 30–page cost analysis that agency personnel had prepared for internal use in developing the fee schedule included in the proposed rule. But the court of appeals found the cost analysis to be unintelligible to

---

42. *Id.* at 1100–07.

43. United States v. Nova Scotia Food Products, Corp., 568 F.2d 240, 251–52 (2d Cir. 1977); see *Weyerhaeuser*, 590 F.2d at 1028–31 (agency must disclose data on which it calculated effluent limitation adopted in final rule). Agencies typically describe some of the information underlying a rulemaking proposal in the NPRM, and include the remainder in the public docket of the rulemaking proceeding. CORNELIUS M. KERWIN, RULEMAKING: HOW GOVERNMENT AGENCIES WRITE LAW AND MAKE POLICY 64 (1994).

44. *Natural Resources Defense Council*, 279 F.3d at 1186; see *Nova Scotia Food Products*, 568 F.2d at 252.

45. *Connecticut Light & Power*, 673 F.2d at 530.

46. *Nova Scotia Food Products*, 568 F.2d at 252.

47. Portland Cement Ass'n v. Ruckelshaus, 486 F.2d 375, 393 (D.C.Cir. 1973), cert. denied, 417 U.S. 921 (1974).

48. Engine Mfgrs. Ass'n v. EPA, 20 F.3d 1177, 1181 (D.C.Cir. 1994).

49. 20 F.3d 1177 (D.C.Cir. 1994).

anyone outside the agency. The court thus directed EPA to provide "a reasonable explanation" of the cost analysis permitting interested members of the public to understand the agency's decisionmaking sufficiently to offer meaningful comment on the proposal fee schedule.[50]

The judicial gloss on the notice requirement of section 553(b) to include public disclosure of the information and studies underlying agency rulemaking proposals is in obvious tension with *Vermont Yankee*, and indeed, the Supreme Court has hinted at its disapproval of this innovation. In *Federal Communications Commission v. WNCN Listeners Guild*,[51] which the Court decided several years after *Vermont Yankee*, the justices upheld a rule even though the agency had failed to disclose a relevant staff study. Conceding the possibility that the agency's failure to disclose the study constituted "a procedural lapse," the Court, without explanation, concluded that the failure was not "a sufficient ground for reopening the [rulemaking] proceeding."[52] Despite the Supreme Court's cold shoulder in *WNCN Listeners Guild*, lower courts have continued to require agencies to disclose the information that informed their rulemaking proposals as an aid to public comment.[53]

Reviewing courts appear less certain about requiring agencies to disclose for public comment relevant information they acquires *after* publication of the notice of proposed rulemaking. In *Portland Cement Association v. Ruckelshaus*,[54] decided five years before *Vermont Yankee* and during the heyday of judicial hybrid rulemaking, the D.C. Circuit suggested that agencies were under a continual obligation throughout a rulemaking proceeding to disclose "information that is material to the subject at hand . . . as it becomes available." Such a requirement would serve the salutary goal of testing all of the factual material upon which agencies rely when drafting a final rule. But imposing a continual duty on administrators to disclose relevant facts that come to their attention during a rulemaking proceeding might trigger a perpetual cycling of notice-and-comment periods that would make informal rulemaking virtually impossible.[55]

More recently, the D.C. Circuit outlined a nuanced approach to the agency's duty to disclose relevant information it learns during a rulemaking proceeding. In *Building Industry Association of Superi-*

---

50. *Id.* at 1181.

51. 450 U.S. 582 (1981).

52. *Id.* at 592 n.22.

53. See, e.g., *Connecticut Light & Power*, 673 F.2d at 530–31; see also Air Transport Ass'n of America v. FAA, 169 F.3d 1, 7 (D.C.Cir. 1999); *Engine Mfgrs.*

Ass'n, 20 F.3d at 1181; Solite Corp. v. EPA, 952 F.2d 473, 484 (D.C.Cir. 1991).

54. 486 F.2d 375, 394 (D.C.Cir. 1973).

55. Building Industry Ass'n of Superior California v. Norton, 247 F.3d 1241, 1246 (D.C.Cir. 2001).

or California v. Norton,[56] the court of appeals upheld a rule that had "relie[d] heavily" on an outside study that was released after the agency published its notice of proposed rulemaking. The agency had received the study during the comment period, but it did not make the study available for public comment. The court of appeals, noting the perpetual cycling concern, held that the agency's failure to disclose the study did not violate the APA. It was important to the court, however, that the study, "while the best available," simply supported the agency's findings and decisions included in the NPRM. The D.C. Circuit suggested that if the new study had "reject[ed] or modif[ied]" the agency's initial position as described in the NPRM, "additional comment" on the study may have been "necessary."[57]

(b) Public Participation and Agency Consideration

The Public's Right to Comment. Section 553(c) of the Administrative Procedure Act requires that agencies "give interested persons an opportunity to participate in the rule making through submission of written data, views or arguments with or without opportunity for oral presentation." The Supreme Court in *Vermont Yankee* made clear that section 553(c) imposes a baseline requirement on agencies only to provide the public an opportunity to submit written comments on rulemaking proposals. Congress (in an enabling act) or agencies (in their discretion) may provide for some form of oral hearing as well, but reviewing courts cannot require public participation in rulemaking proceedings beyond the opportunity to submit written comments on rulemaking proposals (see § 6.2).

The D.C. Circuit has described the public's right to comment on agency rulemaking proposals as a "particularly important component of the [agency's] reasoning process."[58] It is significant that section 553(c) extends the right to comment in informal rulemaking proceedings to "interested *persons*" (emphasis added), while the APA limits participation rights in formal proceedings to "interested *parties*" (see APA § 554(c) (emphasis added)). The APA defines "party" as a "person . . . named or admitted as a party, or properly seeking or entitled as of right to be admitted as party, in an agency

---

56. 247 F.3d 1241 (D.C.Cir. 2001).

57. *Id.* at 1245–46; see also Idaho Farm Bureau Federation v. Babbitt, 58 F.3d 1392, 1402 (9th Cir. 1995) ("agency may use supplementary data, unavailable during the notice and comment period, that expands on and confirms information contained in the proposed rulemaking and addresses alleged deficiencies in the pre-existing data, so long as no prejudice is shown"); Internation-

al Fabricare Inst. v. EPA, 972 F.2d 384, 398–400 (D.C.Cir. 1992) (agency may rely on studies conducted by private laboratories confirming the reliability of a proposed method for measuring chemical concentration without providing specific notice and opportunity for comment on the studies).

58. See *Connecticut Light and Power*, 673 F.2d at 528.

proceeding" (APA § 551(3)). Section 553(c)'s use of "person" rather than "party" to describe the public participants in informal rulemakings therefore signals that commenters need not be formally "admitted as a party" or be specifically entitled to party status in the proceeding. Nor is there case law suggesting that section 553(c)'s use of the modifier "interested" requires that commenters demonstrate their legal standing to participate in the rulemaking. Anyone who is sufficiently "interested" in a rulemaking proceeding to prepare comments may submit them.[59]

The Administrative Procedure Act does not prescribe a minimum comment period. The *Attorney General's Manual* advised agencies to allow interested persons "sufficient time" to prepare their comments.[60] Similarly, reviewing courts require that comment periods extend for a reasonable amount of time, measured in light of the relative simplicity or complexity of the issues raised by a rulemaking proposal.[61] In relatively complex or controversial rulemaking proceedings, agencies typically allow at least 60 days for public comment,[62] but reviewing courts have upheld shorter comment periods that were reasonable under the circumstances.[63] Agencies may accept late comments at their discretion.[64]

The APA does not specify a maximum time-period for agencies to complete a rulemaking proceeding, but a number of enabling acts, particularly statutes authorizing environmental regulation, provide rulemaking deadlines. In the absence of a statutory deadline, agencies are expected to conclude their rulemaking proceedings within a "reasonable time."[65]

The Agency's Duty to Consider Public Comments. In addition to assuring interested members of the public a right to comment on agency rulemaking proposals, section 553(c) correspondingly obligates agencies to "consider ... the relevant matter presented" in the rulemaking proceeding. But section 553(c) does not, in contrast to the APA's provisions governing formal proceed-

---

59. For discussion of who actually participates in administrative rulemaking proceedings, as well as of the effectiveness of such participation, see KERWIN, RULEMAKING, *supra* note 43, at 191–210; Stephen P. Croley, *Theories of Regulation: Incorporating the Administrative Process*, 98 COLUM. L. REV. 1, 119–42 (1998).

60. *Attorney General's Manual, supra* note 8, at 29.

61. See *Connecticut Light and Power*, 673 F.2d at 534.

62. See JEFFREY S. LUBBERS, A GUIDE TO FEDERAL AGENCY RULEMAKING 278 (4th ed. 2006).

63. See, e.g., *Florida Power & Light*, 846 F.2d at 772 (15 days); *Connecticut Light and Power*, 673 F.2d at 534 (30 days).

64. LUBBERS, GUIDE TO RULEMAKING, *supra* note 62, at 279.

65. SECTION OF ADMINISTRATIVE LAW AND REGULATORY PRACTICE OF THE AMERICAN BAR ASSOCIATION, A BLACKLETTER STATEMENT OF FEDERAL ADMINISTRATIVE LAW 25 (2004). The APA authorizes courts "to compel agency action unlawfully withheld or unreasonably delayed" (APA § 706(1)). The Supreme Court has interpreted that authority narrowly, however (see § 8.8).

ings (see APA § 556(e)), limit the agency to considering only the submissions of interested persons. Informal rulemaking is not "on the record." Agencies are free to tap their institutional knowledge and experience when formulating rules. They also may look to sources of information outside the agency and beyond the participants in the rulemaking proceeding.[66] Everything on which the agency relies in formulating a final rule becomes part of the "administrative record" in an informal rulemaking proceeding.[67]

There are times when an agency's "consideration of the relevant matter presented" in a rulemaking proceeding leads it to supplement the rulemaking record after the comment period has closed in order to support its positions on substantive judicial review. It is unsettled whether in such circumstances the APA obligates the agency to provide interested persons an opportunity to comment on the supplemental material. According to the Ninth Circuit, the existence of the public's right to comment depends on the source of the supplemental information. The court of appeals in *Rybachek v. Environmental Protection Agency*[68] permitted EPA to add some 6,000 pages of material to the administrative record after the comment period had closed in order to respond to comments challenging its proposed rule. Interested members of the public, the court wrote, enjoy a right "to comment on the proposed regulations, not to comment in a never-ending way on the [agency's] responses to their comments."[69] Yet several years later, the Ninth Circuit invalidated a rule in *Ober v. Environmental Protection Agency*[70] because the same agency, again after the comment period had closed, invited an "interested party" to submit "new information and data" upon which the agency ultimately relied in formulating its final rule. While an agency can file its *"own* responses to comments received during the comment period," explained the court of appeals, it cannot allow one party a special opportunity to provide "critical" information concerning a rulemaking proposal without permitting other interested parties to comment on the submission.[71]

An additional key to the Ninth Circuit's allowance of EPA's supplementation of the administrative record in *Rybachek* may have been that the new information simply defended the positions the agency already had disclosed in the notice of proposed rulemak-

---

66. See *Attorney General's Manual, supra* note 8, at 31–32. Agencies may be required to disclose for public comment the relevant information not found in the written comments on which they rely in their rulemaking (see § 6.3(a)).

67. See Citizens to Preserve Overton Park, Inc. v. Volpe, 401 U.S. 402, 419–20 (1971); § 8.2.

68. 904 F.2d 1276 (9th Cir. 1990).

69. *Id.* at 1286.

70. 84 F.3d 304 (9th Cir. 1996).

71. *Id.* at 313–15.

ing. Had the supplemental filing supported a significant change in EPA's original positions, the court of appeals might well have required the agency to allow interested parties to comment on the new information supporting the shift before issuing a final rule.[72]

(c) The Final Rule and the Agency's Statement of Basis and Purpose

Agencies publish their final rules in the *Federal Register*, and the rules are eventually codified in the *Code of Federal Regulations*. Section 553(d) of the Administrative Procedure Act establishes a default rule prohibiting administrative rules from taking effect sooner than 30 days after their initial publication. The purpose of the 30–day waiting period is to provide those affected by a new rule "reasonable time to prepare" for complying with any new legal obligation.[73] For rules with a major economic impact, the Small Business Regulatory Enforcement Fairness Act of 1996[74] has created a default waiting period of 60 legislative days. This longer waiting period provides Congress an opportunity to override an agency's rule pursuant to a special fast-track legislative process (see § 2.3(c)).

Section 553(c) of the APA requires that agencies "incorporate in the rules [they adopt] a concise general statement of their basis and purpose." The *Attorney General's Manual* described the statement of basis and purpose as a helpful guide for those who interpret and apply administrative rules.[75] Contemporary courts, however, have emphasized the importance of agency statements of basis and purpose in facilitating judicial review of agency rulemaking. Because statements of basis and purpose contain the agency's contemporaneous explanation and justification of the administrative decisions leading to adoption of the final rule, these statements have become the focal point of the courts' substantive review of agency rulemaking (see § 8.7(b)). Reviewing courts expect an agency's explanation and justification of its rulemaking decisions in the statement of basis and purpose to demonstrate that administrative

---

72. See Idaho Farm Bureau Fed'n v. Babbitt, 58 F.3d 1392, 1402 (9th Cir. 1995) ("agency may use supplementary data, unavailable during the notice and comment period, that expands on and confirms information contained in the proposed rulemaking and addresses alleged deficiencies in the pre-existing data, so long as no prejudice is shown"); see also Building Industry Association of Superior California v. Norton, 247 F.3d 1241, 1245–46 (D.C.Cir. 2001) (permitting failure to disclose for public comment an outside study released after the NPRM where the study, "while the best

available," simply supported the agency's findings and decisions included in the NPRM; "additional comment" on the study may have been "necessary" had new study "reject[ed] or modif[ied]" the agency's initial position as described in the NPRM).

73. *Attorney General's Manual, supra* note 8, at 36 (quoting congressional reports); see Rowell v. Andrus, 631 F.2d 699, 702 n.2 (10th Cir. 1980).

74. 5 U.S.C. §§ 801–808.

75. See *Attorney General's Manual, supra* note 8, at 32.

officials engaged in a "process of reasoned decision-making" when formulating the rule.[76]

The *Attorney General's Manual* made clear its under-estimation of the value of agency statements of basis and purpose to reviewing courts when it assured administrators that they could keep these statements "concise" and "general," in line with the language of section 553(c). The advice of the *Attorney General's Manual* that statements of basis and purpose need not include an "elaborate analysis" of the rules or of the agency's "considerations" in formulating the rules has not held up.[77] The D.C. Circuit's counter-advice that administrators not indulge "an overly literal reading of the statutory terms 'concise' and 'general' " expresses the consensus of contemporary reviewing courts.[78] Although judges do not expect a statement of basis and purpose to include the formal findings of fact and conclusions of law that are required of agency decisions in formal proceedings (see APA § 557(c)(A)),[79] they regard these statements as the functional equivalent of a judicial opinion explaining and justifying the agency's rulemaking decisions.

Reviewing courts do not demand that an agency's statement of basis and purpose contain "an exhaustive, detailed account of every aspect of the rulemaking proceedings." Judges instead expect these statements to "indicate the major issues of policy that were raised in the proceedings and [to] explain why the agency decided to respond to these issues as it did, particularly in light of the statutory objectives that the rule must serve."[80] Similarly, while agencies need not address "every item of fact or opinion" residing in the public comments,[81] they must respond "in a reasoned manner"[82] to those assertions in the comments that, if true, would have required the agency to change the rule.[83] As the First Circuit explained, "It is not in keeping with the rational process to leave vital questions, raised by comments which are of cogent materiality, completely unanswered."[84]

---

76. *Connecticut Light and Power,* 673 F.2d at 528; *Nova Scotia,* 568 F.2d at 252; see § 8.7(b).

77. See *Attorney General's Manual, supra* note 8, at 32.

78. See Automotive Parts & Accessories Ass'n v. Boyd, 407 F.2d 330, 338 (D.C.Cir. 1968).

79. See, e.g., Independent U.S. Tanker Owners Committee v. Dole, 809 F.2d 847, 852 (D.C.Cir.), cert. denied,

484 U.S. 819 (1987); *Automotive Parts & Accessories,* 407 F.2d at 337–38.

80. *Independent U.S. Tanker Owners,* 809 F.2d at 852.

81. *Automotive Parts & Accessories,* 407 F.2d at 338.

82. Reytblatt v. NRC, 105 F.3d 715, 722 (D.C.Cir. 1997).

83. American Mining Congress v. EPA, 907 F.2d 1179, 1188 (D.C.Cir. 1990).

84. *Nova Scotia,* 568 F.2d at 252.

The level of detail that reviewing courts require in a statement of basis of purpose varies according to the nature of the rule and the content of the public comments.[85] When an agency bases a rulemaking decision "on the existence of certain determinable facts," the statement must articulate and justify sufficient factual findings from evidence in the administrative record.[86] Agencies also must justify their rejection of significant regulatory alternatives to the rules they adopt.[87] Cursory explanations of an agency's key rulemaking decisions will not do.[88] The statement of basis and purpose must provide a "reasoned explanation" of an agency's regulatory choices sufficient to assure the reviewing court that the final rule was neither "arbitrary" nor "capricious" (see § 706(2)(A); § 8.7(b)).[89]

(d) *Vermont Yankee* and Judicial Enhancement of the Administrative Procedure Act's Procedural Requirements for Agency Rulemaking

Does the contemporary legal doctrine interpreting and applying section 553 of the Administrative Procedure Act represent the kind of judicial improvisation that the Supreme Court condemned in *Vermont Yankee*? It is undeniable that a considerable portion of contemporary rulemaking requirements originates from judicial gloss on the statutory text beyond the contemplation of the APA's drafters. Yet there is a significant difference between this judicial gloss and the type of judicial hybrid rulemaking that the Supreme Court condemned in *Vermont Yankee*. In that case, the justices confronted courts of appeals decisions pushing agencies to add oral hearing procedures to the written notice-and-comment process that Congress had established for informal rulemaking. They understandably worried that such an add-on would judicialize the informal rulemaking process, thereby vitiating the APA's fundamental distinction between formal and informal agency proceedings. The decisions discussed in this section, by contrast, seek to reinforce rather than to abandon the APA's notice-and-comment process for informal rulemaking. They build on, rather than depart from, the text of section 553 to require that agencies conduct an adequate "paper hearing" when issuing rules.[90]

85. *Reytblatt*, 105 F.3d at 722.

86. Industrial Union Dep't, AFL–CIO v. Hodgson, 499 F.2d 467, 475–76 (D.C.Cir. 1974).

87. *Nova Scotia*, 568 F.2d at 252; see *Independent U.S. Tanker Owners*, 809 F.2d at 854.

88. See, e.g., *Independent U.S. Tanker Owners*, 809 F.2d at 852; National

Welfare Rights Org. v. Mathews, 533 F.2d 637, 649 (D.C.Cir. 1976).

89. See *Nova Scotia*, 568 F.2d at 252.

90. See Peter L. Strauss, *Changing Times: The APA at Fifty*, 63 U. Chi. L. Rev. 1389, 1405–13 (1996).

Yet these judicially created paper-hearing requirements, like the oral hearing requirement invalidated in *Vermont Yankee*, are subject to the criticism that they have over-formalized (indeed, judicialized) a rulemaking procedure that Congress had designed to be nimble as well as legislative. The judicial gloss on the notice-and-comment requirements of section 553, some have complained, has transformed even ordinary rulemaking proceedings into a time-consuming, expensive, and ultimately unpredictable enterprise that has contributed to the "ossification" of administrative rulemaking processes. This ossification, in turn, has encouraged agencies to escape notice-and-comment rulemaking by attempting to make policy by less burdensome methods, and in some instances, by avoiding new policymaking initiatives altogether.[91]

For what it is worth, the courts of appeals have not revealed any noticeable *Vermont Yankee* concern when expansively interpreting the requirements of section 553, and unlike in *Vermont Yankee*, the justices have exhibited no inclination to confront these courts.

§ 6.4   Ex Parte Communications and Bias in Informal Rulemaking

Ex Parte Communications. Sections 554(d)(1) and 557(d)(1) of the Administrative Procedure Act impose strict limitations on ex parte communications involving agency decisionmakers in formal proceedings (see § 5.6). The APA, however, provides no such limitation for informal proceedings. The starkly different legislative attitude toward ex parte communications reflects the crucial distinction between formal and informal proceedings under the APA: Agency decisions in formal proceedings are "on the record"; agency decisions in informal proceedings are not. The ban on ex parte communications in formal proceedings reinforces the on-the-record requirement by insulating agency decisionmakers from off-the-record discussions with interested parties. The need for such a ban is sharply reduced, if not eliminated, in informal rulemaking proceedings because agency decisionmakers may seek information from any source when formulating a rule.

The APA's limitation of its restrictions on ex parte communications to formal proceedings follows more generally from Congress's selection of a judicial model for formal proceedings and a legislative model for informal rulemaking. Although the prior section illustrates how contemporary courts have glossed the procedural requirements of the notice-and-comment process beyond the spare

---

91. See, e.g., E. Donald Elliott, *Reinventing Rulemaking*, 41 DUKE L.J. 1490, 1492–96 (1992). The classic article diagnosing and decrying the ossification of agency rulemaking is Thomas O. McGarity, *Some Thoughts on "Deossifying" the Rulemaking Process*, 41 DUKE L.J. 1490, 1385 (1992).

text of section 553, informal rulemaking remains far less formal—and far less judicial—than formal adjudication. The Supreme Court's decision in *Vermont Yankee* remains a bulwark against judicial transformation of agency rulemaking from a legislative to a judicial model of decisionmaking.

Despite the APA's explicit limitation of its restrictions on ex parte communications to formal proceedings, reviewing courts have extended the ban to at least some informal rulemaking proceedings. The pioneering decision was by the D.C. Circuit in *Sangamon Valley Television Corp. v. United States*.[1] Sangamon challenged a rule of the Federal Communications Commission switching a license to operate a television station from Springfield, Illinois, to St. Louis. Sangamon opposed the switch because it expected to receive the license if the license remained in Springfield. Signal Hill favored the switch because it stood to receive the license upon a move to St. Louis. After the FCC published notice of the proposed switch, representatives of both broadcasters privately contacted members of the Commission to press the case for their city of choice. The court of appeals invalidated the FCC's rule because of Signal Hill's and Sangamon's ex parte communications with the Commission members. The D.C. Circuit, however, limited its decision to rules that were, like the FCC's station switch, "quasi-judicial" in nature. The key to *Sangamon* was that the FCC rule resembled an adjudication resolving "conflicting private claims to a valuable privilege." When an agency uses a rulemaking proceeding to settle a dispute between private parties, the court held, "basic fairness" demands that administrators conduct the proceeding "in the open."[2]

The D.C. Circuit extended *Sangamon*'s limited ban on ex parte communications to *all* informal rulemaking proceedings in *Home Box Office, Inc. v. Federal Communications Commission*.[3] According to *Home Box Office*, after an agency issues a notice of proposed rulemaking, "any agency official or employee who is or may reasonably be expected to be involved in the decisional process of the rulemaking proceeding" should not discuss matters relevant to the proceeding with interested private parties or their representatives. If such an ex parte communication occurs, the court in *Home Box Office* held, the agency must "immediately" disclose the substance of the communication in the public rulemaking file and afford interested members of the public an opportunity to comment. *Home Box Office* required an agency to disclose an ex parte communication occurring before the NPRM only if the communicated information "forms the basis for agency action."[4]

§ 6.4

1. 269 F.2d 221 (D.C.Cir. 1959).

2. *Id.* at 224.

3. 567 F.2d 9 (D.C.Cir.), cert. denied, 434 U.S. 829 (1977).

4. *Id.* at 57.

The D.C. Circuit decided *Home Box Office* in 1977 at the height of the judicial hybrid rulemaking movement (see § 6.1). Moreover, the previous year, Congress had enacted the Government in the Sunshine Act, which had amended the APA to require agency decisionmakers in formal proceedings to disclose on the public record all ex parte communications after the notice of hearing with interested persons concerning matters "relevant to the merits of the proceeding." (APA § 557(d)(1); see § 5.6). *Home Box Office* applied the new APA requirement to informal rulemaking proceedings because the D.C. Circuit concluded that ex parte communications subvert every type of administrative decisionmaking, whether formal or informal, rulemaking or adjudication. The court of appeals in *Home Box Office* found that ex parte communications hampered informal rulemaking proceedings in two distinct ways. First, they undermined the notice-and-comment process by denying interested members of the public the opportunity to respond to "secret" submissions to agency rulemakers by other interested persons. And to the extent that such secret submissions, rather than publicly disclosed information, supplied the actual bases for the agency's final rule, ex parte communications also frustrated judicial review.[5]

The Supreme Court's decision in *Vermont Yankee*, which came just one year after *Home Box Office*, called into question the legitimacy of a judicially imposed, across-the-board ban on ex parte communications in informal rulemaking proceedings.[6] Just as the APA's reservation of a hearing requirement for formal proceedings disabled judges from extending that requirement to informal proceedings (absent the demands of procedural due process), the APA's restriction of the limitations on ex parte communications to formal proceedings should similarly block reviewing courts from applying these limitations in the general run of informal rulemaking proceedings.[7] The D.C. Circuit in *Home Box Office* attempted to ground its across-the-board rule against ex parte communications on "fundamental notions of fairness implicit in due process."[8] Procedural due process norms, however, do not apply to the typical informal rulemaking proceeding, which culminates in a rule establishing a generally applicable norm of conduct.[9] The D.C. Circuit also tried to

---

5. *Id.* at 54–55.

6. The D.C. Circuit has acknowledged the tension between *Home Box Office* and *Vermont Yankee*. See *Air Transport Ass'n of America v. FAA*, 169 F.3d 1, 7 n.5 (D.C.Cir. 1999) ("*Home Box Office* ... could be thought to be undermined by *Vermont Yankee*").

7. See *United Steelworkers of America v. Marshall*, 647 F.2d 1189, 1214 (D.C.Cir. 1980), cert. denied, 453 U.S.

913 (1981) (*Home Box Office* "went beyond the strict terms of the APA" in imposing a ban on ex parte communications in informal rulemaking proceedings that are not "quasi-adjudicatory" in nature).

8. *Home Box Office*, 567 F.2d at 56.

9. *Bi-Metallic Investment. Co. v. State Bd. of Equalization*, 239 U.S. 441 (1915); see *Steelworkers*, 647 F.2d at 1215 n.28 (court "very wary of extend-

justify the *Home Box Office* rule against ex parte communications by analogizing it to the judicial requirement that agencies disclose the information on which they rely in formulating rulemaking proposals.[10] That disclosure requirement has survived *Vermont Yankee*, at least in the lower courts (see § 6.3(a)). But while the requirement that agencies disclose the information underlying a notice of proposed rulemaking, like *Home Box Office*'s ban on ex parte communications, is not stated in section 553 of the APA, the ban on ex parte communications, unlike the disclosure requirement, is the kind of judicial importation of adjudicatory decision-making into informal rulemaking that the justices so forcefully rejected in *Vermont Yankee* (see §§ 6.2, 6.3(d)).

Although the D.C. Circuit has never overruled *Home Box Office*, the court of appeals has since limited the ban on ex parte communications in informal rulemaking to "quasi-adjudicatory" proceedings that, as in *Sangamon*, involve the "resolution of conflicting private claims to a valuable privilege."[11] This trimming began in the very year the D.C. Circuit decided *Home Box Office*, when a different panel of the court of appeals in *Action for Children's Television v. Federal Communications Commission*[12] refused to apply the newly minted, across-the-board ban on ex parte communications retroactively because it marked "a clear departure from established law." The D.C. Circuit panel in *Action for Children's Television* made clear its disagreement with *Home Box Office*'s extension of *Sangamon* to "every case of informal rulemaking." As if in anticipation of the Supreme Court's impending decision in *Vermont Yankee*, the panel wrote, "If Congress wanted to forbid or limit ex parte contacts in every case of informal rulemaking, it certainly had a perfect opportunity of doing so when it [amended the APA to prohibit such contacts in formal proceedings]. . . . That it did not extend the ex parte contact provisions of amended section 557 to section 553 even though such an extension was urged upon it during the hearings is a sound indication that Congress still does not favor a per se prohibition . . . in all such proceedings." The court of appeals in *Action for Children's Television* continued to adhere to *Sangamon*, limiting the rule against ex parte communications in informal rulemaking to proceedings "involv[ing] . . . resolution of conflicting private claims to a valuable privilege."[13]

ing the due process reasoning of *Home Box Office*" to informal rulemaking proceedings that are not "quasi-adjudicatory" in nature); see § 3.1.

10. *Home Box Office*, 567 F.2d at 55.

11. *Steelworkers*, 647 F.2d at 1214, 1215 n.28; see *Sangamon*, 269 F.2d at 224.

12. 564 F.2d 458 (D.C.Cir. 1977).

13. *Id.* at 458, 474–77; see *Sangamon*, 269 F.2d at 224.

In later decisions, the D.C. Circuit has appeared to side decisively with *Action for Children's Television*, holding the *Home Box Office* rule inapplicable to "informal rulemaking of a policymaking sort."[14] Indeed, in *Sierra Club v. Costle*,[15] the court of appeals seemed to have come full circle by endorsing ex parte communications in the typical informal rulemaking proceeding. In the D.C. Circuit's revised view, the "openness, accessibility, and amenability" of agency officials to interested members of the public enhances rather than undermines the "legitimacy" of administrative rulemaking. Echoing *Vermont Yankee*, the court of appeals in *Sierra Club* advised judges to "refrain from the easy temptation to look askance at all face-to-face lobbying efforts, regardless of the forum in which they occur, merely because we see them as inappropriate in the judicial context." Although the D.C. Circuit in *Sierra Club* acknowledged the danger that ex parte communications may provide a secret basis for agency rulemaking unseen by the public, it reminded that on judicial review agencies must justify their rules on the basis of a public administrative record.[16]

Although the D.C. Circuit has limited the *Home Box Office* rule to *Sangamon*-type rulemakings, a number of agencies have adopted broader restrictions on ex parte communications in their rulemaking proceedings.[17]

Prejudgment by Agency Rulemakers. Section 556(b) of the Administrative Procedure Act provides that agency decisionmakers in formal proceedings must perform their responsibilities "in an impartial manner." The APA, however, provides no corresponding guarantee of "impartial" agency decisionmaking in informal rulemaking proceedings. Reviewing courts nevertheless hold open the possibility of disqualifying an agency decisionmaker for prejudgment of the issues relevant to an informal rulemaking proceeding, but they have been extremely reluctant to exercise this authority. The leading decision was by the D.C. Circuit in *Association of National Advertisers, Inc. v. Federal Trade Commission*.[18] In *Association of National Advertisers*, several industry groups challenged the FTC's denial of their petition seeking removal of the Commission chairman from a rulemaking proceeding concerning restrictions on advertising directed at children. These groups claimed that the chairman's public statements concerning regulation of children's advertising proved his "prejudgment of specific factual is-

---

14. Sierra Club v. Costle, 657 F.2d 298, 400 (D.C.Cir. 1981); see Iowa State Commerce Commission v. Office of Federal Inspector, 730 F.2d 1566, 1576 (D.C. Cir. 1984); *Steelworkers*, 647 F.2d at 1214–16.

15. 657 F.2d 298 (D.C.Cir. 1981).

16. *Id.* at 400–04.

17. For a brief discussion of these agencies' limitations on ex parte communications, see JEFFREY S. LUBBERS, A GUIDE TO FEDERAL AGENCY RULEMAKING 339–43 (4th ed., 2006).

18. 627 F.2d 1151 (D.C.Cir. 1979), cert. denied, 447 U.S. 921 (1980).

sues sufficient to preclude his ability to serve as an impartial arbiter." The court of appeals upheld the FTC's decision not to disqualify the chairman because of these statements, explaining that the requirement of "a neutral and detached adjudicator is simply an inapposite role model for an [agency rulemaker] who must translate broad statutory commands into concrete social policies." Writing just one year after the Supreme Court's decision in *Vermont Yankee*, the D.C. Circuit cautioned, "We must not impose judicial roles upon administrators when they perform functions very different from those of judges."[19]

Notwithstanding the D.C. Circuit's pointed refusal in *Association of National Advertisers* to "impose judicial roles" on administrative rulemakers, the court of appeals ruled that persons interested in an agency's rulemaking are entitled to a "fair and open proceeding," including "access to an impartial decisionmaker." The court of appeals reconciled this apparent contradiction by holding open the possibility of disqualifying an agency decisionmaker in an informal rulemaking proceeding, while making clear that the threshold of impartiality was lower for rulemakers than for adjudicators. In order to disqualify an agency decisionmaker for having prejudged relevant issues in an informal rulemaking proceeding, the court held in *Association of National Advertisers*, the challenger must make "a clear and convincing showing" that the decisionmaker "has an unalterably closed mind on matters critical to the disposition of the proceeding."[20] To meet this standard, the challenger must overcome the reviewing courts' presumption that agency decisionmakers handle their rulemaking obligations with "an open mind," albeit "not an empty one."[21]

The demanding disqualification standard of *Association of National Advertisers* coupled with the presumption of regularity courts afford administrative decisionmakers have slammed the door on efforts to remove agency decisionmakers for prejudgment of informal rulemaking proceedings.[22] For example, in *C & W Fish Co. v. Fox*,[23] the D.C. Circuit rejected a challenge to an agency rule prohibiting the use of drift gillnets in certain waters on the ground that an agency decisionmaker had an "unalterably closed mind," thus satisfying the *Association of National Advertisers* standard for disqualification. The official, while head of a state marine fisheries

---

19. *Id.* at 1155, 1168–69.

20. *Id.* at 1170, 1174.

21. PLMRS Narrowband Corp. v. FCC, 182 F.3d 995, 1002 (D.C.Cir. 1999).

22. See, e.g., *id.* at 995, 1002; Lead Industries Ass'n v. EPA, 647 F.2d 1130, 1179–80 (D.C.Cir.), cert. denied, 449

U.S. 1042 (1980); see also JERRY L. MASHAW, et al., ADMINISTRATIVE LAW: THE AMERICAN PUBLIC LAW SYSTEM 584 (5th ed., 2003) (authors unable to find any federal administrative rule that has been invalidated because of prejudgment by an agency decisionmaker).

23. 931 F.2d 1556 (D.C.Cir. 1991).

agency immediately before joining the federal agency, had said, "There's just *no question* that [drift gillnets] should be eliminated." The court ruled that this advocacy did not "even approach" the *Association of National Advertisers* standard.[24]

§ 6.5 Exemptions From the Informal Rulemaking Process

Section 553 of the Administrative Procedure Act establishes a strong default rule requiring that administrative rulemaking observe the notice-and-comment process. The act, however, allows for several exceptions to the general requirement of informal rulemaking procedures. First, as always, other acts of Congress may alter the rulemaking process (see APA § 559). For example, some enabling acts require an agency to use "hybrid" rulemaking procedures, which combine adjudicatory elements with the notice-and-comment process, when issuing rules on particular subjects.[1] Second, section 553(c) provides that "rules … required by statute to be made on the record after opportunity for an agency hearing" are subject to formal rather than informal rulemaking requirements. In formal rulemaking proceedings, agencies replace the public's opportunity to submit written comments on a proposed rule with a full trial-type hearing observing most APA procedures for formal adjudication (see § 4.2(a)).

In addition to allowing for rulemaking processes more formal than the notice-and-comment norm, section 553 explicitly permits agencies to issue certain types of rules without providing for any form of public participation. These exemptions fall into three categories. The first includes rules that are exempt because of their *subject matter*. None of the provisions of section 553 applies to rules involving (1) "a military or foreign affairs function of the United States" or (2) "a matter relating to agency management or personnel or to public property, loans, grants, benefits, or contracts" (§ 553(a)). These subject-matter exemptions are not developed here.[2]

---

24. *Id.* at 1564–65 (emphasis added). For a wide-ranging discussion of the issues raised by the disqualification of agency rulemakers, see Peter L. Strauss, *Disqualification of Decisional Officers in Rulemaking*, 80 COLUM. L. REV. 990 (1980).

§ 6.5

1. See, e.g., Federal Trade Commission Improvement Act of 1980, 15 U.S.C. § 57b–3; Clean Water Act of 1977, 33 U.S.C. § 1317; Clean Air Act Amendments of 1977, 42 U.S.C. § 7607(d); Tox-

ic Substances Control Act of 1976, 15 U.S.C. § 2605(c); Consumer Product Safety Act of 1972, 15 U.S.C. § 2058; Occupational Safety and Health Act of 1970, 29 U.S.C. § 655.

2. For discussion of the subject-matter exemptions from section 553, see *Attorney General's Manual on the Administrative Procedure Act* 26–28 (1947), reprinted in WILLIAM F. FUNK, et al., FEDERAL ADMINISTRATIVE PROCEDURE SOURCEBOOK 33–171 (3d ed. 2000); JEFFREY S. LUBBERS, A GUIDE TO FEDERAL AGENCY RULEMAKING 62–67 (4th ed.,

The second category of exemptions includes (1) "interpretative rules," (2) "general statements of policy," and (3) procedural rules ("rules of agency organization, procedure, or practice") (APA § 553(b)(A)). These three types of agency rules differ in *nature* from the "legislative" (or, "substantive") rules for which the APA requires public participation.[3] The distinctive quality of a legislative rule, according to the *Attorney General's Manual*, is that it, like a statute, regulates private conduct with "the force and effect of law."[4] "[S]ubstantive rights are not at stake" in the same way when agencies issue the rule-types grouped in the second category of rulemaking exemptions.[5] Interpretive rules and policy statements are often called "guidance documents" or "nonlegislative" rules because they lack the force of law. Procedural rules, in contrast to guidance documents, are legally binding, but unlike the legislative rules that require public participation, they do not create or alter *substantive* legal rights held by members of the public. Procedural rules instead govern the processes that agencies follow when making decisions concerning substantive rights.

Finally, section 553 exempts even legislative rules from its procedural requirements when agencies have "good cause" to bypass them. Section 553(b)(B) allows an agency to dispense with the notice-and-comment process when it "for good cause finds" that compliance would be "impracticable, unnecessary, or contrary to the public interest." Section 553(d)(3) allows a legislative rule to take effect immediately upon publication when an agency has "good cause" not to observe the otherwise mandatory 30–day waiting period.

Just as the Supreme Court has disabled judicial efforts to add procedures beyond the section 553 norm of notice and comment,[6] reviewing courts have been hesitant to excuse agencies from observing that statutory baseline of public participation in agency rulemaking. The D.C. Circuit captured the prevailing theme of the case law when it observed that section 553's exemptions have been

---

2006); Arthur Earl Bonfield, *Military and Foreign Affairs Function Rulemaking under the APA*, 71 MICH. L. REV. 221 (1972); Arthur Earl Bonfield, *Public Participation in Federal Rulemaking Relating to Public Property, Loans, Grants, Benefits, or Contracts*, 118 U. PA. L. REV. 540 (1970).

3. The APA uses the term "substantive rule" in section 553(d), but the act nowhere uses the term "legislative rule." The two terms often are used interchangeably in administrative law, but I prefer the modifier "legislative" because it highlights the distinguishing quality of the agency rules that trigger

the procedural requirements of section 553—their legal effect.

4. *Attorney General's Manual, supra* note 2, at 30 n.3.

5. American Hospital Ass'n v. Bowen, 834 F.2d 1037, 1045 (D.C.Cir. 1987).

6. See Vermont Yankee Nuclear Power Corp. v. Natural Resources Defense Council, 435 U.S. 519 (1978) (rejecting judicial hybrid rulemaking); United States v. Florida East Coast Railway, 410 U.S. 224 (1973) (strictly interpreting the APA provision triggering formal rulemaking).

"narrowly construed and only reluctantly countenanced."[7] Reviewing courts have been especially on guard against administrative attempts to abuse these exemptions by issuing substantive, legislative rules on the sly without affording interested members of the public the participation rights guaranteed them by the informal rulemaking process.[8]

This section considers each of the exemptions from section 553's requirements for public participation in agency rulemaking. But first, it describes the nature of the "legislative rules" that Congress had in mind when it designed the notice-and-comment process of section 553.

(a) Legislative Rules

Legislative rules have two distinguishing marks. First and foremost, they establish a standard of public conduct that carries the force of law.[9] The second marker follows from the first. Because legislative rules are legally binding, agencies may issue such rules only if Congress has authorized them to do so.[10] Legislative rules function like statutes. If valid, they create legally enforceable rights for or impose legal obligations on members of the public. They bind the agency and the courts as well.[11] It is the legislative character of these rules that prompted Congress to require public participation before their adoption.

Reviewing courts distinguish legislative rules, which require notice and comment before their adoption, from guidance documents, which require no public participation, by determining whether the document in question has the "legal effects" described in the preceding paragraph.[12] The judicial approaches for detecting the legal effect of an administrative document varies, depending on whether the agency claims that it is a statement of policy or an interpretive rule. The differing approaches for testing the legal effect of agency rules and statements are discussed in section 6.5(b).

---

7. New Jersey Dep't of Environmental Protection v. EPA, 626 F.2d 1038, 1046 (D.C.Cir. 1980); see Professionals and Patients for Customized Care v. Shalala, 56 F.3d 592, 595 (5th Cir. 1995).

8. American Bus Ass'n v. United States, 627 F.2d 525, 528 (D.C.Cir. 1980).

9. Pacific Gas & Electric Co. v. Federal Power Commission, 506 F.2d 33, 38 (D.C.Cir. 1974); see Attorney General's Manual, supra note 2, at 30 n.3.

10. Syncor International Corp. v. Shalala, 127 F.3d 90, 95 (D.C.Cir. 1997); see Attorney General's Manual, supra note 2, at 30 n.3.

11. See Chrysler Corp. v. Brown, 441 U.S. 281, 295 (1979); Morton v. Ruiz, 415 U.S. 199, 232 (1974); Batterton v. Marshall, 648 F.2d 694, 701–02 (D.C.Cir. 1980).

12. See, e.g., Pacific Gas & Electric, 506 F.2d at 38.

Before having that discussion, it is worth noting that some reviewing courts have used an alternative test for distinguishing between legislative rules and guidance documents. These courts have required agencies to proceed through notice and comment whenever a document has "a substantial impact" on the public. The substantial impact test deemed any administrative statement or rule to be a legislative rule if, as a practical matter, it caused individuals to alter their conduct.[13]

The substantial impact test arose as a competitor to the traditional legal effects approach during the heyday of the judicial hybrid rulemaking movement—the period stretching from the late 1960s to the mid–1970s (see § 6.1). Although the substantial impact test has had its academic champions,[14] in recent years reviewing courts have shied away from the test.[15] The problem with the substantial impact test is that an agency's nonlegislative statements, although not legally binding, inevitably influence public conduct. Otherwise, why would an agency bother to issue them? Because guidance documents alter public conduct, judges have worried that adopting the substantial impact test to define legislative rules would largely read out the section 553 exceptions for statements of policy and interpretive rules. Such a judicial override, they have concluded, would be incompatible with the *Vermont Yankee* principle forbidding judges from ordering agencies to observe procedures that Congress consciously had declined to require.[16]

Although the Supreme Court has not ruled on the legitimacy of the substantial impact test, and reviewing courts continue to assess the impact of a rule on the public when determining whether an agency statement or rule has legal effect and thus is legislative in nature,[17] the courts of appeal seem to have abandoned the substantial impact test as an alternative to the legal effects tests when distinguishing between legislative rules and guidance documents.

13. See, e.g., Lewis–Mota v. Secretary of Labor, 469 F.2d 478, 483 (2d Cir. 1972), quoting Texaco, Inc. v. Federal Power Commission, 412 F.2d 740, 744 (3d Cir. 1969).

14. The leading article espousing the substantial impact test over the legal effects test is William T. Mayton, *A Concept of a Rule and the "Substantial Impact" Test in Rulemaking*, 33 EMORY L.J. 889 (1984). For criticism of the substantial impact test, see Michael Asimow, *Nonlegislative Rulemaking and Regulatory Reform*, 1985 DUKE L.J. 381, 399–401.

15. Metropolitan School District v. Davila, 969 F.2d 485, 493 (7th Cir. 1992), cert. denied, 507 U.S. 949 (1993) ("Prevailing authority rejects the proposition that a rule that has substantial impact is necessarily legislative"); see, e.g., Rivera v. Becerra, 714 F.2d 887, 890–91 (9th Cir. 1983), cert. denied, 465 U.S. 1099 (1984); Cabais v. Egger, 690 F.2d 234, 237 (D.C.Cir. 1982).

16. See *Rivera*, 714 F.2d at 890; *Cabais*, 690 F.2d at 237.

17. See *Cabais*, 690 F.2d at 237.

(b) Guidance Documents

Guidance documents (also called "nonlegislative rules") lack the force of law. They are not legally binding on the public, the agency, or the courts. Because guidance documents lack legal effect, section 553(b)(A) of the Administrative Procedure Act exempts them from notice-and-comment requirements, and section 553(d)(2) of the APA exempts them from the 30–day waiting period that legislative rules must observe before taking effect. Congress has required only that agencies publish guidance documents in the *Federal Register* in order to rely on them when taking action affecting members of the public.[18] Section 553(b)(A) identifies two types of guidance documents that enjoy this special treatment— general statements of policy and interpretive rules.

Congress's removal of procedural constraints on the issuance of policy statements and interpretive rules reflects not only the non-legislative character of these instruments, but also the desirability of their use in administrative governance. Policy statements and interpretive rules serve two basic functions. They promote administrative consistency by instructing agency personnel on how to apply broad or ambiguous laws. They also enable agencies to inform interested members of the public of administrative policies and legal interpretations before the agency acts on them.[19]

Reviewing courts have experienced extraordinary difficulty at times when deciding whether an administrative statement or rule is legislative, and thus subject to the notice-and-comment provisions of section 553, or nonlegislative, and thus free from all public participation requirements. Because of the differing natures of agency policy statements and interpretive rules, courts have used different analyses for distinguishing those guidance documents from the legislative rules that trigger the procedural requirements of section 553. The APA's exemptions for policy statements and for interpretive rules are discussed in turn.

Policy Statements. Reviewing courts have tended to follow the *Attorney General's Manual*'s definition of policy statements, which describes these instruments as "statements issued by an agency to advise the public prospectively of the manner in which the agency proposes to exercise a discretionary function."[20] Administrative policy statements assume a variety of forms and proceed under many titles, such as "guidances," "memoranda," "manuals,"

18. 5 U.S.C. § 552(a)(1)(D). In addition, Executive Order 13,422, 72 Fed. Reg. 2,763 (2007), subjects "significant guidance documents" to White House review (see § 2.4 (c)).

19. See Hoctor v. Department of Agriculture, 82 F.3d 165, 167 (7th Cir. 1996); *American Hospital Ass'n*, 834 F.2d at 1045; *Pacific Gas & Electric*, 506 F.2d at 38.

20. *Attorney General's Manual, supra* note 2, at 30 n.3; see, e.g., *Chrysler Corp.*, 441 U.S. at 302 n.31.

"policy letters," "press releases," "staff instructions," "bulletins" and the like.

In distinguishing between legislative rules and policy statements, reviewing courts determine whether the document at issue binds the agency in subsequent administrative adjudications.[21] In administrative adjudications involving a legislative rule, the agency simply interprets the rule and applies it to the facts.[22] The agency cannot alter the rule without satisfying the notice-and-comment requirements of section 553.[23] By contrast, a nonlegislative statement of policy leaves the agency genuinely "free to exercise discretion" when deciding future adjudications.[24] While agency officials may use policy statements to guide their future actions, they may not "apply or rely" on a policy statement "as law."[25] Thus, the absence of legal effect that frees agencies to issue policy statements without public participation and without delay limits an agency's reliance on these statements in future cases.

The D.C. Circuit's decision in *Pacific Gas & Electric Co. v. Federal Power Commission*[26] is the leading authority on the distinction between legislative rules and policy statements. The decision also illustrates the utility of agency policy statements, as well as the difficulties reviewing courts face in distinguishing them from the legislative rules that require notice and comment. *Pacific Gas & Electric* arose against the background of a natural gas shortage that forced pipeline companies to reduce the deliveries of natural gas that they were contractually obligated to provide. The enabling act of the Federal Power Commission (now, the Federal Energy Regulatory Commission) authorized the Commission to relieve a pipeline company of its contractual obligations during a period of short supply upon agency approval of a "just and reasonable" curtailment plan. The FPC issued a "Statement of General Policy"

---

21. *Pacific Gas & Electric*, 506 F.2d at 38; see *American Hospital Ass'n*, 834 F.2d at 1046.

22. *Pacific Gas & Electric*, 506 F.2d at 38.

23. National Family Planning & Reproductive Health Ass'n v. Sullivan, 979 F.2d 227, 234 (D.C.Cir. 1992); see *Chrysler Corp.*, 441 U.S. at 301–02; United States v. Nixon, 418 U.S. 683, 695–96 (1974). Section 551(5) of the APA defines rulemaking to include the administrative process for "amending" or "repealing" a rule.

24. *American Bus Ass'n*, 627 F.2d at 529; see also *Syncor International Corp.*, 127 F.3d at 94 (having issued a policy statement, "[t]he agency retains the discretion and the authority to change its

position—even abruptly—in any specific case"); *American Hospital Ass'n*, 834 F.2d at 1046. For an argument that the reserved discretion of the agency, while relevant, often should not be determinative in distinguishing between a legislative rule and a policy statement, see Robert A. Anthony, *Interpretive Rules, Policy Statements, Guidances, Manuals, and the Like—Should Federal Agencies Use Them to Bind the Public?*, 41 DUKE L.J. 1311, 1359–63 (1992).

25. *Pacific Gas & Electric*, 506 F.2d at 38; see Panhandle Producers & Royalty Owners Ass'n v. Economic Regulatory Administration, 847 F.2d 1168, 1174–75 (5th Cir. 1988).

26. 506 F.2d 33 (D.C.Cir. 1974).

directing all pipeline companies anticipating short supplies of natural gas to submit a curtailment plan for the Commission's approval. The result was a flurry of submissions reflecting a variety of delivery priorities.

In an effort to sharpen its guidance to the pipeline companies, as well as to increase the uniformity of the companies' curtailment plans, the FPC issued a follow-up "Statement of Policy."[27] This second statement delineated a list of delivery priorities that pipeline companies should observe in developing a curtailment plan. For example, the Commission's new statement advised that residential customers should receive priority over large businesses, reasoning that it usually would be easier for businesses to find alternative sources of natural gas. The FPC's statement provided, however, that in each of its administrative proceedings reviewing a curtailment plan, the pipeline companies, as well as their customers, could "challenge or support [the Commission's] policy through factual or legal presentation as may be appropriate in the circumstances presented."[28] As the D.C. Circuit read the FPC's follow-up statement, the Commission remained open to approving curtailment plans that did not observe its list of delivery priorities if it concluded that the plan would better serve the public interest.[29]

Pipeline customers that had been assigned a low priority in the FPC's statement sued, claiming that the statement was a legislative rule rather than a policy statement, and thus that it was invalid because the Commission had issued it without notice and comment. The court of appeals rejected the claim. The focal point of the court's analysis was the *intent* of the Commission in issuing the follow-up statement. The court of appeals found that the Commission had intended for its statement to establish only "initial guidelines as a means of facilitating curtailment planning and the adjudication of curtailment cases." The FPC had made clear that it would "thoroughly consider not only the policy's applicability to the facts ... but also the underlying validity of the policy itself." Had the court found that the Commission had intended that its statement "establish a binding rule of law not subject to challenge in particular cases," the court would have held the statement to have been an invalidly promulgated legislative rule.[30]

In determining the FPC's intent to issue a nonbinding policy statement rather than a legislative rule, the court of appeals

---

27. *Id*. at 36.

28. Federal Power Commission Order No. 467, quoted in Appendix, *Pacific Gas & Electric*, 506 F.2d at 50.

29. *Pacific Gas & Electric*, 506 F.2d at 36.

30. *Id*. at 39–40; see also United States Telephone Ass'n v. FCC, 28 F.3d 1232, 1234 (D.C.Cir. 1994) (the distinction between legislative rules and policy statements "turns on an agency's intention to bind itself to a particular legal policy position").

carefully parsed the text of the statement. The court began with the Commission's characterization of the statement as a policy statement rather than as a legislative rule, but the court hardly rested there.[31] It also satisfied itself that the Commission's statement had not established a legally binding norm that had finally determined the rights of pipeline companies or of their customers. Although the statement identified the delivery priorities for which the FPC had provided "initial and tentative" approval, it was crucial that the statement gave "no assurance" that the Commission ultimately would approve any plan that complied with the statement's priorities. The FPC's statement made equally clear that interested parties in each case would have an opportunity to persuade the Commission not to apply the policy in their circumstances.[32]

The *Pacific Gas & Electric* approach to distinguishing between nonlegislative policy statements and legislative rules is subject to the criticism that the court's reliance on the title and text of an agency statement, together with administrative officials' professed intent in issuing a statement, provides room (and incentive) for agencies to mischaracterize the binding force of their statements in order to avoid the statutory obligations of notice and comment. It tempts agencies, in other words, to camouflage their rules as policy statements.[33] The D.C. Circuit in *Pacific Gas & Electric* was alert to this shortcoming, however, warning the FPC that it would invalidate the Commission's decisions regarding the pipeline companies' fuel-curtailment plans if it found that agency decisionmakers had relied on the statement of delivery priorities as a legally binding rule rather than as a set of guidelines for later discretionary decisions in particular cases.[34]

The D.C. Circuit has made good on this threat in later cases, demonstrating that the court will find an administrative statement to be a legislative rule rather than a policy statement not only if it "appears on its face to be binding," but also if the agency applies the statement "in a way that indicates it is binding."[35] The D.C.

---

31. *Pacific Gas & Electric*, 506 F.2d at 39, 40; see also *American Hospital Ass'n*, 834 F.2d at 1047 ("an agency's characterization of its own actions, while not decisive, is a factor that [reviewing courts] consider"); Community Nutrition Institute v. Young, 818 F.2d 943, 946 (D.C.Cir. 1987) (courts "give some, albeit 'not overwhelming,' deference to an agency's characterization of its statement"; courts "give far greater weight to the language actually used by the agency" in a statement than they do "to

an agency's characterization of its statement").

32. *Pacific Gas & Electric*, 506 F.2d at 40.

33. See United States Telephone Ass'n v. FCC, 28 F.3d 1232, 1235 (D.C.Cir. 1994).

34. *Pacific Gas & Electric*, 506 F.2d at 41.

35. General Electric Co. v. EPA, 290 F.3d 377, 383 (D.C.Cir. 2002); see Hudson v. FAA, 192 F.3d 1031, 1034–35 (D.C.Cir. 1999).

Circuit's decision in *United States Telephone Association v. Federal Communications Commission*[36] is illustrative. *United States Telephone Association* involved the FCC's issuance, without notice and comment, of a penalty schedule for the Commission's use in administrative enforcement proceedings. The schedule established a base fine for each type of offense within the FCC's jurisdiction. The statement also included a series of adjustments to the base fines for specified aggravating and mitigating factors. The FCC, like the FPC in *Pacific Gas & Electric*, had called its penalty schedule a policy statement rather than a rule. And the text of the FCC's statement, like the FPC's statement in *Pacific Gas & Electric*, retained the Commission's discretion not to apply the penalty schedule in particular cases. The court's review of the penalty schedule cast doubt on these representations, however. For one thing, the court was skeptical that an agency would publish "an exhaustive framework for sanctions if it did not intend to use that framework to cabin its discretion." Moreover, the subject matter of the FCC's statement— "a detailed schedule of penalties applicable to specific infractions as well as the appropriate adjustments for particular situations"— struck the court as more fitting for a legislative rule than for a policy statement.[37]

Most importantly, however, the court of appeals in *United States Telephone Association* held a trump card that had been unavailable in *Pacific Gas & Electric*. In *Pacific Gas & Electric*, the court reviewed the agency's statement before officials had applied it in subsequent adjudications. In *United States Telephone Association*, there was a sufficient administrative track record to allow the court to test the agency's claim that the schedule provided nonbinding guidance that administrative adjudicators would feel free to disregard in appropriate cases. This record showed that the agency had assessed fines "exactly as prescribed" by the penalty schedule in virtually all of 300 administrative adjudications. This record convinced the court that the agency's penalty schedule was binding rather than discretionary in practice, and thus was invalid without prior notice and opportunity for public comment.[38]

Interpretive Rules. Reviewing courts have tended to follow the *Attorney General's Manual*'s definition of interpretive rules, which describes these instruments as "rules or statements issued by an agency to advise the public of the agency's construction of the statutes and rules which it administers."[39] As was true of policy

---

36. 28 F.3d 1232 (D.C.Cir. 1994).

37. *Id.* at 1234.

38. *Id.* at 1234–35.

39. *Attorney General's Manual, supra* note 2, at 30 n.3; see, e.g., Shalala v. Guernsey Memorial Hospital, 514 U.S. 87, 99 (1995).

statements, interpretive rules may appear in a variety of agency communications, such as "memoranda," "manuals," and the like.[40]

A judicial examination of whether a particular agency pronouncement is a legislative rule requiring notice and comment or an interpretive rule exempt from all public participation obligations is a highly fact-specific undertaking.[41] In making this determination, the central inquiry is whether the statement or rule *itself* creates or modifies a legal right or obligation (and is thus a legislative rule)[42] or merely explains or clarifies provisions of a statute or regulation (and is thus an interpretive rule).[43] In one influential statement of the test for finding an agency rule to be interpretive rather than legislative, the D.C. Circuit wrote that the rule may do no more than "spell out a duty *fairly encompassed* within the [statute or] regulation that the interpretation purports to construe."[44]

As with policy statements, an agency may not rely on its interpretive rules as binding law in its decisionmaking. An agency that follows an interpretive rule in an adjudicatory proceeding legally bases its decision on the statute or legislative rule subject to interpretation, and not on the interpretive rule itself. The interpretive rule simply sets out the agency's understanding of the law that governs its decisions.[45]

Reviewing courts tend to look closely at agency interpretations of broad, general provisions of an existing statute or legislative rule to ensure that the "interpretation" does not supply the operative content of the interpreted provisions.[46] The Seventh Circuit's decision in *Hoctor v. Department of Agriculture*[47] illustrates this tendency. An agency published a legislative rule, after notice and comment, broadly requiring that facilities housing animals "be constructed of such material and of such strength as appropriate for the animals involved." The agency quantified the appropriate strength requirement in an internal memorandum instructing its inspectors that all "dangerous animals" must be secured inside a perimeter fence at least eight feet high. The agency relied on the

---

40. For helpful commentary on the distinction between administrative policy statements and legislative rules, see Robert A. Anthony, *Interpretive Rules, Policy Statements, Guidances, Manuals, and the Like, supra* note 24.

41. *American Hospital Ass'n*, 834 F.2d at 1045.

42. See *Syncor*, 127 F.3d at 95.

43. *American Hospital Ass'n*, 834 F.2d at 1045; see *Syncor*, 127 F.3d at 94; *Hoctor*, 82 F.3d at 167; Professionals and Patients for Customized Care v.

Shalala, 56 F.3d 592, 602 (5th Cir. 1995); Powderly v. Schweiker, 704 F.2d 1092, 1098 (9th Cir. 1983).

44. Paralyzed Veterans of America v. D.C. Arena L.P., 117 F.3d 579, 588 (D.C.Cir. 1997) (emphasis added).

45. See American Mining Congress v. Mine Safety & Health Administration, 995 F.2d 1106, 1109 (D.C.Cir. 1993).

46. *Syncor*, 127 F.3d at 94 n.6.

47. 82 F.3d 165 (7th Cir. 1996).

eight-foot-fence rule stated in the memorandum when finding a dealer who kept dangerous animals within a six-foot fence to be in violation of the appropriate strength regulation.[48]

The court of appeals held that the agency could not enforce the eight-foot-fence rule against the dealer because it was a legislative rather than an interpretive rule, and the agency had not observed the notice-and-comment procedures of section 553 before its adoption. The eight-foot-fence rule was legislative, the court held, because the agency had not derived the rule from the appropriate strength regulation "by a process reasonably described as interpretation." The agency had not construed the terms "appropriate" and "strength" to mean "eight feet." Rather, the internal memorandum had transformed the "appropriate strength" requirement into a new and distinct eight-foot-fence requirement for housing dangerous animals.[49]

Although reviewing courts are wary of agencies using interpretive rather than legislative rules to flesh out broad and general legal provisions, they uphold such efforts where the interpretation "supplies crisper and more detailed lines than the authority being interpreted" without establishing a new and distinct standard of conduct.[50] The D.C. Circuit's decision in *Paralyzed Veterans of America v. D.C. Arena L.R.*[51] provides an example of a true interpretive rule adding specificity to the interpreted law. The Americans with Disabilities Act required that certain newly constructed facilities be "readily accessible to and usable by individuals with disabilities." Using its rulemaking authority granted by the act, the Justice Department issued a legislative rule requiring newly constructed facilities to include wheelchair areas providing people with physical disabilities "lines of sight comparable to those for members of the general public." Later, the Department, in a manual published without notice and comment, interpreted the rule's lines-of-comparable-sight requirement to mean sightlines over standing spectators in arenas where spectators can be expected to stand (such as a sports facility). The court of appeals held that this interpretation was not a legislative rule. In this instance, the court of appeals was satisfied that the Justice Department's statement in the manual was "not sufficiently distinct or additive to the regulation to require notice and comment." The interpretation in the manual, the court found, had been "driven by the actual meaning

---

48. *Id.* at 167–68.

49. *Id.* at 169–71; see also *Syncor*, 127 F.3d at 95 (agency "notice" that it would require certain manufacturers to comply with several statutory provisions was legislative rather than interpretive because it "[did] not purport to construe any language in a relevant statute or regulation; it [did] not interpret anything").

50. *American Mining Congress*, 995 F.2d at 1112.

51. 117 F.3d 579 (D.C.Cir. 1997).

[the Department] ascribe[d] to the phrase 'lines of sight compara-ble.' "[52] Thus the legal basis of any Justice Department action pursuant to its manual's interpretation would be the legislative rule it had issued pursuant to notice and comment. The same could not be said of the agency action pursuant to the eight-foot-fence rule that the Seventh Circuit invalidated in *Hoctor*.

(c) Procedural Rules

The Administrative Procedure Act exempts procedural rules (or in the language of section 553(b)(A), "rules of agency organiza-tion, procedure, or practice") from the requirements of notice and comment in order to provide agencies flexibility in "organizing their internal operations."[53] This exemption generally is available for administrative rules governing the conduct of an agency's proceedings, as well for rules allocating authority and assigning duties within an agency.[54] The procedural rules that govern agency proceedings, unlike the other section 553(b)(A) exemptions, often carry the force of law. When they do, procedural rules, like legisla-tive rules, are binding on the agency as well as on members of the public who invoke the agency's decisionmaking processes. But unlike legislative rules requiring notice and comment, procedural rules do not alter the substantive rights or interests held by members of the public.[55] Rather, they control how individuals assert their rights and protect their interests in administrative proceed-ings.[56]

As students of federal civil procedure know all too well from their struggles with the doctrine spawned by *Erie Railroad Co. v. Thompkins*,[57] the distinction between substance and procedure can be as elusive as the distinction between legislative rules and guid-ance documents. The enduring difficulty has been that procedure affects substance. Parties who fail to observe procedural rules sometimes lose substantive rights.[58] There have been occasions when reviewing courts have treated rules governing agency proce-dure as legislative rules requiring notice and comment because the substantive impact of the rule convinced the judges that public participation in the rulemaking was appropriate.[59] And some re-

52. *Id*. at 587–88.

53. Batterton v. Marshall, 648 F.2d 694, 707 (D.C.Cir. 1980).

54. See LUBBERS, GUIDE TO RULEMAK-ING, *supra note* 2, at 68.

55. *Batterton*, 648 F.2d at 707; see also James V. Hurson Associates, Inc. v. Glickman, 229 F.3d 277, 280 (D.C.Cir. 2000) (quoting *Batterton*).

56. *Batterton*, 648 F.2d at 707; see also *James V. Hurson Associates*, 229 F.3d at 280 (quoting *Batterton*).

57. 304 U.S. 64 (1938).

58. See *Chamber of Commerce*, 174 F.3d at 211 ("distinction [between legis-lative rules and procedural rules] is of-ten difficult to apply, as even a purely procedural rule can affect the substan-tive outcome of an agency proceeding").

59. See, e.g., Air Transport Ass'n of America v. Department of Transporta-

viewing courts, at least, hold out the possibility of finding an agency's regulation of its procedure to be substantive when it "encodes a substantive value judgment"[60] or severely restricts substantive rights.[61] But just as reviewing courts in recent years have resisted defining legislative rules by their "substantial impact" on the public (see § 6.5(a)), contemporary courts generally refuse to require procedural rules to observe the notice-and-comment requirements of section 553 because of their impact on the parties in administrative proceedings.[62] As the D.C. Circuit recently put it, "an otherwise-procedural rule does not become a substantive one, for notice-and-comment purposes, simply because it imposes a burden on regulated parties."[63]

A comparison of the D.C. Circuit's decisions in *Pickus v. Board of Parole*[64] and in *National Whistleblower Center v. Nuclear Regulatory Commission*[65] illustrates the distinction between the substantive, legislative rules that require notice and comment and the procedural rules that do not. In *Pickus*, the court of appeals held a rule revision by the Parole Board to be substantive rather than procedural in nature, and thus to require notice and comment pursuant to section 553. Before the revision, the Parole Board had followed published guidelines delineating many of the criteria its members considered when deciding whether to release federal prisoners on parole. The Board restricted its decisionmaking discretion when it replaced those guidelines with "a complex, detailed table" specifying the prison time the Board would require an inmate to serve before parole, based on such criteria as the severity of the inmate's offense. The new rules were substantive rather than procedural because they established the criteria by which the Board would make the substantive determination whether to grant parole. A procedural rule exempt from notice and comment, the court reminded, only regulates "the form of agency action and proceedings."[66]

tion, 900 F.2d 369, 375–78 (D.C.Cir. 1990), vacated as moot, 933 F.2d 1043 (D.C.Cir. 1991) (holding agency rules establishing a formal adjudication scheme for civil penalty proceedings to be substantive rather than procedural because the rules "substantially affected civil penalty defendants' rights to avail themselves of an administrative adjudication").

60. See JEM Broadcasting Co., Inc. v. FCC, 22 F.3d 320, 328 (D.C.Cir. 1994) ("the procedural exception to notice and comment does not apply [if the rule] 'encodes a substantive value judgment'"), quoting American Hospital Ass'n v. Bowen, 834 F.2d 1037, 1047 (D.C.Cir. 1987).

61. National Whistleblower Center v. NRC, 208 F.3d 256, 262 (D.C.Cir. 2000) (procedural rules that "foreclose effective opportunity to make one's case on the merits" must observe the notice-and-comment process).

62. *American Hospital Ass'n*, 834 F.2d at 1047.

63. *James V. Hurson Associates*, 229 F.3d at 281.

64. 507 F.2d 1107 (D.C.Cir. 1974).

65. 208 F.3d 256 (D.C.Cir. 2000).

66. *Pickus*, 507 F.2d at 1111, 1113; see also *Chamber of Commerce*, 174 F.3d at 211–12 (holding an agency directive providing that each employer in selected

In *National Whistleblower Center*, the D.C. Circuit held a rule revision by the Nuclear Regulatory Commission to be procedural rather than substantive in nature, and thus exempt from the public participation requirements of section 553. The NRC's rule revision tightened the standard used by the Commission to rule on requests by third parties for an extension of time to file contentions in support of a motion to intervene in license-renewal proceedings. Although the new rule in *National Whistleblower Center*, like the revised rule in *Pickus*, restricted agency discretion by changing the criteria of agency decisionmaking, the *Whistleblower* rule change governed purely procedural decisions. It revised the "timetable for asserting substantive rights," rather than the substantive rights themselves. The new rule in *Pickus*, by contrast, changed the criteria the Parole Board used to determine eligibility for parole, and thereby modified the substantive rights of inmates to parole.[67]

(d) The Good Cause Exemptions

Two provisions of the Administrative Procedure Act offer "good cause" exemptions from section 553's procedural requirements for substantive, legislative rulemaking by agencies. The first, section 553(b)(B), exempts legislative rules from notice and comment if "the agency for good cause finds (and incorporates the finding and a brief statement of reasons therefor in the rules issued) that notice and public procedure thereon are impracticable, unnecessary, or contrary to the public interest." The second, section 553(d)(3), exempts legislative rules from the 30–day waiting period between the rule's publication and its effective date when an agency finds "good cause" and publishes an explanation of the cause with the rule. Section 553(d)(3), unlike section 553(b)(B), does not delineate specific grounds for finding good cause to exempt a rule from the 30–day waiting period. To bypass the 30–day waiting period, reviewing courts expect agencies generally "to balance the necessity for immediate implementation" of a rule against the fairness of providing affected members of the public sufficient time to bring themselves into compliance with the new rule.[68]

industries would be inspected unless it adopted an acceptable safety and health program to be a substantive, legislative rule rather than a procedural rule).

67. *National Whistleblower Center*, 208 F.3d at 258, 262; see also *James V. Hurson Associates*, 229 F.3d at 281 (agency's abolition of so-called "face-to-face" process of reviewing food labeling was procedural rather than substantive because it "did not alter the substantive criteria by which [the agency] would approve or deny proposed labels; it simply changed the procedures [the agency]

would follow in applying those substantive standards"); *JEM Broadcasting*, 22 F.3d at 327 (agency's so-called "hard look" rules, under which the agency summarily dismissed flawed license applications without allowing the applicant to correct its error, were procedural rather than substantive because the rules "did not change the *substantive standards* by which the [agency] evaluate[d] license applications").

68. United States v. Gavrilovic, 551 F.2d 1099, 1105 (8th Cir. 1977); see Riv-

This section discusses section 553(b)(B)'s good cause exemption from the usual notice-and-comment requirements of legislative rulemaking. Section 553(b)(B) lists three distinct (yet overlapping) "good cause" exemptions. An agency has "good cause" to avoid notice and comment if observing those procedures would be (1) "impracticable," (2) "unnecessary," *or* (3) "contrary to the public interest."[69] To invoke one of these exemptions, an agency must support its finding of good cause to the satisfaction of a reviewing court.[70] And as with the other section 553 exceptions, judges "narrowly" construe the good cause exemptions to avoid any unnecessary evasion of the notice-and-comment obligations that usually are a prerequisite for legislative rulemaking.[71]

Impracticability. The *Attorney General's Manual* advised that notice and comment would be "impracticable" within the meaning of the good cause exemption if following that process would impede an agency's "due and timely execution of its functions."[72] Or as the Ninth Circuit explained this exemption, notice and comment is "impracticable" if an agency cannot "both follow section 553 and execute its statutory duties."[73] Viewed in this light, the impracticability exemption is an expression of the general principle that statutory directives in an agency's enabling act may override the provisions of the APA (see APA § 559; § 4 (Intro.)).

The conflict between an agency's statutory obligations to administer its enabling act and to observe the public participation requirements of section 553 occurs when an agency must act more quickly than the notice-and-comment process would allow. Thus, the *Attorney General's Manual*'s illustration of the impracticability exemption hypothesized a situation where an agency learned from the investigation of an airline accident that a rule regulating air safety should be revised immediately in order to save lives. In such

erbend Farms, Inc. v. Madigan, 958 F.2d 1479, 1485–86 (9th Cir. 1992).

69. *Attorney General's Manual, supra* note 2, at 30.

70. See Tennessee Gas Pipeline Co. v. FERC, 969 F.2d 1141, 1145 (D.C.Cir. 1992). For commentary on the inconsistent judicial enforcement of the requirement that agencies publish their findings and reasons for invoking one of the good cause exemptions, see Juan J. Lavilla, *The Good Cause Exemption to Notice and Comment Rulemaking Requirements under the Administrative Procedure Act*, 3 ADMIN. L.J. AM. U. 317, 399–403 (1989).

71. United States Steel Corp. v. EPA, 595 F.2d 207, 214 (5th Cir. 1979); see Air Transport Ass'n of America v.

Department of Transportation, 900 F.2d 369, 379 (D.C.Cir. 1990), vacated as moot, 933 F.2d 1043 (D.C.Cir. 1991); Levesque v. Block, 723 F.2d 175, 184 (1st Cir. 1983). For detailed discussions of the good cause exemptions to the notice-and-comment requirements of section 553, see Lavilla, *Good Cause Exemption, supra* note 70; Ellen R. Jordan, *The Administrative Procedure Act's "Good Cause" Exemptions*, 36 ADMIN. L. REV. 113 (1984).

72. *Attorney General's Manual, supra* note 2, at 30.

73. *Riverbend Farms*, 958 F.2d at 1484–85 & n.2, quoting *Levesque*, 723 F.2d at 184; see United States Steel Corp. v. EPA, 605 F.2d 283, 287 (7th Cir. 1979).

a case, the *Attorney General's Manual* advised, the agency would be justified in finding notice and comment to be "impracticable" because of the overriding need to ensure air safety by immediately issuing a new rule.[74]

Agencies commonly invoke the impracticability exemption when they are under pressure to issue legislative rules before a congressional or judicial deadline. The mere existence of such a deadline, even if "strict," does not justify an exemption from notice and comment.[75] Reviewing courts, however, have held that the combination of a strict deadline and a particularly complex rulemaking may make notice and comment "impracticable" and thus within the good cause exemption.[76] Yet even in a complex rulemaking, the good cause exemption should not be available if the deadline leaves the agency adequate time to comply with the procedural requirements of section 553.[77] Nor should reviewing courts allow agencies to "abuse" the good case exemption by procrastinating until just before a deadline and then claiming insufficient time to proceed with notice and comment.[78]

Public Interest. According to the *Attorney General's Manual*, notice and comment is "contrary to the public interest" when "advance notice" of new rules "tend[s] to defeat their purpose."[79] The classic example here is administrative rulemaking establishing price controls. An agency might reasonably fear that providing advance notice of a price freeze would stimulate a stampede by firms to raise prices and to complete transactions before the controls take effect.[80] When invoking the "public interest" exemption

---

74. *Attorney General's Manual, supra* note 2, at 30–31.

75. See Petry v. Block, 737 F.2d 1193, 1203 (D.C.Cir. 1984); *Levesque*, 723 F.2d at 184; *United States Steel*, 595 F.2d at 213.

76. See, e.g., Methodist Hospital of Sacramento v. Shalala, 38 F.3d 1225, 1236–37 (D.C.Cir. 1994) (upholding agency's invocation of good cause exemption for "the daunting task of preparing regulations to implement a complete and radical overhaul of the Medicare reimbursement system" within a statutory deadline of just over four months where enabling act manifested Congress's "clear intent that APA notice and comment procedures need not be followed"); *Petry*, 737 F.2d at 1200–03 (upholding agency's invocation of good cause exemption for rulemaking to implement a particularly complex enabling act within a 60–day deadline); *United States Steel*, 605 F.2d at 286–89 (upholding agency's invoca-

tion of good cause exemption for "time-consuming" rulemaking under "a series of tight statutory deadlines" prompted by "Congressional concern over the seriously adverse health consequences" resulting from agency's prior delays in issuing these rules).

77. See American Federation of Government Employees v. Block, 655 F.2d 1153, 1158 (D.C.Cir. 1981); New Jersey v. EPA, 626 F.2d 1038, 1047 (D.C.Cir. 1980).

78. Council of Southern Mountains, Inc. v. Donovan, 653 F.2d 573, 581 (D.C.Cir. 1981); see *Air Transport Ass'n*, 900 F.2d at 379; National Ass'n of Farmworkers Organizations v. Marshall, 628 F.2d 604, 622 (D.C.Cir. 1980).

79. *Attorney General's Manual, supra* note 2, at 31; see *Riverbend Farms*, 958 F.2d at 1484 n.2.

80. *United States Steel*, 595 F.2d at 214 n.15; see, e.g., DeRieux v. Five Smiths, 499 F.2d 1321, 1332 (Temp.

in such situations, however, agency officials must be prepared to demonstrate to a reviewing court's satisfaction the substantiality of their fear that regulated entities will take actions that undermine the contemplated regulation while the rulemaking proceeding is pending.[81]

In an emergency situation, the public interest exemption overlaps with the impracticability exemption, and agencies sometimes rely on both to justify issuing a legislative rule without notice and comment. For example, the Fourth Circuit upheld INS's rule, issued without notice and comment during the Iranian hostage crisis in 1980, limiting the time that certain Iranian nationals were permitted to stay in the United States.[82] And reviewing courts have been receptive to agency findings that public health and safety emergencies justify dispensing with notice-and-comment procedures.[83] By contrast, an agency's claim that immediate publication of a final rule would promote efficiency, save money, or otherwise further Congress's general regulatory goals ordinarily should not be sufficient to invoke the public interest or impracticability exemption. An agency could make such a claim for almost any rule. In order to invoke these exemptions, agencies must be able to demonstrate some extraordinary need to issue a rule immediately.[84]

Interim Rules. It has become common, and expected, for agencies invoking the impracticability and public interest exemptions from notice and comment to issue final rules on an "interim" basis, coupled with the announced attention of replacing these "interim-final" rules with permanent rules after notice and comment. Although the Administrative Procedure Act does not require agencies to issue interim rules when invoking the impracticability or public interest exemptions, reviewing courts are more likely to allow those exemptions when agencies issue final rules on an "interim" basis.[85]

Emer. Ct. App.1974), cert. denied, 419 U.S. 896 (1974); Amalgamated Meat Cutters & Butcher Workmen v. Connally, 337 F.Supp. 737, 761–62 (D.D.C. (1971) (three-judge court)).

81. See *Tennessee Gas Pipeline*, 969 F.2d at 1145 (denying good cause exemption for an interim rule requiring advance notice and disclosure of the construction or replacement of facilities by natural gas pipeline companies; agency contended interim rule was needed "to prevent the environmental damage that might result from a speedup in construction and replacement as pipeline compa-

nies seek to avoid the unknown burdens of a final rule").

82. Malek-Marzban v. Immigration and Naturalization Service, 653 F.2d 113, 115 (4th Cir. 1981).

83. See Jordan, *"Good Cause" Exemptions*, *supra* note 71, at 122–29.

84. See *Levesque*, 723 F.2d at 184.

85. See, e.g., *American Federation of Government Employees*, 655 F.2d at 1157–58; cf. *Tennessee Gas Pipeline*, 969 F.2d at 1144–45 (although "the interim status of [a] challenged rule is a significant factor in the good cause analysis," interim status, alone, does not exempt a rule from notice and comment).

The interim final rulemaking process is a highly desirable administrative innovation. It allows agencies to fulfill the obligations of their enabling acts by immediately promulgating rules when time is of the essence as well as to honor the public participation requirements of section 553 before formulating the permanent regulation. The APA does not explicitly authorize the process of "interim final rulemaking," but there is no legal impediment to its adoption so long as the agency is justified in its invocation of a good cause exemption from notice-and-comment requirements.[86]

Unnecessary. The *Attorney General's Manual* advised that notice and comment would be "unnecessary," and therefore would not be required, for "the issuance of a minor rule or amendment in which the public is not particularly interested."[87] An example of such a non-controversial rule would be a requirement that parties sign loan agreements in ink rather than in pencil. A study conducted in the late 1980s found that roughly one quarter of the administrative rules adopted pursuant to the good cause exemptions were grounded on the agency's claim that the minor or technical nature of the rulemaking suggested that the public would have no interest in commenting.[88]

Agencies have cited this good cause exemption, with mixed success, when making what they regard as "technical" amendments to legislative rules. In *Chlorine Institute, Inc. v. Occupational Safety and Health Administration*,[89] for example, the Fifth Circuit allowed OSHA to correct a "clerical mistake" in its rule governing exposure to chlorine. The court of appeals ruled that the "unnecessary" exemption enabled agencies to correct "inadvertent and ministerial" errors in their legislative rules, unless the "correction" was "a guise for changing previous decisions because the wisdom of those decisions appears doubtful in the light of changing policies."[90] But in *Utilities Solid Waste Activity Group v. Environmental Protection Agency*,[91] the D.C. Circuit denied the good cause exemption to EPA's attempt to correct a ministerial mistake in its rules governing PCBs. The court of appeals found that "members of the public were greatly interested" in the agency's amendment because the change had "greatly expanded the regulated community and increased the regulatory burden."[92]

---

86. For a discussion and defense of interim final rulemaking, see Michael Asimow, *Interim-Final Rules: Making Haste Slowly*, 51 Admin. L. Rev. 703, 719–20 (1999).

87. *Attorney General's Manual, supra* note 2, at 31; see also *Levesque*, 723 F.2d at 184 (notice and comment is "unnecessary" when "the regulation is technical or minor").

88. Lavilla, *Good Cause Exemption, supra* note 70, at 342 & n.92.

89. 613 F.2d 120 (5th Cir. 1980).

90. *Id.* at 123–24.

91. 236 F.3d 749 (D.C. Cir. 2001).

92. *Id.* at 754–55; see also Texaco, Inc. v. Federal Power Commission, 412 F.2d 740, 743 (3d Cir. 1969) (holding amendment to a rule requiring natural

Direct Final Rulemaking. The Environmental Protection Agency pioneered a legislative rulemaking innovation that has gained traction in recent years. This innovation, called "direct final rulemaking," is reserved for instances when agency officials believe that following the notice-and-comment process is unnecessary because the rules will not stir controversy. Section 553(b)(B), as we have just seen, provides a good cause exemption from notice and comment in such circumstances, but an agency invoking the exemption risks invalidation of its rule if a reviewing court disagrees with the agency's prediction of the public's lack of interest in its rulemaking. Direct final rulemaking allows agencies to test their belief that notice-and-comment procedures are unnecessary in a rulemaking. In this process, the agency publishes a final rule, together with a statement of basis and purpose, without having gone through the notice-and-comment process. The publication states that the rule will become effective at a later date if the agency receives no significant adverse comment. Should the agency receive such comment, it withdraws the rule and proceeds through the notice-and-comment process.[93]

The Administrative Procedure Act does not explicitly authorize direct final rulemaking, and courts have yet to settle its legality. The direct final rulemaking process is permissible, of course, if public participation is "unnecessary" within the meaning of the good cause exemption of section 553(b)(B). Indeed, in such a case, direct final rulemaking provides *more* procedure than is statutorily required. But what of rules with sufficient impact on the regulated public to rule out a conclusion that they are minor or technical? An agency may be expected to answer this question by claiming that the absence of public comment demonstrates the lack of public interest in the rulemaking.[94] But it is not certain that the absence of public comment, without more, establishes that an agency rule is technical or minor or that notice and comment otherwise is unnecessary.[95]

A proponent of direct final rulemaking has argued that the process substantially complies with the notice-and-comment requirements of section 553 even if the good cause exemption is not applicable to a particular rulemaking proceeding. The argument here is that the direct final rulemaking process affords interested

---

gas companies to pay compound interest on refunds ordered by the agency did not qualify for the "unnecessary" exception because the amendment "would affect numerous jurisdictional natural gas companies and potentially involves large sums of money").

93. See Lars Noah, *Doubts about Direct Final Rulemaking*, 51 ADMIN. L. REV.

401, 406–07 (1999); Ronald M. Levin, *Direct Final Rulemaking*, 64 GEO. WASH. L. REV. 1, 1 (1995).

94. See Levin, *Direct Final Rulemaking*, *supra* note 93, at 11–15.

95. See Noah, *Doubts about Direct Final Rulemaking*, *supra* note 93, at 416.

members of the public both notice of the agency's rulemaking intention as well as the opportunity to block the rulemaking by submitting substantial adverse comment.[96] But it is far from certain that reviewing courts would accept derivations of the notice-and-comment process for legislative rules for which they have found public participation to be necessary, and thus outside the good cause exemption.[97]

96. See Ronald M. Levin, *More on Direct Final Rulemaking: Streamlining, Not Corner–Cutting*, 51 ADMIN. L. REV. 757, 758–63 (1999); Levin, *Direct Final Rulemaking, supra* note 93, at 15–18.

97. See Noah, *Doubts about Direct Final Rulemaking, supra* note 93, at 417–23.

Chapter 7

THE AVAILABILITY AND TIMING OF JUDICIAL REVIEW

The final component of the traditional model of administrative law (see § 1.4) provides for judicial review of agency action (and sometimes inaction) to ensure its legality, and thus its legitimacy. This judicial role of testing the exercise of administrative power for its fidelity to law is crucial in a polity committed to the rule of law.

Some form of judicial review has always been part of the administrative process in the United States. From the beginning, courts have checked the legality of administrative decisions before enforcing them in a civil or criminal proceeding. Early courts also drew on the common law remedies that America inherited from English legal practice to review official action. Individuals challenged actions by public officials that violated their common law rights by filing suits for damages, at least as permitted by the doctrine of sovereign immunity. English common law also provided a network of prerogative writs—most prominently, the writs of mandamus and of habeas corpus—from which American judges might select in order to control the legality of government action.[1] For example, in *Marbury v. Madison*,[2] the justices used a writ of

---

1. For a discussion of the prerogative writs providing for judicial review of administrative action, see Louis L. Jaffe, Judicial Control of Administrative Action 165–93 (1965).

2. 5 U.S. (1 Cranch) 137 (1803). For a revealing analysis of *Marbury* from an

mandamus to review Secretary of State James Madison's refusal to deliver William Marbury's commission to serve as justice of the peace for the District of Columbia. When the common law provided no remedy, courts drew on their equitable powers, such as the power to issue injunctions, to protect individuals from unlawful government action.[3]

Yet for a variety of reasons, these traditional remedies fell short of making judicial review generally available for monitoring the legality of federal agency action. This shortcoming perhaps was acceptable in early America, when federal administrators seldom acted in ways that directly compromised individual rights. But Congress disturbed the early American equilibrium in the late nineteenth and early twentieth centuries by adopting a series of enabling acts creating modern federal agencies and equipping them with formidable regulatory powers (see § 1.5(b)). Some, but not all, of these enabling acts explicitly provided for judicial review of the regulatory actions they authorized.

The interaction of common law traditions and statutory judicial review provisions created a vexing tangle of court proceedings, subjecting agencies to widely varying forms, and at times to no form, of judicial review. One of Congress's central purposes in adopting the Administrative Procedure Act in 1946 was to clarify and to unify the process of judicial review over agency action. Sections 701–705 of the APA, which are the subject of this chapter, govern the availability and process of judicial review. Section 706, which is the subject of the Chapter 8, codifies the scope of judicial review.

§ 7.1 The Administrative Procedure Act's Roadmap for Judicial Review

Section 704 of the Administrative Procedure Act provides for two tracks of judicial review over agency action. The first track is "special statutory review" (APA § 703), which section 704 describes as "[a]gency action made reviewable by statute," typically the enabling act. The second track of judicial review provided for in section 704 is usually described as "APA review," or as "general statutory review." APA review is available for "final agency action for which there is no other adequate [judicial] remedy" (APA § 704). A third and final track of judicial review is available for at least some agency action that is not reviewable according to processes prescribed by either the enabling act or by the APA. This

administrative law perspective, see Henry P. Monaghan, Marbury *and the Administrative State*, 83 Colum. L. Rev. 1 (1983).

3. See, e.g., American School of Magnetic Healing v. McAnnulty, 187 U.S. 94 (1902).

third track of judicial review is described as "nonstatutory review."
(See Figure 7–1.)

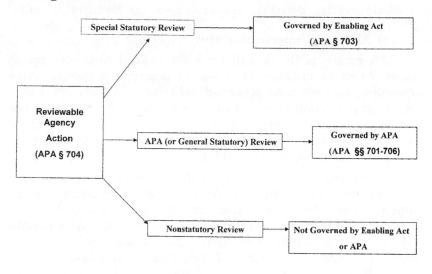

Figure 7-1: The APA's Roadmap to Judicial Review

(a) Special Statutory Review

Special statutory review is appropriate where the agency's
enabling act prescribes a particular form of judicial review proceeding for the relevant administrative action. Special statutory review
provisions are most common in enabling acts authorizing government regulation through formal adjudication. Many of these enabling acts instruct challengers to file a petition for review directly
in a circuit court of appeals (sometimes, specifically the D.C.
Circuit), instead of filing the more customary complaint in a federal
district court.[1] Congress often has considered review by a trial court
to be unnecessary in such cases because the formal administrative
hearing process has framed the issues and has closed the evidentiary record. A reviewing court need only assess the legality of the
agency's decision based on the administrative hearing record, which
of course, is how appellate courts normally proceed.

The linkage between formal administrative adjudication and
direct review in the appellate courts is incomplete, however. Congress has subjected some administrative rulemaking proceedings to
direct review in the appellate courts.[2] And some enabling acts

§ 7.1

1. See *Attorney General's Manual on
the Administrative Procedure Act* 97
(1947), reprinted in WILLIAM F. FUNK, et

al., FEDERAL ADMINISTRATIVE PROCEDURE
SOURCEBOOK 33–171 (3d ed. 2000).

2. See Harold H. Bruff, *Coordinating
Judicial Review in Administrative Law*,
39 U.C.L.A. L. REV. 1193, 1196 (1992).

create special statutory review proceedings in federal district court. The most prominent example of special district court review applies to administrative decisions concerning Social Security benefits.[3]

(b) APA (or General Statutory) Review

APA review is the default track for judicial review of agency action. When an enabling act does not prescribe a special review proceeding, and when no other judicial remedy is adequate, courts review agency action pursuant to the provisions of the Administrative Procedure Act. This chapter focuses on APA review rather than on special statutory review because the latter proceedings are creatures of their particular enabling acts.

APA review proceedings are dictated by sections 701–706 of the Administrative Procedure Act. APA review proceedings also are subject to the rules of jurisdiction and procedure that apply generally to federal litigation.[4] In brief, Section 702 of the APA permits any person who is injured by final agency action, and who otherwise has standing to sue (see § 7.2(c)), to seek APA review of that action. (Section 551(2) of the APA defines "person" to include not only individuals, but also corporations, partnerships, associations, and the like.) Although section 704 of the APA creates a cause of action for judicial review of final agency action when no other judicial remedy is adequate,[5] the APA itself does not provide federal jurisdiction over such actions.[6] Jurisdiction in federal district court is readily available for suits against federal agencies, however, pursuant to the general federal question statute (28 U.S.C. § 1331). Courts also review agency action pursuant to the APA when agencies seeks judicial enforcement of their orders (APA § 703).

APA actions may be filed in any "court of competent jurisdiction" (typically a federal district court), and they may take "any applicable form of legal action," including actions for declaratory and injunctive relief (APA § 703). Section 702 waives the sovereign immunity of the United States for actions "seeking relief other than money damages." (Other federal statutes waive immunity from certain damages claims against federal agencies.) Filing an APA action does not automatically stop agency action from taking effect, but the APA gives reviewing courts authority "to postpone the effective date of an agency action or to preserve status or rights pending conclusion of the review proceeding" (APA § 705).

---

3. See David P. Currie & Frank J. Goodman, *Judicial Review of Federal Administrative Action: Quest for the Optimal Forum*, 75 COLUM. L. REV. 1, 5–7 (1975).

4. See *Attorney General's Manual*, *supra* note 1, at 93.

5. Japan Whaling Ass'n v. American Cetacean Society, 478 U.S. 221, 231 n.4 (1986).

6. Your Home Visiting Nurse Services, Inc. v. Shalala, 525 U.S., 449, 457–58 (1999); Califano v. Sanders, 430 U.S. 99, 104–07 (1977).

(c) Nonstatutory Review

The broad availability of judicial review over agency action provided by the Administrative Procedure Act has made the traditional common law and equitable forms of action largely obsolete. Yet those forms of action may spring to life in the unusual case where the APA or its review provisions do not apply to the acting agency or to a particular agency action. In these instances, contemporary courts may fall back on their general authority to provide injunctive and other forms of equitable relief, declaratory judgments (28 U.S.C. § 2201), and writs of mandamus (28 U.S.C. § 2201). Although these forms of relief often are authorized by acts of Congress, administrative lawyers have grouped them under the unfortunate rubric "nonstatutory review" because they are not based on an agency's enabling act or on the APA.

§ 7.2   The Availability of Judicial Review

The Administrative Procedure Act codifies a "strong presumption" favoring judicial review of administrative action.[1] Accordingly, even when an enabling act is completely silent concerning the availability of judicial review over the agency action it authorizes, section 704 of the Administrative Procedure Act typically authorizes APA review.[2] The APA, however, makes the presumption favoring judicial review of agency action rebuttable in two instances. Section 701(a) provides that APA review is unavailable "to the extent that (1) statutes preclude judicial review or (2) agency action is committed to agency discretion by law." This section considers these exceptions in turn.

(a) Statutory Preclusion of Judicial Review

The Administrative Procedure Act withdraws its provisions for judicial review "to the extent that statutes preclude judicial review" (APA § 701(a)(1)). Section 701(a)(1)'s allowance for statutory preclusion of judicial review follows the general scheme of the APA, which establishes a generally applicable set of default rules governing the administrative process, subject to override by other acts of Congress (see APA § 559).

§ 7.2

1. INS v. St. Cyr, 533 U.S. 289, 298 (2001); Bowen v. Michigan Academy of Family Physicians, 476 U.S. 667, 670 (1986); see also Califano v. Sanders, 430 U.S. 99, 104 (1977) (APA embodies the "intention and understanding" of Congress that judicial review of agency action should be "widely available"). For a critique of the presumption of reviewability as a canon of statutory interpretation, see Daniel B. Rodriguez, *The Presumption of Reviewability: A Study in Canonical Construction and its Consequences*, 45 VAND. L. REV. 743 (1992).

2. See Sierra Club v. Peterson, 185 F.3d 349, 366 (5th Cir. 1999).

It is rare for Congress to completely insulate agency action from judicial review. It is not unusual, however, for an enabling act to limit judicial review or to channel review to a specific court. The prefatory language "to the extent" in section 701(a) makes clear that Congress is free to partially preclude judicial review of an agency's action. But because of the APA's "strong presumption" favoring judicial review of administrative action,[3] reviewing courts, following the legislative history of the APA, require "clear and convincing evidence of a . . . legislative intent" to preclude judicial review, wholly or partially, before applying section 701(a)(1).[4]

Implied Preclusion of Judicial Review. The Supreme Court has interpreted acts of Congress to preclude judicial review even when the acts have not expressly so provided.[5] In determining whether an enabling act implicitly precludes judicial review of agency action, reviewing courts assess the overall "statutory scheme," asking whether the statute's text, its regulatory purpose, or the legislative history manifests a congressional intention to preclude judicial review.[6]

An implication of congressional intent to preclude judicial review may arise when an enabling act expressly identifies particular parties who may seek review of agency action or particular types of agency action that are subject to judicial review, but remains silent regarding other parties or types of action. The Court has made clear that such statutory silences do not necessarily imply a congressional intention to preclude judicial review.[7] For example, in *Abbott Laboratories v. Gardner*,[8] pharmaceutical companies had sued to challenge a rule of the Food and Drug Administration regulating the labeling of prescription drugs. FDA argued that Congress had intended to preclude pre-enforcement review of such regulations. In the agency's reading, the enabling act's creation of a special procedure for pre-enforcement judicial review of other types of regulation signaled that Congress had intended to preclude pre-enforcement review of labeling regulations. The Court rejected FDA's interpretation. The justices assessed "the entire legislative scheme" governing judicial review of FDA regulations and conclud-

---

3. *St. Cyr*, 533 U.S. at 298.

4. Abbott Laboratories v. Gardner, 387 U.S. 136, 141 (1967); see *Bowen*, 476 U.S. at 671–72; Nathaniel L. Nathanson, *Some Comments on the Administrative Procedure Act*, 41 ILL. L. REV. 368, 415 (1946) (quoting the relevant legislative history of the APA).

5. See Morris v. Gressette, 432 U.S. 491, 501 (1977); Switchmen's Union of North America v. National Mediation Board, 320 U.S. 297 (1943); *Attorney General's Manual on the Administrative*

Procedure Act 94 (1947), reprinted in WILLIAM F. FUNK, et al., FEDERAL ADMINISTRATIVE PROCEDURE SOURCEBOOK 33–171 (3d ed. 2000).

6. Block v. Community Nutrition Institute, 467 U.S. 340, 345 (1984); see *Bowen*, 476 U.S. at 673; Thunder Basin Coal Co. v. Reich, 510 U.S. 200, 207 (1994).

7. See *Bowen*, 476 U.S. at 674; *Abbott Laboratories*, 387 U.S. at 141.

8. 387 U.S. 136 (1967).

ed that Congress had intended the special review procedure to add a remedy for certain types of rules and not to eliminate the "more traditional channels of review" for other FDA rules.[9]

The justices, however, have interpreted statutes similar to the FDA's enabling act in *Abbott Laboratories* to implicitly preclude judicial review of agency action when they have become convinced that allowing review of the relevant action would disrupt the administrative scheme Congress had envisioned. *Thunder Basin Coal Company v. Reich*,[10] for example, involved an enabling act that required mining companies to allow a representative authorized by their workers to join agency officials when they inspected the companies' mines. A company sued in federal district court challenging the selection of union employees as its miners' representatives. The Court held that the "structure" of the enabling act demonstrated Congress's intention to preclude the mining company's suit. The act established a special process for administrative enforcement proceedings and provided for exclusive jurisdiction in the federal courts of appeals for challenges by companies to adverse administrative enforcement decisions. The Court believed that allowing mining companies to file pre-enforcement suits in federal district court to head off administrative enforcement proceedings would undermine the statutory enforcement scheme.[11]

Similarly, in *Block v. Community Nutrition Institute*,[12] the Court disallowed the ultimate consumers of dairy products from suing to challenge milk-price supports issued by the Department of Agriculture. The enabling act's provision of review rights to the producers and handlers of dairy products, the justices found, implied that Congress had intended to preclude legal challenges by consumers. As in *Thunder Basin*, the Court in *Block* concluded that allowing consumer suits would "severely disrupt" the "complex and delicate administrative scheme" established by the enabling act.[13]

Constitutional Limits on Statutory Preclusion of Judicial Review. Although the justices have hinted at the existence of "constitutional constraints" on Congress's authority to preclude judicial review of agency action,[14] they have never invalidated a statutory provision precluding such review.[15] The Court, however,

---

9. *Id.* at 139–48; see also *Bowen*, 476 U.S. at 674–78 (rejecting similar implied preclusion arguments regarding the Medicare program).

10. 510 U.S. 200 (1994).

11. *Id.* at 207–12.

12. 467 U.S. 340 (1984).

13. *Id.* at 345–48.

14. *Bowen*, 476 U.S. at 672–73.

15. See AMERICAN BAR ASSOCIATION SECTION OF ADMINISTRATIVE LAW AND REGULATORY PRACTICE, A BLACKLETTER STATEMENT OF FEDERAL ADMINISTRATIVE LAW 46 (2004).

has clearly marked statutory preclusion of constitutional claims against federal agencies as an area of special sensitivity.

The scope of congressional power to deny the federal judiciary its accustomed authority to hear constitutional claims remains one of the great unanswered questions of constitutional law.[16] The justices have avoided that question in administrative litigation by steadfastly interpreting statutory provisions generally precluding judicial review not to reach constitutional claims.[17] The Supreme Court's decision in *Johnson v. Robison*[18] is illustrative. *Johnson* involved a constitutional challenge to the Veterans Administration's refusal to pay education benefits to conscientious objectors who had satisfactorily completed two years of civilian service in lieu of military service. The enabling act explicitly denied courts the power to review VA benefits decisions on "any question of law or fact." The justices, however, worried that interpreting the statutory preclusion provision to bar constitutional challenges to VA decisions would raise "serious" constitutional questions. They thus invoked the "cardinal principle that this Court ... first ascertain whether a construction of the statute is fairly possible by which the [constitutional] question[s] may be avoided." Noting that the enabling act did not explicitly earmark constitutional claims for preclusion, the Court held that the enabling act's provision generally precluding judicial review of VA benefits decisions did not preclude the conscientious objector's suit.[19]

The Supreme Court also has expressed doubt over Congress's power to preclude judicial review of agency decisions on "a pure question of law."[20] Accordingly, reviewing courts have resisted interpreting statutory provisions generally precluding judicial review to bar purely legal challenges to agency action. Federal courts are most likely to honor statutory provisions precluding judicial review of agency findings of fact and of agency applications of law to fact.[21]

16. See, e.g., Hamdan v. Rumsfeld, ___ U.S. ___, 126 S.Ct. 2749, 2762–64 (2006); Ex parte Yerger, 75 U.S. (8 Wall.) 85 (1868); Ex parte McCardle, 74 U.S. (7 Wall.) 506 (1868). The law-review literature considering this issue is extensive, but the fountainhead is Henry M. Hart, Jr., *The Power of Congress to Limit the Jurisdiction of Federal Courts: An Exercise in Dialectic*, 66 HARV. L. REV. 1362 (1953).

17. See Lepre v. Department of Labor, 275 F.3d 59, 75 (D.C.Cir. 2001) (Silberman, J., concurring) (it is "doubt[ful] that the Supreme Court has left ... any principled ground upon which a Court of Appeals judge can honor a congressional preclusion of review of a constitutional claim").

18. 415 U.S. 361 (1974).

19. *Id.* at 366–74; see also McNary v. Haitian Refugee Center, Inc., 498 U.S. 479 (1991) (enabling act's provision precluding judicial review of determinations by the Attorney General concerning applications by undocumented workers for adjustment of status did not bar constitutional challenge to the administration of the act).

20. *St. Cyr*, 533 U.S. at 308.

21. See Ronald M. Levin, *Understanding Unreviewability in Administrative Law*, 74 MINN. L. REV. 689, 739–40

(b) Agency Action Committed to Agency Discretion

The Administrative Procedure Act withdraws its provisions for judicial review "to the extent that . . . agency action is committed to agency discretion by law" (APA § 701(a)(2)). In contrast to the statutory preclusion exemption of section 701(a)(1), the committed-to-agency-discretion exemption of section 701(a)(2) does not hinge on an explicit or implicit congressional intention to override the usual presumption of reviewability.[22] Rather, an action is committed to agency discretion by law where an enabling act provides *complete* decisionmaking discretion to administrators.[23]

An agency has complete decisionmaking discretion, the Supreme Court held in *Citizens to Preserve Overton Park v. Volpe*, in those rare instances when a reviewing court has "no law to apply" in reviewing an administrative decision.[24] A reviewing court has no law to apply, the Court later explained in *Heckler v. Chaney*,[25] when the enabling act "is drawn so that a court would have no meaningful standard against which to judge the agency's exercise of discretion." The absence of "judicially manageable standards" to review agency action makes it "impossible" for courts to evaluate whether the agency has abused its decisionmaking discretion, as required by section 706(2)(A) of the APA.[26]

On the relatively few occasions in recent years that the Supreme Court has applied section 701(a)(2)'s committed-to-agency-discretion exemption, the justices have used the "no law to apply" test in anything but a mechanical fashion. The Court instead has approached the exemption as an administrative law counterpart to the political question doctrine, which intertwines interpretation of the constitutional text and a host of prudential considerations to insulate certain decisions by the political branches of the federal government from review in the courts. In similar fashion, when invoking the committed-to-agency-discretion exemption, the justices have integrated their interpretation of an enabling act's standards with a general assessment of the propriety of reviewing the type of agency action at issue. This approach has led the Court largely to limit the committed-to-agency-discretion exemption to the types of administrative decisions that the justices traditionally have regarded as unsuitable for judicial review.[27]

(1990); see, e.g., Lindahl v. OPM, 470 U.S. 768, 778–91 (1985).

22. Heckler v. Chaney, 470 U.S. 821, 830 (1985).

23. See *Attorney General's Manual*, *supra* note 5, at 94–95.

24. 401 U.S. 402, 410 (1971).

25. 470 U.S. 821 (1985).

26. *Id.* at 830. For criticism of the no-law-to-apply test as "simplistic, historically unfounded, and needlessly rigid," see Levin, *Understanding Unreviewability*, *supra* note 21, at 692, 704–10.

27. Lincoln v. Vigil, 508 U.S. 182, 191 (1993); see, e.g., ICC v. Brotherhood of Locomotive Engineers, 482 U.S. 270, 282 (1987) (citing "tradition of nonre-

For example, in *Lincoln v. Vigil*,[28] the Court held that a decision by the Indian Health Service to discontinue a regional health program for Indian children was not subject to judicial review. The agency decided to reallocate the money it had spent for the discontinued regional program to a national Indian health-care program. Congress had never appropriated funds expressly for the regional program. Instead, Congress funded all of the agency's Indian health programs collectively through annual lump-sum appropriations. The justices noted that they "traditionally" have regarded an agency's allocation of funds from a lump-sum appropriation "as committed to agency discretion." They explained, "[T]he very point of a lump-sum appropriation is to give an agency the capacity to adapt to changing circumstances and meet its statutory responsibilities in what it sees as the most effective or desirable way."[29]

The Court's decision in *Webster v. Doe*[30] provides another example of the justices' use of the committed-to-agency-discretion exemption to steer clear of agency decisions that they traditionally have been reluctant to review. In *Webster*, the director of the Central Intelligence Agency fired an agency employee because the director believed that the employee's homosexuality made him a security risk. A statute authorized the director, "in his discretion, [to] terminate the employment of any officer or employee of the Agency whenever he shall deem such termination necessary or advisable in the interests of the United States." The employee claimed, among other things, that the firing had violated that statutory provision because his dismissal was not "necessary or advisable in the interests of the United States." The Court refused to consider whether or not the director had been correct in concluding that the employee posed a security risk, holding that the statute committed the dismissal of CIA employees completely to the discretion of the director. The Court in *Webster* noted that the legislative text did not limit the director's power to fire CIA employees to instances where the firing was necessary or advisable in the interests of the United States. The statute's language instead authorized a firing whenever the director *deemed* it to be necessary or advisable in the interests of the United States. Interpreting the statute to provide the director complete discretion to fire CIA employees made sense to the justices because "employment with the CIA entails a high degree of trust that is perhaps unmatched in Government service."[31]

viewability" regarding agency refusals to reconsider their decisions for material error).

28. 508 U.S. 182 (1993).

29. *Id.* at 190–95.

30. 486 U.S. 592 (1988).

31. *Id.* at 599–600.

Agency Decisions not to Commence Enforcement Actions. *Heckler v. Chaney*[32] represents the Court's most striking use of the committed-to-agency-discretion exemption to avoid reviewing traditionally non-reviewable administrative decisions. Although the Administrative Procedure Act defines "agency action" to include an agency's "failure to act" (APA § 551(13)), the Court in *Chaney* flipped the usual presumption of reviewability for agency decisions not to begin an investigation or an enforcement action. *Chaney* held such "failure[s] to act" to be presumptively committed to agency discretion. The Court grounded *Chaney*'s presumption of non-reviewability on the tradition of unfettered executive discretion to decline prosecution in particular cases, as well as on "the general unsuitability" of judicial review of administrative decisions not to commence an enforcement proceeding. Agencies seldom pursue every law violation within their jurisdiction. The justices explained, "[A]n agency decision not to enforce often involves a complicated balancing of a number of factors which are peculiarly within its expertise. Thus, the agency must not only assess whether a violation has occurred, but whether agency resources are best spent on this violation or another, whether the agency is likely to succeed if it acts, whether the particular enforcement action requested best fits the agency's overall policies, and, indeed, whether the agency has enough resources to undertake the action at all." Administrators, the Court believed, were "far better equipped" than judges to juggle these "variables."[33]

Chaney's presumption of non-reviewability for decisions by agencies not to commence an enforcement proceeding is not absolute, however. A court has "law to apply," and thus may review, an agency's decision not to proceed against a possible law violation where the enabling act "has provided guidelines for the agency to follow in exercising its enforcement powers."[34] *Dunlop v. Bachowski*[35] involved such statute. In *Bachowski*, the Secretary of Labor had rejected a union member's request that the agency file suit to set aside a union election. The enabling act provided that, upon the complaint by a union member, the Secretary of Labor "*shall* investigate such complaint and, if he finds probable cause to believe that a violation ... has occurred ... he *shall* ... bring a civil action" (emphasis added). Judicial review of the Labor Secretary's refusal to commence an enforcement proceeding was proper, the Court in *Chaney* later explained, because the enabling act had "required," and had not merely authorized, "the Secretary to file

32. 470 U.S. 821 (1985).

33. *Id.* at 830–38. For criticism of *Chaney*, see Cass R. Sunstein, *Reviewing Agency Inaction after* Heckler v. Chaney, 52 U. Chi. L. Rev. 653 (1985).

34. *Chaney*, 470 U.S. at 832–33.

35. 421 U.S. 560 (1975).

suit if certain clearly defined factors were present."[36] The Court's willingness to review agency decisions not to take enforcement action when an enabling act requires an agency to act in specified circumstances aligns the committed-to-agency-discretion exemption of section 701(a)(2) with section 706(1) of the Administrative Procedure Act, which requires reviewing courts to "compel agency action unlawfully withheld."[37]

Agency Denials of Rulemaking Petitions. The Administrative Procedure Act provides "interested person[s] the right to petition [an agency] for the issuance, amendment, or repeal of a rule" (APA § 553(e)). The APA reinforces this right by requiring any agency denying a rulemaking petition to provide "a brief statement of the grounds for denial" (APA § 555(e)). Before *Chaney*, courts had regularly reviewed the lawfulness of agency denials of rulemaking petitions.[38] But even though the *Chaney* decision had made clear that the justices had not considered the reviewability of agency denials of rulemaking petitions,[39] *Chaney*'s holding that agency decisions not to commence an enforcement proceeding were presumptively non-reviewable placed the rulemaking precedent in doubt.[40]

The justices largely removed the *Chaney* cloud hovering over the reviewability of agency denials of rulemaking petitions in *Massachusetts v. Environmental Protection Agency*.[41] In *Massachusetts*, the Court held that denial of a rulemaking petition was more "susceptible to judicial review" than an agency's decision not to initiate an enforcement action. Several "key differences" between these two forms of agency inaction accounted for the inapplicability of *Chaney*'s presumption of non-reviewability to rulemaking denials. "In contrast to nonenforcement decisions," the justices noted in *Massachusetts*, "agency refusals to initiate rulemaking 'are less frequent, more apt to involve legal as opposed to factual analysis, and subject to special formalities, including a public explanation.' "[42] It also has been significant to reviewing courts that the

---

36. *Chaney*, 470 U.S. at 833–34; see also National Wildlife Federation v. EPA, 980 F.2d 765, 773–74 (D.C.Cir. 1992) (holding presumption of non-reviewability of agency non-enforcement decisions to be rebutted because the enabling act had "withdraw[n] discretion from the agency and [had] provide[d] guidelines for the exercise of enforcement power").

37. See Norton v. Southern Utah Wilderness Alliance, 542 U.S. 55, 63 (2004) (the only "agency action that can be compelled under the APA is action legally *required*"); § 8.8.

38. See, e.g., Public Citizen Health Research Group v. Auchter, 702 F.2d 1150 (D.C.Cir. 1983).

39. *Chaney*, 470 U.S. at 825 n. 2.

40. American Horse Protection Ass'n, Inc. v. Lyng, 812 F.2d 1, 4 (D.C.Cir. 1987).

41. ___ U.S. ___, 127 S.Ct. 1438 (2007).

42. *Id*. at 1459, quoting, *American Horse Protection Ass'n*, 812 F.2d at 4.

APA created "a procedural right" for "interested person[s]" to file a rulemaking petition with an agency (APA § 553(e)).[43]

Courts review agency denials of rulemaking petitions by determining whether the denial was "arbitrary, capricious, an abuse of discretion, or otherwise not in accordance with law" (see APA § 706(2)(A)).[44] While judicial review under the "arbitrary-or-capricious" standard always is limited and deferential,[45] the Court in *Massachusetts* cautioned that judicial review of agency denials of rulemaking petitions should be "extremely limited" and "highly deferential."[46] Judicial review of such denials, the justices also advised, must be informed by the understanding that "an agency has broad discretion to choose how best to marshal its limited resources and personnel to carry out its delegated responsibilities."[47]

Constitutional Claims. The Court has resisted the conclusion that agency action which is committed to agency discretion within the meaning of section 701(a)(2) is immune from constitutional review. In *Webster v. Doe*,[48] for example, the justices limited the non-reviewability of the CIA director's decision to fire agency employees on security grounds, in the language of the section 701(a) of the APA, only "to the extent" an employee challenges the firing on statutory grounds. Federal courts, the Court held in *Webster*, remained open to an employee's "colorable constitutional claims" against the director.[49] For such a claim, of course, the Constitution itself provides reviewing courts with the necessary "law to apply."[50]

The justices in *Webster*, as they have when addressing statutory preclusion claims, made no secret of their desire "to avoid the serious constitutional question that would arise if a federal statute were construed to deny any judicial forum for a colorable constitutional claim." In navigating the committed-to-agency-discretion exemption, as in interpreting statutes precluding judicial review, the Court therefore will interpret an enabling act to deny constitutional review of agency action only if Congress makes such a denial "clear." In such a case, the Court finally would be confronted with

---

43. *Massachusetts*, 127 S.Ct. at 1459; *American Horse Protection Ass'n*, 812 F.2d at 4.

44. See *American Horse Protection Ass'n*, 812 F.2d at 4.

45. The "arbitrary-or-capricious" standard is discussed in § 8.7.

46. *Massachusetts*, 127 S.Ct. at 1459, quoting, National Customs Brokers & Forwarders Ass'n of America, Inc. v. United States, 883 F.2d 93, 96 (D.C.Cir. 1989); see also *American Horse Protec-*

tion Ass'n, 812 F.2d at 5 (agency refusal to initiate rulemaking proceeding is to be overturned "only in the rarest and most compelling of circumstances").

47. *Massachusetts*, 127 S.Ct. at 1459; *American Horse Protection Ass'n*, 812 F.2d at 4.

48. 486 U.S. 592 (1988).

49. *Id*. at 601–05.

50. See Sunstein, *Reviewing Agency Inaction, supra* note 33, at 658.

the issue it steadfastly has avoided, that is, whether Congress may strip the federal judiciary of the power to review the constitutionality of administrative action.[51]

(c) Standing

Article III of the Constitution extends the federal judicial power to several types of "Cases" or "Controversies." The Supreme Court has inferred an important limitation on federal jurisdiction from that power grant: Article III contains a "case-or-controversy requirement" that restricts federal courts to deciding legal questions only as appropriate to resolve an actual case. The bedrock principle of the case-or-controversy requirement is the rule prohibiting federal courts from issuing "advisory opinions," that is, legal opinions provided outside the confines of a pending case. The case-or-controversy requirement of Article III signals that judicial review of agency action is not an *end* in itself, but rather is a *means* of deciding cases, and thereby protecting individuals from unlawful infringements on their legal rights.

Over the years, the Court has refined the case-or-controversy requirement to ensure that "cases" within the meaning of Article III are "of the sort traditionally amenable to, and resolved by, the judicial process."[52] These refinements include constitutional limitations on federal jurisdiction, which are mandatory for Congress and the courts, as well as prudential limitations, which are binding neither on Congress nor on the courts.[53] The principle of standing— that a proper plaintiff is necessary for there to be a proper case—is the most important of these case-or-controversy refinements.

The essence of the standing requirement may be stated simply: A plaintiff must have a "personal stake in the outcome of the controversy."[54] The details of standing doctrine are not so simple. Standing doctrine embodies an interaction of constitutional, statutory, and judge-made law that is as complex as it is controversial. A full treatment of the subject is best left to texts on federal courts and jurisdiction. This section presents only the essentials of standing doctrine as it applies to federal litigation challenging the legality of agency action.

The Supreme Court has created no less than six criteria for determining whether a plaintiff has standing to sue in federal court. The first three criteria are "constitutional" (or "Article III") requirements that the justices have derived from the case-or-con-

---

51. *Webster,* 486 U.S. at 601–05.

52. See Steel Co. v. Citizens for a Better Environment, 523 U.S. 83, 102 (1998).

53. See Bennett v. Spear, 520 U.S. 154, 162 (1997).

54. See Warth v. Seldin, 422 U.S. 490, 498–99 (1975); Baker v. Carr, 369 U.S. 186, 204 (1962).

troversy limitation of Article III. These requirements are that the plaintiff (1) has suffered, or imminently will suffer, "personal injury" (2) that is "fairly traceable" to the defendant's allegedly unlawful conduct and (3) that is "likely to be redressed" by the court should the plaintiff prevail in the litigation.[55] The three constitutional standing requirements, as a group, are designed to prevent federal courts from issuing advisory opinions. They also help to ensure that lawsuits challenging agency action honor the essential attributes of a traditional case.

Because Congress cannot expand the jurisdiction of federal courts beyond the limits of Article III,[56] none of the three constitutional standing requirements may be abrogated by statute.[57] Nor may litigants or the courts waive them. Plaintiffs, without exception, must allege, and prove, each of the three constitutional requirements in order to establish their standing to sue in federal court.[58] It is not unusual for courts to hold a threshold evidentiary hearing to determine a plaintiff's standing.

If a plaintiff satisfies the three constitutional requirements, and thus establishes the court's Articles III power to resolve the case, a court still may dismiss the suit if the plaintiff trips over any of the three "judicially self-imposed limits" on litigant standing.[59] These "prudential" considerations generally deny standing to plaintiffs asserting (1) "generalized grievance[s] shared in substantially equal measure by all or a large class of citizens";[60] (2) claims that are outside the "zone of interests" protected by the law upon which the plaintiff relies; and (3) "third party claims," that is, the assertion of someone else's legal rights.[61] The three prudential considerations, like the three constitutional requirements, help ensure that lawsuits challenging agency action resemble traditional cases. But because the prudential considerations are not compelled by the Constitution, Congress may override them by statute.[62] Even

---

55. See *Bennett*, 520 U.S. at 162; Allen v. Wright, 468 U.S. 737, 751 (1984).

56. Marbury v. Madison, 5 U.S. (1 Cranch) 137, 173–80 (1803).

57. Lujan v. Defenders of Wildlife, 504 U.S. 555, 571–78 (1992). For an argument against reading Article III to limit the power of Congress to create litigant standing by authorizing causes of action, see Cass R. Sunstein, *Standing and the Privatization of Public Law*, 88 COLUM. L. REV. 1432, 1461–80 (1988). For an argument that the existence of such a limit is historically grounded, see Ann Woolhandler & Caleb Nelson, *Does History Defeat Standing Doctrine?*, 102 MICH. L. REV. 689 (2004).

58. *Lujan*, 504 U.S. at 561, 576.

59. See *Allen*, 468 U.S. at 751.

60. *Warth*, 422 U.S. at 499.

61. *Allen*, 468 U.S. at 751. The zone-of-interests test is the only prudential consideration considered in this section. For analysis of the generalized grievance criterion, see Gene R. Nichol, Jr., *Standing on the Constitution: The Supreme Court and* Valley Forge, 61 N.C. L. REV. 798 (1983). For analysis of the third party claim criterion, see Henry P. Monaghan, *Third Party Standing*, 84 COLUM. L. REV. 277 (1984).

62. See *Bennett*, 520 U.S. at 162.

in the absence of a statutory override, a court in its discretion may decline to apply a prudential consideration in a particular case.

The justices have acknowledged that each of the six elements of standing doctrine is pliable. Even the nondiscretionary constitutional requirements are "not susceptible of precise definition." In close cases, the requirement that a plaintiff suffer (or imminently will suffer) injury often morphs into an inquiry of whether a plaintiff has suffered *sufficient* injury to establish standing. The flexibility of the remaining two constitutional standing requirements is apparent in their formulation: A plaintiff's injury must be "fairly" traceable to the challenged action, and a favorable judicial decision must be "likely" to remedy the injury. It should come as no surprise, then, that the Court's implementation of the standing criteria has been anything but "a mechanical exercise."[63]

Injury. The injury requirement often is the focus of judicial attention when a plaintiff's standing to sue is at issue. Federal courts traditionally enforced this requirement by applying the "legal interest" (or "legal right") test, which demanded that a plaintiff seeking judicial review of agency action allege injury to an interest protected by the Constitution or by an act of Congress or an interest analogous to some common law right.[64] In *Association of Data Processing Service Organizations, Inc. v. Camp*,[65] the Supreme Court discontinued the legal interest test because the justices believed that it conflated standing, a jurisdictional requirement, with the merits of the plaintiff's substantive claim. *Data Processing* reoriented the injury inquiry to a determination of whether the plaintiff has suffered (or imminently will suffer) some "injury in fact."[66]

Although the Court has continued to stress that a plaintiff's standing to sue "in no way depends on the merits of the plaintiff's contention that [the defendant's] conduct is illegal,"[67] the injury

---

63. See *Allen*, 468 U.S. at 751.

64. See Association of Data Processing Service Organizations, Inc. v. Camp, 397 U.S. 150, 153 (1970); Joint Anti–Fascist Refugee Comm. v. McGrath, 341 U.S. 123, 153 (1951) (Frankfurter, J., concurring).

65. 397 U.S. 150 (1970).

66. *Id.* at 152. The relative merits of the legal interest test and the injury-in-fact alternative were the subject of a storied debate between two leading administrative law scholars on the heels of the *Data Processing* decision, see Kenneth Culp Davis, *The Liberalized Law of Standing*, 37 U. CHI. L. REV. 450 (1970);

Louis Jaffee, *Standing Again*, 84 HARV. L. REV. 633 (1971).

67. See *Warth*, 422 U.S. at 500. Many observers suspect that at least on occasion, a court's view on the merits of a controversy informs its ruling on litigant standing. See, e.g., Jonathan D. Varat, *Variable Justiciability and the Duke Power Case*, 58 TEX. L. REV. 273 (1980). For criticism of contemporary standing doctrine as fostering politically result-oriented manipulation by the courts, see Richard J. Pierce, Jr., *Is Standing Law or Politics?*, 77 N.C.L. REV. 1741 (1999). The leading defense of a court's use of standing, together with the other justiciability doctrines, to

determination nevertheless may turn on "the nature and source" of the plaintiff's substantive claim.[68] The Court since *Data Processing* has revived the traditional "legal interest" test at least to some degree by requiring that plaintiffs not only plead and prove "injury in fact," but also that they demonstrate their injury is "legally and judicially cognizable."[69] The justices have yet to pin down the requirements of this additional showing, but for an injury to be legally and judicially cognizable, it must at least (1) result from "invasion of a [plaintiff's] legally protected interest" and (2) arise in a dispute that is "traditionally thought to be capable of resolution through the judicial process."[70]

The justices have warned that generalizations about standing requirements are treacherous,[71] but they have often repeated several descriptions of the type of injury necessary to support litigant standing. First and foremost, an injury also must be "actual or imminent."[72] The injury also must be sufficiently "particularized," "distinct," and "personal" to distinguish the plaintiff's interest in the outcome of the litigation from those of the public at large.[73] And finally, an injury must be "palpable" and "concrete," rather than "abstract," "conjectural," or "hypothetical."[74]

A trio of the Supreme Court's environmental decisions helps to clarify the nature of the injury necessary to secure a plaintiff's standing to sue. In *Sierra Club v. Morton*,[75] an environmental organization had sued to challenge the legality of a permit granted by the U.S. Forest Service for development of a recreational facility in a national forest. The Sierra Club had alleged that the development would harm "the aesthetics and ecology of the area." The Court readily accepted that aesthetic and environmental harms, although non-economic in nature, could satisfy the injury requirement of Article III. The Court insisted, however, that a plaintiff must be "among the injured" in order to have standing. Sierra Club failed to satisfy that requirement because it had not alleged that either "it or its members would be affected in any of their activities or pastimes by the ... development." The organization had grounded its standing to sue on its "special interest in the conservation and the sound maintenance of the national parks,

---

avoid legal issues it deems inadvisable to decide is ALEXANDER M. BICKEL, THE LEAST DANGEROUS BRANCH: THE SUPREME COURT AT THE BAR OF POLITICS 111–98 (2d ed. 1986).

68. *Warth*, 422 U.S. at 500; see Raines v. Byrd, 521 U.S. 811, 818 (1997).

69. *Raines*, 521 U.S. at 819; see *Allen*, 468 U.S. at 753–56; *Warth*, 422 U.S. at 514.

70. *Raines*, 521 U.S. at 819.

71. See *Data Processing*, 397 U.S. at 151.

72. See *Bennett*, 520 U.S. at 167.

73. See *Raines*, 521 U.S. at 818–19; *Lujan*, 504 U.S. at 560; *Allen*, 468 U.S. at 751.

74. See *Bennett*, 520 U.S. at 167; *Allen*, 468 U.S. at 751.

75. 405 U.S. 727 (1972).

game refuges and forests of the country." But that ideological interest, the Court held, was too abstract to support standing.[76]

The Court followed *Sierra Club* in *Lujan v. Defenders of Wildlife*,[77] where another environmental organization had sued to challenge the legality of an administrative rule making the Endangered Species Act inapplicable to federal participation in actions taken in foreign countries. The Defenders of Wildlife had claimed that the new rule would hasten the extinction of certain endangered and threatened species. Citing *Sierra Club*, the Court ruled that "the desire to use or observe an animal species, even for purely esthetic purposes, [was] undeniably a cognizable interest for purpose of standing." But the Defenders of Wildlife, like the Sierra Club, was unable to satisfy the justices that it or its members had suffered a sufficient injury to that interest.[78]

In contrast to the Sierra Club, however, the Defenders of Wildlife had submitted affidavits by two of its members claiming personal injury. One member stated that she had traveled to Egypt recently and that she had "observed the traditional habitat of the endangered Nile crocodile there." This member also stated that she intended to return to Egypt to observe the crocodile again, but that the American role in projects along the Nile River threatened the crocodile's habitat. The other member stated that she had traveled to Sri Lanka some years earlier and had observed the habitat of such endangered species as the Asian elephant and the leopard. That habitat had become the site of a project funded by a federal agency. This second member claimed that the project would "seriously reduce endangered, threatened, and endemic species habitat including areas that I visited . . . [, which] may severely shorten the future of these species." The second member also stated that she intended to return to Sri Lanka with the hope of "spotting" the endangered elephant and leopard.[79]

The Court in *Lujan* denied the members' standing, and thus the standing of the Defenders of Wildlife, because the affidavits failed to show how diminution of the species threatened by the projects had injured the two members. Their past visits to foreign project areas "prove[d] nothing" to the justices. And the members'

---

76. *Id*. at 730, 734–35, 738–40. The Court similarly has held that a plaintiff's interests as U.S. citizen or as federal taxpayer are too abstract to support standing to challenge the legality of actions taken by the federal government. See Schlesinger v. Reservists Committee to Stop the War, 418 U.S. 208, 220–21 (1974) (citizens); Frothingham v. Mellon, 262 U.S. 447, 487 (1923) (taxpayers). For the classic argument that a plaintiff's ideological interest in the sub-

ject of the litigation should be sufficient to sustain standing, see Louis L. Jaffee, *The Citizen as Litigant in Public Actions: The Non–Hohfeldian or Ideological Plaintiff*, 116 U. Pa. L. Rev. 1033, (1968).

77.   504 U.S. 555 (1992).

78.   *Id*. at 562–64.

79.   *Id*. at 563–64.

professed intention to return to those project areas, without any "concrete plans" or indication of when they intended to return, was insufficient to demonstrate the "actual or imminent injury" necessary for litigant standing. The Court in *Lujan* repeated *Sierra Club*'s message that "a plaintiff claiming injury from environmental damage must use the area affected by the challenged activity" in order to satisfy the injury-in-fact requirement.[80]

In the third decision, *Friends of the Earth v. Laidlaw Environmental Services (TOC), Inc.*,[81] an environmental organization managed to satisfy the injury requirement. Friends of the Earth had alleged that Laidlaw had illegally discharged pollutants into a waterway in violation of the Clean Water Act. Laidlaw challenged the organization's standing, claiming that none of its members could have been injured "in fact" by the company's discharges because the district court had found no proof that the discharges had harmed the environment.

The Court in *Laidlaw* was not concerned by the absence of proof on environmental harm. "The relevant showing for purposes of Article III standing," explained the justices, was "injury to the plaintiff," not injury to the environment. The organization had secured its standing, the Court held, by demonstrating that Laidlaw's discharges had injured several of its members. The justices highlighted the affidavit of one of the organization's members who lived near Laidlaw's facility. This member "occasionally drove over" the river into which Laidlaw allegedly had discharged pollutants. He stated that the river "looked and smelled polluted." The member also stated that "he would like to fish, camp, swim, and picnic in and near the river between 3 and 15 miles downstream from the facility, as he did when he was a teenager," but that he "would not do so because he was concerned that the water was polluted by Laidlaw's discharges." This affidavit satisfied the justices that the member's "reasonable concerns about the effects of [Laidlaw's] discharges directly affected" his recreational and aesthetic interests in the area.[82] In *Laidlaw*, then, at least one member of Friends of the Earth, and thus the organization itself, had standing to sue because, in the language of *Sierra Club*, the member was "among the injured."[83]

Taken together, *Sierra Club*, *Lujan*, and *Laidlaw* open federal courts to plaintiffs claiming environmental, aesthetic, recreational, and other non-economic injuries, but these decisions make clear that the justices closely scrutinize such claims to ensure that the

---

80. *Id.* at 562–66.

81. 528 U.S. 167 (2000).

82. *Id.* at 180–85.

83. *Sierra Club*, 405 U.S. at 735.

plaintiff actually has suffered, or imminently will suffer, a distinct and personal injury.

Traceability and Redressability. The second and third constitutional requirements of litigant standing—that the plaintiff's injury be "fairly traceable" to the defendant's actions and "likely redressable" by a federal court—are often mirror images of an inquiry into causation. Traceability "examines the causal connection between the assertedly unlawful conduct and the alleged injury," while redressability "examines the causal connection between the alleged injury and the judicial relief requested."[84] If the plaintiff's injury was caused by the challenged action of the defendant, the injury can be fairly traced to the defendant, and a remedial order of the court addressed to the defendant typically can redress the injury.

Traceability and redressability often break down when "the independent action of some third party not before the court" is the immediate cause of the plaintiff's injury.[85] The Court's decision in *Simon v. Eastern Kentucky Welfare Rights Organization*[86] illustrates the third party causation problem. Indigents had sued the Secretary of the Treasury and the Commissioner of Internal Revenue challenging the legality of an IRS revenue ruling declining to revoke the tax-exempt status of nonprofit hospitals that offer only emergency-room services to indigents. The justices were willing to assume that at least some of the plaintiffs had been denied hospital services because they were indigent. But this injury, the Court held, was directly caused by the decision of the hospitals to deny them services, and not by the IRS's revenue ruling. Although the plaintiffs had alleged that the revenue ruling had "encouraged" hospitals to deny services to indigents, the Court believed it to be "purely speculative whether the denials of service . . . fairly can be traced to [federal officials'] 'encouragement' or instead result from decisions made by the hospitals without regard to the tax implications." The speculative nature of the relationship between the revenue ruling and the hospital's decision to deny non-emergency services to indigents also undermined the redressability element of the standing requirement. The Court found "no substantial likelihood" that a remedial order requiring IRS to withhold tax-exempt status from hospitals that deny non-emergency services to indigents "would result in [plaintiffs'] receiving the hospital treatment they desire."[87]

"Indirect injuries" such as those experienced by the indigent plaintiffs in *Simon* often defeat standing.[88] But not always. The

---

84. *Allen*, 468 U.S. at 753 n.19.

85. *Bennett*, 520 U.S. at 167.

86. 426 U.S. 26 (1976).

87. *Id.* at 40–46.

88. See *id.* at 44–45; see, e.g., *Allen*, 468 U.S. at 756–60 (1984); *Warth*, 422

Court's decision in *Bennett v. Spear*[89] provides the unusual coun-
terexample. Water users had sued the Fish and Wildlife Service to
challenge the legality of a "biological opinion" the Service had
prepared concerning an irrigation project operated by the Bureau of
Reclamation. The Service and the Bureau are both agencies within
the Department of the Interior. The Service's biological opinion
stated that the Bureau's irrigation project jeopardized the continued existence of two endangered fish species and recommended that
the Bureau maintain water levels that would protect the fish. The
Bureau notified the Service that it intended to impose water-level
restrictions in line with the recommendations of the biological
opinion. The water users claimed that the Bureau's new restrictions threatened to reduce the amount of water previously available
to them from the irrigation project.

The government contested the plaintiffs' standing to sue the
Service, arguing that the claimed injury (a decrease in their water
supply from the irrigation project) was neither "fairly traceable" to
the biological opinion nor "likely redressable" by a judicial ruling
invalidating the opinion. This was because the Bureau, like the
hospitals in *Simon*, had made the decision that directly caused the
threatened injured to the plaintiffs (imposing water-level restrictions), not the Service. But the Court distinguished *Simon* because
the Service's biological opinion had "a virtually determinative
effect" on the Bureau's decision to impose the new water-level
restrictions. Although federal agencies were "technically free to
disregard" the Service's biological opinions, they did so "very
rarely." And indeed, the Bureau's adoption of water-level restrictions in response to the Service's biological opinion reflected a
change from the Bureau's longstanding practice of not restricting
water levels. The Court thus concluded that the Bureau's imposition of water-level restrictions was "fairly traceable" to the biological opinion, and that a judicial order invalidating the opinion would
make it "likely" that the Bureau would eliminate the restrictions.[90]

Although the traceability and redressability elements of Article
III standing usually are opposite sides of the same causation coin, it

U.S. at 504–07; Linda R.S. v. Richard D.,
410 U.S. 614, 617–19 (1973).

89. 520 U.S. 154, 168–71 (1997).

90. *Id.* at 168–71; see also Massachusetts v. EPA, ___ U.S. ___, 127 S.Ct.
1438 (2007). *Massachusetts* involved a
challenge to EPA's denial of a petition to
regulate greenhouse gas emissions from
automobiles. EPA claimed that the challengers lacked standing, arguing that its
failure to regulate auto emissions had
not caused global warming, and that
new limits on emissions would not pre-

vent global warming, because of the existence of other sources of greenhouse
gas emissions throughout the world. The
Court held that the challengers nevertheless had satisfied the traceability and
redressability requirements. Because
U.S. auto emissions "make a meaningful
contribution to greenhouse gas concen-
trations," the Court reasoned, "[a] reduction in [such] emissions would slow
the pace of global emissions increases."
Id. at 1457–58.

is possible for the analyses of these criteria to diverge in particular cases. This divergence may occur, for example, when the relief a plaintiff seeks extends beyond the scope of the defendant's allegedly illegal conduct,[91] or when a court for some reason lacks the power to provide the relief necessary to redress the plaintiff's injury.[92]

The Relevance of the Administrative Procedure Act. The Administrative Procedure Act contains a standing provision. Section 702 extends the right of judicial review to any "person suffering legal wrong because of agency action, or adversely affected or aggrieved by agency action within the meaning of a relevant statute."

A person challenging agency action pursuant to the Administrative Procedure Act, like all plaintiffs in federal court, nevertheless must satisfy each of the Article III requirements of litigant standing—injury, traceability, and redressability.[93] In addition, the Court has read section 702 to obligate plaintiffs to prove that their interests at stake in the litigation are "arguably within the zone of interests to be protected or regulated by the statute or constitutional guarantee in question."[94] The zone-of-interests test is a prudential consideration rather than a constitutional requirement of standing. Congress therefore is as free to override the zone-of-interests requirement of section 702 in a different statute as it is to override any other provision of the APA (see APA § 559).[95]

Zone of Interests. The zone-of-interests element of standing requires that the interests of the plaintiff affected by agency action be "arguably within the zone of interests to be protected or regulated by the statute or constitutional guarantee" that the agency's action allegedly has violated.[96] The zone-of-interests consideration typically comes into play when a plaintiff is incidentally injured by agency action that directly controls the conduct of some third party.[97] Whether the interests of a plaintiff affected by such an action satisfy the zone-of-interests requirement turns on the reviewing court's interpretation of the statutory provision allegedly violated by the agency. Although courts often consult the legislative intent when interpreting the relevant statutory provision, a plain-

---

91. *Allen,* 468 U.S. at 753 n.19.

92. Steel Co. v. Citizens for a Better Environment, 523 U.S. 83, 102 (1998).

93. See, e.g., National Credit Union Administration v. First National Bank & Trust Company, 522 U.S. 479, 488 (1998); *Simon,* 426 U.S. at 39.

94. Association of Data Processing Service Organizations, Inc. v. Camp, 397 U.S. 150, 153 (1970); see *National Credit Union Administration,* 522 U.S. at 488.

95. *Bennett,* 520 U.S. at 163–64.

96. *Data Processing,* 397 U.S. at 153; see *National Credit Union Administration,* 522 U.S. at 488. Some scholars believe that the zone-of-interests test may be applicable only to suits brought pursuant to the Administrative Procedure Act. See ERWIN CHEMERINSKY, FEDERAL JURISDICTION 105 (5th ed. 2007).

97. See CHEMERINSKY, FEDERAL JURISDICTION, *supra* note 96, at 100.

tiff need not show that Congress "specifically intended to benefit" his or her interests in order to fit within the zone of interests arguably protected by the provision. Rather, courts simply (1) "discern the interests 'arguably ... to be protected' by the statutory provision at issue," and then (2) "inquire whether the plaintiff's interests affected by the agency action in question are among them."[98]

The Court's decision in *National Credit Union Administration v. First National Bank & Trust Company*[99] illustrates the justices' focus on the interests actually protected by the relevant statutory provision rather than on the interests Congress had intended to protect by enacting the provision. Several commercial banks sued the National Credit Union Administration challenging that agency's decision to expand the types of employer groups eligible to form a federal credit union beyond the limits the agency previously had set pursuant to its enabling act. By relaxing restrictions on the formation of credit unions, the agency's action injured commercial banks, which compete with credit unions for customers. The agency argued, however, that the banks' injury was not within the zone of interests served by the provision of its enabling act restricting the formation of credit unions. When Congress wrote those restrictions into law, the agency argued, the legislators were not concerned with the interests of a credit union's competitors. Indeed, the agency claimed that Congress's purpose in writing the statutory provision at issue was to enable credit unions to reach the small borrowers that banks did not serve. The Court rejected the agency's zone-of-interests challenge to the banks' standing. The justices explained, "[E]ven if it cannot be said that Congress had the specific purpose of benefiting commercial banks, one of the interests 'arguably ... to be protected' by [the statutory provision at issue was] an interest in limiting the markets that federal credit unions can serve." Banks were within the zone of interests served by the statutory restrictions on the markets that credit unions could serve simply because they benefited from those restrictions.[100]

Not only must one take care to identify the interests actually served by a statute when applying the zone-of-interests consideration, but also one must focus on the interests protected by the particular statutory provision at issue rather than by the statute as a whole. The Court's decision in *Bennett v. Spear*[101] teaches this lesson. Water users sued the Fish and Wildlife Service pursuant to the Administrative Procedure Act, claiming that a biological opinion prepared by the Service had wrongly concluded that an irriga-

---

98. *National Credit Union Administration*, 522 U.S. at 492, 498.

99. 522 U.S. 479 (1998).

100. *Id.* at 492–93, 495–96.

101. 520 U.S. 154 (1997).

tion project operated by the Bureau of Reclamation threatened endangered fish species. The plaintiffs claimed that the Service's opinion violated the Endangered Species Act and that the Bureau's decision to follow the Service's opinion threatened to reduce the supply of water from the project that they had enjoyed over the years. A lower court had found that the plaintiffs lacked standing to make this claim because they were outside the zone of interests protected by the Endangered Species Act. Congress had designed that act, reasoned the lower court, to preserve species, and not to protect those who were adversely affected by species preservation. But the provision of the act that the Service allegedly had violated required federal agencies to "use the best scientific and commercial data available" when determining whether an endangered species was in jeopardy. That language, the Court held, served dual objectives: It safeguarded endangered species from under-enforcement of the act's requirements, as it protected those affected by agency action protecting species from "needless economic dislocation" caused by over-enforcement of the act.[102] The water users, who claimed that their water supply had been put at risk by an erroneous jeopardy determination, fit within the interest against administrative over-enforcement served by the statutory provision at issue.

As the discussion of *National Credit Union Administration* and *Bennett* suggests, the zone-of-interests consideration seldom poses a difficult barrier to the standing of a plaintiff who otherwise satisfies the Article III requirements. The Supreme Court's decision in *Air Courier Conference v. American Postal Workers Union*,[103] however, reminds that there is at least occasional bite in the zone-of-interests element. Postal employee unions had claimed that regulations by the Postal Service partially suspending the Service's monopoly over the international carriage of letters from the United States violated the Private Express Statutes (PES). The PES gave the Postal Service its monopoly, but these statutes also authorized the Postal Service to suspend the monopoly in the "public interest." The suspension of the monopoly allowed private couriers to compete in the international mailing market, and thus threatened the jobs of the union's members. Although this threatened injury was sufficient to satisfy Article III, the Court held that the union lacked standing because the job security of postal workers was not within the zone of interests protected by the PES grant of a monopoly over international mailing to the Postal Service. The statutory provision at issue made the monopoly contingent on the interests of the

102. *Id.* at 175–77.   **103.** 498 U.S. 517 (1991).

public at large, rather than on the special interests of the postal workers.[104]

Associational Standing. An association may sue as the representative of its members where the association itself has not been injured, and thus lacks standing to sue on its own behalf.[105] The Court's acceptance of "associational" or "representative" standing flows from the justices' recognition that people form organizations to promote their shared interests. The existence of shared interests inspires confidence in the courts that an association will faithfully promote the interests of its members in the litigation.[106]

Federal courts grant associations standing to sue on behalf of their members if three conditions are met.[107] First, at least one of the association's members must have standing to sue. This first condition ensures the presence of a case or controversy, and thus it is "an Article III necessity for an association's representative suit."[108] Second, the interests of the members that the organization seeks to protect in the litigation must be "germane to the organization's purpose."[109] The germaneness requirement provides assurance that the association has a stake in the outcome of the litigation sufficient for it "to serve as the defendant's natural adversary."[110] The third and final condition for associational standing provides that "neither the claim asserted nor the relief requested" by the organization must "require the participation of individual members in the lawsuit."[111] This final condition is a prudential consideration rather than a constitutional requirement. It is attuned to the "administrative convenience and efficiency" of permitting an association to represent its members' interests in litigation. It does not state a condition for the existence of an Article III case or controversy.[112]

Courts typically require the participation of an association's members, and thus deny associational standing, when the nature of the association's claim or the nature of its requested relief obligates the court "to consider the individual circumstances" of the injured members of the association.[113] Whether a court must consider the

---

104. *Id.* at 524–31.

105. Warth v. Seldin, 422 U.S. 490, 511 (1975).

106. International Union, UAW v. Brock, 477 U.S. 274, 290 (1986).

107. Hunt v. Washington State Apple Advertising Comm'n, 432 U.S. 333, 343 (1977); see Friends of the Earth, Inc. v. Laidlaw Environmental Services (TOC), Inc., 528 U.S. 167, 181 (2000); *International Union*, 477 U.S. at 281–82; *Warth*, 422 U.S. at 511.

108. United Foods & Commercial Workers Union Local 751 v. Brown Group, Inc., 517 U.S. 544, 555 (1996).

109. *Hunt*, 432 U.S. at 343.

110. *United Foods & Commercial Workers*, 517 U.S. at 555–56.

111. *Hunt*, 432 U.S. at 343.

112. *United Foods & Commercial Workers*, 517 U.S. at 554–58.

113. *International Union*, 477 U.S. at 287.

individual circumstances of an association's members typically depends on whether an association seeks prospective or compensatory relief. If an association seeks a declaratory judgment, an injunction, or some other form of prospective relief, courts usually assume that the association's members share a common injury and that "the remedy, if granted, will inure to [their] benefit." Claims for compensatory relief are different. A claim for damages or some other form of compensation typically is unique to each individual member allegedly suffering injury. In order to determine the proper amount of compensation, a court needs "individualized proof" on the "the nature and extent" of each member's injuries. Courts therefore typically require each member seeking compensation to become a party to the suit, and they deny associations standing to seek damages on behalf of their members.[114] But because the necessity of individual participation by an association's members is prudential rather than constitutional in nature, Congress is free to override this consideration by statute.[115]

§ 7.3   The Timing of Judicial Review

Before reaching the merits of a lawsuit challenging agency action, a reviewing court must satisfy itself that the plaintiff has not filed suit prematurely.[1] Reviewing courts first test the timeliness of administrative litigation by ensuring that the agency action at issue is "final." In addition to being final, the challenged agency action must be "ripe" for judicial review. As a final timing consideration, reviewing courts traditionally have required that challengers exhaust all available administrative remedies as a predicate for seeking judicial review. The exhaustion requirement, however, has been sharply restricted in recent years. This section discusses this complementary set of timing doctrines in turn.

(a) Finality

The Administrative Procedure Act only authorizes lawsuits challenging "final agency action" (APA § 704). As a general rule, litigants filing suit pursuant to the APA may challenge the "preliminary, procedural, or intermediate" decisions an agency makes during an administrative proceeding only "on the review of the final agency action" (APA § 704).

---

114. *Warth*, 422 U.S. at 515–16.

115. *United Food and Commercial Workers*, 517 U.S. at 558.

§ 7.3

1. A lawsuit also may be filed too late, and thus be "moot." Because the

mootness doctrine has no special application in administrative law, it is not considered here. For a helpful, introductory discussion of the mootness doctrine, see ERWIN CHEMERINSKY, FEDERAL JURISDICTION 120–47 (5th ed. 2007).

Section 551(13) of the Administrative Procedure Act defines "agency action" as the issuance or denial of "an agency rule, order, license, sanction, relief" or their equivalent. Each of the five administrative actions listed in the APA's definition—rule, order, license, sanction, and relief—is defined elsewhere in section 551. Section 551(13) also defines "agency action" to include an agency's "failure to act." The legislative history of the APA suggests that Congress intended for the term "agency action" to provide "complete coverage of every form of agency power, proceeding, action, or inaction."[2] But the Supreme Court recently limited the meaning of "agency action" to the "circumscribed, discrete [categories of] agency actions" listed in section 551(13), that is, rules, orders, licenses, sanctions, relief, their equivalents, and under certain conditions, the failure of agencies to take such actions.[3] Litigants thus may file suit pursuant to the APA only to challenge agency conduct or programs that take the form of one of the categories of "agency action" listed in section 551(13).

In *Lujan v. National Wildlife Federation,*[4] for example, the Court refused to entertain an environmental group's challenge to the Bureau of Land Management's administration of the so-called "land withdrawal review program." This program implemented a statutory scheme directing the BLM to decide on an ongoing basis whether to open public lands to private uses, such as mining, grazing and the like. The environmental group claimed that the BLM had been guilty of "rampant" legal violations in its administration of the program. But the justices refused to entertain such a "wholesale" challenge to the BLM's administration of the land withdrawal review program because the program, as such, was "no more an identifiable 'agency action' . . . than a 'weapons procurement program' of the Department of Defense or a 'drug interdiction program' of the Drug Enforcement Administration." Section 704 of the Administrative Procedure Act, the Court ruled, only permitted plaintiffs to challenge "some particular 'agency action' that causes it harm."[5]

In contrast to the term "agency action," which received a layered set of definitions in the Administrative Procedure Act, the other key term of section 704, "final," was left undefined. The Supreme Court has devised a two-part requirement to fill that gap. To be final, and thus subject to judicial review pursuant to the APA, agency action first must be "the consummation of the agen-

---

2. S. Doc. No. 248, 79th Cong., 2d Sess. 255 (1946), quoted in Federal Trade Commission v. Standard Oil Company of California, 449 U.S. 232, 238 n.7 (1980).

3. Norton v. Southern Utah Wilderness Alliance, 542 U.S. 55, 61–65 (2004).

The appropriate conditions for challenging an agency's failure to act are the subject of § 8.8.

4. 497 U.S. 871 (1990).

5. *Id.* at 890–91.

cy's decisionmaking process." If an agency's action is "tentative or interlocutory," it is not final. In addition to completing the administrative decisionmaking process, agency action, to be final, must determine "rights or obligations" or have some other kind of "legal consequences."[6] Reviewing courts have applied each of the finality requirements flexibly and pragmatically.[7] The requirements are discussed in turn.

Agency Action Consummating the Administrative Decisionmaking Process. The consummation element of the APA's finality requirement resembles the final judgment rule, which generally prevents interlocutory appeals in judicial litigation.[8] By eliminating "piecemeal review" of administrative proceedings, the consummation element promotes administrative as well as judicial efficiency. Withholding judicial review until completion of the agency's decisionmaking process prevents the intolerable delays that would attend court challenges of preliminary, procedural or intermediate administrative orders as they are entered. It also allows an agency to correct administrative errors that occur during a proceeding. In some cases, postponing judicial review avoids the necessity of review altogether, either because the agency ultimately decides in favor of the complaining party or because the parties settle their dispute. When review proves necessary, the consummation element still fosters judicial efficiency by enabling the court to consider in one sitting every contested agency action in an administrative proceeding.[9]

The Supreme Court's decision in *Federal Trade Commission v. Standard Oil Company of California (Socal)*[10] illustrates the consummation element of section 704's finality requirement. In *Socal*, the justices held that the FTC's issuance of a complaint commencing a formal adjudicatory proceeding was not "final agency action" and thus was insulated from judicial review until the conclusion of the proceeding. The company argued that the complaint was unlawful because the Commission had not conducted a sufficient investigation. But the complaint, explained the Court, stated only that the Commission had "reason to believe" that the company had engaged in unlawful activity. It represented the agency's "threshold determination that further inquiry [was] warranted," rather than "a definitive statement of position" on the legality of the company's conduct. The Court expected the company to use the adjudicatory

---

6. See Bennett v. Spear, 520 U.S. 154, 177–78 (1997).

7. See *id.* at 177; Federal Trade Commission v. Standard Oil Company of California (Socal), 449 U.S. 232, 239–43 (1980); Abbott Laboratories v. Gardner, 387 U.S. 136, 149 (1967).

8. See American Airlines, Inc. v. Herman, 176 F.3d 283, 288 (5th Cir. 1999); PepsiCo, Inc. v. Federal Trade Commission, 472 F.2d 179, 185 (2d Cir. 1972), cert. denied, 414 U.S. 876 (1973).

9. See *Socal*, 449 U.S. at 242; *Pepsi-Co*, 472 F.2d at 185.

10. 449 U.S. 232 (1980).

proceeding initiated by the complaint to challenge the Commission's position. Were the Commission to conclude after completing the proceeding that the company had engaged in unlawful conduct, judicial review would then be available.[11]

Just as judicial review of an allegedly defective complaint in an administrative adjudicatory proceeding typically must await the agency's final order concluding the proceeding, judicial challenges to the sufficiency of a notice of proposed rulemaking must await issuance of the agency's final rule. A notice of proposed rulemaking, like an administrative complaint, is a threshold determination that reflects only the agency's tentative course of action. A rulemaking proceeding is not consummated until an agency announces its final rule.[12]

The requirement that courts await the consummation of an administrative proceeding before engaging in judicial review is not absolute. The text of section 704 itself—which postpones judicial review of "preliminary, procedural, or intermediate agency action or ruling *not directly reviewable*" until review of the final agency action (emphasis added)—suggests that there are at least some such actions that are "directly reviewable" before completion of the administrative proceeding.[13] The courts' pragmatic approach to the finality requirement enables judges to review interlocutory administrative decisions when they conclude that it would be improper to await completion of the agency's proceeding. For example, in *Pepsi-Co, Inc. v. Federal Trade Commission*, the Second Circuit suggested that commencement of an administrative proceeding that is "plainly beyond [the agency's] jurisdiction as a matter of law" or that "cannot result in a valid order" may be a proper subject of judicial review.[14]

The D.C. Circuit exhibited similar flexibility in *Alabama Power Co. v. Federal Energy Regulatory Commission*[15] by reviewing the legality of FERC's decision to investigate whether certain power companies had charged excessive rates. The companies claimed that the rate investigation would violate their settlement agreement with FERC restricting such investigatory proceedings to three-year intervals. Relying on *Socal* and similar decisions, FERC argued that commencement of its investigation was not reviewable because it was a threshold rather than a final agency action. But the court of appeals distinguished the *Socal* line of precedent because those

---

11. *Id.* at 239–43; see also *American Airlines*, 176 F.3d at 289 (agency decision denying a motion for summary judgment in a formal adjudicatory proceeding is not final agency action within the meaning of section 704 of the Administrative Procedure Act).

12. *Abbott Laboratories*, 387 U.S. at 149–52.

13. See *PepsiCo*, 472 F.2d at 186.

14. *Id.* at 187.

15. 993 F.2d 1557 (D.C.Cir. 1993).

decisions did not involve the commencement of administrative proceedings that allegedly were in breach of contract. If the companies' interpretation of their agreement with FERC was correct, allowing the investigatory proceeding to go forward would not simply have subjected the power companies to the usual costs of participation. It also, crucially, would have denied the companies their "contractual right" to be free from rate investigations between the three-year intervals. The companies' contract right would be violated regardless of the agency's conclusion on the legality of the companies' rates. The court of appeals therefore agreed to rule on the companies' claim that the rate investigation violated the settlement agreement.[16]

Agency Action Determining or Affecting Individual Rights or Obligations. The second element of the finality requirement of section 704—that agency action determine or affect individual rights or obligations—often goes hand-in-hand with the first element, that the action complete the agency's decisionmaking process. An agency's interlocutory decisions during an ongoing administrative proceeding—like issuance of an administrative complaint or publication of a notice of proposed rulemaking—typically fail both elements of the finality requirement: They neither consummate the agency's decisionmaking process nor alter the legal rights or obligations of interested parties. By the same token, agency actions that consummate administrative adjudicatory or rulemaking proceedings typically constitute final agency action because these actions—orders and legislative rules—alter the legal rights or obligations of interested parties.

Some administrative actions, however, consummate the agency's decisionmaking process (satisfying the first element of the finality requirement) but are advisory rather than legally binding (putting into question the second element). This occurs, for example, when an agency recommends that another regulatory authority take some action. In *Chicago & Southern Air Lines, Inc. v. Waterman S.S. Corp.*,[17] for example, the Supreme Court held an agency's order granting an operating license to an air carrier and denying a license to a rival carrier to be non-reviewable. The order was not final, the Court held, because it did not take effect until the president approved it. The justices explained, "To revise or review an administrative decision, which has only the force of a recommendation to the President, would be to render an advisory opinion in its most obnoxious form."[18] Similarly, in *Dalton v. Specter*,[19] the Court held unreviewable an agency's recommendation to the president that certain military bases be closed. That action was not

16. *Id*. at 1566–67.

17. 333 U.S. 103 (1948).

18. *Id*. at 113–14.

19. 511 U.S. 462 (1994).

final, held the justices, because the president was free to accept or to reject the agency's recommendation when making the ultimate decision whether to close any of the bases.[20]

Yet, as was true of the first finality element requiring that agency action consummate the administrative decisionmaking process, reviewing courts approach the second finality element pragmatically rather than rigidly. A reviewing court may consider agency action that is not legally binding to be final, and thus reviewable, if the action has an effect similar to administrative pronouncements with the force of law. The Supreme Court's decision in *Bennett v. Spear*[21] is illustrative. *Bennett* involved a lawsuit by water users challenging the legality of a "biological opinion" prepared by the Fish and Wildlife Service concerning an irrigation project operated by the Bureau of Reclamation. The Service and the Bureau are both agencies within the Department of the Interior. The Service's biological opinion stated that the Bureau's irrigation project jeopardized the continued existence of two endangered fish species and recommended that the Bureau maintain water levels that were sufficient to protect the fish. The Bureau notified the Service that it intended to impose water-level restrictions in line with the recommendations of the biological opinion. The water users claimed that the Bureau's new restrictions threatened to reduce the amount of water previously available to them from the irrigation project.

The government argued that the Service's biological opinion, like the administrative advisory opinions in *Chicago & Southern Air Lines* and in *Dalton*, was not final because it merely recommended that the Bureau take action to protect the threatened species. But the Court distinguished *Bennett* from those decisions because the Service's biological opinion had "a virtually determinative effect" on the Bureau's decision. Although federal agencies were "technically free to disregard" biological opinions, they did so "very rarely." The Court thus concluded that the Service's biological opinion was final because it had "direct and appreciable legal consequences."[22]

Administrative policy statements and interpretive rules provide a common example of agency action that consummates an administrative decisionmaking process but that do not have the force of law (see § 6.5(b)). These so-called "guidance documents" (or, "nonlegislative rules") thus satisfy the first element of the finality requirement but place into doubt the second element. Reviewing courts

---

20. *Id.* at 468–71; see also Franklin v. Massachusetts, 505 U.S. 788, 796–801 (1992) (submission of a census report by the Secretary of Commerce to the president was not final agency action because

the president could revise the report before submitting it to Congress).

21. 520 U.S. 154 (1997).

22. *Id.*, at 169–70, 177–78.

may review guidance documents only if the document at issue has an effect similar to that of a legislative rule, which is legally binding. In *Flue-Cured Tobacco Cooperative Stabilization Corporation v. Environmental Protection Agency*,[23] for example, the Fourth Circuit declined to review a report of the Environmental Protection Agency classifying second-hand tobacco smoke as a known human carcinogen because the report did not constitute final agency action. EPA's report, which the court regarded as a policy statement, created "no legal rights or obligations" and had "no direct regulatory effect" on the challengers.[24] The EPA report on second-hand smoke thus resembled the administrative advisory opinions in *Chicago & Southern Air Lines* and in *Dalton*. It had no effect other than to set the stage for possible future action.

The D.C. Circuit's decision in *Appalachian Power Company v. Environmental Protection Agency*,[25] by contrast, reveals that guidance documents with more direct regulatory effect may be reviewable as final agency action. In *Appalachian Power*, the court of appeals agreed to review the validity of an EPA guidance document entitled "Periodic Monitoring Guidance." An EPA regulation required certain states to include "periodic monitoring" as a condition of permits for the operation of stationary sources of air pollution. The challenged EPA document elaborated the "periodic monitoring" requirement established by the regulation. EPA instructed its personnel to follow the guidance when reviewing permits and "insist[ed]" that state and local authorities comply with the guidance document when establishing the terms and conditions of operating permits. Under these circumstances, EPA's document, the court of appeals held, constituted final agency action because it "reflect[ed] a settled agency position which has legal consequences both for State agencies administering their permit programs and for companies ... [that] must obtain ... permits in order to continue operating."[26] The guidance document resembled the biological opinion in *Bennett* more than the administrative advisory opinions in *Chicago & Southern Air Lines* and in *Dalton*. It had, in the language of *Bennett*, "a virtually determinative effect" on the future issuance of operating permits.[27]

(b) Ripeness

Reviewing courts must ensure not only that the challenged agency action is final, but also that it is "ripe for judicial resolu-

---

23. 313 F.3d 852 (4th Cir. 2002).

24. *Id*. at 858–62.

25. 208 F.3d 1015 (D.C. Cir. 2000).

26. *Id*. at 1017–23; cf. National Park Hospitality Ass'n v. Department of the Interior, 538 U.S. 803, 812 (2003) (hold-

ing an agency policy statement to be final agency action within the meaning of the Administrative Procedure Act, although not ripe for judicial review).

27. *Bennett*, 520 U.S. at 170.

tion."[28] In contrast to the finality requirement, ripeness doctrine is not limited to suits bought pursuant to the Administrative Procedure Act. All federal litigation must be ripe. Ripeness, like standing, is an element of the case-or-controversy requirement of Article III of the Constitution, as well of a mix of judge-made prudential considerations that courts traditionally have consulted when deciding whether to award declaratory or injunctive relief.[29] The ripeness and finality requirements, however, serve similar interests in administrative and judicial efficiency. As the Supreme Court observed, the ripeness requirement protects agencies from "judicial interference until an administrative decision has been formalized and its effects felt in a concrete way by the challenging parties." It also protects courts by steering them clear of "premature adjudication" that would entangle them in "abstract disagreements over administrative policies."[30]

The Supreme Court established modern ripeness doctrine in *Abbott Laboratories v. Gardner*.[31] The *Abbott Laboratories* criteria for assessing the ripeness of agency action for judicial review require courts to determine (1) whether the issues presented in the litigation are ready for judicial decision and (2) whether delaying decision would cause "hardship to the parties."[32]

An agency's final order concluding an adjudicatory proceeding usually is ripe for judicial review because it usually compels a party to take or to cease some particular action. There typically is no reason for a reviewing court to delay assessing the legality of such an order. Any issue arising from the order should be ready for judicial review because it presumably has been a subject of the administrative adjudicatory proceeding. Delaying review typically would impose unnecessary hardship on the losing party by requiring the party either to incur the costs of complying with the agency's order or to violate the order and trigger an enforcement proceeding.

The ripeness of final agency rules for judicial review is less clear cut. The longstanding issue has been whether an administrative rule is ripe for judicial review before the agency has enforced it against the challenger. Reviewing courts are most likely to engage

---

28. Abbott Laboratories v. Gardner, 387 U.S. 136, 148 (1967); see National Park Hospitality Ass'n v. Department of the Interior, 538 U.S. 803 (2003) (holding an agency action to be final within the meaning of the Administrative Procedure Act but not ripe for judicial review).

29. See *National Park Hospitality Ass'n*, 538 U.S. at 808; Reno v. Catholic Social Services, Inc., 509 U.S. 43, 58 n.18 (1993). For an argument that the

doctrine of ripeness should not apply to suits filed pursuant to the Administrative Procedure Act, see John F. Duffy, *Administrative Common Law in Judicial Review*, 77 TEX. L. REV. 113, 162–81 (1998).

30. *Abbott Laboratories*, 387 U.S. at 148–49.

31. 387 U.S. 136 (1967).

32. *Id.* at 149.

in pre-enforcement review of a legislative rule that "as a practical matter requires the plaintiff to adjust his conduct immediately."[33] *Abbott Laboratories* is the Court's leading decision supporting pre-enforcement review of such rules. *Abbott Laboratories* involved a lawsuit by drug companies challenging a rule of the Food and Drug Administration imposing new labeling requirements for prescription drugs. The companies claimed that the labeling regulation exceeded the rulemaking authority that Congress had provided FDA in the enabling act. FDA urged dismissal of the suit, arguing that its rule would be ripe for judicial review, and thus subject to challenge, only as a defense in an enforcement proceeding against a drug company for failing to comply with the regulation.

The Court in *Abbott Laboratories* rejected FDA's argument, holding the companies' pre-enforcement challenge to the labeling rule to be ripe for review. The justices first found that the issue raised in the companies' lawsuit was ready for judicial resolution in advance of an enforcement proceeding. The only issue was the "purely legal" question whether FDA had properly interpreted the provisions of the enabling act governing its rulemaking authority.[34] The justices next concluded that pre-enforcement review of the FDA's rule was "appropriate" because the rule had a "sufficiently direct and immediate" impact on the drug companies. The labeling rule was "clear-cut." Moreover, the rule took effect "immediately upon publication," and FDA expected "immediate compliance" by the companies. The challenged rule thus posed a "dilemma" that produced "a direct effect on the day-to-day business of all prescription drug companies": The companies either could incur the costs of complying with the new labeling requirement or they could violate the rule and thereby "risk prosecution." This is the same dilemma faced by losing parties in administrative adjudicatory proceedings, and the justices concluded that it imposed sufficient hardship on the companies to justify pre-enforcement review of FDA's labeling rule.[35]

The Court made clear in a companion decision, *Toilet Goods Association, Inc. v. Gardner*,[36] that *Abbott Laboratories* did not open all legislative rules to pre-enforcement judicial review. *Toilet Goods Association* involved a pre-enforcement challenge to an FDA rule authorizing immediate suspension of certification services to cosmetics manufacturers that deny FDA inspectors "free access" to the manufacturers' "facilities, processes, and formulae." As had the drug companies in *Abbott Laboratories*, cosmetics manufacturers claimed that the access rule exceeded FDA's rulemaking authority.

---

33. Lujan v. National Wildlife Federation, 497 U.S. 871, 891 (1990).

34. *Abbott Laboratories*, 387 U.S. at 149.

35. *Id*. at 152–53.

36. 387 U.S. 158 (1967).

Yet the Court in *Toilet Goods Association* held that the cosmetics manufacturers' pre-enforcement challenge to the access rule was not ripe for review.

The justices acknowledged that the issue presented by the cosmetics manufacturers' statutory claim, like the issue in *Abbott Laboratories*, was "purely legal." The Court nevertheless held that the issue of FDA's authority to issue the access rule was not ready for judicial resolution at the pre-enforcement stage. FDA had pinned its authority to issue the access rule on a provision of the enabling act empowering the agency to issue rules "for the efficient enforcement" of the act. The justices felt unable to determine whether the access rule promoted efficient statutory enforcement because they had "no idea whether or when" FDA would order an inspection of a cosmetics manufacturer. Nor did they know the justification the agency would cite when ordering an investigation. The Court thus concluded that judicial review would "likely . . . stand on a much surer footing in the context of a specific application of [the access] regulation."[37]

The Court also found that the access rule in *Toilet Goods Association* imposed less hardship on cosmetics manufacturers than the labeling rule in *Abbott Laboratories* had imposed on drug manufacturers. In contrast to the drug-labeling requirement, the access rule did not immediately affect the day-to-day affairs of those subject to the regulation. FDA's rule in *Abbott Laboratories* required drug manufacturers immediately to change their labeling practices, while the access rule in *Toilet Goods Association* merely warned cosmetics manufacturers that the agency *may* suspend certification of their products *if* they denied access to their facilities or records. Even if FDA ordered suspension, the Court noted, the cosmetics manufacturers would suffer "no irremediable adverse consequences" because FDA's procedural rules permitted a manufacturer to challenge a suspension "promptly." If that challenge proved unsuccessful, judicial review offered manufacturers "an adequate forum for testing the regulation in a concrete situation."[38]

The distinction between *Abbott Laboratories* and *Toilet Goods Association* suggests that a reviewing court may determine that a pre-enforcement challenge to an agency rule is not ripe where (1) a judicial decision on the validity of the rule depends on how the rule is applied or (2) the rule does not require immediate changes in the conduct of those affected by the regulation. In the former case, the issues presented by the challenge would not be ready for judicial resolution. In the latter case, the parties would not suffer undue hardship if judicial resolution of the challenge awaited enforcement.

37. *Id*. at 162–63.   **38.** *Id*. at 164–66.

The Supreme Court has followed this understanding of the *Abbott Laboratories/Toilet Goods Association* distinction when evaluating the ripeness of administrative actions other than rules. For example, in *Ohio Forestry Association, Inc. v. Sierra Club*,[39] the justices dismissed an environmental group's lawsuit challenging a federal land and resource management plan that the United States Forest Service had adopted for a national forest in Ohio. Sierra Club claimed that the plan violated several federal statutes by allowing for too much logging and clearcutting of timber. The Court held, however, that the suit did not satisfy either of the two *Abbott Laboratories* criteria for ripeness.

The justices first concluded that dismissal of Sierra Club's challenge to the Forest Service's plan would not cause the organization or its members any "significant hardship." *Ohio Forestry Association* differed crucially from *Abbott Laboratories* because the Forest Service plan, unlike the labeling regulation, "create[d] no legal rights or obligations." Sierra Club, in contrast to the drug companies in *Abbott Laboratories*, had thus suffered no "adverse effects of a strictly legal kind." Nor had the plan "force[d]" Sierra Club "to modify its behavior in order to avoid future adverse consequences."[40]

Moreover, the Forest Service plan did not inflict "significant practical harm" on Sierra Club's ability to contest logging or cutting operations in the forest that it regarded as unlawful. Before any such activity could occur, the Forest Service would have to identify a particular site, propose a specific harvesting method, prepare an environmental review, offer the public an opportunity to be heard, and if sued, justify the proposal to a reviewing court. This process, like the administrative and judicial review processes in *Toilet Goods Association*, gave Sierra Club "ample opportunity later to bring its legal challenge at a time when harm is more imminent and more certain." The justices acknowledged Sierra Club's point that it would be "easier" and less expensive to challenge the plan as a whole rather than to challenge each particular logging or cutting decision as it arose, but "litigation cost saving," the justices ruled, did not "justify review in a case that would otherwise be unripe."[41]

The Court in *Ohio Forestry Association* also concluded that a reviewing court would be better able to evaluate the legal authority of the Forest Service to permit logging and clearcutting operations in the forest if it awaited the Service's decision on particular proposals. The justices anticipated that the agency might "refine its policies" on logging and clearcutting as it moved through the

39. 523 U.S. 726 (1998).   **41.** *Id.* at 733–35.
40. *Id.* at 733–34.

process of permitting specific timber operations. They also believed that judicial review of the lawfulness of these activities would "benefit" from "the focus that a particular logging proposal could provide." Reviewing the logging and clearcutting provisions at the initial planning stage, rather than awaiting a specific decision permitting such activity, would "threaten the kind of abstract disagreements over administrative policies that the ripeness doctrine seeks to avoid."[42]

(c) Exhaustion of Administrative Remedies

Reviewing courts traditionally have required, at least as a default rule, that plaintiffs exhaust all administrative remedies that may resolve their dispute before initiating a lawsuit.[43] The exhaustion requirement protects administrative autonomy by ensuring that agencies have "the first chance to exercise [their] discretion or to apply [their] expertise" in resolving administrative matters.[44] And as with the requirement of finality, exhaustion doctrine reflects "the commonsense notion of dispute resolution that an agency ought to have an opportunity to correct its own mistakes with respect to the programs it administers before it is haled into federal court."[45] The exhaustion requirement also reinforces the requirements of finality and ripeness by promoting judicial efficiency. Agencies may settle disputes before they reach court. For those disputes that remain, the exhaustion requirement allows agencies to assist courts by compiling "a useful record" for review.[46]

In contrast to the finality and ripeness requirements, exhaustion doctrine is wholly a judicial creation. It is rooted neither in the Administrative Procedure Act nor in the case-or-controversy requirement of Article III. Perhaps for that reason, reviewing courts have exhibited considerable flexibility when formulating and applying exhaustion doctrine.[47] They treat the exhaustion requirement as a default rule, retaining discretion to waive exhaustion whenever they conclude that "the interest of the individual in retaining

---

42. *Id.* at 735–37; see also National Park Hospitality Ass'n v. Department of the Interior, 538 U.S. 803 (2003) (holding National Park Service's policy statement that its concession contracts are not subject to the Contract Disputes Act was not ripe for judicial review upon its issuance).

43. McCarthy v. Madigan, 503 U.S. 140, 144–45 (1992); Myers v. Bethlehem Shipbuilding Corp., 303 U.S. 41, 50–51 (1938).

44. McKart v. United States, 395 U.S. 185, 194–95 (1969); see *McCarthy,* 503 U.S. at 145.

45. *McCarthy,* 503 U.S. at 145; see Weinberger v. Salfi, 422 U.S. 749, 765 (1975); *McKart,* 395 U.S. at 195.

46. *McCarthy,* 503 U.S. at 145; see Weinberger, 422 U.S. at 765; *McKart,* 395 U.S. at 195. For a critique of the purposes often attributed to the exhaustion requirement, see Marcia R. Gelpe, *Exhaustion of Administrative Remedies: Lessons from Environmental Cases,* 53 GEO. WASH. L. REV. 1 (1985).

47. See Bowen v. City of New York, 476 U.S. 467, 484 (1986) (exhaustion doctrine "intensely practical").

prompt access to a federal judicial forum" outweighs the "counter-vailing institutional interests favoring exhaustion."[48]

In a recent synthesis of exhaustion doctrine, the Supreme Court identified "at least three broad sets of circumstances" in which reviewing courts have proved willing to waive the exhaustion requirement.[49] Each set of exceptional circumstances ties waiver of the exhaustion requirement to the ineffectiveness of the administrative remedies available to the plaintiff. The first set of circumstances arises when requiring exhaustion "may occasion undue prejudice" to the plaintiff's lawsuit.[50] Such prejudice may occur when an individual may "suffer irreparable harm" without "immediate judicial consideration of [the] claim."[51] It also may occur when an agency will take an "unreasonable or indefinite" length of time to make its decision.[52] The second set of circumstances in which reviewing courts have waived the exhaustion requirement occurs when there is "some doubt as to whether the agency [is] empowered to grant effective relief."[53] This doubt may arise when an individual has challenged the legal sufficiency of the agency's procedures governing the relevant administrative remedy.[54] It also may arise when an individual has challenged the constitutionality of a statute the agency administers, a challenge that agencies are not competent to resolve.[55] The final group of exhaustion exceptions takes hold when the agency is "biased or has otherwise predetermined the issue."[56]

Another consequence of the prudential nature of the exhaustion requirement is that it is subject to congressional override.[57] Because statutes generally trump common law, reviewing courts will honor an act of Congress that eliminates the exhaustion requirement. The Administrative Procedure Act contains just such a provision. Section 704 provides that a plaintiff need not pursue an available administrative appeal from an adverse agency decision in order to seek judicial review of the decision pursuant to the APA,

---

48. *McCarthy*, 503 U.S. at 146; see *Bowen*, 476 U.S. at 484; Mathews v. Eldridge, 424 U.S. 319, 330 (1976).

49. *McCarthy*, 503 U.S. at 146.

50. *Id*. at 146–47.

51. *Id*. at 147; see, e.g., *Bowen*, 476 U.S. at 482–86.

52. *McCarthy*, 503 U.S. at 147; see, e.g., Coit Independence Joint Venture v. FSLIC, 489 U.S. 561, 587 (1989) (exhaustion not required because agency did not place "a reasonable time limit" on its consideration of the relevant claims).

53. *McCarthy*, 503 U.S. at 147, quoting Gibson v. Berryhill, 411 U.S. 564, 575 n.14 (1973).

54. *McCarthy*, 503 U.S. at 148; see, e.g., Barry v. Barchi, 443 U.S. 55, 63 n.10 (1979); Mathews v. Eldridge, 424 U.S. 319, 330–32 (1976).

55. *McCarthy*, 503 U.S. at 147–48; see, e.g., Mathews v. Diaz, 426 U.S. 67, 76 (1976).

56. *McCarthy*, 503 U.S. at 148; see *Gibson*, 411 U.S. at 575 n.14. For a critique of the exhaustion exceptions, see Gelpe, *Exhaustion of Administrative Remedies*, supra note 46, at 25–64.

57. *McCarthy*, 503 U.S. at 144.

unless (1) an act of Congress expressly so requires or (2) the agency's rules both require an administrative appeal and make the decision inoperative during the appeal. If the conditions of section 704 are not met, the doctrine of exhaustion of administrative remedies only applies "in cases not governed by the APA."[58]

Although the Supreme Court has held that reviewing courts must enforce a clear statutory requirement of exhaustion,[59] lower federal courts have expressed uncertainty over whether they may apply the traditional judge-made exceptions to exhaustion to escape a statutory requirement. The Supreme Court has instructed reviewing courts not to waive a statutory exhaustion requirement unless the waiver would be "consistent with [congressional] intent."[60] But where Congress has expressed no intent on waiver, it is hardly clear whether the statutory exhaustion requirement reflects a legislative understanding that the requirement is absolute or an understanding that the requirement incorporates the traditional limitations and exceptions to exhaustion included in the common law doctrine. The First Circuit, while acknowledging that statutory exhaustion requirements are "more rigid" than the judicially created doctrine, nevertheless claimed authority to waive a statutory requirement at least "where a resort to the agency would be futile because the challenge is one that the agency has no power to resolve in the applicant's favor."[61] But the D.C. Circuit has asked, if courts lack power to require exhaustion when Congress has excused it, does it make sense to say that courts can excuse exhaustion when Congress has required it?[62] The D.C. Circuit's question awaits an authoritative answer.

58. Darby v. Cisneros, 509 U.S. 137, 144–45, 153–54 (1993); see Volvo GM Heavy Truck Corp. v. United States Department of Labor, 118 F.3d 205, 209 (4th Cir. 1997). For an approving analysis of *Darby* as "a heartening sign" that federal common law "is receding in administrative law," see Duffy, *Administrative Common Law*, *supra* note 29, at 156–62.

59. See *McCarthy*, 503 U.S. at 144 (1992); *Coit Independence Joint Venture*, 489 U.S. at 579.

60. *Coit Independence Joint Venture*, 489 U.S. at 580.

61. Sousa v. INS, 226 F.3d 28, 32 (1st Cir. 2000).

62. Marine Mammal Conservancy v. Department of Agriculture, 134 F.3d 409, 411 (D.C.Cir. 1998).

Chapter 8

THE NATURE AND SCOPE OF SUBSTANTIVE JUDICIAL REVIEW

The essential role of reviewing courts in the administrative process is to ensure the legality of agency action (and sometimes, of agency inaction) affecting individual rights and obligations. In performing this role, courts may exercise three types of review.

A court may engage in *constitutional review*, determining whether the enabling act or the administrative action at issue complies with the Constitution. Section 706(2)(B) of the Administrative Procedure Act provides that reviewing courts "shall ... hold unlawful and set aside agency action ... found to be ... contrary to constitutional right, power, privilege, or immunity." The constitutional requirements that arise most commonly in administrative litigation involve the separation of powers and procedural due process. Chapters 2 and 3 of this book examine those requirements.

A court also may engage in *procedural review*, determining whether the agency's decisionmaking procedures comply with the Administrative Procedure Act and other statutes, as well as with

308

the agency's procedural rules. Section 706(2)(D) of the APA provides that reviewing courts "shall ... hold unlawful and set aside agency action ... found to be ... without observance of procedure required by law." The procedural requirements of the APA are canvassed in Chapters 4, 5, and 6 of this book.

Finally, a court may engage in *substantive review*, determining whether the agency has appropriately exercised the substantive authority provided by its enabling act. In reviewing the substantive validity of agency action, section 706(2) of the APA instructs courts to ensure that the agency has acted within the scope of its statutory authority, that it has adequate support for its factual findings, and that it has exercised its decisionmaking discretion responsibly. The nature and scope of substantive judicial review of agency action is the subject of this chapter.

Each of the three types of judicial review requires judges to maintain a delicate balance. They must be sufficiently assertive to assure themselves (and the public) of the legality, and thus the legitimacy, of agency action affecting individual rights. Yet judges must not become so assertive that they usurp the role of the agency as the primary administrative authority. Reviewing courts must walk a tightrope, respecting administrative autonomy while enforcing the rule of law.

Striking the proper balance of the judicial role in the administrative process has proven to be most difficult when courts engage in substantive review. Several characteristics of the American system of government administration contribute to this difficulty. First and foremost, judicial review of administrative action raises the same "countermajoritarian difficulty" that arises when courts review the constitutionality of legislative or presidential actions.[1] Although administrative decisionmakers are unelected, they are at least indirectly answerable to the public through their accountability to the president and Congress. Federal judges, with their constitutional guarantees of life tenure and salary, are the least accountable decisionmakers in the American system. This insularity creates institutional advantages for the courts, enabling them to avoid political pressure when ruling on the legality of controversial agency action. But the disconnect between the judgment of the courts and the will of the people becomes a de-legitimizing liability if judges stray beyond the boundaries of law and into the realm of politics. Distinguishing law from politics in the substantive judicial review of agency action is notoriously difficult.

---

1. See ALEXANDER M. BICKEL, THE LEAST DANGEROUS BRANCH: THE SUPREME COURT AT THE BAR OF POLITICS 16–23 (2d ed., 1986). For an argument that judicial review of the exercise of administrative discretion poses no countermajoritarian difficulty, see Matthew D. Adler, *Judicial Restraint in the Administrative State: Beyond the Countermajoritarian Difficulty*, 145 U. PA. L. REV. 759 (1997).

Another characteristic of the American system of government administration that contributes to the difficulty of substantive judicial review is Congress's tendency to delegate broad regulatory authority to agencies through enabling acts containing indeterminate standards defining the reach of administrative power. Judge Harold Leventhal of the D.C. Circuit, a leading judicial voice on administrative law, once suggested that Congress has delegated broad authority to agencies only because judicial review keeps administrators "within statutory limits."[2] The opaqueness of many statutory standards, however, makes it difficult for courts to discern the limits that Congress had in mind when it authorized the agency action they must review.

The indeterminacy of statutory standards governing agency action is exacerbated by the indeterminacy of the APA's standards governing the scope of substantive judicial review. Two prominent administrative law scholars once famously observed, "[T]he rules governing judicial review have no more substance at the core than a seedless grape."[3] The key APA terms—"arbitrary," "capricious," "abuse of discretion," and "substantial evidence"—while certainly suggestive, are hardly self-defining in concrete cases (see APA § 706(2)(A),(E)).

The vagueness of the APA's standards governing the scope of substantive judicial review may be linked, at least in part, to the number and variety of federal agencies and administrative programs that come before the courts. The diversity of administrative action subject to substantive judicial review virtually rules out concrete APA standards.[4] But something else is at work here as well. The APA's indeterminate standards of substantive review reflect Congress's recognition that it is undesirable, and perhaps impossible, to reduce this crucial judicial function to words. Justice Felix Frankfurter noted the inevitability of indeterminate standards of review, writing, "[T]he precise way in which courts [review agency action] cannot be imprisoned within any form of words.... There are no talismanic words that can avoid the process of judgment. The difficulty is that we cannot escape, in relation to this problem, the use of undefined defining terms." The APA's standards of judicial review reflect a strategic decision by Congress that substantive judicial review cannot be dictated by, in Justice Frankfurter's language, "a body of rigid rules assuring sameness of

2. Ethyl Corp. v. EPA, 541 F.2d 1, 68 (D.C.Cir.) (Leventhal, J., concurring), cert. denied, 426 U.S. 941 (1976). For a law-and-economics perspective on why Congress entrusts courts with the duty to police statutory limits on agency action, see William M. Landes & Richard A. Posner, *The Independent Judiciary in* *an Interest–Group Perspective*, 18 J.L. & ECON. 875 (1975).

3. Ernest Gellhorn & Glen O. Robinson, *Perspectives in Administrative Law*, 75 COLUM. L. REV. 771, 780–81 (1975).

4. See United States v. Mead Corp., 533 U.S. 218, 235–37 (2001).

applications." Rather, Congress probably did the best it could by delineating general "standard[s] for judgment" to guide reviewing courts when evaluating the substantive validity of agency action.[5]

There is one final factor contributing to the difficulty of substantive judicial review of agency action. The administrative process in the United States, unlike in a number of other countries, assigns judicial review authority primarily to courts of law rather than to specialized administrative courts.[6] This choice requires generalist judges, who trained in the law, to review the non-legal decisions of specialist administrators who trained in the disciplines relevant to their decisionmaking. Judge David Bazelon of the D.C. Circuit memorably lamented the challenge of having "technically illiterate judges" reviewing the substance of scientifically sophisticated administrative decisions.[7] Moreover, a generalist judge's chance encounter with an administrative program on judicial review may lead to a distorted view of the nature and function of the program, risking a decision that impairs the operations of the agency.

Notwithstanding the awkwardness that it engenders, Congress's choice of ordinary courts of law over specialized tribunals for reviewing most agency decisions makes a profound statement about the nature and responsibility of administrative decisionmaking in the United States. Assigning courts of law the primary responsibility of reviewing the legality of administrative action brings agencies "into harmony with the totality of the law."[8] The requirement that agencies account for their actions in the law courts is the primary vehicle by which American administrative law enforces the rule of law. Although judges are not experts on the substance of the administrative matters that come before them, they are (or should be) attuned to their *Marbury* responsibility of ensuring that government officials observe the law when individual rights are at stake. Judicial review over the substance of agency decisions also tempers the American reliance on technocratic expertise. Because judges lack technical and scientific expertise, judicial

5. Universal Camera Corp. v. NLRB, 340 U.S. 474, 487, 489 (1951).

6. Several specialized courts dot the American judicial landscape, however. The Court of Claims, the Court of International Claims, and the United States Tax Court have jurisdiction over certain types of claims against the federal government and its agencies. The United States Court of Appeals for the Federal Circuit hears appeals from judgments by the Court of Claims, as well patent cases, international trade cases, and several other types of cases.

Because the D.C. Circuit reviews far more agency actions than do the other courts of appeals, it might qualify as "a semi-specialized administrative court." Still, a substantial majority of administrative review cases occur in courts other than the D.C. Circuit. See Harold H. Bruff, *Coordinating Judicial Review in Administrative Law*, 39 U.C.L.A. L. REV. 1193, 1202, 1203, 1205 (1992).

7. *Ethyl Corp.*, 541 F.2d at 67 (Bazelon, J., concurring).

8. LOUIS L. JAFFE, JUDICIAL CONTROL OF ADMINISTRATIVE ACTION 590 (1965).

review requires agency experts to translate their decisions and their decisionmaking into language that lay people can understand, and endorse. In this important sense, judicial review in a generalist rather than in a specialized court fosters the democratic accountability of agency decisionmakers by obligating them to make a public explanation of their decisions that the interested public can understand and accept as legitimate.[9]

§ 8.1   The Framework of Substantive Judicial Review

The framework of substantive judicial review of administrative action is constituted by a handful of fundamental administrative law principles. The first, and most basic, of these principles holds that Congress has entrusted agencies, and not reviewing courts, with the primary role of deciding how best to administer an enabling act. The role of reviewing courts is crucial, yet secondary: Judges determine whether administrative decisions are lawful. This limited understanding of the judicial role underlies the further principle that courts determine the validity of agency action by considering only "the grounds upon which the [agency] itself based its action."[1] If the court holds those grounds to be "inadequate or improper," the court may not uphold the agency action "by substituting what it considers to be a more adequate or proper basis. To do so would propel the court into the domain which Congress has set aside exclusively for the administrative agency."[2]

These basic administrative law principles informed the Supreme Court's resolution of the *Chenery* litigation, which provided much of the framework of contemporary substantive judicial review of agency action. In *Securities and Exchange Commission v. Chenery Corp. (Chenery I)*,[3] the justices reviewed an order of the SEC requiring the managers of a company to surrender stock in their company that they had purchased while the company was proceeding through an agency-supervised reorganization. The Commission had based its order on principals of equity that it had derived from court decisions. The Court held that the SEC had misinterpreted those decisions, and that equity jurisprudence did not support the surrender order. The Commission's lawyers nevertheless asked the justices to uphold the order on the ground that it was supported by the standards in the enabling act governing reorganization. The

---

9.   For fuller consideration of the relative roles and merits of generalized and specialized courts in the administrative process, see Harold H. Bruff, *Specialized Courts in Administrative Law*, 43 ADMIN. L. REV. 329 (1991); Ellen R. Jordan, *Specialized Courts: A Choice?*, 76 Nw. U. L. REV. 745 (1981); Richard L. Revesz, *Specialized Courts and the Administra-* *tive Lawmaking System*, 138 U. PA. L. REV. 1111 (1990).

§ 8.1

1.   SEC v. Chenery Corp., 318 U.S. 80, 88 (1943) (*Chenery I*).

2.   SEC v. Chenery Corp., 332 U.S. 194, 196 (1947) (*Chenery II*).

3.   318 U.S. 80 (1943).

Court refused the request, because the Commission had not relied on the statutory standards when ordering the managers to surrender their stock. The justices explained that Congress had authorized the SEC, not reviewing courts, to make the primary decision of how to apply the standards of its enabling act. For that reason, it would be improper to allow "judicial judgment" of how best to apply the statute to replace "administrative judgment." The Court explained, "For purposes of affirming no less than reversing its orders, an appellate court cannot intrude upon the domain which Congress has exclusively entrusted to an administrative agency."[4]

The Court's disposition of *Chenery I* established an important corollary to the principle that courts review agency action only on the grounds invoked by the agency. Having decided that the judicial precedent cited by the SEC did not justify the surrender order, the Court in *Chenery I* vacated the administrative order and directed the court of appeals to remand the matter back to the SEC "for such further proceedings, not inconsistent with this opinion, as may be appropriate." The Administrative Procedure Act tracks this corollary by instructing reviewing courts simply to "hold unlawful and set aside the agency action" that they determine to be invalid (APA § 706(2)). In the typical case, once a reviewing court invalidates agency action, its only recourse is to remand the matter back to the agency for further consideration. It cannot resolve the matter on its own.[5]

On remand, the SEC applied the standards of its enabling act and again ordered the corporate managers to surrender their stock.

---

4. *Id.* at 88–95; see also Motor Vehicle Manufacturers Ass'n of United States, Inc. v. State Farm Mutual Automobile Insurance Co., 463 U.S. 29, 50 (1983) ("It is well-established that an agency's action must be upheld, if at all, on the basis articulated by the agency itself.").

5. *Chenery I*, 318 U.S. at 95; see, e.g., INS v. Ventura, 537 U.S. 12, 16–17 (2002); Florida Power & Light Co. v. Lorion, 470 U.S. 729, 744 (1985); FPC v. Transcontinental Gas Pipe Line Corp., 423 U.S. 326, 331–34 (1976). The Court has recognized, however, that in some "exceptional situation[s]" a "crystal-clear" administrative error may make "a remand an unnecessary formality." NLRB v. Food Store Employees Union, Local 347, 417 U.S. 1, 8 (1974). Such situations may occur, for example, when an agency has violated a non-discretionary duty or where an agency repeatedly has rejected the only rational outcome available under its enabling act. Moreover, some (but not all) reviewing courts, led by the D.C. Circuit, have issued so-called "remand-only" orders to cure administrative decision-making defects without vacating the agency's order. Courts have issued such orders when they have found that the agency's error was minor and that vacating the administrative order would cause undue disruption to the regulatory program. The Supreme Court, however, has not ruled on whether section 706(2) of the APA permits remand-only orders. For a discussion of these variations on the *Chenery* norm, see SECTION OF ADMINISTRATIVE LAW AND REGULATORY PRACTICE OF AMERICAN BAR ASSOCIATION, A GUIDE TO JUDICIAL AND POLITICAL REVIEW OF FEDERAL AGENCIES 205–09 (John F. Duffy & Michael Herz, eds., 2005); Ronald M. Levin, *"Vacation" at Sea: Judicial Remedies and Equitable Discretion in Administrative Law*, 53 DUKE L.J. 291 (2003).

The Supreme Court upheld the new order in *Securities and Exchange Commission v. Chenery Corp. (Chenery II).*[6] *Chenery I*, the *Chenery II* Court explained, had resolved "no more and no less than that the [SEC's] first order was unsupportable for the reasons supplied by that agency." The question whether the managers could retain their stock thus "lacked a final and complete answer." The SEC's order on remand, the Court in *Chenery II* continued, had "avoid[ed] the fatal error of relying on judicial precedents which [did] not sustain it." The justices were satisfied that the new surrender order was consistent with the governing standards of the enabling act, "a basis upon which it clearly reste[d]."[7]

Chenery II provided another important corollary to the rule of *Chenery I* limiting judicial review of agency action to the grounds cited by the agency. "If the administrative action is to be tested by the basis upon which it purports to rest," the justices added in *Chenery II*, "that basis must be set forth with such clarity as to be understandable. It will not do for a court to be compelled to guess at the theory underlying the agency's action; nor can a court be expected to chisel that which must be precise from what the agency has left vague and indecisive."[8] This corollary underlies the Supreme Court's decision in *Citizens to Preserve Overton Park, Inc. v. Volpe*,[9] which is another foundational case establishing the framework of substantive judicial review. *Overton Park* involved a challenge to a decision by the Secretary of Transportation authorizing federal funding for the construction of an interstate highway through a city park. The challengers claimed that the Transportation Secretary's decision violated his enabling act, which prohibited federal funding of a highway through parkland unless there was no "feasible and prudent alternative" route and the highway plan minimized damage to the park.[10]

The Court in *Overton Park* found itself unable to review the legality of the Secretary's funding decision because he had not prepared a contemporaneous explanation of his decision. The Secretary had written no decision including the relevant factual findings or stating his rationale for funding the park route. Because the funding decision was an instance of informal rather than of formal adjudication, the Secretary had been under no procedural obligation to write formal findings of fact or a statement of reasons (see § 4.2(b)). But the absence of administrative findings and rationale left the justices in the dark about the grounds for the Secretary's

6. 332 U.S. 194 (1947).

7. *Id.* at 199–200, 204–09.

8. *Id.* at 196–97. The Court has since instructed courts to review administrative decisions "of less than ideal clarity if the agency's path may reasonably be discerned." Bowman Transportation, Inc. v. Arkansas–Best Freight System, 419 U.S. 281, 286 (1974).

9. 401 U.S. 402 (1971).

10. *Id.* at 404–05.

funding decision. The Department's lawyers had attempted to address this deficiency by submitting affidavits, "prepared specifically for [the] litigation," in support of the Secretary's funding decision. But the justices considered such "post hoc rationalizations" of agency action to provide "an inadequate basis for review."[11] The Court insisted on reviewing the actual grounds of the funding decision based on "the full administrative record that was before the Secretary at the time he made his decision."[12]

Having refused to review the Secretary's funding decision without a contemporaneous administrative record, the Court in *Overton Park* ignored the instruction of *Chenery I* to remand the matter to the agency. The justices instead remanded the case to the district court with instructions to reconstruct the Secretary's funding decision and to compile the administrative record on which the Secretary had made his decision. In the event the record failed to include the grounds of the Secretary's decision, the justices instructed the district court to fill in the gaps by ordering the administrators involved in the Secretary's funding decision to testify.[13] The result was a 27–day trial, culminating in the invalidation of the Secretary's funding decision.

The justices have since backtracked from the trial remedy they had ordered in *Overton Park*. In *Pension Benefit Guarantee Corp. v. LTV Corp.*,[14] the Court returned to the *Chenery* practice of remanding to the agency "for additional investigation or explanation" as the "preferred course" even when, as in *Overton Park*, a reviewing court "cannot evaluate the challenged agency action on the basis of the record before it."[15] In *Pension Benefit Guarantee Corp.*, the Court also acknowledged a long simmering "tension" between *Overton Park*'s requirement that agencies provide a contemporaneous explanation of their decisions, and *Vermont Yankee*'s holding that courts may not add procedural requirements for agency action beyond those found in acts of Congress or in the procedural rules of agencies (see § 6.2).[16] The justices distinguished *Overton Park* from *Vermont Yankee* by noting that section 706 of the Administrative

---

11. *Id.* at 409, 417, 419; see also Motor Vehicles Manufacturers Ass'n of United States, Inc. v. State Farm Mutual Automobile Insurance Co., 463 U.S. 29, 50 (1983) ("courts may not accept appellate counsel's *post hoc* rationalizations for agency action").

12. *Overton Park*, 401 U.S. at 420; see also Camp v. Pitts, 411 U.S. 138, 142 (1973) ("the focal point for judicial review should be the administrative record already in existence, not some new record made initially in the reviewing court").

13. *Overton Park*, 401 U.S. at 420–21.

14. 496 U.S. 633 (1990).

15. *Id.* at 654 (1990); see Florida Power & Light Co. v. Lorion, 470 U.S. 729, 744 (1985).

16. *Pension Benefit Guarantee Corp.*, 496 U.S. at 654; see Vermont Yankee Nuclear Power Corp. v. Natural Resources Defense Council, Inc., 435 U.S. 519 (1978).

Procedure Act requires that courts review agency action on the
"whole record." A reviewing court thus enforces rather than cir-
cumvents the APA by demanding that agencies provide a complete
administrative record of their decisions.[17]

§ 8.2   The Administrative Record

The Supreme Court has described *Overton Park*'s requirement
that courts review agency action on the basis of "the full administrative record" that was before the agency when the agency made
its decision as a "fundamental principle of judicial review."[1] The
administrative record serves as the "focal point" of substantive
judicial review.[2] The justices have explained, "The task of the
reviewing court is to apply the appropriate APA standard of review
to the agency decision based on the record the agency presents to
the reviewing court."[3] Judicial review on the administrative record
poses no difficulty when an agency's decision is the product of a
formal proceeding. The Administrative Procedure Act requires that
an agency conducting a formal proceeding base its decision exclusively on an evidentiary record generated by the proceeding (see
§ 5.3). On judicial review, the agency simply transfers to the court
the record that the agency already has made for its decision.

Submission of the administrative record of an informal agency
proceeding often is not so straightforward. The APA does not
require that agencies base their decisions in informal proceedings
on a "focused and defined record."[4] It therefore is necessary, as the
Court in *Overton Park* held, for agencies to assemble an administrative record of their decisions. Although the APA does not prescribe
the contents of the administrative record in informal proceedings,
reviewing courts uniformly have required that the record include,
first, all submissions by interested parties during the proceeding
that the agency was required to consider (for example, the public
comments in a rulemaking proceeding). In addition, the administrative record must include all other materials that agency decisionmakers and staff actually considered in making their decision,
unless that material is privileged.[5] A reviewing court may allow

---

17. *Pension Benefit Guarantee Corp.*,
496 U.S. at 654–55.

§ 8.2

1. *Florida Power & Light*, 470 U.S.
at 743.

2. See *Camp*, 411 U.S. at 142 ("the
focal point for judicial review should be
the administrative record already in existence, not some new record made initially in the reviewing court").

3. *Florida Power & Light*, 470 U.S.
at 743–44.

4. See William F. Pederson, Jr., *Formal Records and Informal Rulemaking*,
85 YALE L.J. 38, 61 (1975).

5. For an excellent discussion of the
required contents of an administrative
record, see Richard McMillan, Jr. &
Todd D. Peterson, *The Permissible
Scope of Hearings, Discovery and Additional Factfinding During Judicial Review of Informal Agency Action*, 1982
DUKE L.J. 333, 341–43.

discovery if a challenger raises "legitimate concerns" that the administrative record produced by the agency is incomplete. The purpose of discovery in these circumstances is to verify the completeness of the record.[6]

Federal agencies may assert the privileges that are available to any litigant, such as the attorney-client privilege and the attorney work-product privilege. Agencies enjoy several special governmental privileges as well. The governmental privilege that agencies invoke most frequently in administrative litigation is the deliberative process privilege. This privilege covers an agency's "internal memoranda embodying the deliberative processes of the agency and its staff."[7] Examples of agency memoranda that may fall within the deliberative process privilege include staff recommendations, analyses, work product, and legal opinions. The deliberative process privilege does not protect statements of fact appearing in agency memoranda when the facts are necessary for judicial review and are not otherwise disclosed in the administrative record. A reviewing court also may require an agency to disclose internal memoranda otherwise subject to the deliberative process privilege when the agency has adopted the memoranda as the basis of its decision.[8]

Reviewing courts strictly enforce *Overton Park*'s requirement that agencies support their decisions on the basis of a contemporaneous administrative record. They consistently reject any party's efforts to introduce evidence outside the administrative record for the purpose of challenging or supporting the "propriety" of an agency decision.[9] Permitting such a showing would violate *Chenery I*'s limitation of judicial review to the actual grounds of the agency's decision, as well as *Overton Park*'s prohibition of post hoc rationalizations for agency action.[10] But the record requirement of *Overton Park* is not absolute. Courts permit the introduction of supplemental information that facilities judicial review by completing the picture of the agency's decisionmaking.[11] For example, courts may allow "background information" illuminating the administrative record.[12] This supplemental information, of course, may not provide any "new rationalization" of the agency's decision.[13] Reviewing

6. *Id.* at 339, 340–50.

7. National Courier Ass'n v. Board of Governors of Federal Reserve System, 516 F.2d 1229, 1241–43 (D.C.Cir. 1975).

8. See *id.* at 1241–43; McMillan & Peterson, *Permissible Scope of Hearings*, *supra* note 5, at 342–43, 382–89.

9. Environmental Defense Fund v. Costle, 657 F.2d 275, 285–86 (D.C. Cir. 1981); see ASARCO, Inc. v. EPA, 616 F.2d 1153, 1160 (9th Cir. 1980).

10. See Kunaknana v. Clark, 742 F.2d 1145, 1152 (9th Cir. 1984); *Environmental Defense Fund*, 657 F.2d at 285–86.

11. See *Camp*, 411 U.S. at 142–43.

12. *ASARCO*, 616 F.2d at 1160; Association of Pacific Fisheries v. EPA, 615 F.2d 794, 811–12 (9th Cir. 1980); see *Environmental Defense Fund*, 657 F.2d at 285.

13. *Environmental Defense Fund*, 657 F.2d at 285; see Bunker Hill Co. v.

courts also may allow evidence outside the administrative record to help them determine "whether the agency considered all the relevant factors or fully explicated its course of conduct or grounds of decision."[14]

§ 8.3   The Three Elements of Agency Decisionmaking

Administrative law has avoided defining the scope of substantive judicial review of agency decisions, as such. Instead, it has divided agency decisionmaking into three elements, and has prescribed a distinct standard of review for each element. The Administrative Procedure Act describes the three elements of agency decisionmaking as involving agency decisions on questions of "fact," "law," and "discretion" (APA § 557(c)(A)). Although this APA reference concerns administrative decisions in formal adjudication, it is the premise of scope-of-review doctrine that every agency action—whether rulemaking or adjudication, formal or informal—requires agency decisions on questions of law, fact, and discretion.

Each of the three elements of agency decisions represents a distinct stage of the agency's decisionmaking. An agency finds facts relevant to its decision by gathering and evaluating an evidentiary record. Whether an agency's factual determinations are adequately supported by the evidentiary record is a question of fact. An agency also interprets the standards of its enabling act to define the scope of its decisionmaking authority. Whether an agency has interpreted its enabling act properly is a question of law. To complete its decision, an agency applies its interpretation of the enabling act to its factual findings. Whether an agency has properly applied the enabling act to the facts is a mixed question of law and fact. At bottom, though, the agency's ultimate decision on how best to apply its enabling act to the relevant facts is an exercise of policymaking judgment or discretion.

The central task of scope-of-review doctrine is to define the respective roles of agencies and of the courts with respect to each element of an agency's decision.[1] We now turn to that task.

EPA, 572 F.2d 1286, 1292 (9th Cir. 1977).

14. *ASARCO*, 616 F.2d at 1160; see *Environmental Defense Fund*, 657 F.2d at 286. For an argument that the exceptions reviewing courts have made to *Overton Park*'s record requirement have so eroded the requirement that parties may evade it at will, see Steven Stark & Sarah Wald, *Setting No Records: The Failed Attempts to Limit the Record in*

Review of Administrative Action, 36 Ad. Min. L. Rev. 333 (1984).

§ 8.3

1. See Section of Administrative Law and Regulatory Practice of the American Bar Association, A Blackletter Statement of Federal Administrative Law 29 (2004).

§ 8.4   Judicial Review of Agency Findings of Fact

The typical enabling act authorizes agencies to regulate only on the basis of particular factual circumstances. For example, the Occupational Safety and Health Act of 1970 authorized the Department of Labor to issue rules that were "reasonably necessary or appropriate" to provide a "safe and healthful" workplace. Before the Labor Department could issue such a rule, it had to make factual findings regarding current working conditions to determine whether the conditions were unsafe.[1] The Federal Highway Act of 1968 authorized the Department of Transportation to fund the construction of a highway through parkland only if there was "no feasible or prudent alternative [route]" and the highway plan "minimize[d] harm to [the] park." The Transportation Department had to make factual findings to make those determinations.[2] All enabling acts place factual limits on administrative authority. When an agency acts on the basis of an incorrect understanding of the relevant facts, its action violates the statutory standards establishing its authority just as if the agency had misinterpreted those standards.[3]

Section 706 of the Administrative Procedure Act provides two standards for courts reviewing factual determinations by administrative agencies. Section 706(2)(E) requires reviewing courts to invalidate factual findings by agencies in formal proceedings if they are "unsupported by substantial evidence." Section 706 does not explicitly provide a standard of review for an agency's factual determinations in informal proceedings. For that reason, the general "catchall" provision of section 706(2)(A) applies, requiring courts to invalidate factual findings if they are "arbitrary, capricious, an abuse of discretion, or otherwise not in accordance with law."[4]

Both the substantial evidence standard and the arbitrary-or-capricious standard operate on the premise that agencies are the factfinder in administrative proceedings, not the courts. Congress and the courts have long regarded the task of factfinding to be part of an agency's responsibility to administer regulatory programs. Moreover, the specialization and expertise of administrative agencies often give them an advantage over courts in factfinding, especially with respect to scientifically or technologically sophisti-

---

§ 8.4

1. See Industrial Union Department, AFL–CIO v. American Petroleum Institute, 448 U.S. 607, 642 (1980).

2. See Citizens to Preserve Overton Park, Inc. v. Volpe, 401 U.S. 402, 416 (1971).

3. ICC v. Louisville and Nashville Railroad Co., 227 U.S. 88, 92 (1913).

4. See American Paper Institute, Inc. v. American Electric Power Service Corp., 461 U.S. 402, 412 n.7 (1983); Association of Data Processing Service Organizations, Inc. v. Board of Governors of Federal Reserve System, 745 F.2d 677, 683 (D.C.Cir. 1984).

cated matters.[5] The question for the court on judicial review of administrative factfinding, then, is not whether the court agrees or disagrees with an agency's determinations. Courts do not retry administrative matters. Their job is simply to ensure that the agency has handled its factfinding role responsibly.

(a) Formal Proceedings

Section 706(2)(E) of the Administrative Procedure Act requires reviewing courts to invalidate factual findings by agencies in formal proceedings if they are "unsupported by substantial evidence." The "substantial evidence" standard predates the APA. Congress had incorporated it in a variety of early enabling acts, and when Congress had failed to prescribe a standard of judicial review for administrative factual determinations, the Supreme Court sometimes had adopted the substantial evidence standard on its own.[6] Yet reviewing courts had experienced difficulty translating the substantial evidence standard into a workable legal test until, in 1938, the Supreme Court finally defined it to mean "such relevant evidence as a reasonable mind might accept as adequate to support a conclusion."[7] As so formulated, the substantial evidence standard resembled the standard that courts traditionally had used when reviewing jury findings.

In the leading case of *Universal Camera Corp. v. National Labor Relations Board,*[8] the Supreme Court interpreted Congress's retention of the "familiar" substantial evidence standard in section 706(2)(E) as a signal that the APA had created no "drastic" revision of the scope of judicial review of administrative factual findings. Yet the Court found in the legislative history of the APA an unmistakable legislative intention that reviewing courts "assume more responsibility for the reasonableness and fairness" of administrative findings than some courts had before the APA. The justices in *Universal Camera* attempted to honor the subtle legislative message that reviewing courts invigorate their scrutiny of administrative factual findings within the preexisting substantial evidence standard. They ruled that administrative factual findings, though "entitled to respect, . . . must nonetheless be set aside when the [administrative] record . . . clearly precludes the [agency's] decision from being justified by a fair estimate of the worth of the testimony of witnesses or its informed judgment on matters within

5. Dickinson v. Zurko, 527 U.S. 150, 160–61 (1999).

6. See *id.* at 157 (1999); ICC v. Union Pacific Railroad Co., 222 U.S. 541, 548 (1912); E. Blythe Stason, *"Substantial Evidence" in Administrative Law,* 89 U. PA. L. REV. 1026, 1026–29 (1941); Robert L. Stern, *Review of Findings of*

Administrators, Judges and Juries: A Comparative Analysis, 58 HARV. L. REV. 70, 75–76 (1944).

7. Consolidated Edison Co. v. NLRB, 305 U.S. 197, 229 (1938).

8. 340 U.S. 474 (1951).

its special competence or both." In making this determination, the Court in *Universal Camera* stressed, a reviewing court must consider the "whole record," as section 706 of the APA instructs. This whole record requirement means that in evaluating the substantiality of the evidence supporting an agency's findings of fact, the reviewing court "must take into account whatever in the record fairly detracts from [the] weight" of those findings.[9]

Reviewing courts have continued to give the substantial evidence standard of section 706(2)(E) its traditional meaning. They uphold agency findings of fact if they determine that the evidence in the administrative record "*could* satisfy a reasonable factfinder."[10] This reasonableness review maintains the tradition of judicial deference toward administrative factfinding. At the same time, reasonableness review has an accordion-like quality that offers reviewing courts sufficient flexibility to ensure, in the language of *Universal Camera*, "the reasonableness and fairness" of administrative findings.[11]

A reviewing court may be expected to intensify its reasonableness review when the factual findings of the administrative law judge are overturned during the administrative appeals process (see § 5.5). This is especially the case when the findings turn on the credibility of witnesses that the ALJ had observed during the hearing.[12] The ALJ's findings are part of the administrative record of the agency's decision (APA § 557(c)), and thus they weigh against any contrary findings by the agency.[13] An agency must provide a reasoned explanation of why it disregarded an ALJ's findings.[14]

As the courts' insistence on a reasoned explanation for an agency's departure from the factual findings of an ALJ demon-

9. See *id*. at 487–90; see *Attorney General's Manual on the Administrative Procedure Act* 110 (1947), reprinted in WILLIAM F. FUNK, et al., FEDERAL ADMINISTRATIVE PROCEDURE SOURCEBOOK 33–171 (3d ed. 2000).

10. Allentown Mack Sales and Service, Inc. v. NLRB, 522 U.S. 359, 377 (1998); see *Dickinson*, 527 U.S. at 162. The Supreme Court regards the reasonableness review of the substantial evidence standard as more deferential to administrative factual findings than the "clearly erroneous" standard that federal appellate courts apply to a district judge's findings. *Dickinson*, 527 U.S. at 162. The Supreme Court has defined the clearly erroneous standard as asking whether an appellate court has a "definite and firm conviction" that a trial judge's factual finding is mistaken. United States v. United States Gypsum Co., 333 U.S. 364, 395 (1948).

11. *Universal Camera*, 340 U.S. at 490.

12. *Id*. at 496; see *Attorney General's Manual, supra* note 9, at 84; see, e.g., Penasquitos Village, Inc. v. NLRB, 565 F.2d 1074, 1078–80 (9th Cir. 1977).

13. See *Universal Camera*, 340 U.S. at 492–97.

14. See Patricia M. Wald, *Some Thoughts on Beginnings and Ends: Court of Appeals Review of Administrative Law Judges' Findings and Opinions*, 67 WASH. U.L.Q. 661, 666 (1989); see, e.g., ITT Continental Baking Co. v. FTC, 532 F.2d 207, 219 (2d Cir. 1976).

strates, the traditional translation of the substantial evidence standard into a reasonableness requirement prescribes a norm of administrative decisionmaking as well as a benchmark for judicial review. Administrative factfinding must be reasoned in order to be reasonable. Congress wrote the Administrative Procedure Act to ensure that agency action affecting individual rights be the product of "reasoned decisionmaking," and not merely the arbitrary exercise of governmental power.[15] As one of the most thoughtful commentators on the subject of judicial review of agency action explained, the substantial evidence standard tests not only whether "there is record evidence which provides a rational or logical basis" for an administrative finding, but also whether an agency's findings are "the product of reasoning from evidence."[16]

(b) Informal Proceedings

The traditional understanding holds that the arbitrary-or-capricious standard that section 706(2)(A) of the Administrative Procedure Act provides for judicial review of administrative factual determinations in informal proceedings is "more lenient" than the substantial evidence review prescribed by section 706(2)(E) for agency findings of fact in formal proceedings.[17] The original intention of the Congress that adopted the APA is obscure on this point, however. As introduced in the Senate, the APA would have required a trial de novo in district courts to determine the "relevant facts" when reviewing agency action "in all cases in which adjudications are not required by statute to be made upon agency hearing."[18] The thought behind this original provision seems clear. In formal adjudicatory proceedings, an agency makes findings of the relevant facts from the evidentiary record of a trial-type hearing. The losing party is not entitled to a second trial in the reviewing court, and the court reviews the agency's findings deferentially according to the substantial evidence standard. But in informal adjudication, where the agency is not required to hold a trial-type hearing, this original provision would have offered losing parties their first opportunity to prove their case in the district court reviewing the agency action. Informal rulemaking, which was not a common regulatory practice when Congress drafted the APA, seems to have been off the legislative radar.

---

15. *Allentown Mack*, 522 U.S. at 374.

16. Louis L. Jaffe, Judicial Control of Administrative Action 601 (1965).

17. American Paper Institute, Inc. v. American Electric Power Service Corp., 461 U.S. 402, 412 n.7 (1983); see Abbott Laboratories v. Gardner, 387 U.S. 136, 143 (1967) (substantial evidence standard affords "considerably more general ous judicial review" than does the arbitrary-or-capricious test).

18. See *Attorney General's Manual on the Administrative Procedure Act* 109 (1947), reprinted in William F. Funk, et al., Federal Administrative Procedure Sourcebook 33–171 (3d ed. 2000).

Although the provision for de novo judicial review of administrative factual determinations in informal adjudicatory proceedings was dropped in committee, the *Attorney General's Manual* reports "repeated statements" in the legislative history that the APA contemplated such review.[19] But in the end, this was not what the APA provided. Section 706(2)(F) limits trial de novo of administrative factual determinations on judicial review "to the extent that the facts are subject to trial de novo by the reviewing court." This occurs when agency action is challenged on constitutional grounds. It also occurs when a statute requires courts to review agency action on the basis of the court's independent factfinding. An example of such a statute is the Freedom of Information Act (5 U.S.C. § 552), which contemplates trial de novo in a district court when reviewing an agency's denial of a request for records. De novo judicial review of agency factfinding in contemporary administrative law otherwise is rare.

The traditional understanding that the APA provides for less demanding review of administrative factfinding in informal proceedings than in formal proceedings turns the original position of those who drafted the statute on its head. Still, subjecting agency factfinding in informal proceedings and in formal proceedings to different standards of review respects Congress's decision in section 706(2)(E) to limit the substantial evidence standard to formal proceedings. And lowering the standard of review for informal proceedings may follow from Congress's decisions to designate a specific standard for formal proceedings ("substantial evidence") and to consign agency factfinding in informal proceedings to the general, catchall, arbitrary-or-capricious standard of section 706(2)(A).

Contrary to the initial view of the APA's drafters, the informality of an administrative proceeding may argue for a lesser standard of judicial review of agency factfinding as well. The APA requires agencies in formal proceedings to make specific findings of fact based solely on an evidentiary record generated by an administrative trial-type hearing. Tasking a reviewing court to ensure that an agency's findings have a reasonable basis in that evidentiary record helps to ensure that the agency discharged that statutory obligation. Informal agency action is not "on the record" in that formal sense. The administrative record of informal agency action often lacks the tidiness of formal findings of fact and a discrete evidentiary record (see § 8.2). Moreover, an agency's factual determinations in informal proceedings, especially rulemaking, may be seamlessly interwoven with administrative policy judgments guiding the challenged action. The fluid structure of informal agency decisionmak-

19. *Id.*

ing, and the resulting amorphousness of the administrative record, may justify courts in lowering their expectations when reviewing the evidentiary support of the factual determinations that underlie informal agency action.

Justice Antonin Scalia, while still a member of the D.C. Circuit, challenged the conventional wisdom that substantial evidence review of factual findings in formal administrative proceedings is more demanding than arbitrary-or-capricious review of such findings in informal proceedings. In *Association of Data Processing Service Organizations, Inc. v. Board of Governors of Federal Reserve System*,[20] Justice Scalia, writing for the court of appeals, ruled that "in their application to the requirement of factual support the substantial evidence test and the arbitrary or capricious test are one and the same." In Justice Scalia's rendering, the substantial evidence standard applicable to formal administrative proceedings is "only a specific application" of the arbitrary-or-capricious standard that applies generally to all administrative proceedings.[21]

According to Justice Scalia's opinion for the D.C. Circuit in *Data Processing*, the difference between the substantial evidence standard and the arbitrary-or-capricious standard does not lie in the degree of deference that reviewing courts owe to administrative factual findings. Both standards require reasonableness review. The difference between the two standards lies in the nature of the record that the court reviews for evidentiary support of the agency's findings. In a formal proceeding governed by the substantial evidence standard, evidentiary support of administrative factual findings must be present in the formal hearing record. In an informal proceeding governed by the arbitrary-or-capricious standard, evidentiary support may appear anywhere in the information that agency decisionmakers consulted when making their decision.[22]

There is much to be said for Justice Scalia's equation of the substantial evidence and arbitrary-or-capricious standards of judicial review of agency factfinding. Indeed, before the APA some reviewing courts related substantial evidence review to the more established arbitrary-or-capricious standard.[23] The court's role when reviewing administrative factual determinations in informal proceedings is no different than its role when reviewing administrative factual determinations in formal proceedings. In each instance, the reviewing court must determine "whether the [administrative] record supports whatever factual conclusions underlie the [agency action]."[24] Should reviewing courts be any less concerned with the

---

20.   745 F.2d 677 (D.C.Cir. 1984).

21.   *Id.* at 683.

22.   *Id.* at 683–84.

23.   See Stason, *Substantial Evidence, supra* note 6, at 1026.

24.   See McGregor Printing Corp. v. Kemp, 20 F.3d 1188, 1194 (D.C.Cir. 1994).

soundness of administrative factual determinations in informal proceedings than with the soundness of such determinations in formal proceedings, as the traditional understanding would have it? The APA requires that agencies engage in reasoned decisionmaking in informal as well as in formal proceedings. In each case, if an agency gets the relevant facts wrong, its decision likely will be mistaken as well. And while section 706 of the Administrative Procedure Act uses different language to describe the standards of review of factual determinations in formal and in informal proceedings, once the substantial evidence standard is translated into reasonableness review, may a lesser standard plausibly be ascribed to arbitrary-or-capricious review?[25] It is difficult to imagine a judicial decision upholding an unreasonable administrative factual finding because it is not arbitrary or capricious. As one reviewing court explained, an administrative finding that is not arbitrary or capricious "must necessarily be supported by the evidence in the record."[26]

Justice Scalia's approach for the D.C. Circuit in *Data Processing* to arbitrary-or-capricious review of factual findings in informal proceedings has attracted a significant following,[27] but some courts of appeals have continued to follow the traditional understanding of arbitrary-or-capricious review as more deferential than substantial evidence review.[28] The Supreme Court has noted Justice Scalia's equation of the two standards in *Data Processing*, without either approving or disapproving the equation.[29] The judicial disagreement over the relative strengths of substantial evidence review and arbitrary-or-capricious review becomes most acute in cases involving enabling acts that require courts to use the substantial evidence standard when reviewing administrative factual determinations in an informal proceeding.[30] (Section 559 of the Administrative Procedure Act provides that statutes enacted after the APA may supersede or modify provisions of the act if they do so expressly.) Some

---

25. See *Data Processing*, 745 F.2d at 683–84.

26. Central States Enterprises, Inc. v. ICC, 780 F.2d 664, 674 n.10 (7th Cir. 1985).

27. See, e.g., GTE South, Inc. v. Morrison, 199 F.3d 733, 745 n.5 (4th Cir. 1999) ("[w]ith respect to review of factfindings, there is no meaningful difference between [the arbitrary-or-capricious] standard and the substantial evidence standard"); *Central States Enterprises*, 780 F.2d at 674 n.10 ("the difference between the arbitrary and capricious standard of review and the substantial evidence standard of review is primarily a semantic distinction").

28. See, e.g., Corrosion Proof Fittings v. EPA, 947 F.2d 1201, 1213–14 (5th Cir. 1991).

29. Dickinson v. Zurko, 527 U.S. 150, 158 (1999). The Second Circuit similarly noted the *Data Processing* position without deciding whether to accept it. Browning–Ferris Industries of South Jersey, Inc. v. Muszynski, 899 F.2d 151, 194 (2d Cir. 1990).

30. For a partial listing of such enabling acts, see Matthew J. McGrath, Note, *Convergence of the Substantial Evidence and Arbitrary and Capricious Standards of Review During Informal Rulemaking*, 54 Geo. Wash. L. Rev. 541, 542 n.5 (1986).

reviewing courts have interpreted these substantial evidence review provisions to require them to "take a harder look" at the evidentiary support for administrative factual determinations than they ordinarily would when applying the arbitrary-or-capricious standard.[31] Other courts have expressed some bewilderment over how to "apply the substantial evidence standard of review to an informal [proceeding] during which the agency decisionmaker receives information through nonadversary proceedings and written submissions, rather than formal, trial-type hearings."[32] Amidst this confusion, Justice Scalia in *Data Processing* advised against reading an enabling act prescribing substantial evidence review for administrative factfinding in an informal proceeding to heighten the level of review unless Congress had made that intention clear.[33]

The courts of appeals that continue to find substantial evidence review to be more rigorous than arbitrary-or-capricious review do not cite specific differences between the two standards. These courts seem to believe that section 706's provision of two standards of judicial review for administrative factual determinations, in the language of *Universal Camera*, expresses a "mood [that] must be respected," even though it "cannot be imprisoned within any form of words."[34] Reasonableness review has an accordion-like quality, which courts can expand or contract as they deem appropriate. Reviewing courts that sense a congressional "mood" that the arbitrary-or-capricious standard is less demanding than the substantial evidence standard may simply relax their reasonableness review when evaluating administrative factual determinations in informal proceedings.[35]

§ 8.5   Judicial Review of Agencies' Interpretations of Their Enabling Acts

All enabling acts contain at least some standard marking the boundaries of the agency's decisionmaking authority. (A standardless delegation of administrative power violates the nondelegation doctrine (see § 2.3(a)).) Accordingly, before an agency takes any action—rulemaking or adjudication, formal or informal—administrators must interpret the relevant statutory standards to deter-

---

31. Aqua Slide 'N' Dive Corp. v. CPSC, 569 F.2d 831, 837 (5th Cir.1978); see AFL–CIO v. OSHA, 965 F.2d 962, 970 (11th Cir. 1992); *Corrosion Proof Fittings,* 947 F.2d at 1213–14.

32. Aircraft Owners & Pilots Ass'n v. FAA, 600 F.2d 965, 969 (D.C.Cir. 1979); see, also Industrial Union Dep't, AFL–CIO v. Hodgson, 499 F.2d 467, 469–70 (D.C.Cir. 1974) (describing the "anomaly" of exercising substantial evi-

dence review over administrative factfinding in an informal proceeding).

33. *Data Processing,* 745 F.2d at 686.

34. *Universal Camera,* 340 U.S. at 487, 489.

35. See, e.g,. *AFL-CIO,* 965 F.2d at 970; *Corrosion Proof Fittings,* 947 F.2d at 1213–14; *Aqua Slide 'N' Dive,* 569 F.2d at 837.

mine whether the contemplated action is within the scope of the agency's authority. On judicial review, should the court independently interpret the statutory standards governing the agency's authority or should the court defer to the agency's interpretation, as it does to administrative factual determinations? This basic question is perhaps the most vexing in all of administrative law.

While courts have had no difficulty accepting agencies as the primary factfinders in administrative proceedings, judges have manifested considerable "ambivalence" regarding their responsibility to review agency interpretations of their enabling acts.[1] Two opposing sentiments have competed for supremacy. On one hand, American judicial tradition at least since *Marbury v. Madison* has held, "It is emphatically the province and duty of the judicial department to say what the law is."[2] This tradition dictates independent judicial review of administrative interpretations. Section 706 of the Administrative Procedure Act appears to incorporate the *Marbury* tradition by providing that "the reviewing court shall decide all relevant questions of law." On the other hand, reviewing courts at times have sensed that the *Marbury* tradition may not apply fully to the administrative process. These courts have reasoned that because agencies have the responsibility to administer their enabling acts, they also should have the primary responsibility of interpreting these acts. Indeed, *Marbury*'s author, Chief Justice John Marshall, was willing to respect an agency's "uniform construction" of "doubtful" statutory provisions.[3] Agencies know better than courts how to make a statutory program work, this reasoning goes, and agencies therefore are in a better position than courts to interpret their enabling acts. This reasoning, of course, dictates deferential judicial review of administrative interpretations.

The uncertainty created by the opposing sentiments favoring independent and deferential judicial review of an agency's interpretations of its enabling act has been exacerbated by a lack of precision in discussing this subject. Some have framed the issue as defining the scope of judicial review on questions of law. But that is too broad a frame. It is generally accepted that courts should independently review administrative interpretations of constitutional provisions, statutes of general application, and judicial precedent. The only questions of law on which reviewing courts consider

---

§ 8.5

1. See Pittston Stevedoring Corp. v. Dellaventura, 544 F.2d 35, 49 n.15 (2d Cir. 1976), affirmed sub nom., Northeast Marine Terminal Co. v. Caputo, 432 U.S. 249 (1977).

2. 5 U.S. (1 Cranch) 137, 177 (1803).

3. See United States v. Vowell, 9 U.S. (5 Cranch) 368, 372 (1810).

deferring involve interpretation of the enabling acts and regulations that agencies administer.

Within that narrowed frame, a further distinction must be made. Agencies interpret their enabling acts in two distinct ways before reaching a decision. They must first define the statutory standards that govern their action. Reviewing courts have described this first type of interpretation as raising a "naked"[4] or "pure"[5] question of statutory interpretation because the question of law is unadorned by the specific facts of any particular case. In reaching their ultimate decision, an agency also must apply the statutory standards, as defined, to the facts of the particular proceeding. Reviewing courts have described this second type of administrative interpretation as raising a "mixed" question of law and fact. The second type of administrative interpretation is the subject of § 8.7. This section examines only the scope of judicial review of an agency's pure interpretation of its enabling act.

(a) The Traditional Doctrine: *Skidmore* Deference

The judiciary's traditional approach to reviewing agency's interpretations of its enabling act was characterized by a subtle, and at times inconsistent, effort by courts to balance the sentiments of judicial independence and deference. The justices succinctly described this balancing act in the leading case of *National Labor Relations Board v. Hearst Publications, Inc.*,[6] which the Court decided just two years before Congress adopted the Administrative Procedure Act. In *Hearst*, the justices assigned to reviewing courts the responsibility of resolving "questions of statutory interpretation." But when interpreting enabling acts, the justices instructed courts to give "appropriate weight to the judgment of those whose special duty is to administer the questioned statute."[7]

This nuanced incorporation of judicial deference within an overall framework of judicial independence has come to be known as *Skidmore* deference, so named because this traditional approach to administrative statutory interpretations received its best exposition in *Skidmore v. Swift & Co.*[8] The Court in *Skidmore* underscored that it "has long given considerable and in some cases decisive weight" to an agency's interpretation of its enabling act. Such administrative interpretations are "entitled to respect," the Court explained, because agencies interpret their enabling acts pursuant to "official duty" and based on "specialized expertise."[9]

---

4. See, e.g., Packard Motor Car Co. v. NLRB, 330 U.S. 485, 493 (1947).

5. See, e.g., N.L.R.B. v. United Food & Commercial Workers Union, Local 23, AFL–CIO, 484 U.S. 112, 123 (1987).

6. 322 U.S. 111 (1944).

7. *Id.* at 130–31.

8. 323 U.S. 134 (1944).

9. *Id.* at 139–40.

The *Skidmore* Court's location of statutory interpretation within the "official duty" of agencies honored the administrative authority that Congress has entrusted to agencies. The justices' nod toward the "specialized expertise" of agencies credited not only the technological and scientific knowledge essential for some administrative decisions, but also the accumulated experience that all agencies develop through their day-to-day administration of a statutory program.

The justices in *Skidmore* did not accept an agency's interpretations of its enabling act as "controlling upon the courts by reason of their authority." Rather, they regarded these administrative interpretations as "a body of experience and informed judgment to which courts and litigants may properly resort for guidance." In the end, *Skidmore* provided, the "weight" of any particular administrative interpretation would vary from case to case, depending on "the thoroughness evident in [the agency's] consideration, the validity of its reasoning, its consistency with earlier and later pronouncements, and all those factors which give it power to persuade, if lacking power to control."[10]

The starting point for *Skidmore* deference, paradoxically, is judicial independence. In *Skidmore* deference, the balance of interpretive power was with the courts, and not with the agencies. Reviewing courts remained the "final authorities on issues of statutory construction,"[11] as *Marbury* and section 706 of the Administrative Procedure Act would have it. *Skidmore* deference was a matter of prudence rather than of right. It was discretionary, not mandatory.[12]

A reviewing court, as the authoritative interpreter of administrative enabling acts, was free to look at all of the traditional elements of statutory interpretation in its "search for legislative intention."[13] These familiar elements included a careful parsing of the statutory text, a review of the legislative history, and an occasional reference to the traditional canons of statutory interpretation. In effect, *Skidmore* deference added another element to a reviewing court's interpretation of enabling acts—the agency's interpretation of the relevant statutory provisions.[14] *Skidmore* deference never pressured reviewing courts to accept administrative interpretations that conflicted with their understanding of statuto-

---

10. *Id*. at 140.

11. Volkswagenwerk v. Aktiengesellschaft v. FMC, 390 U.S. 261, 272 (1968).

12. See BATF v. FLRA, 464 U.S. 89, 98 n.8 (1983).

13. See Robert L. Stern, *Review of Findings of Administrators, Judges and*

Juries: A Comparative Analysis, 58 Harv. L. Rev. 70, 106–09 (1944).

14. See Zuber v. Allen, 396 U.S. 168, 192 (1969) (administrative interpretation was "only one input in the interpretational equation").

ry language or congressional purpose.[15] But if the court's review of the statutory materials suggested that an agency's interpretation was permissible, *Skidmore* encouraged the court to consider accepting the agency's interpretation as correct, or at least, as acceptable—that is, to defer.

A reviewing court's decision on whether, in the absence of clear direction from Congress, to accept an agency's interpretation of its enabling act or to soldier on and reach its own judgment of the best interpretation of the statute depended on the "weight" that the court assigned to the administrative interpretation "in a particular case." That weight, in turn, depended on the court's evaluation of "all those factors" giving the agency's interpretation "power to persuade."[16] The court's assessment of the quality of the agency's reasoning often was the most important factor in calibrating the weight of an administrative interpretation. A well reasoned interpretation might convince a reviewing court that the agency's reading was correct. Even if a court remained unconvinced, it still might be comforted that the agency had carefully reviewed the statutory question, and therefore be more inclined to defer to the agency as the institution with primary authority to administer the statute in question.[17]

Courts exercising *Skidmore* deference, however, considered a wide variety of factors when measuring the weight of an administrative interpretation.[18] For example, reviewing courts traditionally were more inclined to defer to statutory interpretations that an agency consistently had followed. Such a track record provided courts some assurance that the interpretation had been correct. Moreover, as with longstanding judicial precedent, reviewing courts were hesitant to disturb the settled expectations of interested parties that a longstanding administrative interpretation typically created. By contrast, reviewing courts were somewhat less likely to defer to statutory interpretation that an agency recently had adopted. An administrative interpretation reflecting a reversal of position typically encountered outright skepticism.

A reviewing court also was more likely to defer to an interpretation that an agency had adopted soon after enactment of the relevant statute, especially if the agency had been involved in the

15. See, e.g., SEC v. Sloan, 436 U.S. 103, 117–23 (1978); *Volkswagenwerk*, 390 U.S. at 272–78.

16. *Skidmore*, 323 U.S. at 140.

17. See Thomas W. Merrill, *Judicial Deference to Executive Precedent*, 101 YALE L.J. 969, 973–74 (1992).

18. This discussion of the factors traditionally influencing the weight of

an administrative interpretation under *Skidmore* deference is drawn from Stephen Breyer, *Judicial Review of Questions of Law and Policy*, 38 ADMIN. L. REV. 363, 365–72 (1986); Merrill, *Judicial Deference*, supra note 17, at 972–75; David R. Woodward & Ronald M. Levin, *In Defense of Deference: Judicial Review of Agency Action*, 31 ADMIN. L. REV. 329, 333–35 (1979).

legislative drafting process. Similarly, courts looked to whether Congress had explicitly or implicitly endorsed a contested administrative interpretation. Congressional approval of an administrative interpretation might be shown by the legislators' rejection of a bill to overturn the interpretation or by their reenactment of the relevant statute in a manner signaling their comfort with the administrative interpretation.

And finally, reviewing courts traditionally evaluated the relative competencies of judges and agencies to interpret the relevant statutory provision. A court was more likely to defer when an interpretation called for technical or scientific expertise beyond the skill sets of most federal judges. This was especially the case when Congress had drafted the statutory language in broad terms with the apparent intent of creating administrative flexibility. Reviewing courts were more likely to take the interpretive lead when the relevant statutory provision might be understood in the light of judicial precedent or of constitutional or common law principles. And some reviewing courts found it essential to their review function to assume primary responsibility for tying down statutory provisions defining the central mission of an agency, while leaving minor interpretive issues to the agency.

To summarize, the balance of interpretive power over an agency's enabling act traditionally lay with reviewing courts. But when a court regarded an enabling act as unclear, it would consider how much weight, if any, to accord the particular administrative interpretation at issue. The result of *Skidmore* deference was to create a sliding scale of judicial deference,[19] depending on the court's assessment of the factors contributing to or detracting from the persuasiveness of the agency's interpretation. As two careful commentators nicely put it, reviewing courts deployed *Skidmore* deference "as the most constructive and prudent way to *reach a correct* decision about the meaning of a disputed statutory term."[20]

(b) The *Chevron* Revolution

The Supreme Court's decision in *Chevron U.S.A., Inc. v. National Resources Defense Council, Inc.*[21] built upon, as it broke with, the *Skidmore* deference that reviewing courts traditionally had accorded to an agency's interpretations of its enabling act. The result was a revolution in scope-of-review doctrine.[22] A leading

19. See Merrill, *Judicial Deference, supra* note 17, at 972.

20. See Woodward & Levin, *Defense of Deference, supra* note 18, at 336.

21. 467 U.S. 837 (1984).

22. It is not clear whether the *Chevron* Court intended the revolution it in-

stigated, however. See Thomas W. Merrill & Kristin E. Hickman, Chevron's *Domain,* 89 Geo. L.J. 833, 838 (2001); Cass R. Sunstein, Chevron's *Step Zero,* 92 Va. L. Rev. 187, 188 & n.2 (2006).

commentator has aptly described *Chevron* as the Supreme Court's "most important decision about the most important issue in modern administrative law—the allocation of power between courts and agencies 'to say what the law is.' "[23]

Chevron involved an ordinary administrative law problem. Congress had amended the Clean Air Act to address the failure of a number of states to satisfy the air-quality standards established by the act. The Clean Air Act Amendments imposed strict permitting requirements on those who desired to build or to modify a "major stationary source" of air pollution in the so-called "non-attainment states." Prodded by the D.C. Circuit, the Environmental Protection Agency issued a rule that defined "stationary source" as meaning the construction or installation of any new or modified piece of equipment that emitted air pollutants. EPA repealed that rule the following year, replacing it with a new rule adopting a plant-wide definition of "stationary source." The rule change was important because the new definition allowed someone who built or modified equipment in a plant to avoid the permitting process by offsetting any increase in pollution caused by the equipment with reductions of emissions from elsewhere within the plant. As framed by the justices in *Chevron*, EPA's rule change presented a "naked question of law"[24]—whether EPA's plant-wide definition of "stationary source" as used in the Clean Air Act Amendments was valid.[25]

The D.C. Circuit had addressed that question in line with the traditional *Skidmore* approach (see § 8.5(a)). The court of appeals had acknowledged that Congress had not defined the term "stationary source," but it nevertheless had concluded that EPA's plant-wide definition was inconsistent with the legislative purpose underlying the Clean Air Act Amendments. Congress had designed the amendments to improve rather than to maintain the substandard air quality in non-attainment states. The court of appeals had invalidated the new EPA rule because the offsetting feature exempted from the permitting process the construction of equipment that would maintain rather than improve air quality in non-attainment states.[26]

The Supreme Court reversed the D.C. Circuit's ruling in *Chevron*, chastising the lower court (as it had in *Vermont Yankee* (see § 6.2)) for over-reaching its review powers. According to the justices, the court of appeals had committed a "basic legal error" when it had decided that a plant-wide definition of the term

---

23. Thomas W. Merrill, *The* Mead *Doctrine: Rules and Standards, Meta–Rules and Meta–Standards*, 54 ADMIN. L. REV. 807, 809 (2002).

24. See Packard Motor Car Co. v. NLRB, 330 U.S. 485, 493 (1947).

25. See *Chevron*, 467 U.S. at 839–40.

26. See NRDC v. Gorsuch, 685 F.2d 718, 720 & n.6, 725–28 (D.C. Cir. 1982).

"stationary source" was inconsistent with Congress's purpose to improve air quality. Because Congress had not "commanded" a specific definition of "stationary source," the Supreme Court held, the court of appeals had been obligated to defer to EPA's new rule as "a reasonable construction of the statutory term." It was for the agency to decide whether an equipment-specific or a plant-wide definition of "stationary source" better served the congressional scheme.[27]

In the process of overturning the D.C. Circuit's ruling, the *Chevron* Court created a new two-step analysis that redefined the scope of judicial review of an "an agency's construction of the statute which it administers." First, a reviewing court must determine whether "Congress has directly spoken to the precise question at issue." If so, "that is the end of the matter." Agencies must comply with the "unambiguously expressed intent of Congress." But if, as is often the case, "the statute is silent or ambiguous with respect to the specific issue," the reviewing court moves to the second step of the analysis. Here, "the question for the court is whether the agency's [interpretation] is based on a permissible construction of the statute." A reviewing court need not agree with an administrative interpretation to find it "permissible." The agency's interpretation need only be "reasonable."[28]

The *Chevron* Two Step promised to simplify traditional *Skidmore* deference by limiting the interpretative power of reviewing courts. *Chevron*, like *Skidmore*, begins with a reviewing court exercising its traditional role as "the final authority on issues of statutory construction."[29] But *Chevron*'s conception of this judicial role is far narrower than *Skidmore*'s. Under *Skidmore*, reviewing courts, like the D.C. Circuit in *Chevron*, were free to reach an independent interpretation of an administrative enabling act even where, in *Chevron*'s language, the statute was "silent or ambiguous with respect to the specific issue." Under *Chevron*'s Step One, the independent interpretive authority of a reviewing court is limited to determining whether the legislative materials provide a clear answer to the specific statutory issue. If the court finds that Congress has not clearly answered the relevant question, *Chevron*'s Step Two requires reviewing courts to defer to any reasonable administrative interpretation. This mandatory, across-the-board deference rule is in stark contrast to the traditional *Skidmore* approach, where reviewing courts had decided on an ad hoc basis whether (and how much) to defer to a particular administrative interpretation based

---

27. See *Chevron*, 467 U.S. at 840–45.

28. See *id.* An agency's interpretation of its enabling act need not be explicit to receive *Chevron* deference, at least where the interpretation is a "necessary presupposition" of the agency's decision. National Railroad Passenger Corp. v. Boston & Maine Corp., 503 U.S. 407, 419–20 (1992).

29. *Chevron*, 467 U.S. at 843 n.9.

on a variety of factors. Under *Chevron*, an interpretive gap in an enabling act, without more, entitles the agency possessing administrative authority to deference. Under *Skidmore*, an agency had to earn deference by convincing a reviewing court of the reliability of its interpretive choices. As one commentator put it, "*Chevron* transformed a regime that allowed courts to give agencies deference along a sliding scale into a regime with an on/off switch."[30]

Chevron also reversed traditional scope-of-review doctrine by making agencies rather than courts, as the justices later put it, "the authoritative interpreter (within the limits of reason)" of ambiguous provisions in the statutes they administer.[31] *Chevron* thus has been described as a "counter-*Marbury* for the administrative state."[32] The Court justified *Chevron*'s transfer of power by construing silence or ambiguity in an enabling act on a particular question as an implicit congressional delegation of interpretive authority to the agency rather than to a reviewing court.[33] This made sense to the justices because, as they saw it, the selection of the best interpretation of unclear provisions in administrative enabling acts was more a question of policy than of law. Enabling acts, the Court reminded, delegate "policy-making responsibilities" to agencies, not courts, because administrators, unlike judges, are "experts in the field" and are more politically accountable for their decisions.[34]

Chevron's revision of the traditional *Skidmore* regime was as controversial it was revolutionary. By transferring interpretative authority from reviewing courts to agencies, *Chevron* challenged the conventional understanding of the separation of powers, which assigns to the judiciary the role to "say what the law is."[35] *Chevron*'s role reversal also was in tension with section 706 of the Administrative Procedure Act, which instructs reviewing courts to "decide all relevant questions of law," including interpretation of "statutory provisions."[36] The Court in *Chevron* anticipated these

30. Merrill, *Judicial Deference, supra* note 17, at 977.

31. See National Cable & Telecommunications Ass'n v. Brand X Internet Services, 545 U.S. 967, 983 (2005).

32. Cass R. Sunstein, *Law and Administration After* Chevron, 90 COLUM. L. REV. 2071, 2075 (1990).

33. See *Chevron*, 467 U.S. at 843–44; see also FDA v. Brown & Williamson Tobacco Corp., 529 U.S. 120, 159 (2000) (*Chevron* deference "is premised on the theory that a statute's ambiguity constitutes an implicit delegation from Congress to the agency to fill in the statutory gap"); Pauley v. Bethenergy Mines, Inc., 501 U.S. 680, 696 (1991) (Con-

gress's "introduction of an interpretative gap" in a statute "delegates policy-making authority to an administrative agency").

34. See *Chevron*, 467 U.S. at 864–66; see also *Pauley*, 501 U.S. at 696 ("Judicial deference to an agency's interpretation of ambiguous provisions of the statutes it is authorized to implement reflects the sensitivity to the proper roles of the political and judicial branches.").

35. See Marbury v. Madison, 5 U.S. (1 Cranch) 137, 177 (1803).

36. For an elaboration of the apparent inconsistency between Chevron and section 706 of the APA, see John D.

criticisms by presuming that statutory ambiguity reflected a congressional intention to delegate interpretive authority to the agencies as part of their overall duty to administer the statute. If Congress had intended that agencies rather than courts take the lead in filling interpretive gaps in enabling acts, judicial deference to reasonable administrative interpretations would follow congressional will, as mandated by the separation-of-powers principle of legislative supremacy.[37]

Most observers, however, regard *Chevron*'s presumption that statutory ambiguities in enabling acts reflect a congressional intention to delegate interpretive authority to agencies as a "dubious fiction."[38] Before *Chevron*, of course, Congress had enacted enabling acts against the background of *Skidmore* deference, which had assigned courts, not agencies, primary responsibility for resolving statutory ambiguities. The *Chevron* Court itself underscored the fictional nature of its presumption of congressional intention when it exclaimed that the actual explanation for any particular interpretive gap in an enabling act was irrelevant.[39]

Yet many of *Chevron*'s proponents have argued that the two-step analysis furthers rather than undermines the separation of powers. These proponents rely on the *Chevron* Court's claim that the resolution of ambiguities in enabling acts involves questions of regulatory policy appropriate for agencies rather than questions of law for the courts.[40] They argue that *Chevron*'s Step One satisfies the injunction of *Marbury* and of the APA that courts take primary responsibility for interpreting the law. *Chevron*'s Step Two enforces the opposite side of the coin by reserving the primary policymaking authority for agencies. From this perspective, *Chevron* deference serves the separation of powers by preventing unelected and unaccountable judges from "infus[ing] their personal political philosophies in the Nation's policy making process."[41] *Chevron* reminds judges that they are not to "supervise" agencies as a superior would a subordinate. Rather, they only may review agency action at

Duffy, *Administrative Common Law in Judicial Review*, 77 TEX. L. REV. 113, 193–99 (1998).

37. See Henry P. Monaghan, *Marbury and the Administrative State*, 83 COLUM. L. REV. 1, 25–28 (1983).

38. Merrill, *Judicial Deference*, *supra* note 17, at 998 (1992). Even Justice Antonin Scalia, the staunchest champion of *Chevron* on the High Court, has conceded that the *Chevron* presumption is a fiction. See Antonin Scalia, *Judicial Deference to Administrative Interpretations of Law*, 1989 DUKE L.J. 511, 517.

39. *Chevron*, 467 U.S. at 865.

40. See, e.g., Richard J. Pierce, Jr., Chevron *and its Aftermath: Judicial Review of Agency Interpretations of Statutory Provisions*, 41 VAND. L. REV. 301, 304–05, 308 (1988); Kenneth W. Starr, *Judicial Review in the Post-*Chevron *Era*, 3 YALE J. ON REG. 283, 308–09 (1986).

41. Pierce, Chevron *and its Aftermath*, *supra* note 40, at 313. On the political accountability of administrative agencies, see Jerry L. Mashaw, *Prodelegation: Why Administrators Should Make Political Decisions*, 1 J. L. ECON. & ORG. 81 (1985).

a respectful distance measured by the separation between the distinctive domains of the Article II executive power and the Article III judicial power.[42]

Even accepting the inevitable mixing of legal and policy issues in the interpretation of ambiguous regulatory statutes, it remains uncertain whether the policy mission of agencies invariably makes them better equipped to fill interpretive gaps in their enabling acts. Administrators suffer from something of a conflict-of-interest when they interpret statutory limits on their authority. By disabling reviewing courts from taking the lead in resolving ambiguities concerning the statutory authority of agencies, *Chevron* removes a salutary check on the potential accumulation and abuse of administrative power. *Chevron* thus may threaten the separation of powers by tipping the balance of power in the administrative state dangerously toward the executive.[43]

(c) The *Chevron* Doctrine in Operation

Chevron fundamentally altered scope-of-review doctrine governing an agency's interpretations of its enabling act. When *Chevron* applies, reviewing courts no longer evaluate whether and how much to defer to an administrative interpretation according to the traditional *Skidmore* factors. They now dance the *Chevron* Two Step. It is not clear, however, whether *Chevron*, in operation, has delivered the revolutionary role reversal between courts and agencies that it had seemed to decree. Empirical studies of court decisions have disagreed over whether *Chevron* has contributed to a significant,[44] a minor,[45] or no[46] increase in judicial affirmance rates of agency action. Reviewing courts, led by the justices themselves, have used the two-step framework to invalidate a substantial minority of administrative interpretations. A study of courts of appeals decisions applying *Chevron* during 1995–1996 (just over ten years after the *Chevron* decision) found that the courts accepted 73% of the administrative interpretations they reviewed.[47] Although

---

42. See Starr, *Judicial Review, supra* note 40, at 307–09; see also *Pauley*, 501 U.S. at 696 ("Judicial deference to an agency's interpretation of ambiguous provisions of the statutes it is authorized to implement reflects the sensitivity to the proper roles of the political and judicial branches.").

43. See Cynthia R. Farina, *Statutory Interpretation and the Balance of Power in the Administrative State*, 89 COLUM. L. REV. 452, 499–526 (1989); Jonathan T. Molot, *The Judicial Perspective in the Administrative State: Reconciling Modern Doctrines of Deference with the Judiciary's Structural Role*, 53 STAN. L. REV. 1, 68–99 (2000).

44. Peter H. Schuck & E. Donald Elliott, *To the* Chevron *Station: An Empirical Study of Federal Administrative Law*, 1990 DUKE L.J. 984.

45. Linda R. Cohen & Matthew L. Spitzer, *Solving the* Chevron *Puzzle*, LAW & CONTEMP. PROBS., Spring 1994, at 65.

46. Sidney A. Shapiro & Richard E. Levy, *Judicial Incentives and Indeterminacy in Substantive Review of Administrative Decisions*, 44 DUKE L.J. 1051, 1070 (1995).

47. See Orin S. Kerr, *Shedding Light on* Chevron: *An Empirical Study of the* Chevron *Doctrine in the U.S.*

73% marks a healthy affirmance rate, the fact that reviewing courts reject over one in four administrative interpretations indicates that *Chevron* did not write agencies a blank check.

The potential for active judicial review of administrative interpretations after *Chevron* has been a surprising development to many observers. This activism also has undermined the apparent simplicity, predictability, and objectivity of the two-step framework. As it turned out, each step of *Chevron* analysis contained latent ambiguities. For example, when is a statute sufficiently clear to deny an agency interpretive discretion at Step One? Indeed, how should reviewing courts determine whether the relevant provision of a statute is clear or ambiguous? And what is the court's role when reviewing the reasonableness of an administrative interpretation at Step Two? Should a court's reasonableness review extend beyond the legislative materials to include the agency's reasoning process? And finally, perhaps the most difficult post-*Chevron* question has occurred at what has been called "Step Zero": when should *Chevron* apply?[48] Agencies interpret their enabling acts in a wide variety of contexts. Are there some settings in which administrative interpretations of ambiguous enabling acts do not merit *Chevron* deference? This section explores the ambiguities lurking in each step of the *Chevron* doctrine by evaluating how courts have applied *Chevron*.

Step One: Is the Relevant Statutory Provision Clear or Ambiguous? At the doctrinal level, *Chevron* Step One sharply limited the traditional scope of judicial review of administrative interpretations. Instead of embarking on a quest for the best interpretation of a contested statutory provision,[49] reviewing courts determine whether the provision is clear or ambiguous.

As described in *Chevron*, the first step of a court reviewing an agency's interpretation of its enabling act is to decide whether Congress has "unambiguously expressed [its] intent" on "the precise question at issue."[50] *Chevron* made clear the implications of the Step One determination. If there is no ambiguity, the reviewing court independently decides whether the administrative interpretation is consistent with the clear meaning of the statute.[51] If there is ambiguity, the court moves to Step Two and determines the reasonableness of the administrative interpretation.

Courts of Appeals, 15 YALE J. ON REG. 1, 30 (1998).

48. The term "step zero" was coined by Thomas W. Merrill and Kristin E. Hickman in Chevron's *Domain, supra* note 22.

49. See Pauley v. Bethenergy Mines, Inc., 501 U.S. 680, 702 (1991) (agency's

interpretation need not be "the best or most natural one").

50. *Chevron*, 467 U.S. at 842–43.

51. *Id.* at 843 n.9; see NLRB v. United Food & Commercial Workers Union, Local 23, AFL–CIO, 484 U.S. 112, 123 (1987).

The Court in *Chevron* did not define the meaning of "ambiguity" for purposes of Step One, but the justices later clarified that the key consideration is whether the contested provision has only one "plausible interpretation."[52] If so, it is unambiguous. A statutory term is ambiguous if it is "susceptible to more precise definition and open to varying constructions."[53]

By its terms, the Court's limitation of the *Chevron* Step One inquiry to the question whether a statutory provisions has only one "plausible interpretation" seemed to drastically limit the interpretative discretion of reviewing courts. Since *Chevron*, however, reviewing courts, with the Supreme Court in the lead, have continued their tradition of carefully interpreting enabling acts, as well as their penchant for critically evaluating administrative interpretations. This unanticipated judicial activism is the product of reviewing courts launching a wide-ranging inquiry in determining whether Congress has provided a clear answer to the statutory question before them. The Supreme Court has instructed reviewing courts at Step One not to interpret the relevant statutory provision "in isolation," because "[t]he meaning or ambiguity of certain words or phrases may only become evident when placed in context."[54] Reviewing courts thus examine contested statutory provisions in the light of the broader statutory and regulatory schemes in which they are situated.[55]

Reviewing courts also look at a wide range of evidence in determining whether the legislative intent underlying a contested provision is clear or ambiguous. The *Chevron* Court itself instructed reviewing courts to draw on all of the "traditional tools of statutory construction,"[56] and the *Chevron* opinion included a lengthy consideration of the legislative history of the Clean Air Act Amendments. Since *Chevron*, the justices have looked beyond the statute and its legislative history to the common usage,[57] dictionary definition,[58] and technical meaning[59] of contested statutory language, as well as

---

52. See Rapanos v. United States, ___ U.S. ___, 126 S.Ct. 2208, 2225 (2006).

53. Gonzales v. Oregon, 546 U.S. 243, 258 (2006).

54. FDA v. Brown & Williamson Tobacco Corp., 529 U.S. 120, 132 (2000).

55. See, e.g., Ragsdale v. Wolverine World Wide, Inc., 535 U.S. 81, 86 (2002); *Brown & Williamson*, 529 U.S. at 133; Maslin Industries, U.S., Inc. v. Primary Steel, Inc., 497 U.S. 116, 131 (1990).

56. *Chevron*, 467 U.S. at 843 n.9.

57. See, e.g., Verizon Communications, Inc. v. FCC, 535 U.S. 467, 498 (2002).

58. See, e.g., MCI Telecommunications Corp. v. American Telephone & Telegraph Co., 512 U.S. 218, 225–28 (1994). The Supreme Court's reliance on dictionary definitions to interpret contested statutory language has spiked in recent years, as at least some justices have eschewed legislative history in favor of a textualist approach to statutory interpretation. See Note, *Looking It Up: Dictionaries and Statutory Interpretation*, 107 HARV. L. REV. 1437 (1994).

59. See, e.g., *Verizon*, 535 U.S. at 498–99.

to traditional canons of statutory interpretation.[60] The Court also has interpreted enabling acts in the light of other legislation, "particularly where Congress has spoken subsequently and more specifically to the topic at hand."[61] Most strikingly, the justices even have considered the "economic and political magnitude" of the agency action at issue. When the magnitude of agency action is high, the justices may make the "common sense" judgment that Congress would not delegate administrative authority without doing so expressly.[62]

This eclectic approach to statutory interpretation at *Chevron* Step One has reintroduced a good measure of the analytical flexibility that had characterized the traditional *Skidmore* regime (see § 8.5(a)). In at least some Step One decisions, the justices seem to have enforced their sense of congressional intention where Congress had not spoken unambiguously to "the precise question at issue," as *Chevron* had required.[63] The Court's occasional reversion to its traditional ways has opened the justices to the charge that they have manipulated the traditional tools of statutory interpretation to manufacture statutory clarity in order to limit the scope of administrative authority as they deem appropriate.[64]

Step Two: Is the Administrative Interpretation of an Ambiguous Statute Reasonable? If a reviewing court's interpretation of the relevant statutory provision at Step One fails to yield an unambiguous congressional intent on the precise question at issue, *Chevron* Step Two requires the court to determine whether the agency's interpretation is "permissible."[65]

The conventional understanding of Step Two analysis centers on whether the administrative interpretation of the relevant statutory provision is reasonable.[66] On this understanding, a reviewing

60. See, e.g., Solid Waste Agency of Northern Cook County v. U.S. Army Corps of Engineers, 531 U.S. 159, 172–73 (2001); National Credit Union Administration v. First National Bank & Trust Co., 522 U.S. 479, 501–02 (1998). For a discussion of the application of canons of statutory interpretation at *Chevron* Step One, see SECTION OF ADMINISTRATIVE LAW AND REGULATORY PRACTICE OF AMERICAN BAR ASSOCIATION, A GUIDE TO JUDICIAL AND POLITICAL REVIEW OF FEDERAL AGENCIES 68–81 (John F. Duffy & Michael Herz, eds., 2005); Sunstein, *Law and Administration, supra* note 32, at 2105–19.

61. See *Brown & Williamson*, 529 U.S. at 133.

62. See *id.* at 133, 159–61; *MCI*, 512 U.S. at 231. For the suggestion that these Step One decisions may have sown

the seeds of a "major question" exception to *Chevron*, see Merrill & Hickman, Chevron's Domain, *supra* note 22, at 844–45; Sunstein, Chevron's Step Zero, *supra* note 22, at 236–47.

63. *Chevron*, 467 U.S. at 842–43; see, e.g., FDA v. Brown & Williamson Tobacco Corp., 529 U.S. 120 (2000).

64. See, e.g., Dole v. United Steelworkers of America, 494 U.S. 26, 43–44 (1990) (White, J., dissenting); Ronald M. Levin, Mead *and the Prospective Exercise of Discretion*, 54 ADMIN. L. REV. 771, 779 (2002); Shapiro & Levy, *Judicial Incentives, supra* note 46, at 1070.

65. *Chevron*, 467 U.S. at 843.

66. See, e.g., United States v. Riverside Bayview Homes, Inc. 474 U.S. 121, 131 (1985); National Railroad Passenger Corp. v. Boston and Maine Corp., 503

court determines whether the agency's interpretation "goes beyond the meaning that the statute can bear."[67] At Step Two, as at Step One, reviewing courts draw on the "traditional tools of statutory construction" to determine the reasonableness of an administrative interpretation.[68] For example, in *Babbitt v. Sweet Home Chapter of Communities for a Great Oregon*, the justices evaluated the reasonableness of an administrative interpretation by analyzing the "ordinary" and "dictionary" meanings of the relevant provision; the "statutory context" of the provision; and the "broad purpose" and "legislative history" of the statute.[69]

Because of the "interpretative leeway" that the reasonableness standard of *Chevron* Step Two gives to agencies,[70] it is hardly surprising that reviewing courts are far less likely to invalidate administrative interpretations at Step Two than at Step One.[71] It took the Supreme Court fifteen years to invalidate an administrative interpretation at Step Two. That decision, *AT & T Corp. v. Iowa Utilities Bd.*,[72] offers a helpful illustration of the reasonableness inquiry. In *AT & T*, the justices reviewed regulations adopted by the Federal Communications Commission implementing the Telecommunications Act of 1996. The Telecommunications Act prohibited states from restricting competition in local telephone markets. The act also required telephone companies that had enjoyed a state-created monopoly to operate in a local service area (so called "incumbent local exchange carriers" or "incumbent LECs") to take a number of steps to facilitate market entry by new competitors.[73] The Court held that all but one of the FCC's implementing regulations reflected a reasonable interpretation of the Telecommunications Act's requirements.

The problem regulation was the FCC's "unbundling rule," which identified "network elements" (such as caller I.D. and directory assistance) that incumbent LECs must provide to new competitors entering their markets. Incumbent LECs argued that the unbundling rule reflected the Commission's misinterpretation of the "necessary" and "impairment" standards of the Telecommuni-

U.S. 407, 417–18 (1992); *Chevron*, 467 U.S. at 840, 844, 845.

67. See *MCI*, 512 U.S. at 229; see also Natural Resources Defense Council, Inc. v. Daley, 209 F.3d 747, 753 (D.C.Cir. 2000) ("a court will not uphold [an agency's] interpretation that diverges from any realistic meaning of the statute").

68. *Chevron*, 467 U.S. at 843 n.9.

69. 515 U.S. 687, 696–708 (1995); see also Republican National Committee v. FEC, 76 F.3d 400, 406 (D.C.Cir.1996)

(at Step Two reviewing courts "ask whether the [agency's] interpretation ... is reasonable in light of the language, legislative history, and policies of the statute").

70. *Verizon*, 535 U.S. at 501.

71. See Kerr, *Shedding Light on Chevron*, *supra* note 47, at 47 (citing results of empirical study conducted by author).

72. 525 U.S. 366 (1999).

73. *Id.* at 371–73.

cations Act. These statutory standards deemed it "necessary" for incumbent LECs to provide market entrants with a network element if the failure to do so would "impair" an entrant's ability to provide local service. The FCC had interpreted of the Telecommunications Act's "necessary" standard as requiring an incumbent LEC to provide a network element to a market entrant even if the entrant could obtain the element from another source. The Commission had interpreted the act's "impairment" standard as requiring an incumbent LEC to provide a network element to a market entrant whenever "the failure to do so would decrease the quality, or increase the financial or administrative cost of the service [the entrant] seeks to offer."[74]

The Court in *AT & T* invalidated the unbundling rule because the justices concluded that the FCC's interpretations of the "necessary" and "impairment" standards of the Telecommunications Act had been unreasonable. The Court held that the FCC's interpretation of the act's "necessary" standard was impermissible because it was not "consistent with the statute" for the Commission to ignore "the availability of elements outside the incumbent's network." The Court also ruled out the FCC's position that "*any* increase in cost (or decrease in quality)" experienced by an entrant because of an incumbent LEC's denial of a network element constituted an "impairment" of the entrant's ability to furnish services. This interpretation, the Court held, was "not in accord with the ordinary and fair meaning" of the statutory term. In effect, the Court in *AT & T* found the FCC interpretations to have been unreasonable because they essentially had read the "necessary" and "impairment" standards out of the Telecommunications Act.[75]

The conventional understanding of *Chevron* Step Two's reasonableness inquiry, illustrated in *AT & T*, has come under stiff challenge in recent years. This challenge, which has gained some traction among reviewing courts[76] and commentators,[77] proffers a

74. *Id*. at 388–89.

75. *Id*. at 387–92; compare Republican National Committee v. FEC, 76 F.3d 400, 406 (D.C.Cir.1996) (upholding administrative interpretation at Step Two because the statutory text and the legislative history provided "no basis for questioning the reasonableness" of the interpretation and because the interpretation furthered the purposes of the statute).

76. See, e.g., Sierra Club v. Leavitt, 368 F.3d 1300, 1304 (11th Cir. 2004); Consumer Federation of America v. U.S. Dept. of Health & Human Serv., 83 F.3d 1497 (D.C.Cir. 1996); Madison Gas &

Elec. Co. v. EPA, 25 F.3d 526, 529 (7th Cir. 1994).

77. See ABA GUIDE TO JUDICIAL AND POLITICAL REVIEW, *supra* note 60, at 96–102; Ronald M. Levin, *The Anatomy of Chevron: Step Two Reconsidered*, 72 CHI.-KENT L. REV. 1253 (1997); Mark Seidenfeld, *A Syncopated Chevron: Emphasizing Reasoned Decisionmaking in Reviewing Agency Interpretations of Statutes*, 73 TEX. L. REV. 83 (1994); cf. Molot, *Judicial Perspective, supra* note 43, at 92–94 (noting problems with arbitrary-or-capricious review at Step Two); but see Gary Lawson, *Outcome, Procedure and Process: Agency Duties of Explanation for Legal Conclusions*, 48

revised understanding of Step Two analysis that is not limited to an examination of whether an administrative interpretation is reasonable according to the traditional tools of statutory construction. The alternative approach to *Chevron* Step Two also would incorporate elements of the "arbitrary-or-capricious" review that courts use to evaluate the ultimate decision of an agency in an administrative proceeding (see § 8.7). This revised understanding of *Chevron* Step Two thus would inquire generally whether the administrative interpretation was the product of "reasoned decisionmaking." Advocates of the revised approach would look beyond the legislative materials to examine such factors as the soundness of the agency's decision-making process, the logic of the agency's reasoning, and the sufficiency of the evidentiary record.

A panel of the D.C. Circuit in *Arent v. Shalala*[78] attempted to defend the conventional understanding of *Chevron* Step Two against the revisionist challenge by distinguishing the function of reasonableness review of an agency's statutory interpretation from that of arbitrary-or-capricious review of an agency's ultimate decision. For the *Arent* court, the function of *Chevron* Step Two is to determine the reasonableness of an agency's *interpretation* of its "authority to act under a statute." It therefore, necessarily, is "rooted in statutory analysis." By contrast, the *Arent* Court explained, the function of arbitrary-or-capricious review is to determine the propriety of an agency's decision to *exercise* its statutory authority in a particular manner. A multidimensional analysis of the overall soundness of an agency's decisionmaking, which arbitrary-or-capricious review provides, is necessary for reviewing courts to make that ultimate determination.[79]

The D.C. Circuit in *Arent* correctly stated the conventional understanding of the respective roles of *Chevron* Step Two and arbitrary-or-capricious review. As the Supreme Court put it one year after the *Chevron* decision, judicial review at Step Two "is limited to the question whether [an administrative interpretation] is reasonable, in light of the language, policies, and legislative history of the [relevant statute]."[80] Although the Supreme Court to

---

RUTGERS L. REV. 313, 325–31 (1996) (rejecting arbitrary-or-capricious review at Step Two).

78. 70 F.3d 610 (D.C.Cir. 1995).

79. *Id.* at 615–16; see also Continental Airlines, Inc. v. Dep't of Transp., 843 F.2d 1444, 1452 (D.C.Cir. 1988) ("[I]nterpreting a statute is quite a different enterprise than policymaking.... [M]uch of the 'arbitrary and capricious' style analysis concerned with reasoned agency decisionmaking ... cannot be applied directly to the question of whether

an agency's interpretation of a statute is 'contrary to law.' It would be inappropriate, therefore, to import wholesale that body of law and apply it in a conceptually distinct arena.").

80. United States v. Riverside Bayview Homes, Inc. 474 U.S. 121, 131 (1985); see also National Ass'n of Home Builders v. Defenders of Wildlife, ___ U.S. ___, 127 S.Ct. 2518, 2534 (2007) (upholding administrative interpretation at Step Two as "reasonable in light of the statute's text and the overall statu-

date has followed this conventional understanding of *Chevron* Step Two, the justices have yet to consider the revisionist challenge.

Step Zero: Is *Chevron* Applicable? The Supreme Court made clear in *Chevron* that its new two-step analysis would not apply every time a court reviews statutory interpretations by an administrative agency. The Court limited the application of *Chevron* to judicial review of an agency's interpretation of a "statute which it administers,"[81] that is, an enabling act. This limitation, the Court later explained, established "congressional delegation of administrative authority" as a "precondition to deference under *Chevron*."[82] From that seemingly simple precondition, the justices have spun an intricate web of doctrines that significantly limit *Chevron*'s application.[83]

The Court's reservation of *Chevron* deference for an agency's interpretations of the statutes it administers made it clear that *Chevron* does not apply when a court interprets and enforces constitutional requirements relating to agency action.[84] Similarly, agencies are not entitled to *Chevron* deference when they interpret a judicial opinion, even if the opinion concerns a statute that the agency administers.[85]

The Supreme Court has found *Chevron* inapplicable as well in cases where Congress has not given the agency power to "administer" the statute it has interpreted. For example, the justices have held that *Chevron* does not apply to an administrative interpretation of a statutory provision granting individuals a private right of action in federal court. Congress has given the courts, rather than any agency, power to "administer" such provisions.[86] The Court also has denied *Chevron* deference to administrative interpretations

tory scheme"); Barnhart v. Thomas, 540 U.S. 20, 26–29 (2003) (using statutory interpretation rather than arbitrary-or-capricious review at *Chevron* Step Two).

81.   *Chevron*, 467 U.S. at 842.

82.   Adams Fruit Co., Inc. v. Barrett, 494 U.S. 638, 649 (1990).

83.   Leading explorations of the limited applicability of *Chevron* include Merrill & Hickman, Chevron's *Domain*, *supra* note 22; Sunstein, Chevron's *Step Zero*, *supra* note 22.

84.   See, e.g., Gulf Power Co. v. FCC, 208 F.3d 1263, 1271 (11th Cir. 2000); Rural Telephone Coalition v. FCC, 838 F.2d 1307, 1313 (D.C.Cir. 1988).

85.   See Reno v. Bossier Parish School Bd., 528 U.S. 320, 336 n.5 (2000); see also Jicarilla Apache Tribe v. FERC, 578 F.2d 289, 292–93 (10th Cir. 1978)

(declining to defer to an agency interpretation based on common law principles). In *National Cable & Telecommunications Association v. Brand X Internet Services*, 545 U.S. 967 (2005), however, the Court held that *Chevron* applies where an agency's interpretation of *ambiguous* terms in its enabling act deviates from a prior judicial interpretation. This is so, the Court reasoned, because *Chevron* vests agencies, not reviewing courts, with primary interpretive authority over ambiguities in the statutes they administer. By contrast, the Court in *National Cable* held, prior judicial interpretations of the *unambiguous* terms of enabling acts block agencies from adopting a contrary interpretation. This is because unambiguous terms in enabling acts are capable of only one correct interpretation. *Id.* at 982–86.

86.   *Adams Fruit*, 494 U.S. at 649.

of statutes, such as the Administrative Procedure Act, that apply generally to federal agencies.[87] Because Congress has not provided any particular agency with administrative authority over a generally applicable statute, the justices have reasoned, no agency possesses any special interpretive expertise regarding its provisions.[88] The Court has reserved judgment on whether *Chevron* might apply to a statute for which two or more agencies share administrative responsibility.[89] It might be said that where the agencies sharing administrative authority are few in number, each agency possesses a degree of interpretive expertise that is lacking with respect to a generally applicable statute such as the APA. The D.C. Circuit, however, has ruled against *Chevron* deference regarding statutes providing for shared administrative authority. Applying *Chevron*, noted the court of appeals, would create "a regulatory regime in which either the same statute is interpreted differently by the several agencies or the one agency that happens to reach the courthouse first is allowed to fix the meaning of the text for all."[90]

The Supreme Court even has held *Chevron* inapplicable in some instances where an agency has interpreted a statute that it alone administers. For example, the justices have refused to apply *Chevron* to statutory interpretations that an agency announces for the first time in litigation. These interpretations, the justices have explained, amount to nothing more than "litigating positions" expressing "post hoc rationalizations" by an agency defending its actions.[91] The Court also has held *Chevron* inapplicable to some interpretations that agencies have made of their enabling acts contemporaneously with the agency's action. This final Step Zero limitation on the applicability of *Chevron* is the subject of § 8.5(d).

---

87. See, e.g., Metropolitan Stevedore Co. v. Rambo, 521 U.S. 121, 137 n.9 (1997) (*Chevron* does not apply to administrative interpretations of the APA); Bowen v. American Hospital Association, 476 U.S. 610, 642 n.30 (1986) (plurality opinion) (*Chevron* does not apply to administrative interpretation of the Rehabilitation Act); cf. Chemical Waste Management, Inc. v EPA, 873 F.2d 1477 (D.C.Cir. 1989) (applying *Chevron* to agency decision that a hearing provision in its enabling act did not trigger the formal adjudication requirements of the APA).

88. See *Metropolitan Stevedore Co.*, 521 U.S. at 137 n.9; *Bowen*, 476 U.S. at 642 n.30 (plurality opinion).

89. See Bragdon v. Abbott, 524 U.S. 624, 642 (1998).

90. Rapaport v. United States Dep't of Treasury, Office of Thrift Div., 59 F.3d 212, 216–17 (D.C.Cir. 1995) (holding *Chevron* inapplicable "because that agency shares responsibility for the administration of the statute with at least three other agencies").

91. Martin v. Occupational Safety and Health Review Comm'n, 499 U.S. 144, 156 (1991); see *Bowen*, 488 U.S. at 212–13. The Court, however, has applied *Chevron* to an administrative interpretation announced after notice-and-comment rulemaking that was "prompted by litigation." Smiley v. Citibank, 517 U.S. 735, 741 (1996).

(d) The *Mead* Counter–Revolution

The Supreme Court re-conceptualized *Chevron* and further limited its application in *United States v. Mead Corp.*[92] In *Mead*, the justices held that *Chevron* applies only "when it appears that [1] Congress delegated authority to the agency generally to make rules carrying the force of law, and that [2] the agency interpretation claiming deference was promulgated in the exercise of that authority."[93] After *Mead*, administrative interpretations of ambiguous enabling acts in connection with agency action that does not carry the "force of law" receive *Skidmore* deference, the shorthand reference to the traditional multi-factored, sliding scale doctrine that *Chevron* had replaced (see § 8.5(a)).[94] (See Figure 8–1.)

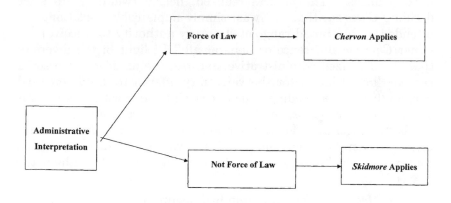

Figure 8-1: Judicial Review of Administrative Interpretations After *Mead*

Mead is best understood as a refinement of *Chevron*'s Step Zero requirement establishing "congressional delegation of administrative authority" as a "precondition to deference under *Chevron*."[95] *Mead* essentially held that an agency "administers" a statute, within the meaning of Step Zero, only when it acts with the force of law. *Mead*'s revision of Step Zero suggested a new understanding of *Chevron* deference. This understanding posits that an enabling act's implicit delegation of *interpretive* authority to an agency is simply the natural byproduct of Congress's broader delegation of *lawmaking* authority to the agency.[96]

---

92.   533 U.S. 218 (2001).

93.   *Id.* at 226–27.

94.   *Id.* at 221, 226–27; see Skidmore v. Swift & Co., 323 U.S. 134 (1944).

95.   Adams Fruit Co., Inc. v. Barrett, 494 U.S. 638, 649 (1990); see *Chevron*, 467 U.S. at 842.

96.   See Merrill & Hickman, *Chevron's Domain, supra* note 22, at 874–82.

Mead's refinement of Step Zero represented a counter-revolution of scope-of-review doctrine because it returned traditional *Skidmore* deference as the default rule when courts review agency interpretations of their enabling acts. *Mead* re-conceptualized the *Chevron* Two Step as an especially strong deference rule applicable only where agencies interpret their enabling acts when exercising lawmaking authority. *Skidmore* applies to all other agency interpretations of their enabling acts.

Mead reaffirmed *Skidmore*'s learning. Because agencies "necessarily make all sorts of interpretive choices" regarding their enabling acts, the Court explained, "[t]he fair measure of deference to an agency administering its own statute" should "vary with circumstances." The justices realized, nearly twenty years after deciding *Chevron*, that "it [was] simply implausible that Congress intended such a broad range of statutory authority to [receive] . . . either *Chevron* deference or none at all." In light of the diversity that characterized administrative statutes, the justices expressed a renewed appreciation for the versatility offered by *Skidmore*'s ad hoc, multi-factored, sliding scale approach to reviewing administrative interpretations. *Skidmore*, the *Mead* Court concluded, provided the better deference doctrine for judicial review of administrative interpretations in the nearly infinite variety of decisionmaking contexts in which agencies execute their enabling acts without the force of law.[97]

The *Mead* counter-revolution had begun to take shape with the Court's revival of *Skidmore* deference in *Equal Employment Opportunity Commission v. Arabian American Oil Co. ("ARAMCO")*.[98] At issue in *ARAMCO* was whether Title VII of the Civil Rights Act of 1964 protected American citizens from discriminatory employment practices by U.S. employers operating in foreign countries. The EEOC, which administers Title VII, had interpreted the act to apply to such practices, but because Title VII did not give the agency authority to issue legally binding rules, the Commission had published its interpretation in nonbinding "guidelines." The Court held that EEOC's interpretation of Title VII did not merit *Chevron* deference because Congress had not provided the Commission with substantive, legislative rulemaking authority (see § 6.5(a)). The Court instead accorded the EEOC's interpretive guidelines *Skidmore* deference.[99]

The Court followed *ARAMCO* in *Christensen v. Harris County*.[100] *Christensen* arose from the provisions of the Fair Labor Standards Act governing compensation for overtime work by state

97. *Mead*, 533 U.S. at 227–28, 236.   **99.** *Id.* at 256–57.

98. 499 U.S. 244 (1991).   **100.** 529 U.S. 576 (2000).

employees. The FLSA permitted states and their political subdivisions to compensate their employees for overtime by granting compensatory time (or "comp time"), which entitled an employee to time off from work with full pay. The act, however, required a state to provide overtime pay to employees who had not used their accumulated comp time. Against the background of these FLSA provisions, Harris County adopted a policy requiring its employees to use their comp time instead of receiving overtime pay. That policy conflicted with a nonbinding "opinion letter" issued by the Department of Labor, the federal agency that administers the Fair Labor Standards Act. The Labor Department's opinion letter had interpreted the FLSA to prohibit states from requiring that their employees use compensatory time (in lieu of receiving overtime pay) unless the employee had agreed to that requirement in advance.

The Court in *Christensen* ruled that the Labor Department's interpretation of the comp time provisions of the FLSA was entitled merely to *Skidmore* deference because the agency's interpretation had appeared in an opinion letter. The Court explained, "Interpretations such as those in opinion letters—like interpretations contained in policy statements, agency manuals, and enforcement guidelines, all of which lack the force of law—do not warrant *Chevron*-style deference." The Labor Department's interpretation would have been entitled to *Chevron* deference, the justices observed, had it been "arrived at after, for example, a formal adjudication or notice-and-comment rulemaking."[101]

Mead extended *ARAMCO* and *Christensen*. At issue in *Mead* was a tariff-classification ruling by the United States Customs Service determining the duty owed on imported merchandise. Unlike the administrative guidelines in *ARAMCO* and the agency opinion letter in *Christensen*, the tariff-classification rulings in *Mead* were legally binding for the particular transaction they addressed. The Court nevertheless held that the Customs rulings lacked the force of law, and thus that they warranted *Skidmore* rather than *Chevron* deference.[102]

The Court in *Mead* looked first at the Customs Service's enabling act authorizing tariff-classification rulings. The justices found no statutory language indicating that "Congress meant to

---

101. *Id.* at 587; see also Reno v. Koray, 515 U.S. 50, 61 (1995) (internal agency guideline not subject to the "rigors" of the notice-and-comment process of the Administrative Procedure Act is entitled only to "some deference"); Martin v. Occupational Safety and Health Review Comm'n, 499 U.S. 144, 157 (1991) (interpretive rules and enforcement guidelines are "entitled to some weight on judicial review," but not to "the same deference as norms that derive from the exercise of the [agency's] delegated lawmaking powers").

102. *Mead*, 533 U.S. at 222, 227, 230, 232.

delegate authority to Customs to issue classification rulings with the force of law." Indeed, there were statutory signals that Congress had no such intent. For example, the enabling act subjected tariff-classification rulings to independent review in the Court of International Trade.[103]

The justices then examined the practice of the Customs Service in making tariff-classification rulings. This practice, the *Mead* Court found, gave no "indication that Customs ever set out with a lawmaking pretense in mind." Forty-six Customs offices issued between 10,000 and 15,000 classification letters each year. Customs typically did not follow notice-and-comment procedures when issuing a tariff-classification ruling. Most classification letters included "little or no reasoning." And finally, the Customs Service's regulations advised that tariff-classification rulings had no precedential effect on other transactions.[104]

The Court in *Mead* concluded that the attributes of non-lawmaking activity revealed by Customs's enabling act and by the agency's practice when making tariff-classification rulings deprived the rulings of the force of law necessary for *Chevron* to apply. *Mead* thus implied that the meaning of "force of law" for purposes of triggering *Chevron* differs from the conventional meaning of "force of law" in administrative law. The conventional understanding has been that agency action carries the "force of law" if it is legally binding on the affected parties in the sense that failure to comply with the action would subject a party to legal sanctions.[105] Customs's tariff-classification rulings were legally binding in that sense, yet they did not carry the force of law sufficient to trigger *Chevron*.

Mead failed to specify just what *was* required for agency action to satisfy its new force-of-law threshold.[106] The Court instead created the open-ended prospect that a congressional delegation of lawmaking authority necessary for *Chevron* to apply "may be shown in a variety of ways." The essential requirement, explained the justices, was that it be "apparent from the agency's generally conferred authority and other statutory circumstances that Congress would expect the agency to be able to speak with the force of

---

103. See *id.* at 231–32.

104. See *id.* at 223–24, 233. The enabling act required Customs to follow notice-and-comment procedures only when revoking or modifying a tariff-classification ruling. *Id.* at 234.

105. This is the definition that distinguishes legislative rules, which re-

quire notice and comment, from guidance documents, which do not (see § 6.5(a)-(b)).

106. For an argument that the Court should adopt the conventional meaning of "force of law" for *Chevron* purposes, see Merrill, Mead *Doctrine, supra* note 23, at 827–33.

law when it addresses ambiguity in the statute or fills a space in the enacted law."[107]

The *Mead* Court, following *Christensen*, left no doubt that Congress's delegation of power to an agency to engage in formal adjudication or in informal rulemaking would satisfy the force-of-law requirement.[108] But while congressional conferral of formal adjudicatory or informal rulemaking authority was *sufficient* to satisfy the force-of-law requirement, it was not *necessary*. "[S]ome other indication of a comparable congressional intent" would suffice as well. The justices suggested that they "generally" would be inclined to find a "comparable congressional intent" to convey administrative lawmaking power when an enabling act provides for "a relatively formal administrative procedure tending to foster the fairness and deliberation that should underlie a pronouncement [carrying the] force [of law]."[109]

Mead's prospect of force-of-law status for administrative interpretations adopted pursuant to procedures sufficiently formal to foster the kind of "fairness and deliberation" that attend notice-and-comment rulemaking and formal adjudication suggests a new process-based justification for *Chevron* deference. According to this justification, an agency earns *Chevron* deference by adopting an interpretation of its enabling act in a proceeding that affords interested parties a meaningful opportunity to participate and that fosters the kind of reasoned decisionmaking that reviewing courts expect when agency action has legal force. By contrast, an agency that opts for the expediency of announcing an interpretation more summarily must earn its deference according to the traditional factors that calibrate *Skidmore*'s sliding scale.[110] As a leading commentator put it, *Mead* may give agencies a choice, "Pay me now or pay me later."[111]

---

107. See *Mead*, 533 U.S. at 227, 230.

108. *Mead*, 533 U.S. at 227; see *Christensen*, 529 U.S. at 587; see also Martin v. Occupational Safety and Health Review Comm'n, 499 U.S. 144, 157 (1991) (administrative interpretations in notice-and-comment rulemaking and in adjudication are "exercise[s] of delegated lawmaking powers"). The *Mead* Court noted, "[T]he overwhelming number of our cases applying *Chevron* deference have reviewed the fruits of notice-and-comment rulemaking or formal adjudication." *Mead*, 533 U.S. at 230.

109. *Mead*, 533 U.S. at 227, 230; see also Edelman v. Lynchburg College, 535 U.S. 106, 114 (2002) ("deference under *Chevron* . . . does not necessarily require an agency's exercise of express notice-and-comment rulemaking power").

110. Merrill & Hickman, *Chevron's Domain*, supra note 22, at 884–88; Sunstein, *Chevron's Step Zero*, supra note 22, at 225–26.

111. Sunstein, *Chevron's Step Zero*, supra note 22, at 225. For an argument against relying on the administrative process underlying an agency's interpretation when determining whether the interpretation carries the force of law, see, Levin, Mead, supra note 64, at 787–98.

The Customs Service's highly informal decisionmaking procedures for issuing tariff-classification rulings, which the *Mead* Court described as "far removed not only from notice-and-comment process, but from any other circumstances reasonably suggesting that Congress ever thought of classification rulings as deserving [*Chevron*] deference,"[112] helped to undermine any prospect of a finding that the rulings carried the force of law. But the *Mead* Court did not deny Customs's tariff-classification rulings *Chevron* deference solely because of a process deficiency. Two additional considerations contributed to the justices' conclusion that the Customs rulings lacked legal force. First, although the rulings were binding on the parties for the particular transaction, they did not serve as precedent for future transactions.[113] Legislative rulemaking and formal adjudicatory orders, by contrast, affect the rights of a broad range of individuals and constrain the future decisionmaking of the agency. *Mead*'s force-of-law requirement thus may rest, at least in part, on a judicial judgment that agencies tend to make statutory interpretations that bind themselves and the public with a seriousness of purpose and a quality of deliberation that warrants *Chevron* deference.[114] But when an agency, as in *Mead*, makes an interpretation that constrains no one other than the immediate party, there exists a risk of arbitrariness that *Skidmore* deference is more adept at uncovering.

The final consideration that seemed important to the *Mead* Court in denying *Chevron* deference was that Customs had issued tens of thousands of tariff-classification rulings through 46 branch offices.[115] By contrast, legislative rules typically are issued at an agency's headquarters, and formal adjudicatory orders, when they are issued at an agency's branch office, typically are subject to centralized internal review. Again, *Mead* may reflect, at least in part, the justices' intuition that agencies will (or should) assert centralized control when they are consciously engaged in lawmaking. The extreme decentralization of Customs's practice regarding tariff rulings made perfect sense for an agency facing the need of making a high number of quick, on-the-spot judgments, but not for an act of lawmaking.

In the end, (1) the Customs Service's highly informal administrative decisionmaking process seemed to combine with (2) the highly diffuse issuance of tariff-classification rulings and (3) the

112. See *Mead*, 533 U.S. at 231.

113. See *id.* at 233; cf. *id.* at 232 ("precedential value alone does not add up to *Chevron* entitlement").

114. See FEC v. National Rifle Association of America, 254 F.3d 173, 185–86 (D.C.Cir. 2001) (post-*Mead* decision ap-

plying *Chevron* to agency action reflecting the "considered judgment" of the agency exercised "pursuant to congressionally delegated lawmaking power" and having "binding legal effect").

115. See *Mead*, 533 U.S. at 233–34.

lack of precedential effect of those rulings to bring home to the *Mead* Court that the rulings did not warrant *Chevron* deference. But the justices' highly contextual approach to the force-of-law requirement in *Mead* left unclear whether administrative action with some (but not all) of the attributes of tariff-classification rulings should qualify for *Chevron* deference. The justices also gave little guidance on how it would treat administrative interpretations in decisionmaking contexts that differed from notice-and-comment rulemaking and formal adjudication in ways other than those that had infected the Customs rulings.

Mead's tentativeness regarding the criteria for its new force-of-law threshold has left *Chevron* Step Zero in a state of confusion.[116] *Mead* is only clear in establishing that *Chevron* generally applies as a matter of course to administrative interpretations in notice-and-comment rulemaking and in formal adjudication.[117] The Court's analysis of the tariff-classification rulings in *Mead* had seemed to make equally clear that reviewing courts should determine on an ad hoc basis whether administrative interpretations in other informal adjudications deserve *Chevron* or *Skidmore* deference. Courts of appeals since *Mead*, however, have readily applied *Chevron* to administrative interpretations in informal adjudications.[118] Even more puzzling is the force-of-law status of legally binding rules that agencies issue without notice and comment, such as procedural rules and interim rules (see § 6.5(c)-(d)). Unlike the tariff-classification rulings in *Mead*, these rules typically are issued at an agency's headquarters and generally bind the agency as well as the public. But agencies may issue these rules without any process fostering the kind of "fairness and deliberation" the *Mead* Court expected of administrative lawmaking.[119]

The uncertainty surrounding *Mead* extends even to the status of administrative interpretations appearing in policy statements, interpretive rules and other nonbinding guidance documents that *Mead*, *ARAMCO*, and *Christensen* had seemed clearly to consign to *Skidmore* rather than to *Chevron* deference.[120] In *Barnhart v. Walton*, the Court seemed to turn away from *Mead*'s force-of-law requirement, holding a nonbinding interpretive rule eligible for

116. See Lisa Schultz Bressman, *How* Mead *Has Muddled Judicial Review of Agency Action*, 58 Vand. L. Rev. 1443, 1444, 1457–74 (2005).

117. See Yellow Transportation, Inc. v. Michigan, 537 U.S. 36, 45 (2002) (applying *Chevron* deference to agency interpretation in notice-and-comment rulemaking); SEC v. Zandford, 535 U.S. 813, 819–20 (2002) (applying *Chevron* deference to agency interpretation in formal adjudication).

118. See, e.g., Mylan Laboratories, Inc. v. Thompson, 389 F.3d 1272, 1279–80 (D.C.Cir. 2004); Davis v. EPA, 336 F.3d 965, 972 n.5 (9th Cir. 2003); Wilderness Society v. U.S. Fish and Wildlife Service, 316 F.3d 913, 921–22 (9th Cir. 2003).

119. See *Mead*, 533 U.S. at 230.

120. See *id*. at 232, 234; *Christensen*, 529 U.S. at 587.

Chevron *deference.*[121] *The applicability of* Chevron, *the* Walton *Court explained, "depend[ed] in significant part upon the interpretive method used and the nature of the question at issue." In* Walton, *the Court concluded that the "interstitial nature of the legal question, the related expertise of the Agency, the importance of the question to administration of the statute, the complexity of that administration, and the careful consideration the Agency has given the question over a long period of time" made* Chevron *deference appropriate for the administrative interpretation there at issue.*[122] *The Court's reasoning in* Walton *is curious because the factors the justices considered traditionally have been used by reviewing courts exercising* Skidmore *deference.* Walton, *therefore, may be true to* Mead, *holding simply that the interpretive rule merited the strong deference associated with* Chevron *because its indicia of reliability scored high on* Skidmore's *sliding scale. The following year the Court suggested that* Walton *had not undone* Mead, *when it once again categorically ruled out* Chevron *deference for administrative interpretations appearing in "policy statements, agency manuals and enforcement guidelines."*[123] *The confusion on display in* Walton *is symptomatic of the confused state of* Chevron *Step Zero in the wake of* Mead.

§ 8.6 Judicial Review of Agencies' Interpretations of Their Rules

Reviewing courts traditionally have deferred to an agency's interpretation of its rules more readily than they have to an agency's interpretation of its enabling act.[1] Just one year before Congress adopted the Administrative Procedure Act, the Supreme Court, in *Bowles v. Seminole Rock & Sand Co.*, ruled that an agency's interpretation of its regulations has "controlling weight unless it is plainly erroneous or inconsistent with the regulation."[2] Reviewing courts have followed the *Seminole Rock* deference rule ever since.

---

121.   535 U.S. 212, 222 (2002).

122.   *Id.* at 222.

123.   Clackamas   Gastroenterology Associates v. Wells, 538 U.S. 440, 449 n.9 (2003); see also Washington State Dep't of Social and Health Services v. Guardianship Estate of Keffeler, 537 U.S. 371, 385–86 (2003) (agency interpretation in guidance documents issued without notice and comment entitled to *Skidmore* deference). *Walton*, however, has prompted at least several courts of appeals to give *Chevron* deference to administrative guidance documents as they

deem appropriate. See, e.g., Kruse v. Wells Fargo Home Mortgage, Inc., 383 F.3d 49, 58–61 (2d Cir. 2004); Schuetz v. Banc One Mortgage Corp., 292 F.3d 1004, 1012 (9th Cir. 2002).

§ 8.6

1. See, e.g., Udall v. Tallman, 380 U.S. 1, 16 (1965) ("When the construction of an administrative regulation rather than a statute is in issue, deference is even more clearly in order").

2.   325 U.S. 410, 414 (1945).

Reviewing courts "presume" that enabling acts delegate to agencies the "power to render authoritative interpretations" of their own rules because this power is a "necessary adjunct" of an agency's authority "to promulgate and to enforce [regulations]." Judges recognize that agencies are "in a better position ... to reconstruct the purpose" of the rules they have issued. And the wide array of problems that agencies encounter when they enforce their regulations yields a unique "expertise" that is valuable when gauging the impact of a rule interpretation on a regulatory program.[3]

The judicial deference that courts accord an agency's interpretation of its rules is often referred to as "*Seminole Rock* deference" or as "*Auer* deference," the latter term referencing the Supreme Court's decision confirming the survival of this distinctive deference principle in the wake of *Chevron*.[4] As a formal matter, *Seminole Rock* and *Chevron* have distinct applications: The former applies to administrative rule interpretations, while the latter applies to administrative statutory interpretations.[5] In operation, however, the two forms of deference are strikingly similar. For example, *Seminole Rock* and *Chevron* deference each require that the interpreted provision be ambiguous.[6] And although some courts of appeals have described *Seminole Rock* deference as granting agencies more interpretive leeway than *Chevron* deference,[7] both deference rules essentially entitle agencies to adopt any reasonable interpretation.[8] It is an open question, however, whether *Seminole Rock* deference, like *Chevron* deference, is subject to the *Mead* requirement that the administrative interpretation carry the force of law.[9]

3. See Martin v. Occupational Safety and Health Review Comm'n, 499 U.S. 144, 151–53 (1991).

4. See Auer v. Robbins, 519 U.S. 452, 461–63 (1997).

5. See Stinson v. United States, 508 U.S. 36, 44–45 (1993).

6. See Christensen v. Harris County, 529 U.S. 576, 588 (2000); *Martin*, 499 U.S. at 150–51.

7. See C.F. Communications Corp. v. FCC, 128 F.3d 735, 738 (D.C.Cir. 1997); Paradissiotis v. Rubin, 171 F.3d 983, 987 (5th Cir. 1999).

8. See, e.g., *Martin*, 499 U.S. at 158 ("the reviewing court should defer to the Secretary only if the Secretary's [rule] interpretation *is* reasonable"); Ehlert v. United States, 402 U.S. 99, 105 (1971) (reviewing courts are "obligated to regard as controlling a reasonable,

consistently applied administration" of an ambiguous agency rule).

9. Cf. *Auer*, 519 U.S. at 461–63 (pre-*Mead* decision deferring to an agency's rule interpretation appearing for the first time in an *amicus* brief, where there was "no reason to suspect that the interpretation does not reflect the agency's fair and considered judgment"). For a discussion of the potential application of *Mead* to *Seminole Rock* deference, see Scott H. Angstreich, *Shoring Up* Chevron: *A Defense of* Seminole Rock *Deference to Agency Regulatory Interpretations*, 34 U.C. DAVIS L. REV. 49 (2000); Robert A. Anthony, *Three Settings in which Nonlegislative Rules Should Not Bind*, 53 ADMIN. L. REV. 1313 (2001); Peter L. Strauss, *Publication Rules in the Rulemaking Spectrum: Assuring Proper Respect for an Essential Element*, 53 ADMIN. L. REV. 803, 822–38 (2001).

The Supreme Court in *Gonzales v. Oregon*[10] placed a distinctive limitation on the applicability of *Seminole Rock* deference. In *Gonzales*, the justices refused to defer to an administrative interpretation of a regulation that did "little more than restate the terms of the statute itself." Agencies are owed *Seminole Rock* deference, the *Gonzales* Court ruled, only when they interpret rules that bring "specificity" to statutes they enforce. An administrative interpretation of a rule that simply repeats the statutory text does not warrant *Seminole Rock* deference, the justices explained, because the interpretation reflects the agency's understanding of Congress's language, not its own.[11]

§ 8.7   Judicial Review of the Ultimate Decision of the Agency

The final element of agency action is the agency's ultimate decision of whether and how to exercise its authority to make a rule or to issue an order. This decision does not raise pure issues of law or of fact. It involves instead the agency's application of law (the relevant standards of the enabling act) to fact (the agency's factual determinations regarding the regulatory matter at issue). Reviewing courts therefore traditionally have described an agency's ultimate decision in a proceeding as raising a "mixed" question of law and fact. In its essence, however, an agency's decision to issue a rule or an order is an exercise of administrative "judgment" and "discretion." An agency's ultimate decision represents policy judgment of how best to resolve a particular proceeding in the light of the agency's statutory mandate.

Because the Administrative Procedure Act does not explicitly provide a standard of judicial review for an agency's ultimate decision to act, section 706(2)(A), the catchall provision, applies. Reviewing courts thus must determine whether the agency's decision is "arbitrary, capricious, an abuse of discretion, or otherwise not in accordance with law." These terms, which often are referred to as the "arbitrary-or-capricious" standard, leave unclear just how carefully reviewing courts should monitor agency decisionmaking for errors in judgment or abuses of discretion, and the proper calibration of this standard of review remains controversial.

(a) The Traditional Approach

Traditionally, judicial review of administrative decisionmaking resembled the highly deferential review that courts now exercise when evaluating whether socioeconomic legislation is consistent with the constitutional requirement of substantive due process.[1]

---

10.   546 U.S. 243 (2006).

11.   Id. at 256–58.

§ 8.7

1.   See Pacific States Box & Basket Co. v. White, 296 U.S. 176, 185–86

Reviewing courts asked only that an agency provide a "rational basis" or a "reasonable ground" for its application of an enabling act to the relevant facts in a proceeding.[2] As the justices once put it, reviewing courts traditionally upheld ultimate administrative decisions that reflected "a sensible exercise of judgment."[3]

The high level of deference that reviewing courts traditionally accorded to an agency's ultimate decision was premised on the enabling act's delegation of administrative authority to agencies. The agency's administrative authority included the power to decide how best to apply its enabling act in regulatory proceedings. Reviewing courts believed that they would subvert this statutory scheme by substituting their judgment for that of agency officials regarding the proper administration of these acts. They also believed that agencies, by virtue of their administrative experience and technical expertise, knew best how to execute regulatory programs.[4]

The traditional understanding that courts should remain highly deferential when reviewing ultimate administrative decisions was entrenched by the time Congress enacted the Administrative Procedure Act. For example, in *SEC v. Chenery Corp.* (*Chenery II*),[5] the Court upheld a decision by the Securities and Exchange Commission requiring the management group of a company to forfeit stock in the company that it had purchased during a reorganization proceeding administered by the SEC. The Commission had concluded that the stock purchases were inconsistent with provisions of its enabling act requiring that reorganization plans be "fair" and "equitable" to the shareholders. The Court upheld the SEC's application of these provisions to the stock purchases because the Commission had "a reasonable basis" for its "value judgment" that corporate managers should not be permitted to trade in their companies' stock during reorganization. The justices spent very little time examining the SEC's judgment on the merits. They emphasized instead that it was the agency's role, and not theirs, to make such a decisionmaking judgment. The Court explained, "The Commission's conclusion here rests squarely in that area where administrative judgments are entitled to the greatest amount of

(1935) (equating the presumptions of regularity applying to legislative action and to administrative action).

2. See, e.g., American Trucking Ass'ns v. United States, 344 U.S. 298, 314 (1953) (invalidation of ultimate administration decision is proper only if the agency had "no reasonable ground for the exercise of judgment"); Mississippi Valley Barge Line Co. v. United States, 292 U.S. 282, 286–87 (1934) ("judicial function is exhausted when there

is found to be a rational basis for the conclusions approved by the administrative body").

3. Gray v. Powell, 314 U.S. 402, 413 (1941).

4. See, e.g., NLRB v. Hearst Publications, Inc., 322 U.S. 111, 130–31 (1944); *Gray*, 314 U.S. at 411–12.

5. 332 U.S. 194 (1947).

weight by appellate courts. It is the product of administrative experience, appreciation of the complexities of the problem, realization of the statutory policies, and responsible treatment of the uncontested facts. It is the type of judgment which administrative agencies are best equipped to make and which justifies the use of the administrative process.... Whether we agree or disagree with the result reached, it is an allowable judgment which we cannot disturb."[6] *Chenery II* expressed the conventional conception of judicial review of ultimate administrative decisions when Congress drafted the "arbitrary-or-capricious" standard of section 706(2)(A) of the APA.

(b) Hard Look Judicial Review

Contemporary courts have intensified their arbitrary-or-capricious review of ultimate agency decisions considerably beyond the minimal review that judges traditionally had exercised. Arbitrary-or-capricious judicial review has remained deferential, however. Contemporary courts, like earlier courts, examine the reasonableness—not the correctness—of an agency's ultimate decision to issue a rule or an order. And also like earlier courts, they do not "substitute [their] judgment for that of the agency."[7] But contemporary courts tend to review more closely the substantive rationality of administrative regulatory decisions. They also look more broadly at the quality of the agency's reasoning process and at the thoroughness of the agency's explanation for its regulatory choices. The Supreme Court underscored the modern shift in intensity when it ruled that contemporary arbitrary-or-capricious review of ultimate administrative decisionmaking is stiffer than the rationality review that applies to substantive due process claims.[8]

Reviewing courts began to heighten their arbitrary-or-capricious review of agency decisionmaking in the late 1960s and early 1970s. This period witnessed an explosion of new enabling acts launching ambitious regulatory undertakings to enhance environmental quality, protect consumers, and generally promote the health and safety of the American public. In implementing this new authority, agencies began to switch from formal adjudication, the traditional regulatory method of choice, to the more streamlined

6. *Id.* at 208–09; see also National Broadcasting Co. v. United States, 319 U.S. 190, 224 (1943) ("Our duty is at an end when we find that the action of the [agency] was based upon findings supported by evidence, and was made pursuant to authority granted by Congress. It is not for us to say that the [statutory standards] will be furthered or retarded by the [agency action]. The responsibility belongs to the Congress for the grant of valid legislative authority and to the Commission for its exercise.").

7. See, e.g., Motor Vehicle Manufacturers Ass'n v. State Farm Mutual Automobile Insurance Co., 463 U.S. 29, 43 (1983); Citizens to Preserve Overton Park, Inc. v. Volpe, 401 U.S. 402, 416 (1971).

8. See *State Farm*, 463 U.S. at 43 n.9.

process of informal rulemaking. The combination of increased regulatory power and reduced decisionmaking procedures alone might have proved combustible. But an additional development made a judicial reaction inevitable. By the 1960s and 1970s, many had abandoned the traditional assumption that agencies, because of their specialization and expertise, could best fulfill their statutory mission with minimal judicial involvement. A new consensus held that agencies were prone to "capture" by the very industries that Congress had charged them to regulate, and thus that agencies were unlikely, at least without prodding, to regulate in the public interest (see § 1.5(e)). As this theory of agency capture took hold, reviewing courts began to shoulder the responsibility of ensuring, as the D.C. Circuit put it at the time, that "important legislative purposes, heralded in the halls of Congress, are not lost or misdirected in the vast hallways of the federal bureaucracy."[9]

This newfound judicial commitment to heightened scrutiny of administrative decisionmaking had both a procedural and a substantive dimension. The intensification of procedural judicial review during this period became known as "hybrid rulemaking." When agencies used informal rulemaking to create important regulatory policy, courts exercising hybrid rulemaking review would consider adding procedural requirements beyond those delineated in the Administrative Procedure Act to ensure that all affected individuals and groups (especially public interest groups) could adequately participate in the administrative proceeding. The infusion of judicially imposed procedural requirements into the APA framework often created something of a "hybrid" process with adjudicatory and rulemaking elements (see § 6.1).

The intensification of substantive judicial review became known as "hard look" judicial review. Over the years, "hard look" has taken on a double meaning: Reviewing courts take a "hard look" at administrative decisionmaking in order to ensure that the agencies themselves have taken a "hard look" at regulatory issues before deciding them.[10]

Hybrid rulemaking procedural review and hard look substantive review share a common spirit. Each seeks to ensure that agencies engage in "reasoned decisionmaking" before acting with the force of law, especially in matters of great public importance.[11]

9. Calvert Cliffs' Coordinating Committee, Inc. v. AEC, 449 F.2d 1109, 1111 (D.C.Cir. 1971).

10. See National Lime Ass'n v. EPA, 627 F.2d 416, 451 n.126 (D.C.Cir. 1980); Greater Boston Television Corp. v. FCC, 444 F.2d 841, 851 (D.C. Cir. 1970), cert. denied, 403 U.S. 923 (1971).

11. *Greater Boston*, 444 F.2d at 852 (hard look review); see Ethyl Corp. v. EPA, 541 F.2d 1, 66 (D.C.Cir.) (Bazelon, C.J., concurring), cert. denied, 426 U.S. 941 (1976) (hybrid rulemaking review).

Yet although both innovations have been controversial, hard look review has had more staying power than hybrid rulemaking review. In *Vermont Yankee Nuclear Power Corp. v. National Resources Defense Council*,[12] the Supreme Court put a halt to the judicial creation of administrative procedural requirements beyond those adopted by Congress or by the agencies themselves (see § 6.2). The spirit of hybrid rulemaking review survives today only to the extent that reviewing courts have derived specific procedural requirements from the general notice-and-comment provisions of section 553 of the APA (see § 6.3).

By contrast, the Supreme Court has endorsed hard look substantive review.[13] The durability of hard look review may be traced, at least in part, to its statutory pedigree. Although the APA does not explicitly mandate the specific elements of hard look judicial review, these elements, like the surviving hybrid rulemaking precedent, can be said to derive from the general text of the APA, in this case the arbitrary-or-capricious standard of section 706(2)(A). It is revealing that in *Vermont Yankee*, as the justices unanimously interred judicially imposed hybrid rulemaking, they unanimously endorsed the essence of hard look substantive review.[14]

During his tenure on the D.C. Circuit, Judge Harold Leventhal was the leading proponent of hard look judicial review of agency decisionmaking. He sketched his conception of heightened arbitrary-or-capricious review in *Greater Boston Television Corp. v. FCC*.[15] Judge Leventhal saw reviewing courts as exercising a crucial "supervisory" role over administrative agencies, a role that obligated them to "intervene not merely in case of procedural inadequacies, or bypassing of the mandate in the legislative charter, but more broadly if the court becomes aware, especially from a combination of danger signals, that the agency has not really taken a 'hard look' at the salient problems, and has not genuinely engaged in reasoned decision-making." Judge Leventhal readily acknowledged the decisonmaking advantages available to agencies by virtue of their specialization and expertise, but he insisted that those advantages were "secured, not crippled" by close, substantive judicial review. Leventhal added, "A court does not depart from its proper function when it undertakes a study of the record, hopefully perceptive, even as to the evidence on technical and specialized matters, for this enables the court to penetrate to the underlying

---

12. 435 U.S. 519 (1978).

13. See *State Farm*, 463 U.S. at 42–44; *Overton Park*, 401 U.S. at 416.

14. See *Vermont Yankee*, 435 U.S. at 549 (stating that the focus of judicial review of agency action under the APA should be on "the propriety" of an agency's "contemporaneous explanation" of its decision, as well as on the sufficiency of "the administrative record" supporting the agency's decision).

15. 444 F.2d 841 (D.C. Cir. 1970), cert. denied, 403 U.S. 923 (1971).

decisions of the agency, to satisfy itself that the agency has exercised a reasoned discretion, with reasons that do not deviate from or ignore the ascertainable legislative intent." To Judge Leventhal, hard look judicial review "combines judicial supervision with a salutary principle of judicial restraint." Where an agency has not "shirked [its] fundamental task" of giving reasoned consideration to the relevant regulatory issues and of providing a reasoned explanation of its decisionmaking, Leventhal would have reviewing courts "exercise restraint and affirm the agency's action" even when they would have decided the administrative matter differently.[16]

Just one year after *Greater Boston*, the Supreme Court endorsed hard look judicial review in *Citizens to Preserve Overton Park, Inc. v. Volpe*.[17] In *Overton Park*, the justices directed reviewing courts to use the arbitrary-or-capricious standard of section 706(2)(A) to engage in a "searching and careful" review of the ultimate agency decision in administrative proceedings.[18] In order to facilitate this newly mandated judicial hard look at administrative decisions, the Court in *Overton Park* required that agencies provide reviewing courts with a contemporaneous administrative record of their decisionmaking (see §§ 8.1–8.2). As one court of appeals explained several years after the *Overton Park* decision, "meaningful" judicial review "requires an adequate record."[19] At the same time, the Court in *Overton Park*, as had Judge Leventhal in *Greater Boston*, tempered its intensification of arbitrary-or-capricious review by cautioning reviewing courts to remain deferential to the decisionmaking judgment of administrators. A reviewing court, the *Overton Park* Court reminded, "is not empowered to substitute its judgment for that of the agency."[20]

In the years since the foundational opinions in *Greater Boston* and *Overton Park*, hard look judicial review has evolved into a flexible network of doctrines allowing courts the latitude to invalidate administrative action whenever they doubt that an agency has engaged in reasoned decisionmaking. The flexibility of hard look judicial review permits courts to review an agency's decisionmaking according to the circumstances of each case. In general, reviewing courts tend to intensify their review of "high-stakes" administrative action, and to relax their scrutiny of more routine agency decisions.[21] In addition, judges may review an agency's decisionmak-

---

16. *Id.* at 850–51.

17. 401 U.S. 402 (1971).

18. *Id.* at 416 ("Section 706(2)(A) [of the APA] requires a finding that the actual choice made was not 'arbitrary, capricious, an abuse of discretion, or otherwise not in accordance with law.' ").

19. United States v. Nova Scotia Food Products Corp., 568 F.2d 240, 249 (2d Cir. 1977).

20. *Overton Park*, 401 U.S. at 416.

21. SECTION OF ADMINISTRATIVE LAW AND REGULATORY PRACTICE OF AMERICAN BAR ASSOCIATION, A BLACKLETTER STATEMENT OF FEDERAL ADMINISTRATIVE LAW 34 (2004).

ing more closely and more skeptically when, in Judge Leventhal's language, "a combination of danger signals" in the administrative record suggests "that the agency has not really taken a 'hard look' at the salient problems, and has not genuinely engaged in reasoned decision-making."[22] And finally, it must be said, the intensity (or lack of intensity) of hard look review may vary with the predilections of the reviewing court.

A court's arbitrary-or-capricious review of ultimate administrative decisions in the contemporary, hard look era is capable of nabbing a variety of decisionmaking errors.[23] These defects may be organized into three loose, and somewhat overlapping, categories. First, an agency's ultimate decision in an administrative proceeding may be substantively irrational. Second, an agency may fail to give adequate consideration to the regulatory issues in an administrative proceeding. Third, and finally, an agency may fail to provide an adequate explanation of its decisionmaking. These three categories are discussed in turn.[24]

A reviewing court will invalidate an agency's ultimate decision as irrational if it finds that the decision is "so implausible that it could not be ascribed to a difference in view or the product of agency expertise."[25] An administrative decision might be "implausible" if, in the language of *Overton Park*, it reflects "a clear error of judgment."[26] Another sign of implausibility fatal to an administrative decision is the absence of a "rational connection between the facts found and the choice made."[27] Similarly, reviewing courts will invalidate as irrational an administrative sanction that is "greatly out of proportion to the magnitude of the violation."[28] Yet as was the case traditionally, it is unusual for contemporary reviewing courts to find ultimate administrative decisions to be substantively irrational.

It is more common for a court exercising arbitrary-or-capricious review today to invalidate an administrative decision because of the agency's failure to give adequate consideration to the regula-

---

22. *Greater Boston*, 444 F.2d at 851. Compare, e.g., Motor Vehicle Manufacturers Association v. State Farm Mutual Automobile Insurance Co., 463 U.S. 29 (1983), with Baltimore and Gas & Electric Co. v. NRDC, 462 U.S. 87 (1983).

23. See Federal Election Com'n v. Rose, 806 F.2d 1081, 1089 (D.D.Cir. 1986).

24. For a fuller discussion of the decisionmaking flaws that may lead to invalidation under the arbitrary-or-capricious standard, see SECTION OF ADMINISTRATIVE LAW AND REGULATORY PRACTICE OF

AMERICAN BAR ASSOCIATION, A GUIDE TO JUDICIAL AND POLITICAL REVIEW OF FEDERAL AGENCIES 177–95 (John F. Duffy & Michael Herz, eds., 2005).

25. *State Farm*, 463 U.S. at 43; see, e.g., Puerto Rico Sun Oil Co. v. EPA, 8 F.3d 73, 78 (1st Cir. 1993).

26. See *Overton Park*, 401 U.S. at 416.

27. Burlington Truck Lines, Inc. v. United States, 371 U.S. 156, 168 (1962).

28. ABA BLACKLETTER STATEMENT, *supra* note 21, at 35.

tory issues in an administrative proceeding. An agency may fail to live up to this decisionmaking duty in a variety of ways. It may, for example, rely on factors that Congress had not intended that the agency consider.[29] Or an agency may fail to give reasoned consideration to the factors relevant to its decision or to an "an important aspect of the regulatory problem."[30] Similarly, reviewing courts will invalidate an administrative decision where the agency has failed to give reasoned consideration to "obvious" alternative solutions to a regulatory problem at issue.[31]

The third, and most common, decisionmaking defect leading to invalidation of agency action as arbitrary or capricious is an agency's failure to adequately explain its decisionmaking. Agencies must provide a reasoned explanation of the important aspects of their decisions.[32] They also must give a reasoned explanation of the various choices they made in reaching their decision.[33] As Judge Leventhal noted in *Greater Boston*, the agency's obligation to provide a reasoned explanation of its decisionmaking assumes a special urgency when warning signs of arbitrariness appear in the record. This occurs, for example, where an agency rejects obvious alternative solutions to a regulatory problem at issue;[34] an agency decision appears to conflict with evidence in the administrative record;[35] and an agency decision is inconsistent with the agency's prior decisions or with its past practice.[36]

The Supreme Court embraced the post-*Overton Park* evolution of hard look doctrine in *Motor Vehicle Manufacturers Association v. State Farm Mutual Automobile Insurance Co.*[37] *State Farm* provides an exemplar of hard look judicial review in operation. The Department of Transportation had issued a rule requiring manufacturers

---

29. See, e.g., *State Farm*, 463 U.S. at 43; *Overton Park*, 401 U.S. at 416.

30. *Id.*; see e.g., *Puerto Rico Sun Oil*, 8 F.3d at 77 (failing to discuss "relevant issues"); *Rose*, 806 F.2d at 1088.

31. City of Brookings Municipal Telephone Co. v. FCC, 822 F.2d 1153, 1169 (D.C.Cir. 1987); see, e.g., *Nova Scotia*, 568 F.2d at 253 (invalidating agency rule regulating processing of smoked fish in part because agency failed to consider a less onerous alternative). Reviewing courts do not require that agencies consider every conceivable alternative to the policy choices they make. See, e.g., *City of Brookings Municipal Telephone*, 822 F.2d at 1169. Nor do courts require that an agency "solve every problem before it in the same proceeding." Mobil Oil Exploration & Producing Southeast Inc. v. United Distribution Companies, 498 U.S. 211, 231 (1991).

32. See, e.g., *Rose*, 806 F.2d at 1088; Industrial Union Dep't, AFL–CIO v. Hodgson, 499 F.2d 467, 479–81, 486–88 (D.C.Cir. 1974). The adequacy of an agency's explanation depends on whether the reviewing court can reasonably discern the path of the agency's decisionmaking. Bowman Transportation, Inc. v. Arkansas–Best Freight System, 419 U.S. 281, 286 (1974).

33. Continental Airlines, Inc. v. Dep't of Transp., 843 F.2d 1444, 1451 (D.C.Cir. 1988).

34. *City of Brookings Municipal Telephone*, 822 F.2d at 1169.

35. See, e.g., *State Farm*, 463 U.S. at 43.

36. See *id.* at 42; Atchison, Topeka & Santa Fe Railway Co. v. Wichita Bd. of Trade, 412 U.S. 800, 808 (1973).

37. 463 U.S. 29 (1983).

to install seatbelts in automobiles. Seatbelts are effective in saving lives and in minimizing injury, but the rule itself had proven ineffective because too few passengers fastened their belts. The Department eventually amended the seatbelt rule, phasing in a requirement that auto manufacturers install passive restraints— passenger-protection systems that do not require the passenger to engage them. Manufacturers could satisfy the passive restraint rule by installing either air bags or automatic seatbelts. The *State Farm* litigation arose from the Transportation Department's rescission of the passive restraint rule shortly before its requirements were to begin phasing in.[38]

The Department based its rescission on a reassessment of the cost-benefit analysis underlying the passive restraint rule. The Department had issued that rule because officials had concluded that the impressive safety benefits promised by passive systems outweighed the costs of compliance.[39] In rescinding the rule, the Department did not question that original assessment. It based the rescission instead on the apparent decision of most auto manufacturers to comply with the rule by installing automatic seatbelts that were detachable. The detachability feature, the Department concluded, undermined its earlier projection of safety benefits accruing from the passive restraint rule because it was impossible to predict how many car owners would detach their automatic belts. The Transportation Department rescinded the rule because officials believed it unreasonable to impose substantial compliance costs on manufacturers (and ultimately on consumers) without greater likelihood of producing significant safety benefits.[40]

Because the Administrative Procedure Act regards an agency's "repealing" of a rule as an act of rulemaking (APA § 551(5)), the Court in *State Farm* used the same scope of review it would have applied to an agency's decision to issue a rule. Thus, the question before the Court was whether the Department's rescission of the passive restraint rule had been arbitrary or capricious (APA § 706(2)(A)).[41] The Transportation Department's rescission of the passive restraint rule could not hold up under the Court's withering hard look review.

All of the justices in *State Farm* agreed that the Department had made a fatal decisionmaking mistake by failing to consider an

---

38. *Id.* at 34–38.

39. *Id.* at 37–38. The passive restraint rule survived an arbitrary-or-capricious challenge in *Pacific Legal Foundation v. Dep't of Transportation*, 593 F.2d 1338 (D.C.Cir.), cert. denied, 444 U.S. 830 (1979).

40. *State Farm*, 463 U.S. at 38–39.

41. *Id.* at 40–42, 46 ("While the removal of a regulation may not entail the monetary expenditures and other costs of enacting a new standard, and accordingly, it may be easier for an agency to justify a deregulatory action, the direction in which an agency chooses to move does not alter the standard of judicial review established by law.").

obvious alternative solution to the problem posed by the decision of auto manufacturers to opt for detachable belts. The Department simply could have amended the passive restraint rule to eliminate that option. By requiring manufacturers to install airbags or non-detachable automatic seatbelts, the Court held, the Department would have revived the prospect of delivering the safety benefits it had projected when issuing the passive restraint rule, and thus the Department would have better served the purposes underlying its enabling act.[42]

A bare five-justice majority of the Court also held in *State Farm* that the Transportation Department had not adequately supported its assumption that the installation of detachable automatic seatbelts in automobiles would fail to produce significant safety benefits. The administrative record lacked any "direct evidence" supporting the Department's assumption that usage would not substantially increase upon the installation of automatic belts that owners could detach. Indeed, the scant evidence in the record concerning whether car owners could be expected to remove detachable automatic seatbelts contradicted the Department's assumption.[43]

Then–Justice Rehnquist, writing for the four partially dissenting justices in *State Farm*, traced the Transportation Department's "changed view" of the passive restraint rule "to the election of a new President of a different political party."[44] (The passive restraint rule had been issued during the Carter Administration and had been rescinded during the Reagan Administration.) But true to hard look judicial review, the *State Farm* majority did not accept political ideology, standing alone, as adequate justification for administrative rulemaking. The rulemaking and judicial review provisions of the APA, the Court in *State Farm* explained, created a "presumption" against rule changes "that are not justified by the rulemaking record."[45]

As *State Farm* illustrates, hard look judicial review of administrative decisionmaking is powerful. Judge Patricia Wald of the D.C. Circuit has stated that the failure by an agency to engage in "reasoned decisionmaking" is "the most frequent cause for overturning agency action" in her court.[46] It should not be surprising, then, that hard look review is controversial. Supporters believe that

42. *Id.* at 46–51, 55–56.

43. *Id.* at 51–57.

44. *Id.* at 59 (Rehnquist, J., concurring in part and dissenting in part).

45. *Id.* at 42.

46. See Patricia M. Wald, *Judicial Review in Midpassage: The Uneasy Partnership Between Courts and Agencies*

Plays On, 32 TULSA L. REV. 221, 234 (1996). For an argument that the Supreme Court has shown little interest in exercising hard look judicial review since *State Farm*, see Michael Herz, *The Rehnquist Court and Administrative Law*, 99 NW. U. L. REV. 297, 308–18 (2004).

hard look review serves the key function of keeping agencies true to their statutory mission.[47] Hard look review discourages agency action that caters to special interest groups, supporters claim, because it forces agencies to expose their reasoning process to close judicial inspection.[48] Supporters also credit hard look judicial review with improving administrative decisionmaking. "It is a great tonic," one commentator (and former EPA official) observed, when agency decisionmakers know that reviewing courts "will inquire into the minute details of methodology, data sufficiency, and test procedure and will send the regulation back if these are lacking." Only "well-documented and well-reasoned" decisions survive hard look judicial review.[49]

Critics of hard look judicial review have questioned from the beginning whether judges are competent to superintend the substantive policy choices of administrative agencies. No one has put this criticism more pointedly than Judge David Bazelon of the D.C. Circuit, who wrote, "substantive review of mathematical and scientific evidence by technically illiterate judges is dangerously unreliable." Judge Bazelon also worried, as have other critics, over the legitimacy of judges involving themselves too deeply in the substance of administrative decisionmaking. Hard look review, Bazalon argued, carries an unacceptable risk that judges will introduce their political and policy preferences into their evaluation of administrative decisionmaking.[50]

Critics more recently have added the charge that the rigors of hard look judicial review, and the unpredictability of outcome it engenders, have contributed to an "ossification" of the regulatory process that has prevented agencies from accomplishing their statutory mission.[51] Put simply, these critics claim that hard look judicial review has made it unacceptably burdensome, expensive, and time

47. See, e.g., Cass R. Sunstein, *Deregulation and the Hard–Look Doctrine*, 1983 Sup. Ct. Rev. 177, 211–12 (hard look judicial review provides "an important, if imperfect, means of promoting agency fidelity to statutory norms").

48. See Mark Seidenfeld, *Demystifying Deossification: Rethinking Recent Proposals to Modify Judicial Review of Notice and Comment Rulemaking*, 75 Tex. L. Rev. 483, 501–02 (1997); Sidney A. Shapiro & Richard E. Levy, *Heightened Scrutiny of the Fourth Branch: Separation of Powers and the Requirement of Adequate Reasons for Agency Decisions*, 1987 Duke L.J. 387, 412–13; Cass R. Sunstein, *In Defense of the Hard Look: Judicial Activism in Administra-*

tive Law, 7 Harv. J.L. & Pub. Pol. 51, 53 (1984).

49. William F. Pederson, Jr., *Formal Records and Informal Rulemaking*, 85 Yale L.J. 38, 60 (1975).

50. Ethyl Corp. v. EPA, 541 F.2d 1, 66 (D.C.Cir.), cert. denied, 426 U.S. 941 (1976) (Bazelon, J., concurring); see, e.g., Richard J. Pierce, Jr., *Two Problems in Administrative Law: Political Polarity on the District of Columbia Circuit and Judicial Deterrence of Agency Rulemaking*, 1988 Duke L.J. 300, 303–07.

51. The leading example is Thomas O. McGarity, *Some Thoughts on "Deossifying" the Rulemaking Process*, 41 Duke L.J. 1385, 1419 (1992).

consuming for agencies to issue rules.[52] The ossification charge resembles a common criticism leveled against hybrid rulemaking review (see § 6.3(d)). In both instances, critics claim that the intensification of judicial review has judicialized the regulatory process,[53] and by doing so, has robbed informal rulemaking of the flexibility and efficiency that have made it an attractive policymaking instrument.[54] Indeed, critics claim that the prospect of hard look review has deterred agencies from using notice-and-comment rulemaking, forcing administrators either to make policy by issuing non-binding guidance documents (see § 6.5(b)),[55] or to leave in place outdated rules that they would prefer to change.[56]

Amid the controversy, reviewing courts continue to exercise hard look judicial review of the ultimate decisions of administrative agencies.

§ 8.8   Judicial Power to Compel Agency Action

Section 706(1) of the Administrative Procedure Act authorizes reviewing courts to "compel agency action unlawfully withheld or unreasonably delayed." The *Attorney General's Manual* described section 706(1) as "apparently intended to codify" the traditional authority of federal courts to issue writs of mandamus compelling administrative officers to perform the ministerial and non-discretionary duties that the law requires of them.[1] The Attorney General's reading of section 706(1) accounted for the provision's language enabling reviewing courts to compel agency action that is "unlawfully withheld," but it seemed to ignore section 706(1)'s application to agency action that is "unreasonably delayed." Congress may have intended, at least in part, that this language provide a means of enforcing the general obligation that section 555(b) of the APA places on agencies to "conclude a matter presented to it . . . within a reasonable time."[2]

52. See *id.* at 1419; Richard J. Pierce, Jr., *Seven Ways to Deossify Agency Rulemaking*, 47 ADMIN. L. REV. 59, 60–62 (1995).

53. See, e.g., JERRY L. MASHAW & DAVID L. HARFST, THE STRUGGLE FOR AUTO SAFETY 20–26 (1990); Stephen Breyer, *Judicial Review of Questions of Law and Policy*, 38 ADMIN. L. REV. 363, 395 (1986).

54. See, e.g., McGarity, *"Deossifying" the Rulemaking Process*, *supra* note 51, at 1385; Pierce, *Seven Ways to Deossify Agency Rulemaking*, *supra* note 52, at 65.

55. See, e.g., E. Donald Elliott, *Reinventing Rulemaking*, 41 DUKE L.J. 1490, 1492–96 (1992).

56. See, e.g., Breyer, *Judicial Review*, *supra* note 53, at 391–93; McGarity, *"Deossifying" the Rulemaking Process*, *supra* note 51, at 1419–20.

§ 8.8

1. *Attorney General's Manual on the Administrative Procedure Act* 108 (1947), reprinted in WILLIAM F. FUNK, et al., FEDERAL ADMINISTRATIVE PROCEDURE SOURCEBOOK 33–171 (3d ed. 2000).

2. See Telecommunications Research and Action Center v. FCC, 750 F.2d 70, 79 (D.C.Cir. 1984).

Reviewing courts traditionally have been reluctant to tap the authority that section 706(1) provides them to compel agency action. The Supreme Court cemented this tradition in *Norton v. Southern Utah Wilderness Alliance ("SUWA"),*[3] where the justices gave section 706(1) a limited reading. The Court held that "a claim under § 706(1) can proceed only where a plaintiff asserts that an agency [1] failed to take a *discrete* agency action [2] that it is *required to take.*"[4]

The first limitation established by the Court in *SUWA* restricted the reach of section 706(1) to an agency's failure to take one of the "discrete" actions listed in the APA's definition of "agency action."[5] These actions include issuing (or denying) "an agency rule, order, license, sanction, relief, or the equivalent thereof" (§ 551(13)).[6] This limitation blocks challenges, like those presented in *SUWA*, which claim broadly that an agency has failed to shoulder its statutory responsibilities.[7]

The second limitation that the Court in *SUWA* placed on the reach of section 706(1) permits courts to compel only agency action that is "legally *required.*" The justices thus followed the *Attorney General Manual* in denying independent significance to the "unreasonably delayed" language of section 706(1). Explained the Court, "[A] delay cannot be unreasonable with respect to action that is not required."[8]

The Court in *SUWA* believed that its narrow reading of section 706(1) was necessary "to protect agencies from undue judicial interference with their lawful discretion, and to avoid judicial entanglement in abstract policy disagreements which courts lack both expertise and information to resolve." Empowering courts "to enter general orders compelling compliance with broad statutory mandates," the justices feared, would make it "the task of the supervising court, rather than the agency, to work out compliance with the broad statutory mandate, injecting the judge into day-to-day agency management." Added the Court, "The prospect of pervasive oversight by federal courts over the manner and pace of agency compliance with such congressional directives is not contemplated by the APA."[9]

---

3.   542 U.S. 55 (2004).

4.   *Id.* at 64.

5.   *Id.* at 61–63.

6.   The APA's definition of "agency action" is discussed in § 7.3(a).

7.   *SUWA*, 542 U.S. at 64–65.

8.   *Id.* at 63–64 & n.1.

9.   *Id.* at 66–67. For an argument that the justices' concern about overreaching by courts pursuant to section

706(1) was not supported by the judicial track record, see William D. Araiza, *In Praise of a Skeletal APA:* Norton v. Southern Utah Wilderness Alliance, *Judicial Remedies for Agency Inaction, and the Questionable Value of Amending the APA,* 56 ADMIN. L. REV. 979, 990–92 (2004). For the Court's approach to agency decisions not to initiate enforcement proceedings and to deny rulemaking petitions, see § 7.2(b).

Table of Cases

A

Abbott Laboratories v. Gardner, 387 U.S. 136, 87 S.Ct. 1507, 18 L.Ed.2d 681 (1967)—§ **1.5, n. 49, 50; § 4.1, n. 10; § 7.2; § 7.2, n. 4, 8; § 7.3; § 7.3, n. 7, 28, 31; § 8.4, n. 17.**

Abrams v. United States, 250 U.S. 616, 40 S.Ct. 17, 63 L.Ed. 1173 (1919)— **§ 3.2, n. 4.**

Action For Children's Television v. F.C.C., 564 F.2d 458, 183 U.S.App. D.C. 437 (D.C.Cir.1977)—§ **6.3, n. 11, 13; § 6.4; § 6.4, n. 12.**

Adams Fruit Co., Inc. v. Barrett, 494 U.S. 638, 110 S.Ct. 1384, 108 L.Ed.2d 585 (1990)—§ **8.5, n. 82, 95.**

Air Courier Conference of America v. American Postal Workers Union AFL–CIO, 498 U.S. 517, 111 S.Ct. 913, 112 L.Ed.2d 1125 (1991)—§ **7.2; § 7.2, n. 103.**

Aircraft Owners and Pilots Ass'n v. Federal Aviation Administration, 600 F.2d 965, 195 U.S.App.D.C. 151 (D.C.Cir.1979)—§ **8.4, n. 32.**

Air Line Pilots Ass'n, Intern. v. Quesada, 276 F.2d 892 (2nd Cir.1960)— **§ 3.1; § 3.1, n. 13.**

Air Transport Ass'n of America v. Department of Transp., 900 F.2d 369, 283 U.S.App.D.C. 385 (D.C.Cir. 1990)—§ **6.5, n. 59, 71.**

Air Transport Ass'n of America v. F.A.A., 169 F.3d 1, 335 U.S.App.D.C. 85 (D.C.Cir.1999)—§ **6.3, n. 53; § 6.4, n. 6.**

Alabama Power Co. v. F.E.R.C., 993 F.2d 1557, 301 U.S.App.D.C. 253 (D.C.Cir.1993)—§ **7.3; § 7.3, n. 15.**

A.L.A. Schechter Poultry Corporation v. United States, 295 U.S. 495, 55 S.Ct. 837, 79 L.Ed. 1570 (1935)—§ **1.5; § 1.5, n. 30; § 2.3; § 2.3, n. 28, 46.**

Alexandria, City of v. United States, 737 F.2d 1022 (Fed.Cir.1984)—§ **2.3, n. 105.**

Allen v. Wright, 468 U.S. 737, 104 S.Ct. 3315, 82 L.Ed.2d 556 (1984)—§ **7.2, n. 55.**

Allentown Mack Sales and Service, Inc. v. N.L.R.B., 522 U.S. 359, 118 S.Ct. 818, 139 L.Ed.2d 797 (1998)—§ **8.4, n. 10.**

Amalgamated Meat Cutters and Butcher Workmen of North America, AFL–CIO v. Connally, 337 F.Supp. 737 (D.D.C.1971)—§ **6.5, n. 80.**

American Airlines, Inc. v. Herman, 176 F.3d 283 (5th Cir.1999)—§ **7.3, n. 8.**

American Bus Ass'n v. United States, 627 F.2d 525, 201 U.S.App.D.C. 66 (D.C.Cir.1980)—§ **6.5, n. 8.**

American Federation of Government Emp., AFL–CIO v. Block, 655 F.2d 1153, 210 U.S.App.D.C. 336 (D.C.Cir. 1981)—§ **6.5, n. 77.**

American Federation of Labor and Congress of Indus. Organizations v. Donovan, 757 F.2d 330, 244 U.S.App.D.C. 255 (D.C.Cir.1985)—§ **6.3, n. 23, 38.**

American Federation of Labor and Congress of Indus. Organizations v. Occupational Safety and Health Admin., United States Dept. of Labor, 965 F.2d 962 (11th Cir.1992)—§ **8.4, n. 31.**

American Horse Protection Ass'n, Inc. v. Lyng, 812 F.2d 1, 258 U.S.App.D.C. 397 (D.C.Cir.1987)—§ **7.2, n. 40.**

American Hosp. Ass'n v. Bowen, 834 F.2d 1037, 266 U.S.App.D.C. 190 (D.C.Cir.1987)—§ **6.5, n. 5, 60.**

American Hosp. Ass'n v. N.L.R.B., 499 U.S. 606, 111 S.Ct. 1539, 113 L.Ed.2d 675 (1991)—§ **4.3, n. 26.**

American Lung Ass'n v. Browner, 884 F.Supp. 345 (D.Ariz.1994)—§ **2.4, n. 103.**

American Medical Ass'n v. Reno, 57 F.3d 1129, 313 U.S.App.D.C. 44 (D.C.Cir. 1995)—§ **Ch. 6, n. 3.**

American Medical Ass'n v. United States, 887 F.2d 760 (7th Cir.1989)— § **6.3, n. 11.**

American Mfrs. Mut. Ins. Co. v. Sullivan, 526 U.S. 40, 119 S.Ct. 977, 143 L.Ed.2d 130 (1999)—§ **3.4; § 3.4, n. 68.**

F

Fahey v. Mallonee, 332 U.S. 245, 67 S.Ct. 1552, 91 L.Ed. 2030 (1947)— **§ 2.3, n. 61.**

Farmers Union Cent. Exchange, Inc. v. F.E.R.C., 734 F.2d 1486, 236 U.S.App.D.C. 203 (D.C.Cir.1984)— **§ 4.2, n. 11.**

F.C.C. v. Allentown Broadcasting Corp., 349 U.S. 358, 75 S.Ct. 855, 99 L.Ed. 1147 (1955)—**§ 5.5, n. 5.**

F.C.C. v. WNCN Listeners Guild, 450 U.S. 582, 101 S.Ct. 1266, 67 L.Ed.2d 521 (1981)—**§ 4.3; § 4.3, n. 27; § 6.3; § 6.3, n. 51.**

Federal Deposit Ins. Corp. v. Mallen, 486 U.S. 230, 108 S.Ct. 1780, 100 L.Ed.2d 265 (1988)—**§ 3.4; § 3.4, n. 146.**

Federal Election Commission v. National Rifle Ass'n of America, 254 F.3d 173, 349 U.S.App.D.C. 96 (D.C.Cir. 2001)—**§ 8.5, n. 114.**

Federal Election Com'n v. Rose, 806 F.2d 1081, 256 U.S.App.D.C. 395 (D.C.Cir.1986)—**§ 8.7, n. 23.**

Federal Maritime Com'n v. South Carolina State Ports Authority, 535 U.S. 743, 122 S.Ct. 1864, 152 L.Ed.2d 962 (2002)—**§ 2.2, n. 5.**

Federal Power Commission v. Hope Natural Gas Co., 320 U.S. 591, 64 S.Ct. 281, 88 L.Ed. 333 (1944)—**§ 2.3, n. 61.**

Federal Power Commission v. Texaco, Inc., 377 U.S. 33, 84 S.Ct. 1105, 12 L.Ed.2d 112 (1964)—**§ 4.3, n. 21.**

Federal Power Commission v. Transcontinental Gas Pipe Line Corp., 423 U.S. 326, 96 S.Ct. 579, 46 L.Ed.2d 533 (1976)—**§ 8.1, n. 5.**

Federal Trade Commission v. Cement Institute, 333 U.S. 683, 68 S.Ct. 793, 92 L.Ed. 1010 (1948)—**§ 5.3, n. 34; § 5.5; § 5.5, n. 4.**

Federal Trade Commission v. Ruberoid Co., 343 U.S. 470, 72 S.Ct. 800, 96 L.Ed. 1081 (1952)—**§ 2.2, n. 2.**

Field v. Clark, 143 U.S. 649, 12 S.Ct. 495, 36 L.Ed. 294 (1892)—**§ 2.3; § 2.3, n. 1, 18.**

Florida East Coast Ry. Co., United States v., 410 U.S. 224, 93 S.Ct. 810, 35 L.Ed.2d 223 (1973)—**§ 4.1, n. 14; § 4.2; § 4.2, n. 5, 14; § 6.5, n. 6.**

Florida Power & Light Co. v. Lorion, 470 U.S. 729, 105 S.Ct. 1598, 84 L.Ed.2d 643 (1985)—**§ 8.1, n. 5, 15.**

Florida Power & Light Co. v. United States, 846 F.2d 765, 269 U.S.App. D.C. 377 (D.C.Cir.1988)—**§ 6.3, n. 10.**

Flue–Cured Tobacco Cooperative Stabilization Corp. v. United StatesE.P.A., 313 F.3d 852 (4th Cir.2002)—**§ 7.3; § 7.3, n. 23.**

Food and Drug Admin. v. Brown & Williamson Tobacco Corp., 529 U.S. 120, 120 S.Ct. 1291, 146 L.Ed.2d 121 (2000)—**§ 8.5, n. 33, 54, 63.**

Franklin v. Massachusetts, 505 U.S. 788, 112 S.Ct. 2767, 120 L.Ed.2d 636 (1992)—**§ 1.2, n. 1; § 7.3, n. 20.**

Freytag v. Commissioner, 501 U.S. 868, 111 S.Ct. 2631, 115 L.Ed.2d 764 (1991)—**§ 2.2, n. 6; § 2.4; § 2.4, n. 12, 19, 31.**

Friends of the Earth, Inc. v. Laidlaw Environmental Services (TOC), Inc., 528 U.S. 167, 120 S.Ct. 693, 145 L.Ed.2d 610 (2000)—**§ 7.2; § 7.2, n. 81, 107.**

F.T.C. v. Standard Oil Co. of California, 449 U.S. 232, 101 S.Ct. 488, 66 L.Ed.2d 416 (1980)—**§ 7.3; § 7.3, n. 2, 7, 10.**

Fuentes v. Shevin, 407 U.S. 67, 92 S.Ct. 1983, 32 L.Ed.2d 556 (1972)—**§ 3.4, n. 46, 138, 154; § Ch. 3, n. 10.**

Furlong v. Shalala, 156 F.3d 384 (2nd Cir.1998)—**§ 3.4, n. 60.**

G

Gavrilovic, United States v., 551 F.2d 1099 (8th Cir.1977)—**§ 6.5, n. 68.**

General Elec. Co. v. E.P.A., 290 F.3d 377, 351 U.S.App.D.C. 291 (D.C.Cir. 2002)—**§ 6.5, n. 35.**

Germaine, United States v., 99 U.S. 508, 25 L.Ed. 482 (1878)—**§ 2.4, n. 30.**

Gibson v. Berryhill, 411 U.S. 564, 93 S.Ct. 1689, 36 L.Ed.2d 488 (1973)— **§ 7.3, n. 53.**

Gilbert v. Homar, 520 U.S. 924, 117 S.Ct. 1807, 138 L.Ed.2d 120 (1997)— **§ 3.4, n. 85, 135, 141.**

Gilligan, Will & Co. v. Securities and Exchange Commission, 267 F.2d 461 (2nd Cir.1959)—**§ 5.5, n. 10.**

Glidden Co. v. Zdanok, 370 U.S. 530, 82 S.Ct. 1459, 8 L.Ed.2d 671 (1962)— **§ 2.5, n. 6.**

Goldberg v. Kelly, 397 U.S. 254, 90 S.Ct. 1011, 25 L.Ed.2d 287 (1970)—**§ 3.3; § 3.3, n. 1; § 3.4; § 3.4, n. 29.**

Gonzales v. Oregon, 546 U.S. 243, 126 S.Ct. 904, 163 L.Ed.2d 748 (2006)— **§ 8.5, n. 53; § 8.6; § 8.6, n. 10.**

J

K

L

N

Index

†